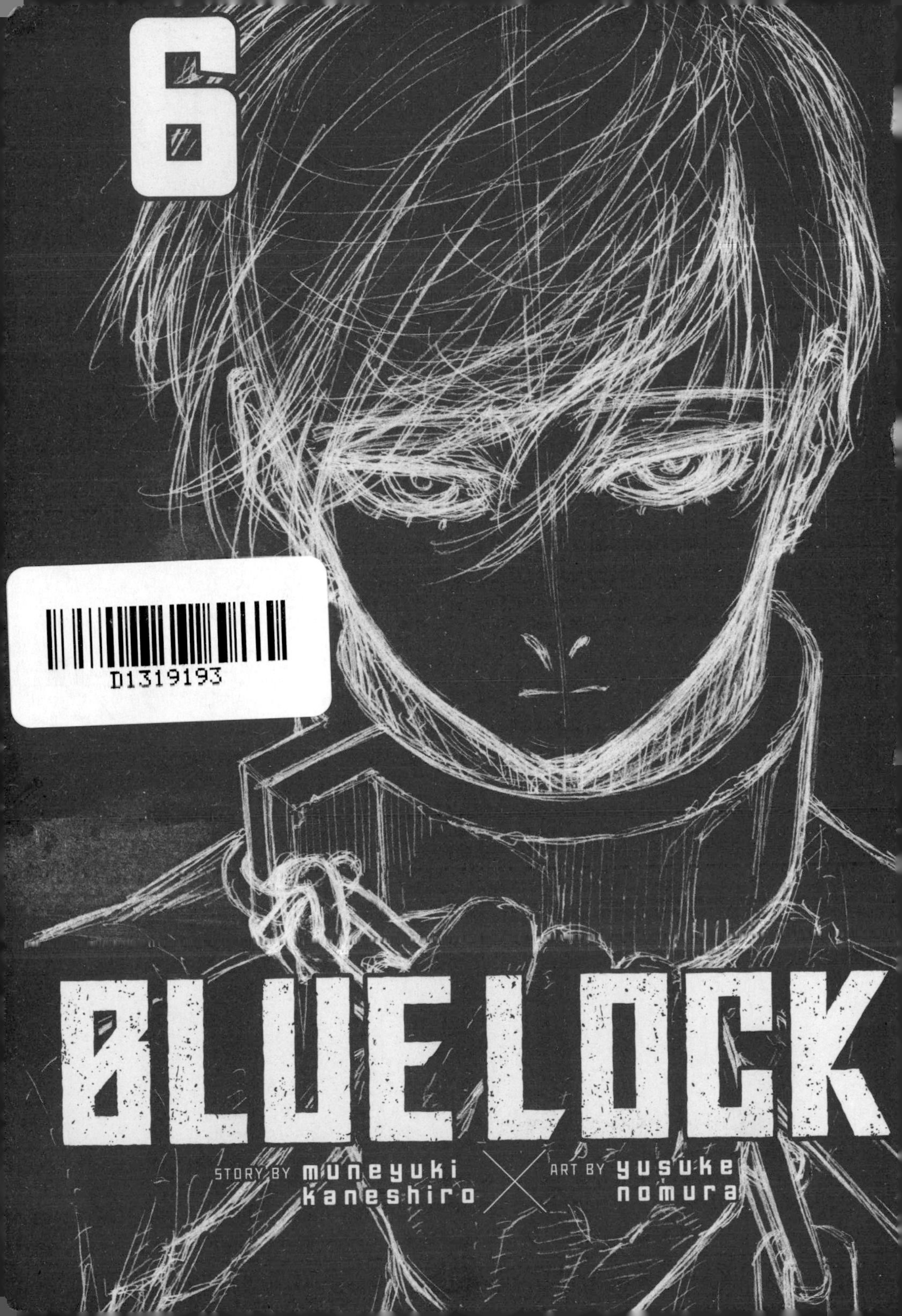
6
BLUE LOCK
STORY BY muneyuki kaneshiro
ART BY yusuke nomura

# CHARACTERS
# TEAM Z

## YOICHI ISAGI

The protagonist. After coming to Blue Lock to change his life, Isagi finds himself struggling hard every day. His weapons are his strong spatial awareness and direct shots.

## TEAM Z CLEARS THE FIRST SELECTION ROUND!!

## MEGURU BACHIRA

A wild forward who plays by following his intuition. His weapons are his dribbling and passing techniques.

## RENSUKE KUNIGAMI

A passionate forward. His weapon is his left leg's shooting power.

## HYOMA CHIGIRI

A cool prodigy forward. His weapon is his incredible speed.

## WATARU KUON

His weapon is his jumping power. Has he redeemed himself after his betrayal?!

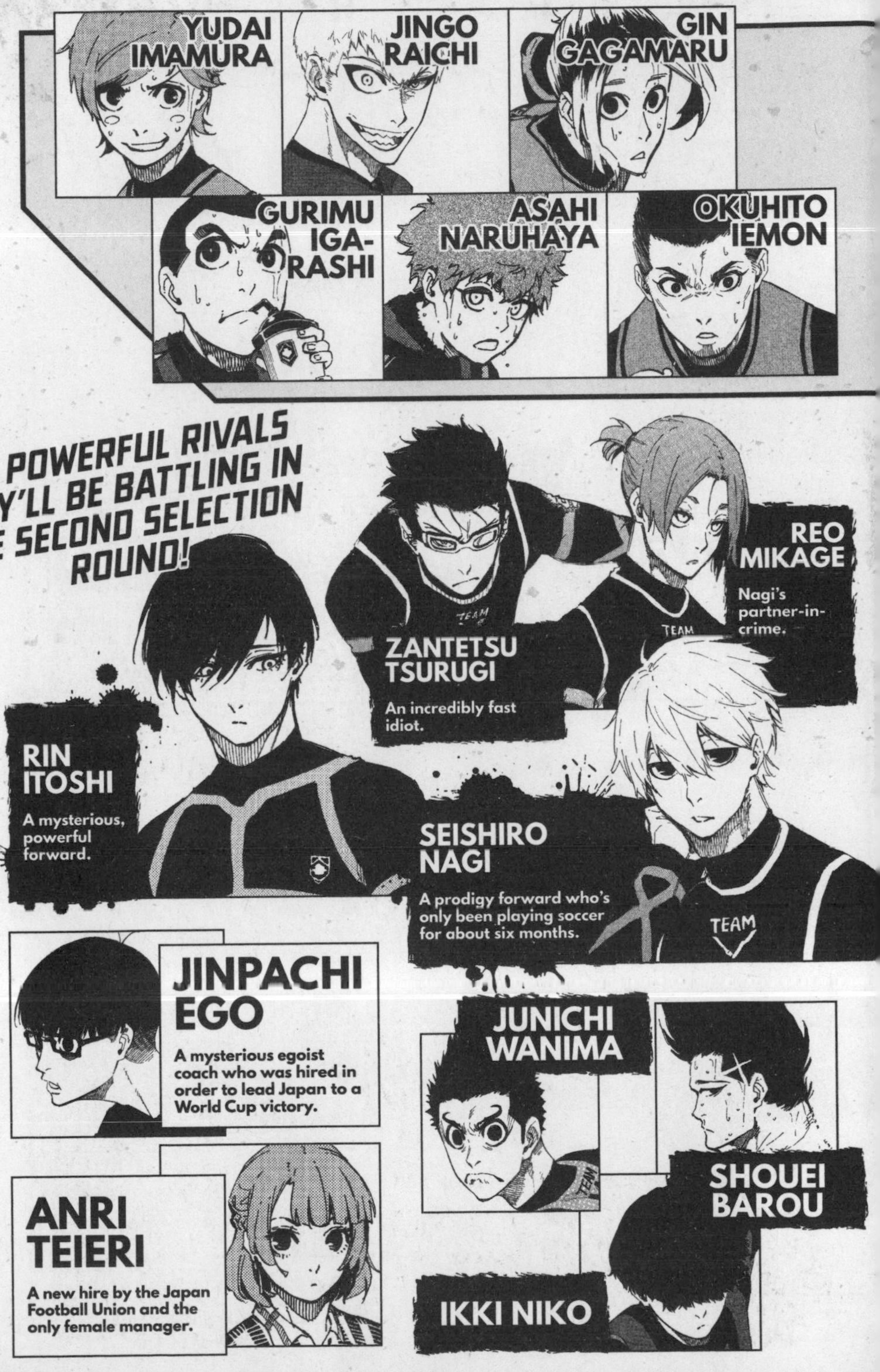

GIN GAGAMARU
JINGO RAICHI
YUDAI IMAMURA
OKUHITO IEMON
ASAHI NARUHAYA
GURIMU IGA-RASHI
THE POWERFUL RIVALS THEY'LL BE BATTLING IN THE SECOND SELECTION ROUND!
REO MIKAGE
Nagi's partner-in-crime.
ZANTETSU TSURUGI
An incredibly fast idiot.
RIN ITOSHI
A mysterious, powerful forward.
SEISHIRO NAGI
A prodigy forward who's only been playing soccer for about six months.
TEAM
SHOUEI BAROU
JUNICHI WANIMA
IKKI NIKO
JINPACHI EGO
A mysterious egoist coach who was hired in order to lead Japan to a World Cup victory.
ANRI TEIERI
A new hire by the Japan Football Union and the only female manager.

# CONTENTS

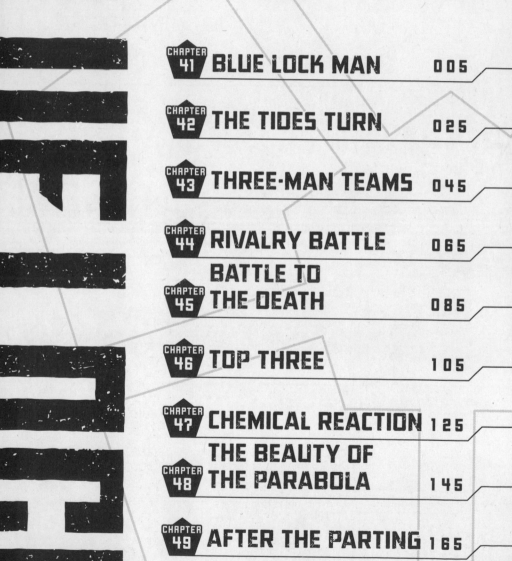

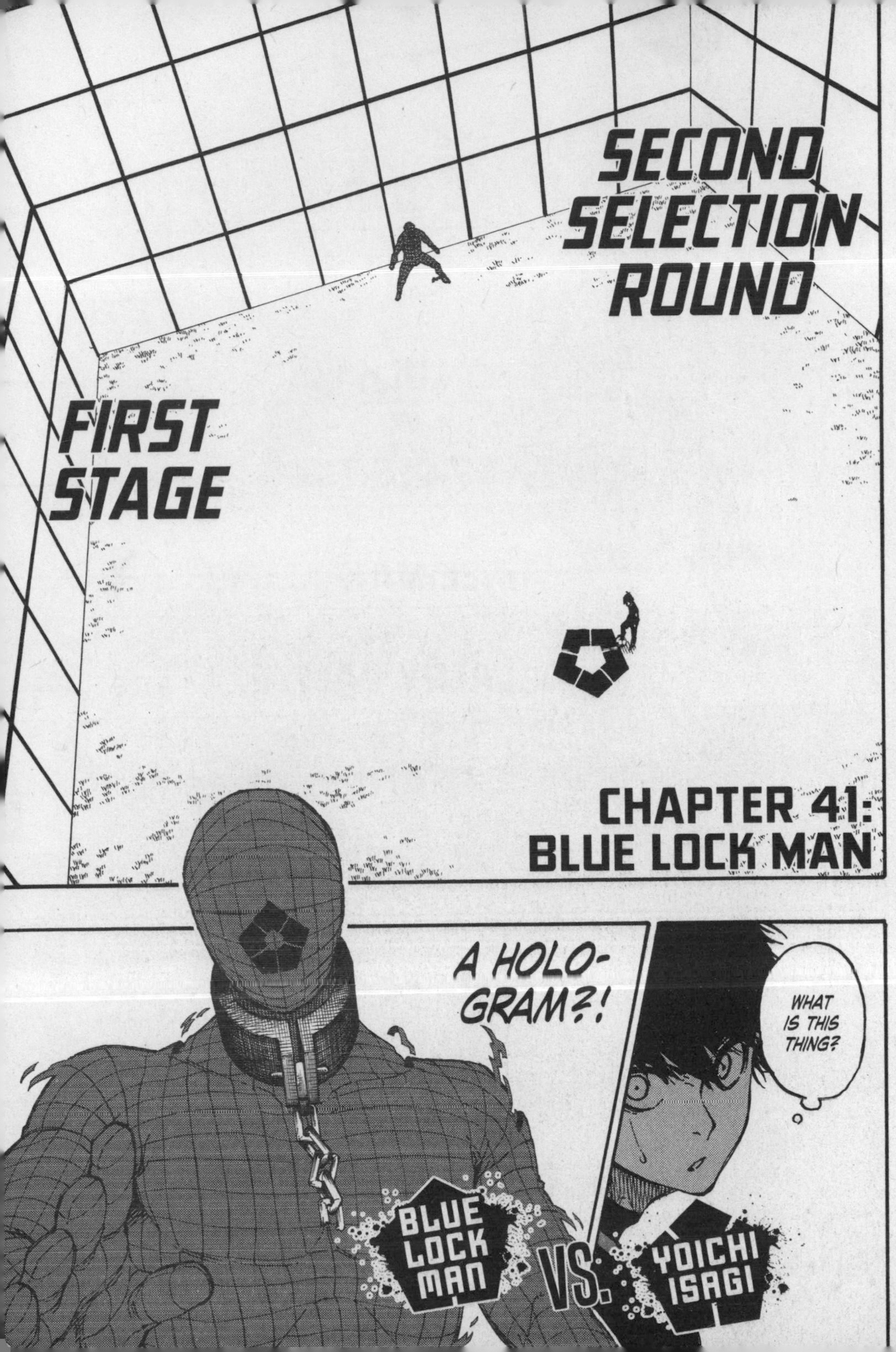
SECOND SELECTION ROUND
FIRST STAGE
CHAPTER 41: BLUE LOCK MAN
WHAT IS THIS THING?
A HOLO-GRAM?!
YOICHI ISAGI
VS.
BLUE LOCK MAN

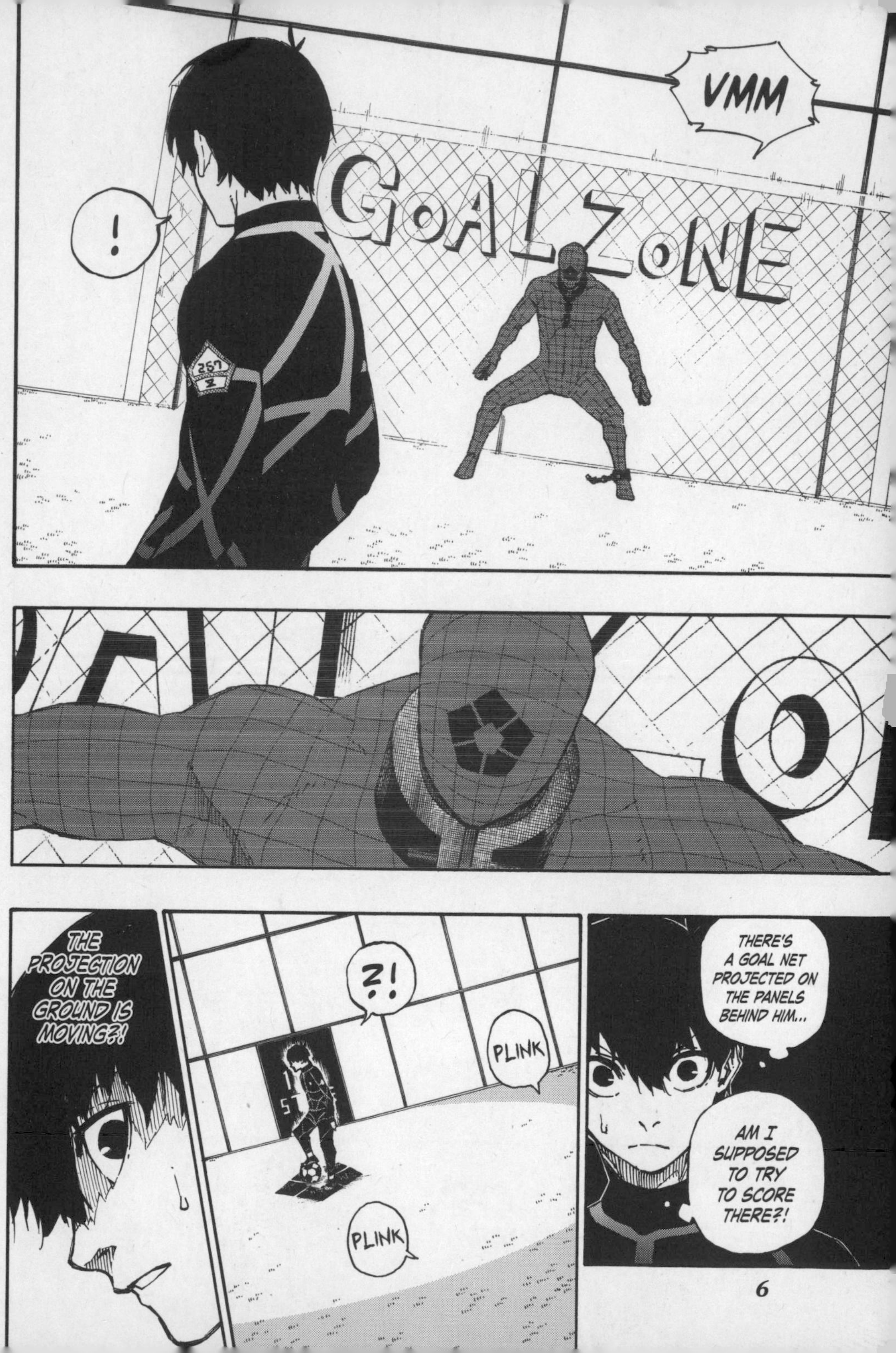
VMM
GOAL ZONE
!
THERE'S A GOAL NET PROJECTED ON THE PANELS BEHIND HIM...
AM I SUPPOSED TO TRY TO SCORE THERE?!
?!
PLINK
PLINK
THE PROJECTION ON THE GROUND IS MOVING?!

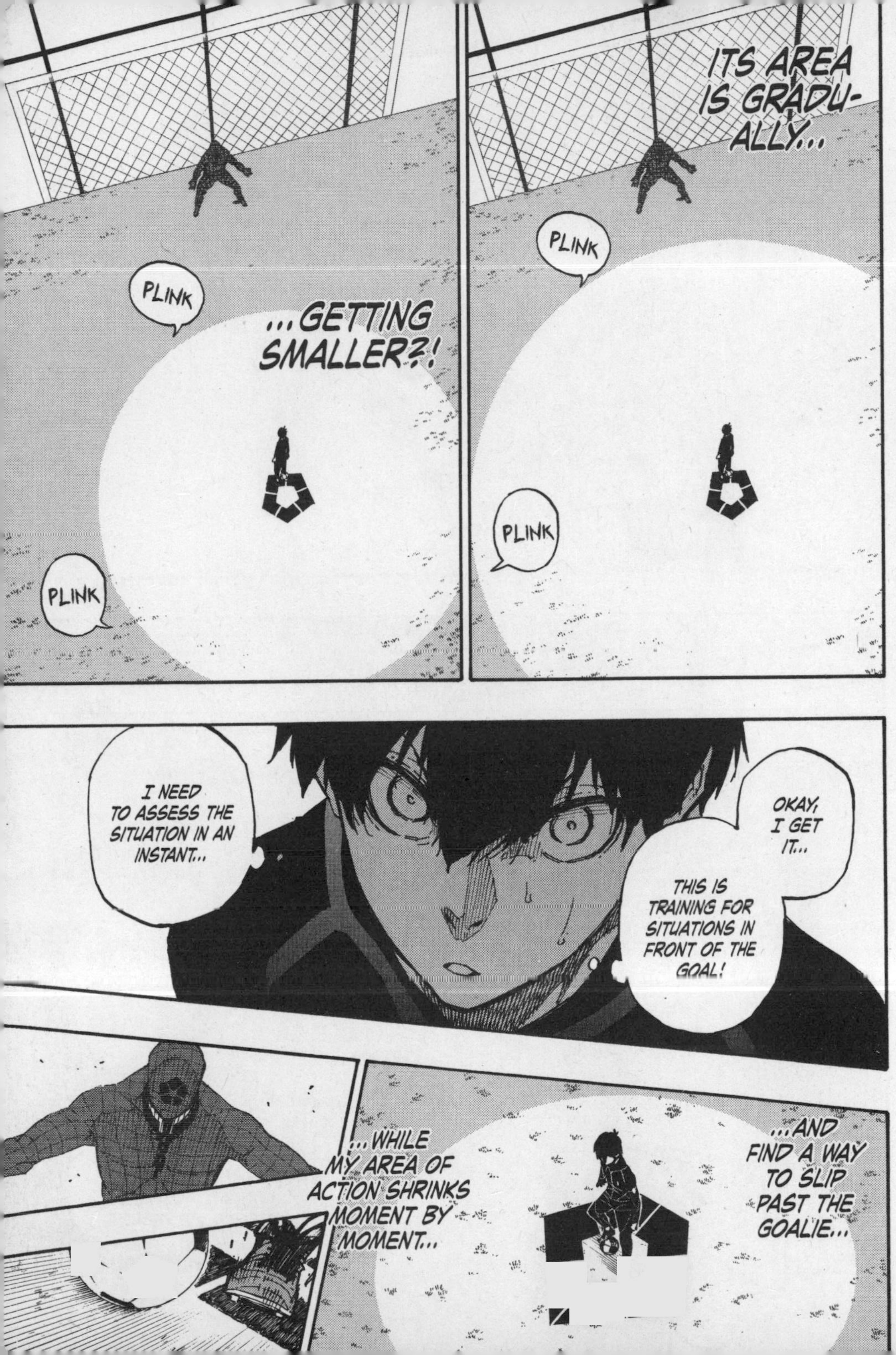
ITS AREA IS GRADU-ALLY...
PLINK
PLINK
PLINK
...GETTING SMALLER?!
PLINK
OKAY, I GET IT...
THIS IS TRAINING FOR SITUATIONS IN FRONT OF THE GOAL!
I NEED TO ASSESS THE SITUATION IN AN INSTANT...
...WHILE MY AREA OF ACTION SHRINKS MOMENT BY MOMENT...
...AND FIND A WAY TO SLIP PAST THE GOALIE...

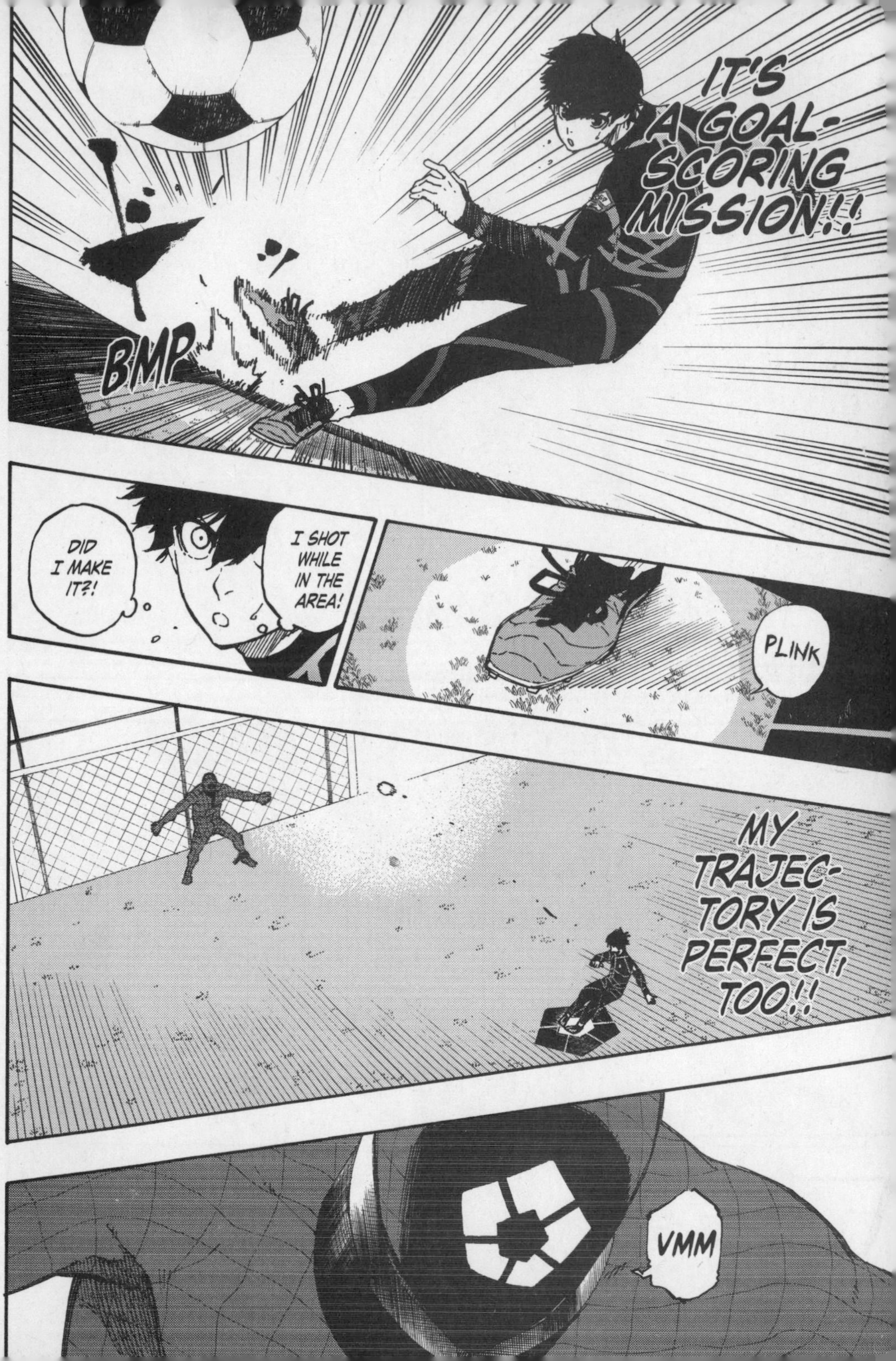
IT'S A GOAL-SCORING MISSION!!
BMP
I SHOT WHILE IN THE AREA!
DID I MAKE IT?!
PLINK
MY TRAJEC-TORY IS PERFECT, TOO!!
VMM

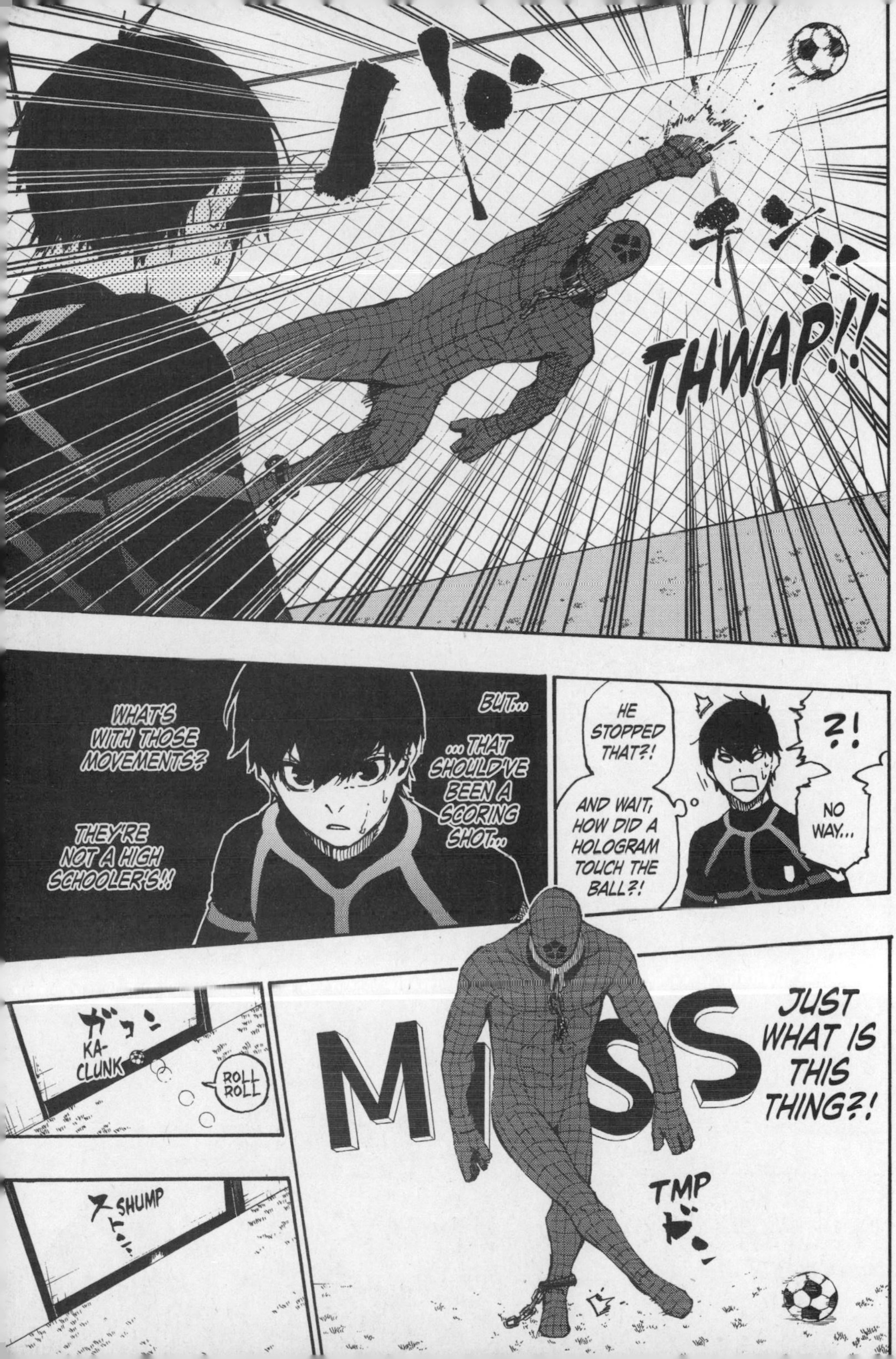
THWAP!!
?!
NO WAY...
HE STOPPED THAT?!
AND WAIT, HOW DID A HOLOGRAM TOUCH THE BALL?!
BUT...
...THAT SHOULD'VE BEEN A SCORING SHOT...
WHAT'S WITH THOSE MOVEMENTS?
THEY'RE NOT A HIGH SCHOOLER'S!!
JUST WHAT IS THIS THING?!
MISS
TMP
KA-CLUNK
ROLL ROLL
SHUMP

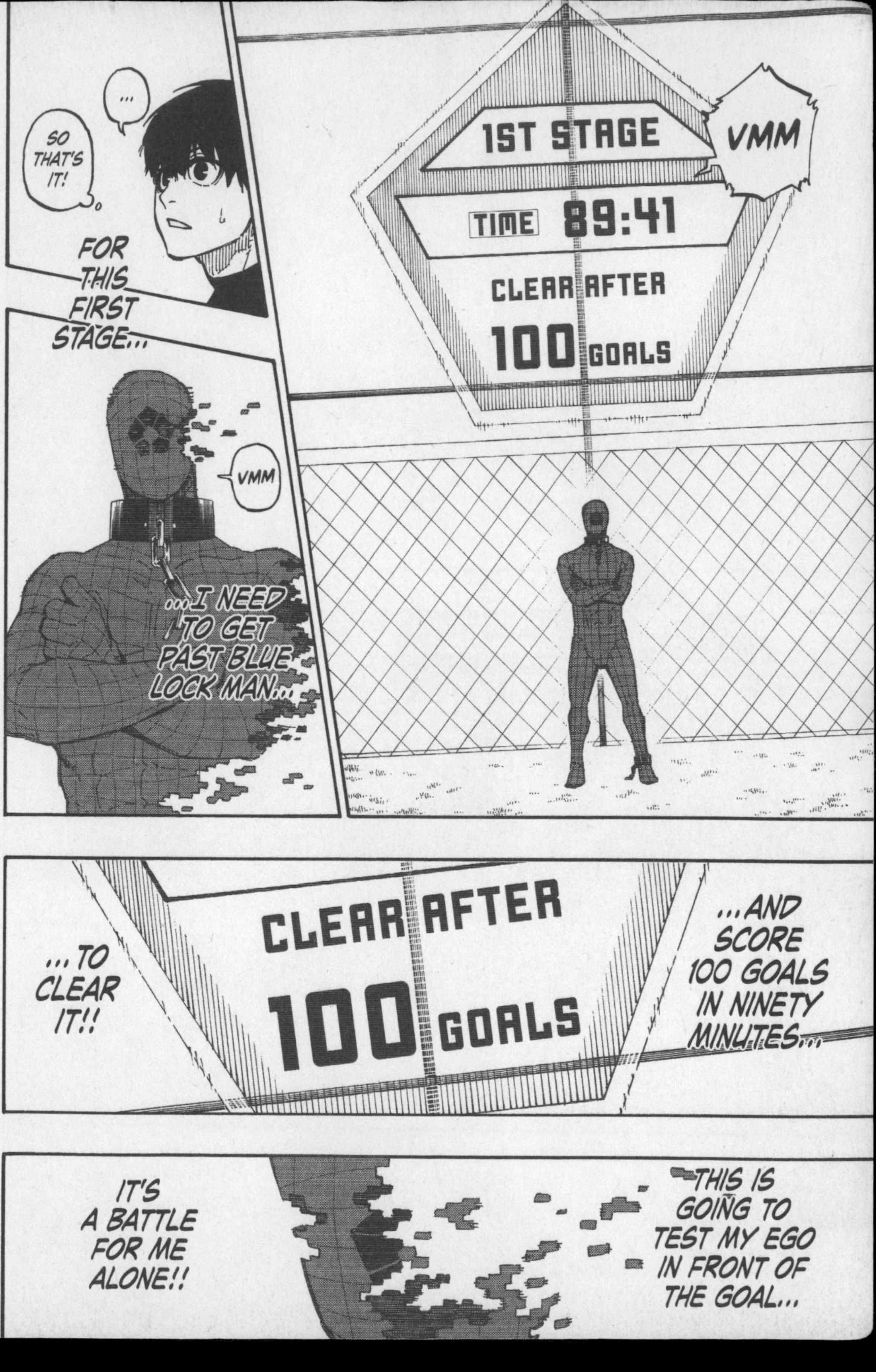

1ST STAGE
VMM
TIME 89:41
CLEAR AFTER 100 GOALS
...
SO THAT'S IT!
FOR THIS FIRST STAGE...
VMM
...I NEED TO GET PAST BLUE LOCK MAN...
...AND SCORE 100 GOALS IN NINETY MINUTES...
CLEAR AFTER 100 GOALS
...TO CLEAR IT!!
THIS IS GOING TO TEST MY EGO IN FRONT OF THE GOAL...
IT'S A BATTLE FOR ME ALONE!!

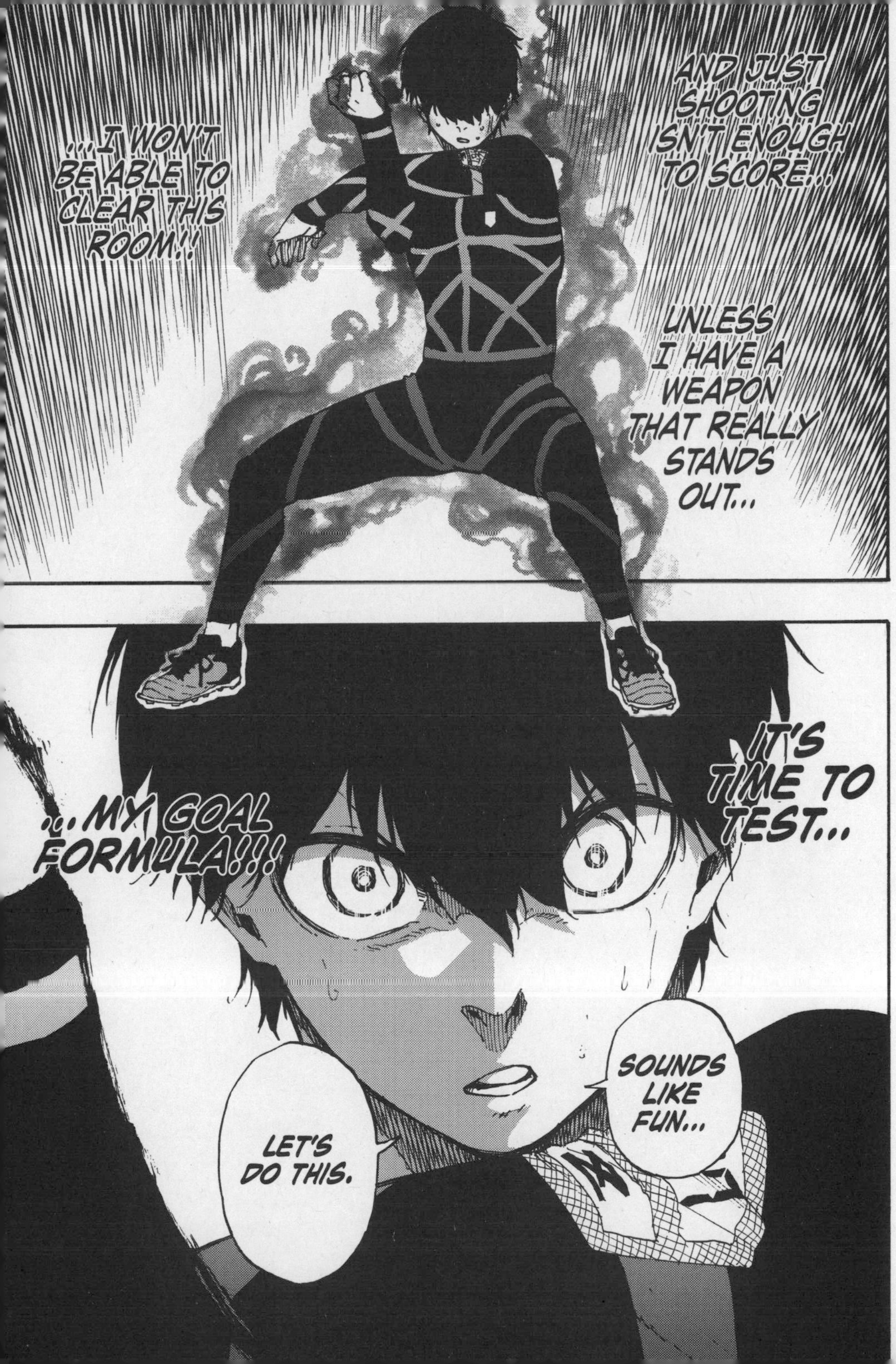
AND JUST SHOOTING ISN'T ENOUGH TO SCORE...
UNLESS I HAVE A WEAPON THAT REALLY STANDS OUT...
...I WON'T BE ABLE TO CLEAR THIS ROOM!!
IT'S TIME TO TEST...
...MY GOAL FORMULA!!!
SOUNDS LIKE FUN...
LET'S DO THIS.

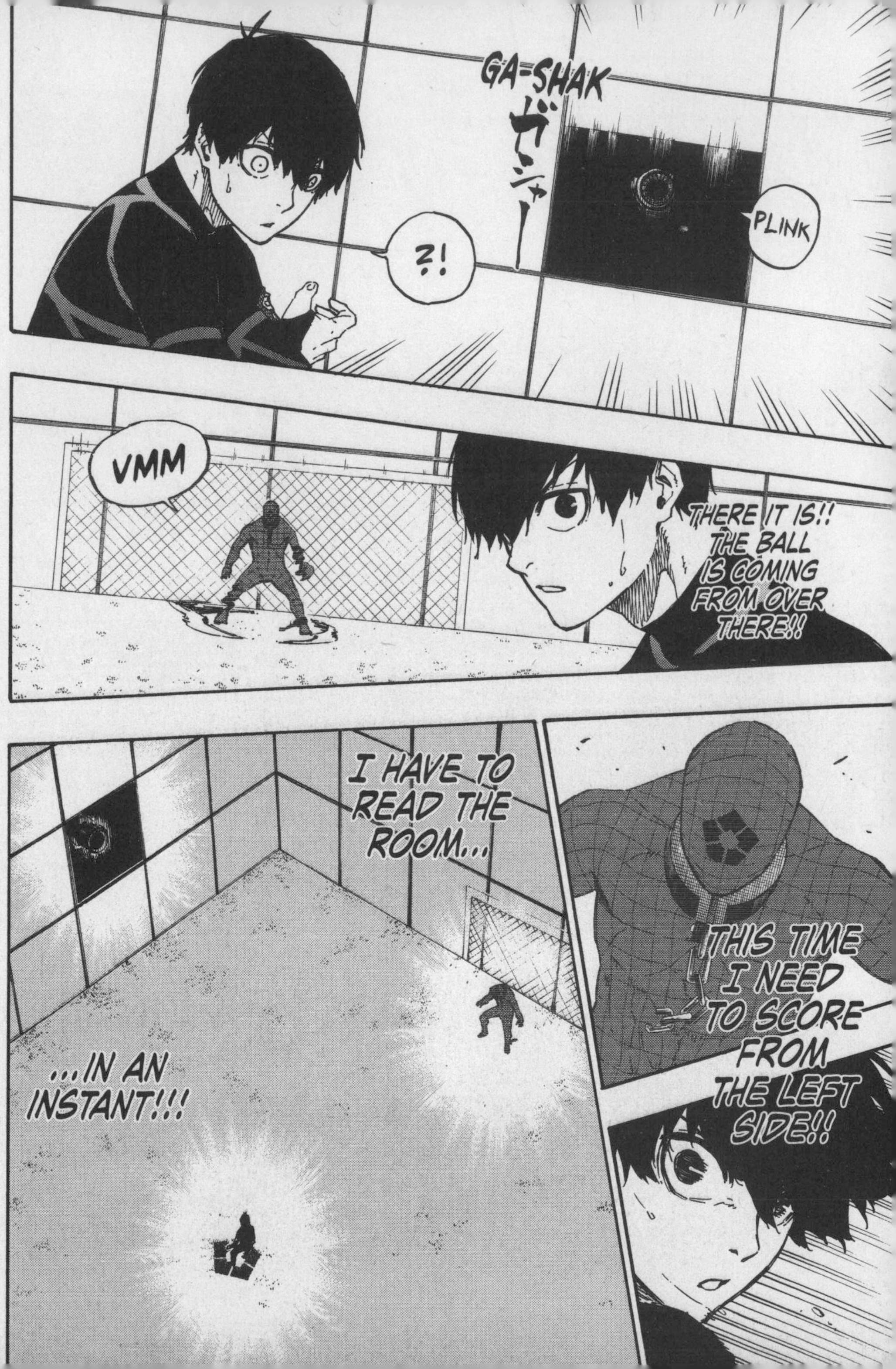
GA-SHAK
ガシャー
PLINK
?!
THERE IT IS!! THE BALL IS COMING FROM OVER THERE!!
VMM
THIS TIME I NEED TO SCORE FROM THE LEFT SIDE!!
I HAVE TO READ THE ROOM...
...IN AN INSTANT!!!

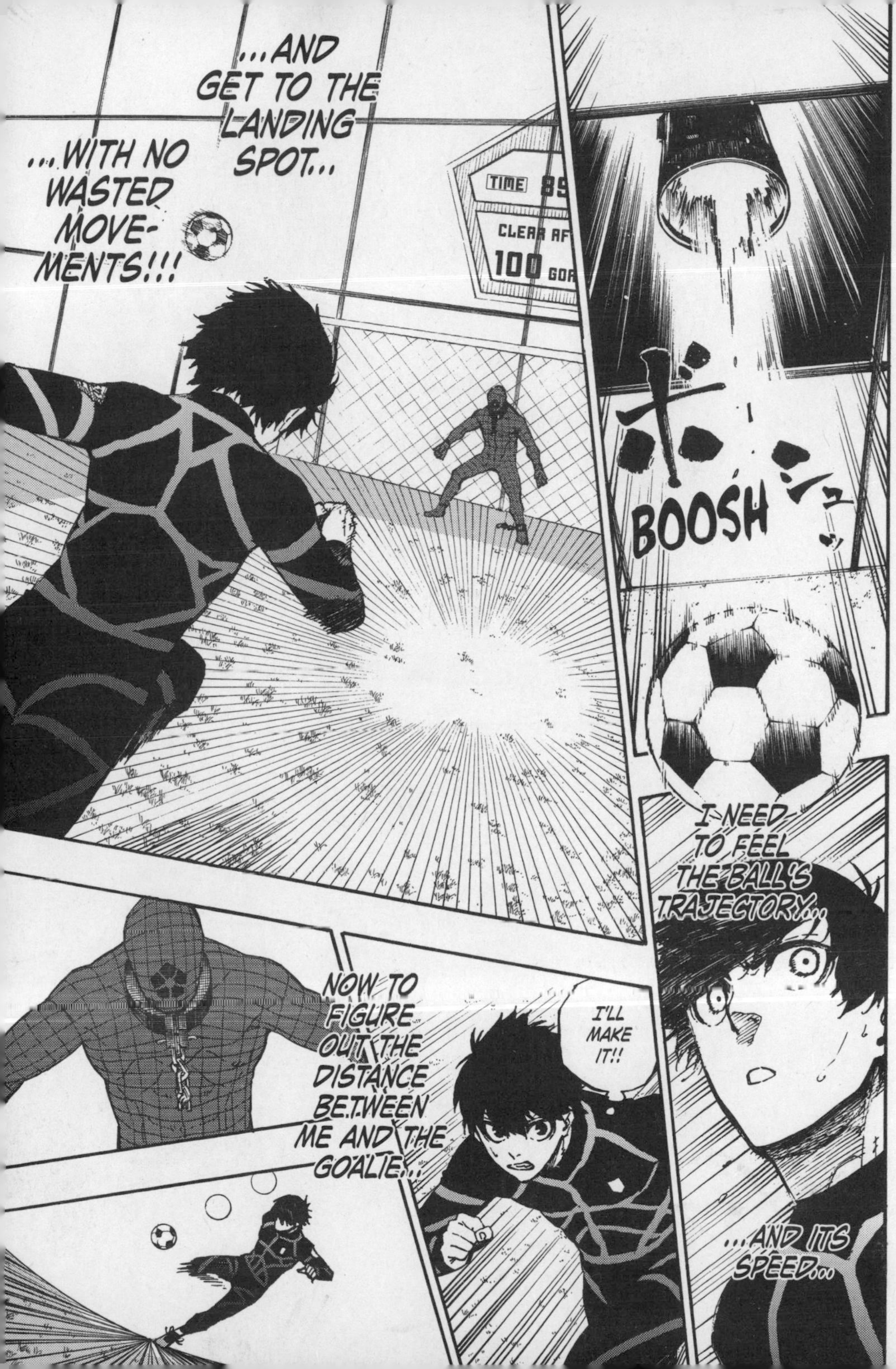

BOOSH
シュッ
...AND GET TO THE LANDING SPOT...
...WITH NO WASTED MOVEMENTS!!!
TIME 89
CLEAR AF
100 GOA
I NEED TO FEEL THE BALL'S TRAJECTORY...
...AND ITS SPEED...
NOW TO FIGURE OUT THE DISTANCE BETWEEN ME AND THE GOALIE...
I'LL MAKE IT!!

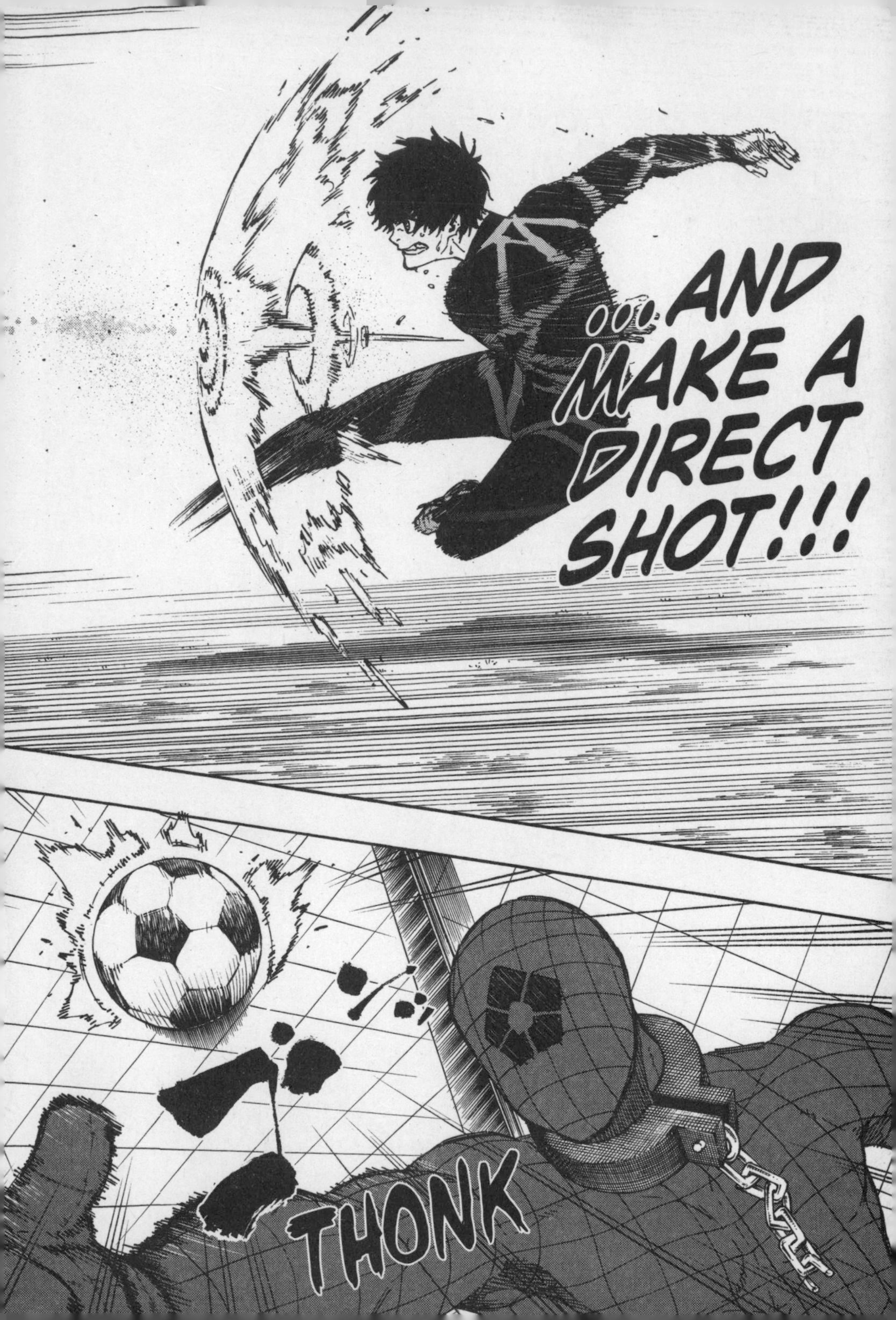
...AND MAKE A DIRECT SHOT!!!
THONK

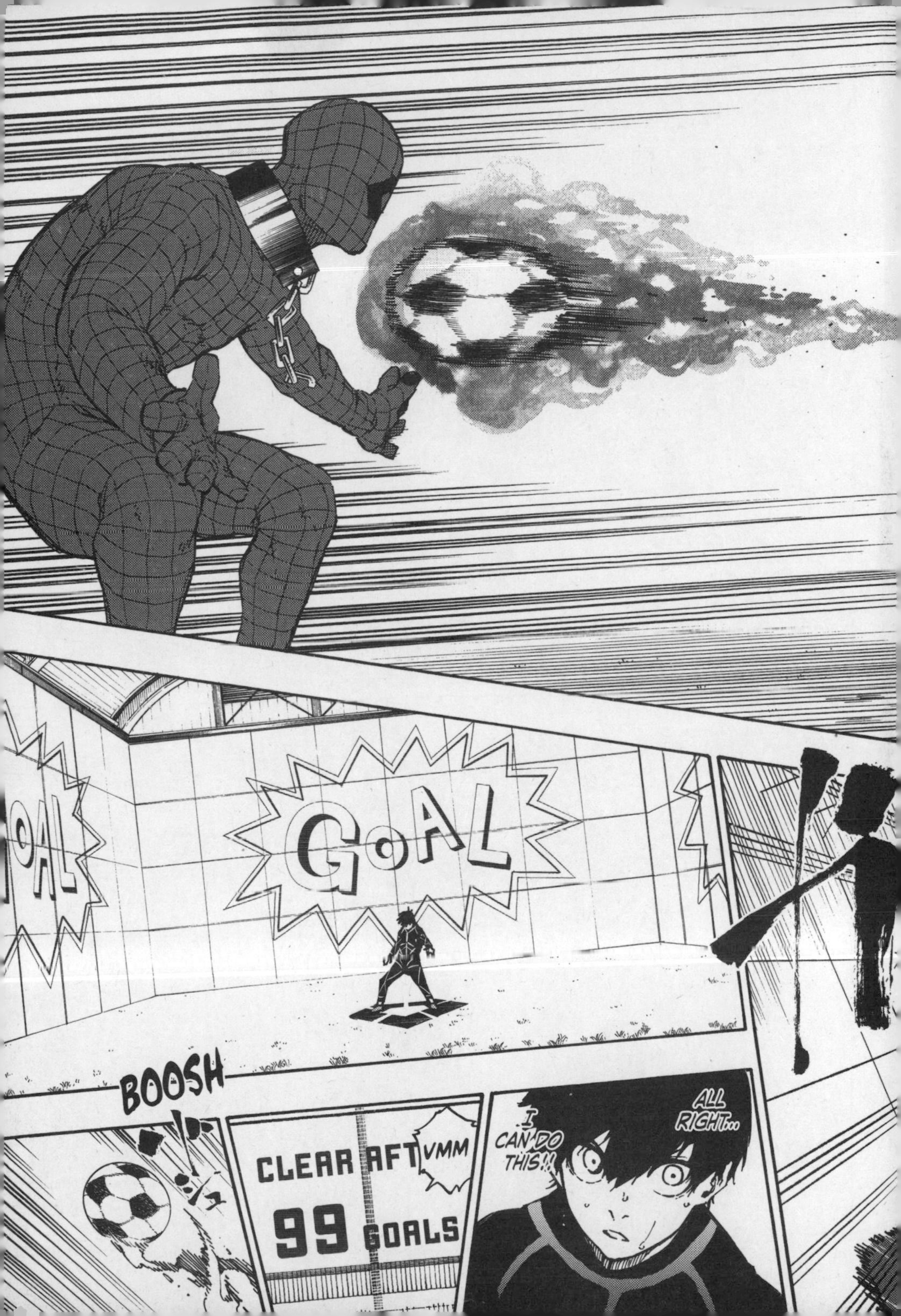
GOAL
OAL
ALL RIGHT...
I CAN DO THIS!!
VMM
CLEAR AFT
99 GOALS
BOOSH

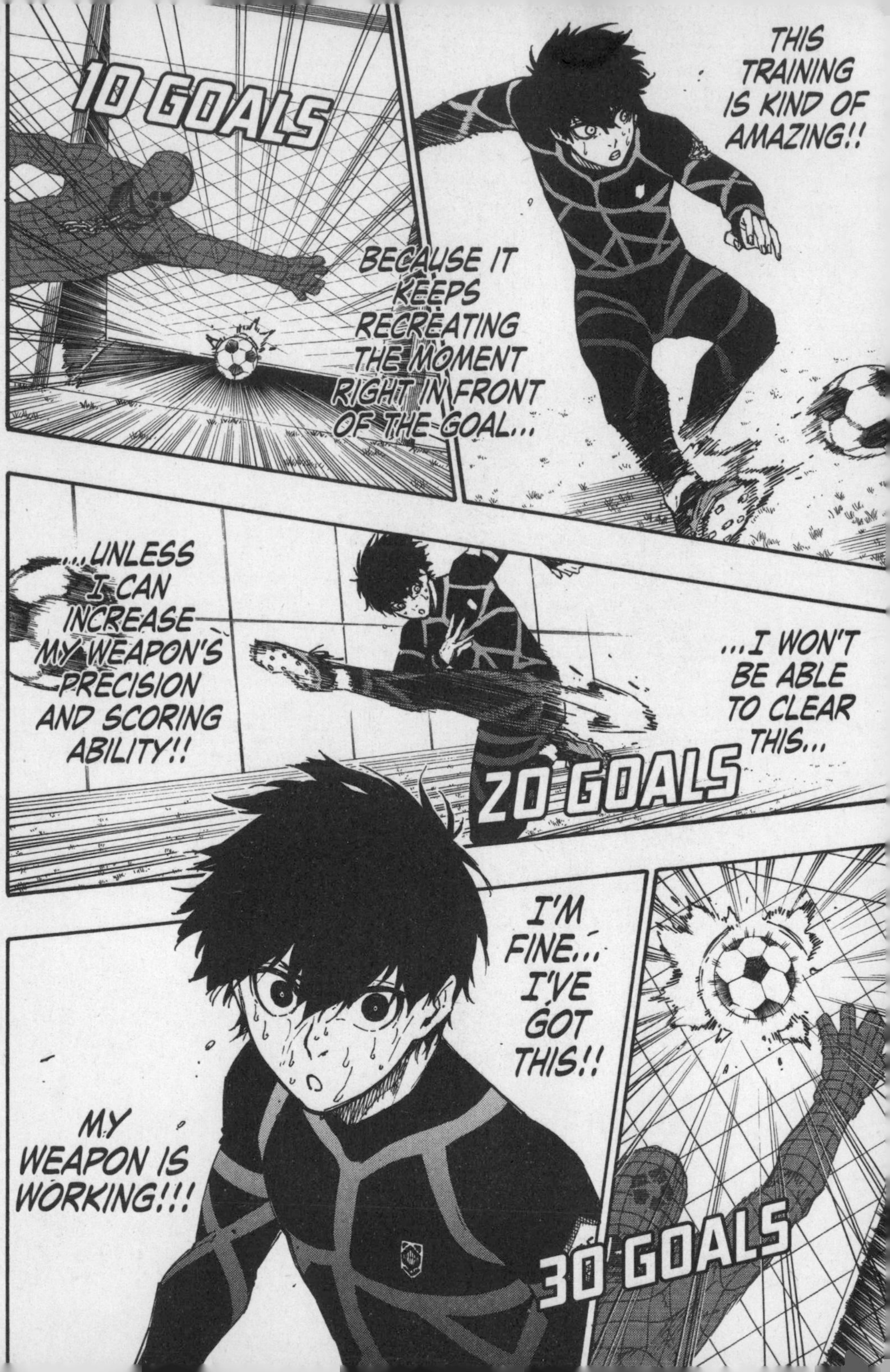
THIS TRAINING IS KIND OF AMAZING!!
BECAUSE IT KEEPS RECREATING THE MOMENT RIGHT IN FRONT OF THE GOAL...
10 GOALS
...I WON'T BE ABLE TO CLEAR THIS...
...UNLESS I CAN INCREASE MY WEAPON'S PRECISION AND SCORING ABILITY!!
20 GOALS
30 GOALS
I'M FINE... I'VE GOT THIS!!
MY WEAPON IS WORKING!!!

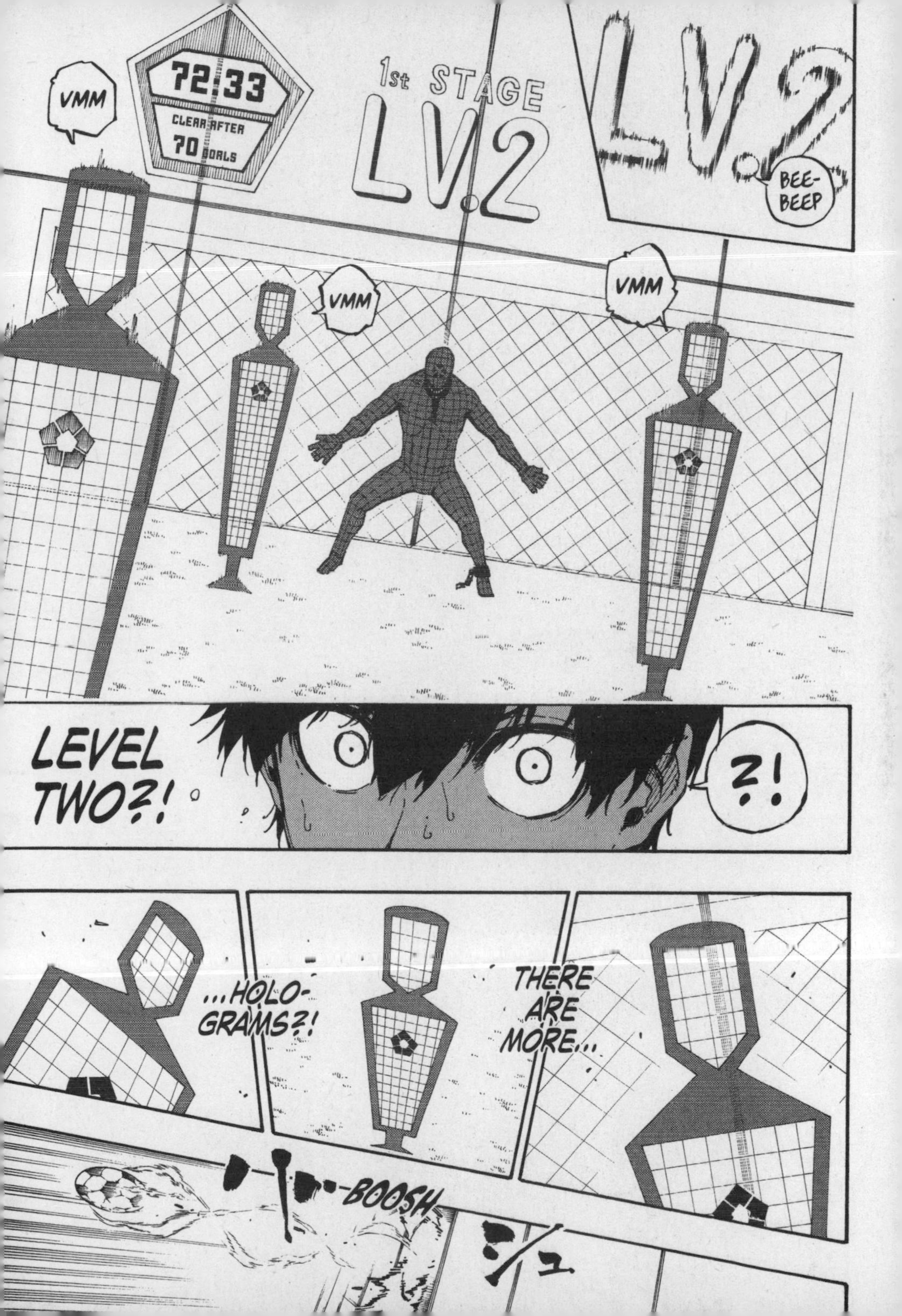
LV.2
BEE-BEEP
VMM
1st STAGE
LV.2
VMM
72:33
CLEAR AFTER
70 GOALS
VMM
?!
LEVEL TWO?!
THERE ARE MORE...
...HOLO-GRAMS?!
BOOSH
シュ

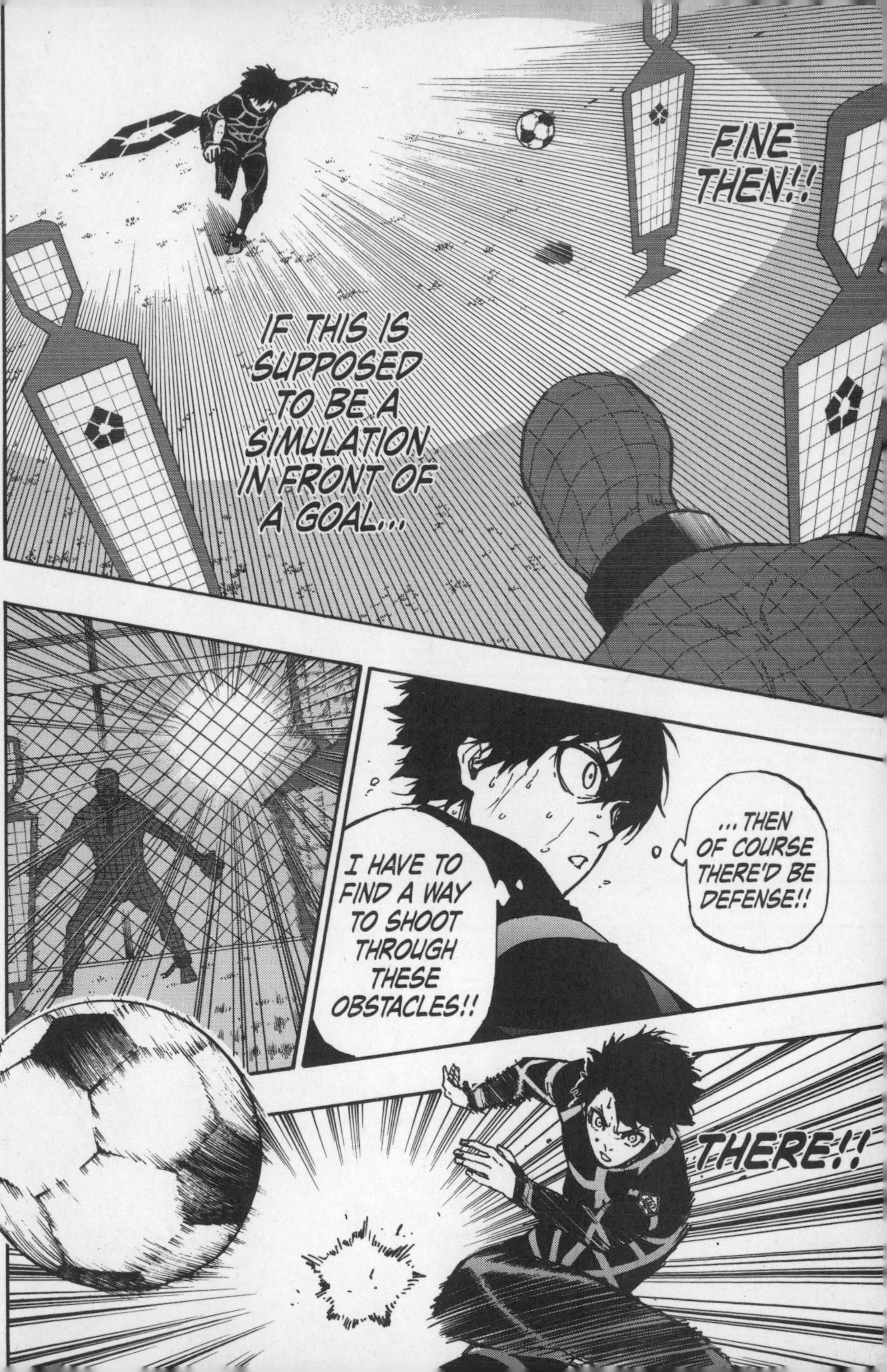
FINE THEN!!
IF THIS IS SUPPOSED TO BE A SIMULATION IN FRONT OF A GOAL...
...THEN OF COURSE THERE'D BE DEFENSE!!
I HAVE TO FIND A WAY TO SHOOT THROUGH THESE OBSTACLES!!
THERE!!

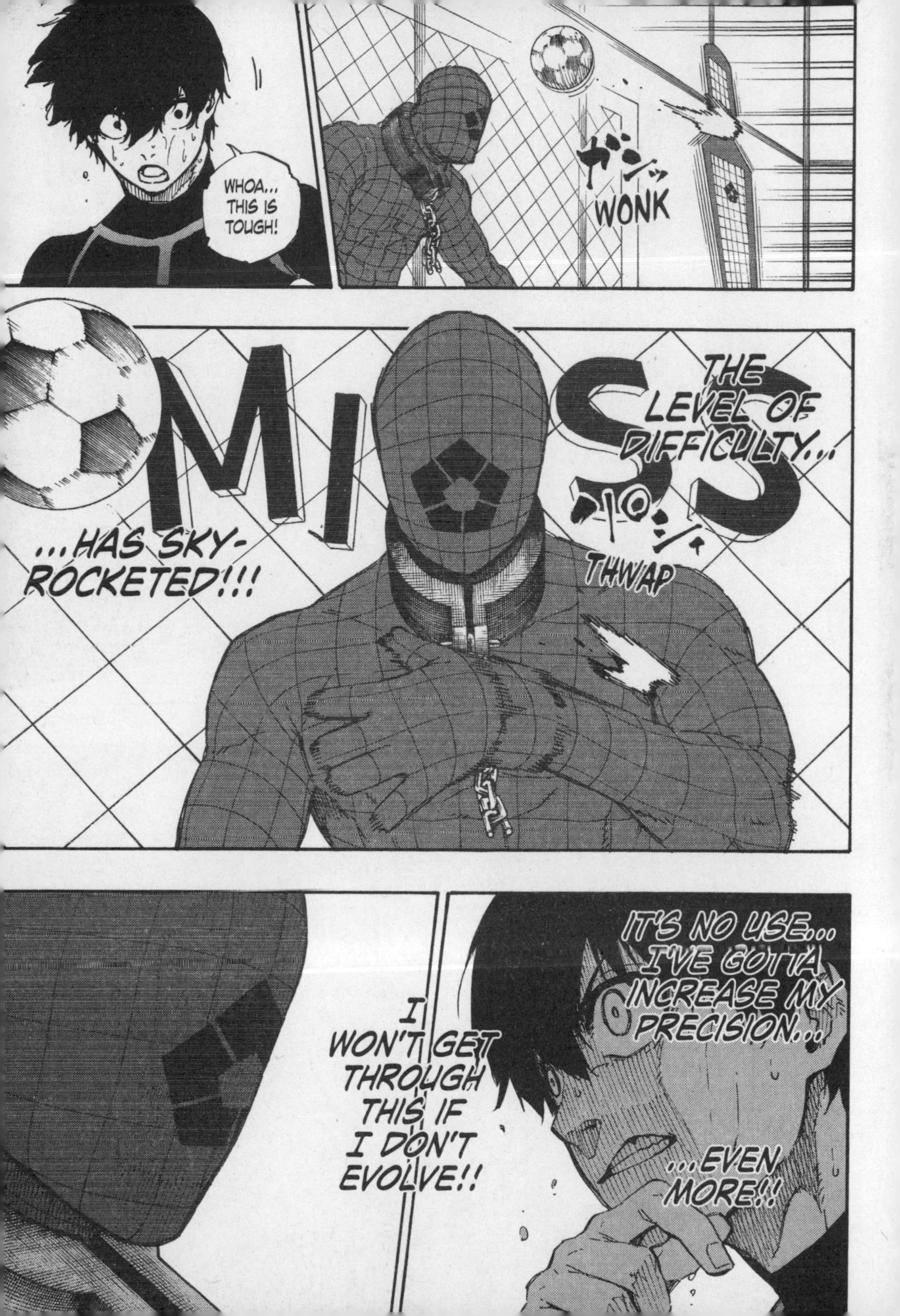
WONK
WHOA... THIS IS TOUGH!
MISS
THE LEVEL OF DIFFICULTY...
THWAP
...HAS SKY-ROCKETED!!!
IT'S NO USE... I'VE GOTTA INCREASE MY PRECISION...
...EVEN MORE!!
I WON'T GET THROUGH THIS IF I DON'T EVOLVE!!

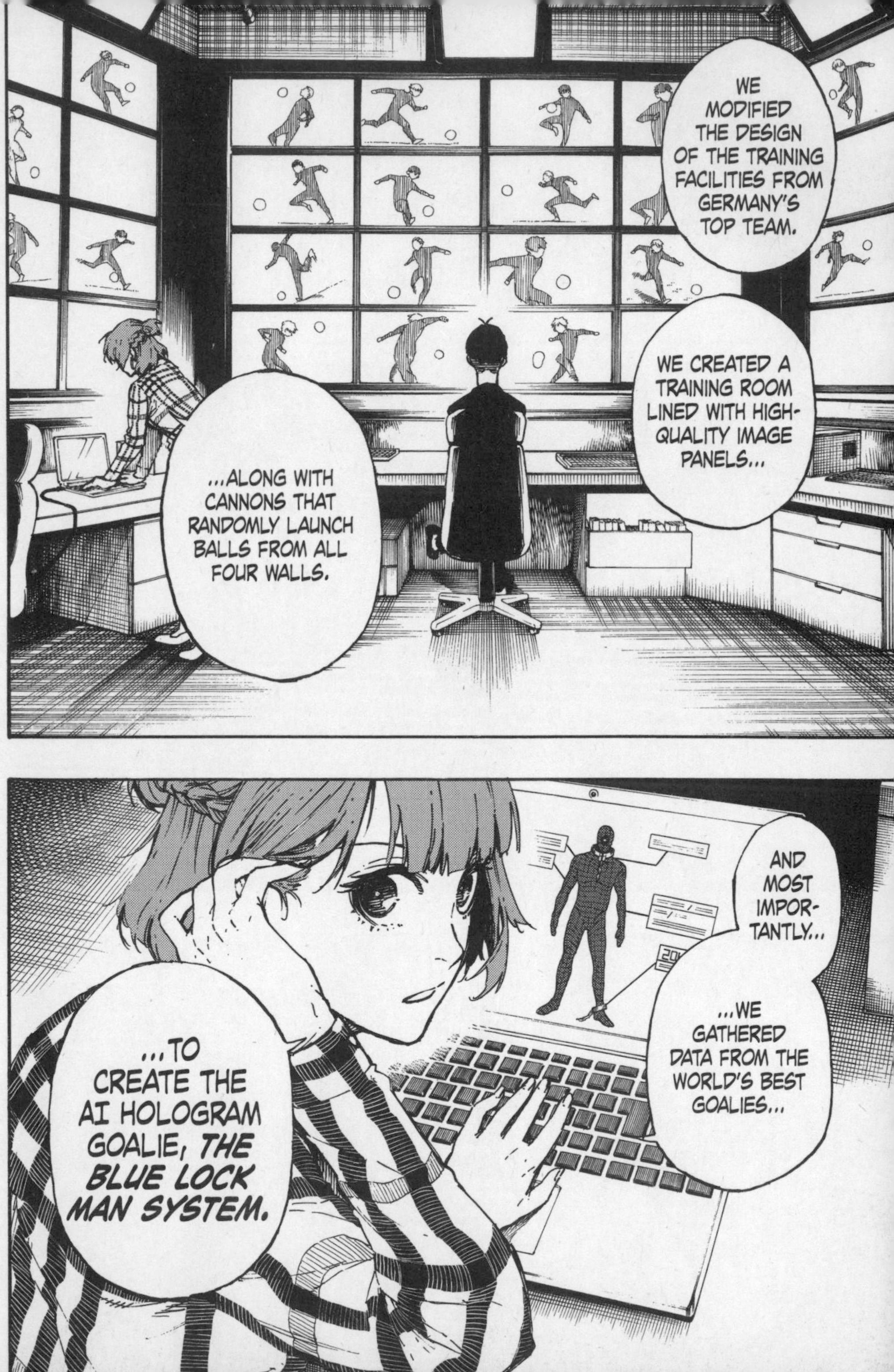
WE MODIFIED THE DESIGN OF THE TRAINING FACILITIES FROM GERMANY'S TOP TEAM.
WE CREATED A TRAINING ROOM LINED WITH HIGH-QUALITY IMAGE PANELS...
...ALONG WITH CANNONS THAT RANDOMLY LAUNCH BALLS FROM ALL FOUR WALLS.
AND MOST IMPOR-TANTLY...
...WE GATHERED DATA FROM THE WORLD'S BEST GOALIES...
...TO CREATE THE AI HOLOGRAM GOALIE, *THE BLUE LOCK MAN SYSTEM.*

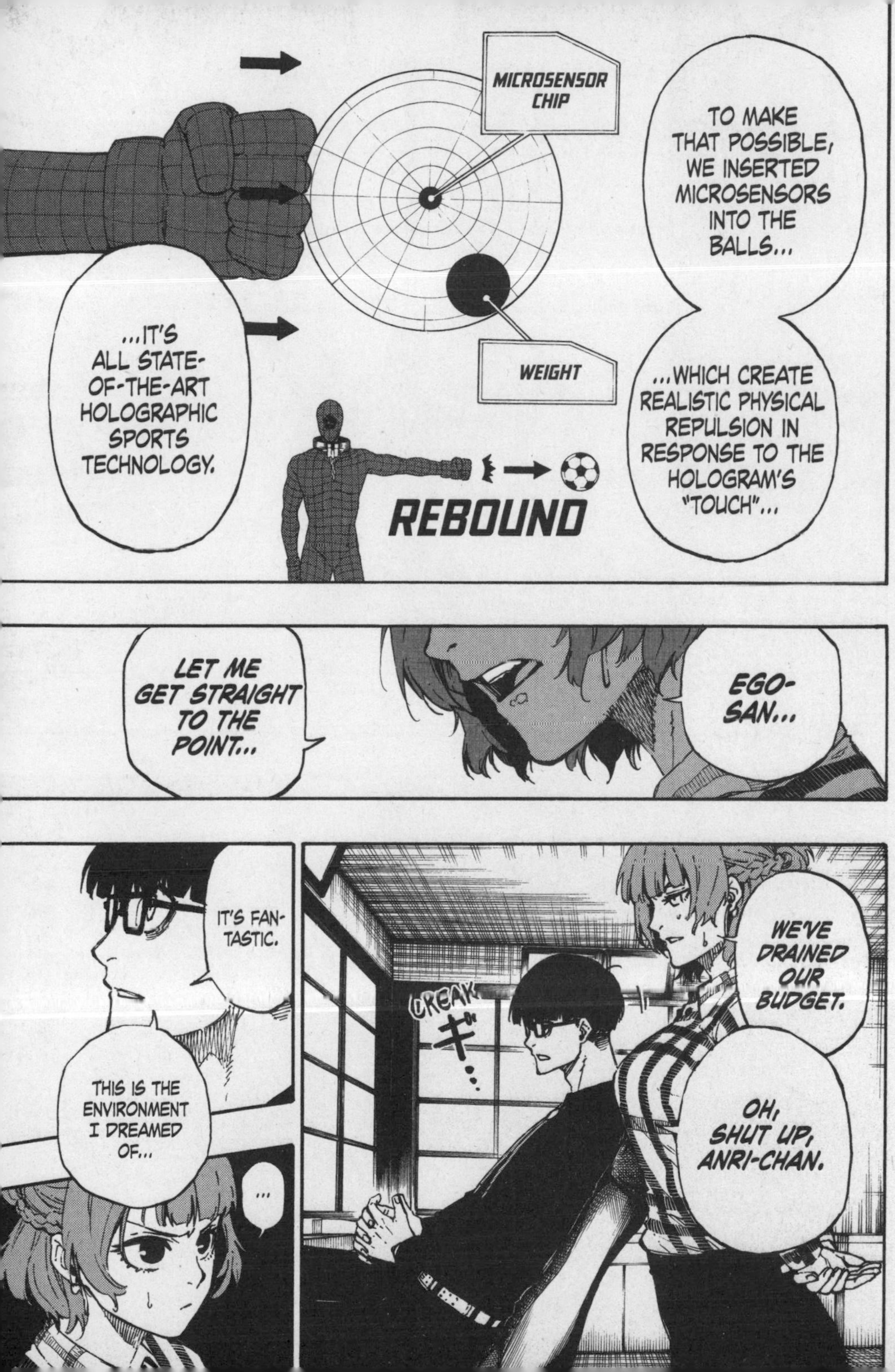
TO MAKE THAT POSSIBLE, WE INSERTED MICROSENSORS INTO THE BALLS...
...WHICH CREATE REALISTIC PHYSICAL REPULSION IN RESPONSE TO THE HOLOGRAM'S "TOUCH"...
MICROSENSOR CHIP
WEIGHT
REBOUND
...IT'S ALL STATE-OF-THE-ART HOLOGRAPHIC SPORTS TECHNOLOGY.
EGO-SAN...
LET ME GET STRAIGHT TO THE POINT...
WE'VE DRAINED OUR BUDGET.
OH, SHUT UP, ANRI-CHAN.
CREAK
IT'S FAN-TASTIC.
THIS IS THE ENVIRONMENT I DREAMED OF...
...

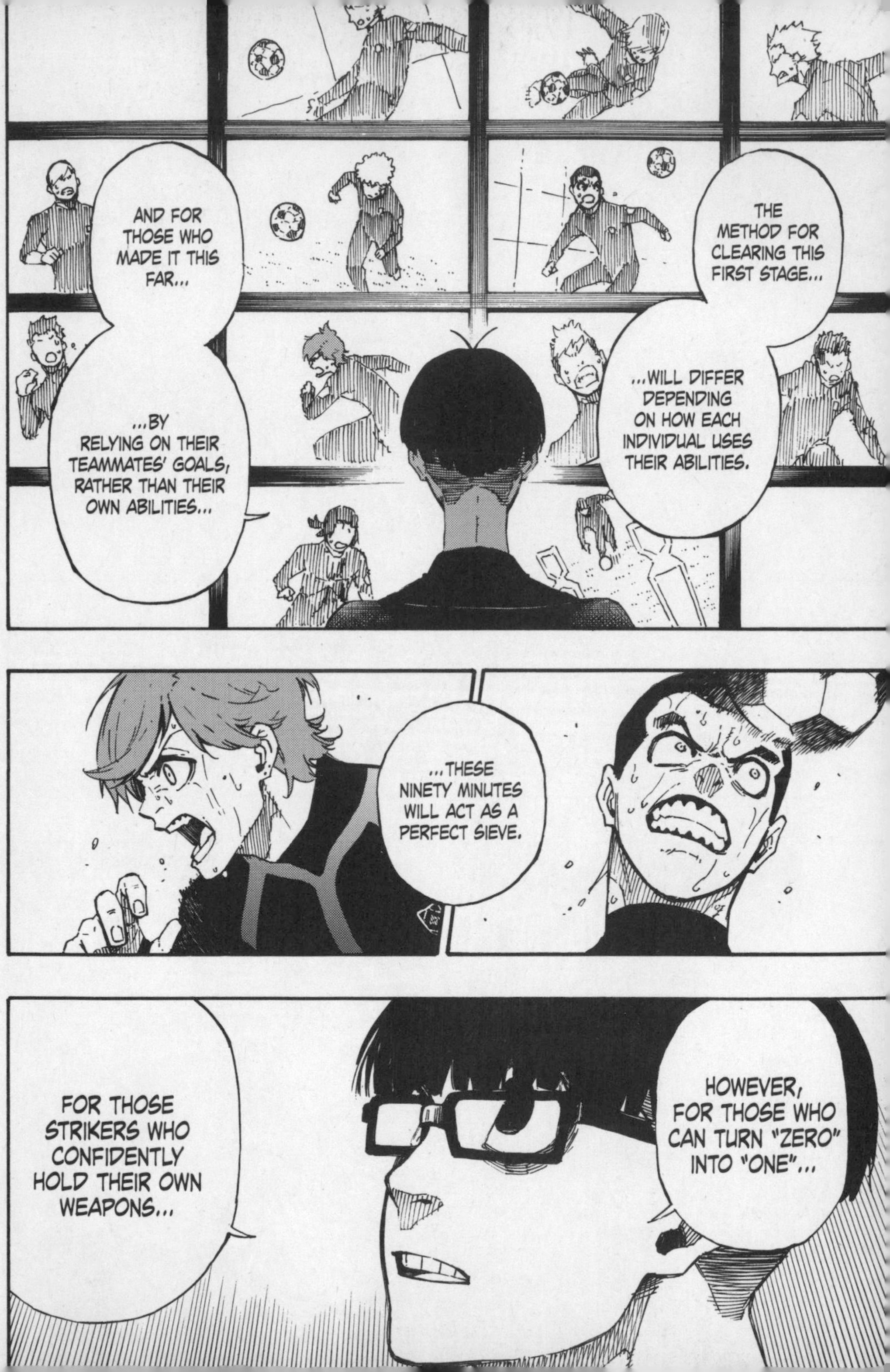
THE METHOD FOR CLEARING THIS FIRST STAGE...
...WILL DIFFER DEPENDING ON HOW EACH INDIVIDUAL USES THEIR ABILITIES.
AND FOR THOSE WHO MADE IT THIS FAR...
...BY RELYING ON THEIR TEAMMATES' GOALS, RATHER THAN THEIR OWN ABILITIES...
...THESE NINETY MINUTES WILL ACT AS A PERFECT SIEVE.
HOWEVER, FOR THOSE WHO CAN TURN "ZERO" INTO "ONE"...
FOR THOSE STRIKERS WHO CONFIDENTLY HOLD THEIR OWN WEAPONS...

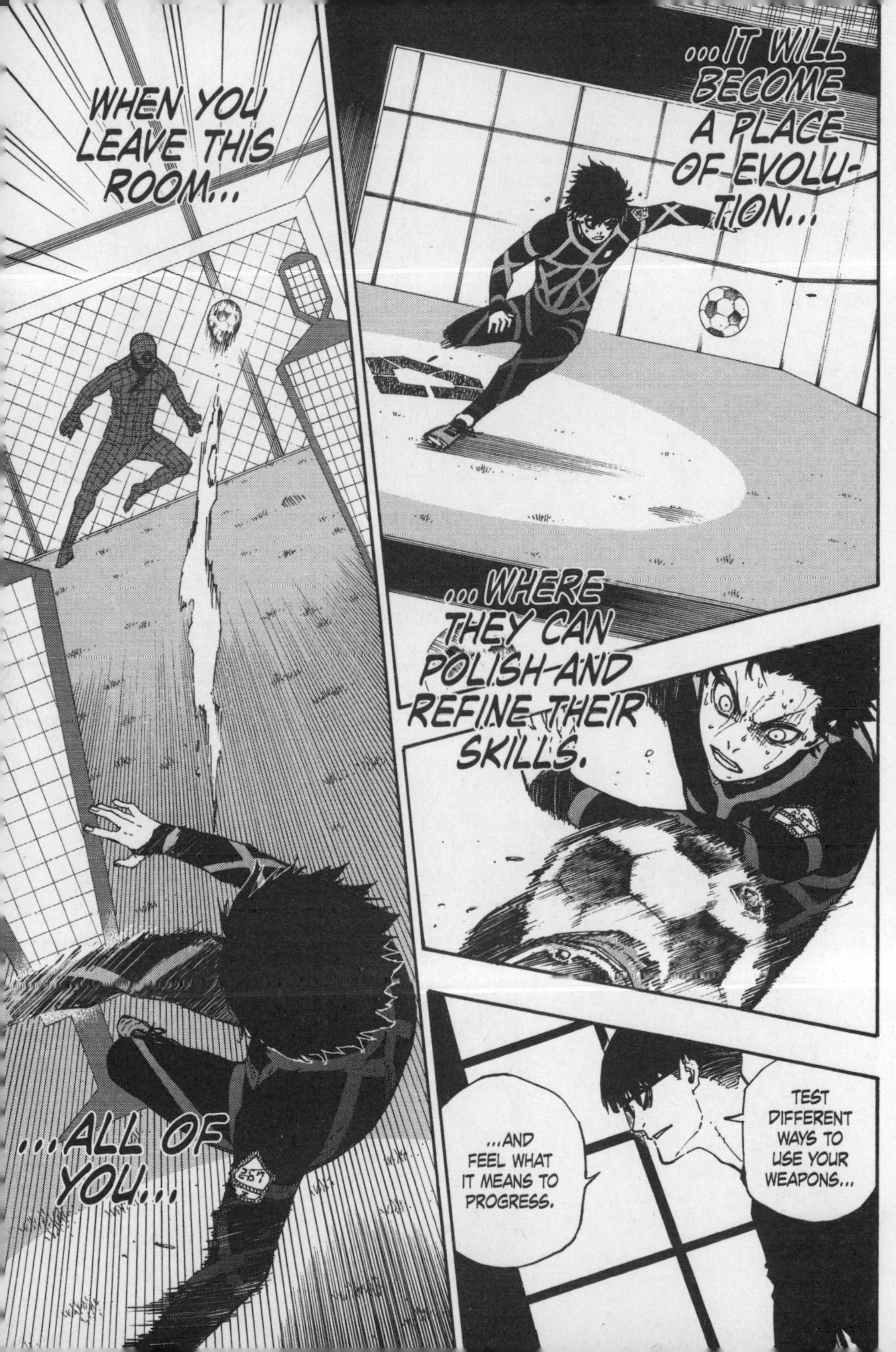
...IT WILL BECOME A PLACE OF EVOLUTION...
...WHERE THEY CAN POLISH AND REFINE THEIR SKILLS.
TEST DIFFERENT WAYS TO USE YOUR WEAPONS...
...AND FEEL WHAT IT MEANS TO PROGRESS.
WHEN YOU LEAVE THIS ROOM...
...ALL OF YOU...

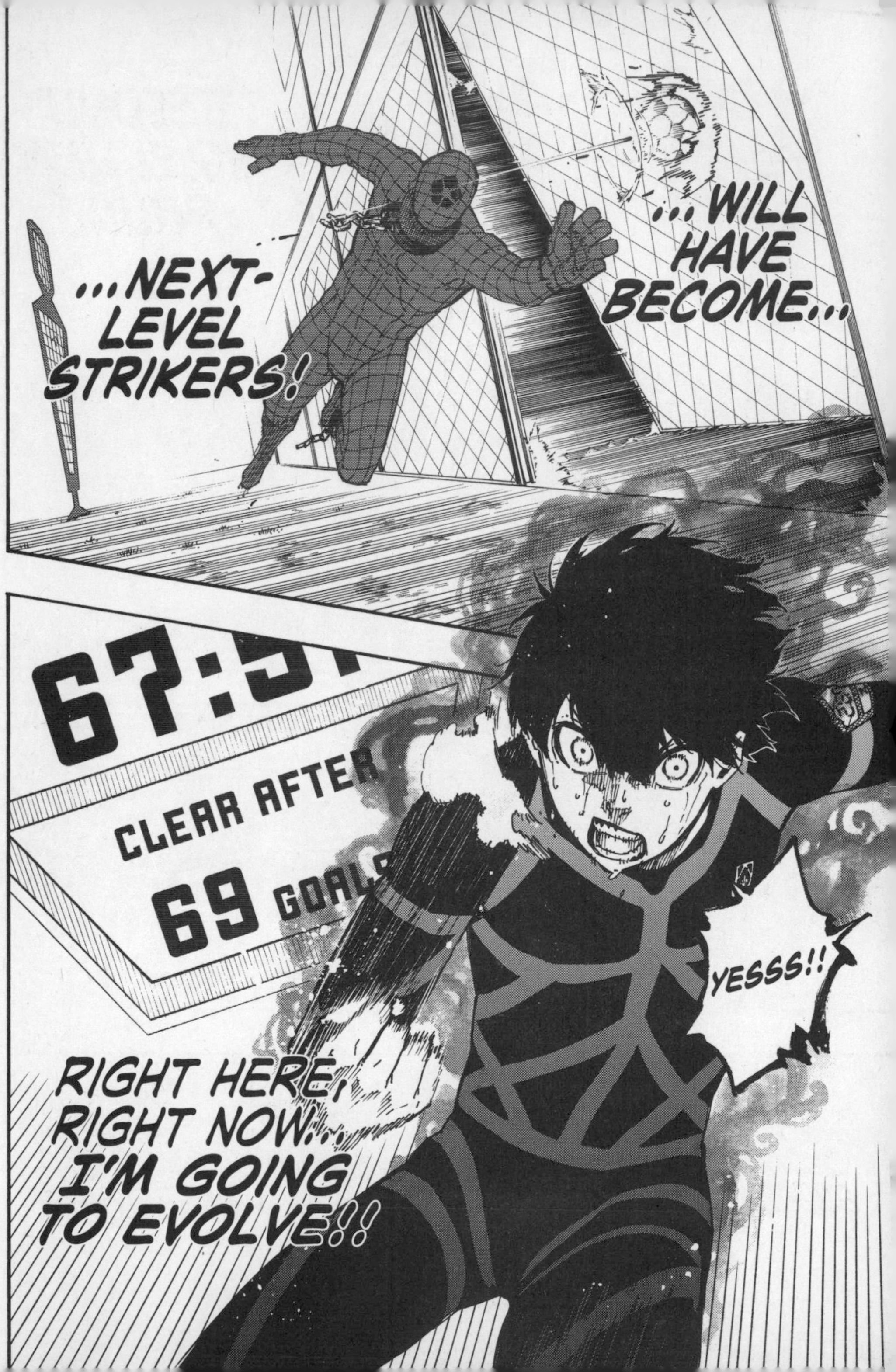
...WILL HAVE BECOME...
...NEXT-LEVEL STRIKERS!
YESSS!!
CLEAR AFTER
69
RIGHT HERE, RIGHT NOW... I'M GOING TO EVOLVE!!

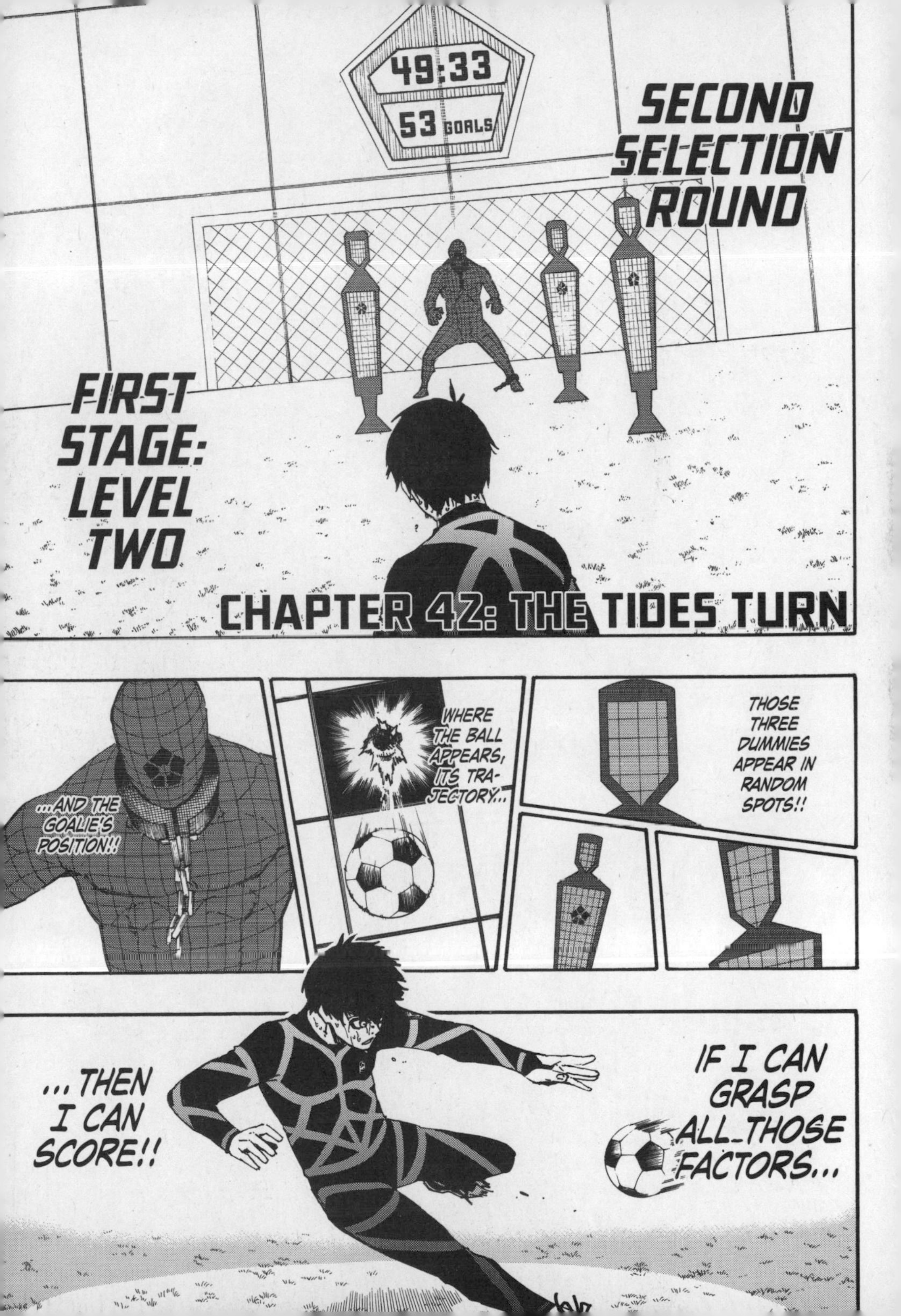
49:33
53 GOALS
SECOND SELECTION ROUND
FIRST STAGE: LEVEL TWO
CHAPTER 42: THE TIDES TURN
THOSE THREE DUMMIES APPEAR IN RANDOM SPOTS!!
WHERE THE BALL APPEARS, ITS TRA-JECTORY...
...AND THE GOALIE'S POSITION!!
IF I CAN GRASP ALL THOSE FACTORS...
...THEN I CAN SCORE!!

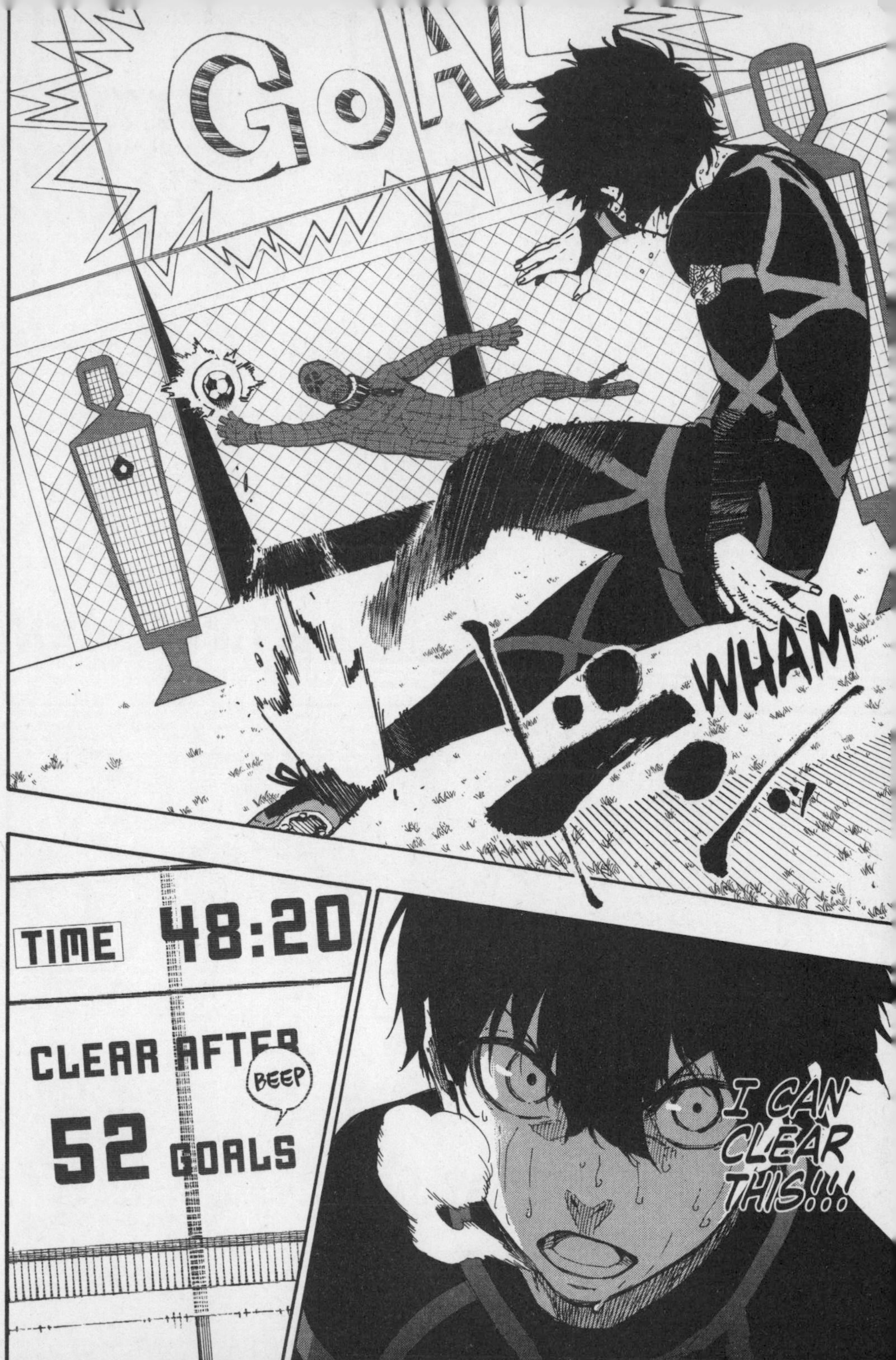

GOA
WHAM
I CAN CLEAR THIS!!!
TIME 48:20
CLEAR AFTER 52 GOALS
BEEP

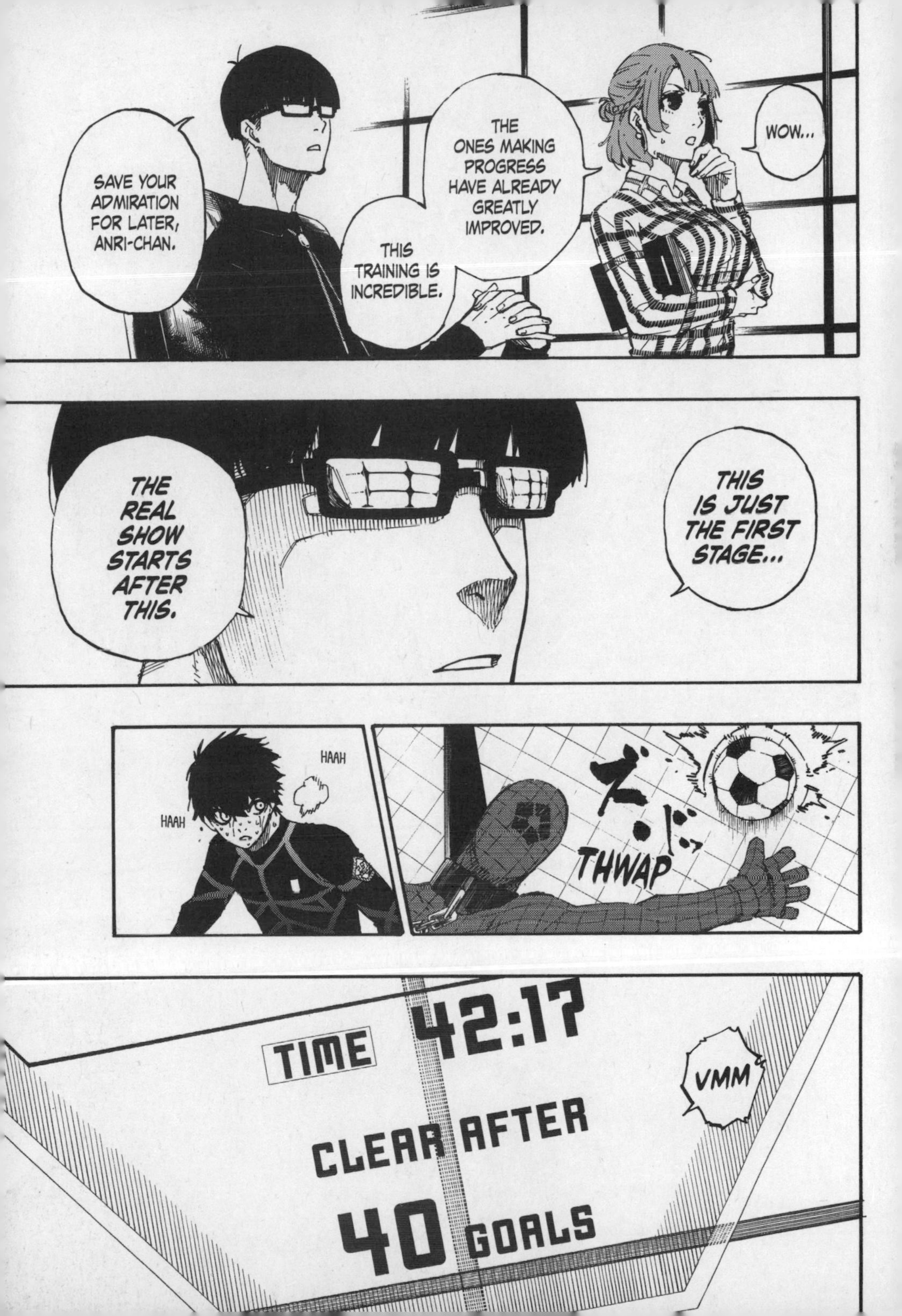
WOW...
THE ONES MAKING PROGRESS HAVE ALREADY GREATLY IMPROVED.
THIS TRAINING IS INCREDIBLE.
SAVE YOUR ADMIRATION FOR LATER, ANRI-CHAN.
THIS IS JUST THE FIRST STAGE...
THE REAL SHOW STARTS AFTER THIS.
THWAP
HAAH
HAAH
VMM
TIME 42:17
CLEAR AFTER 40 GOALS

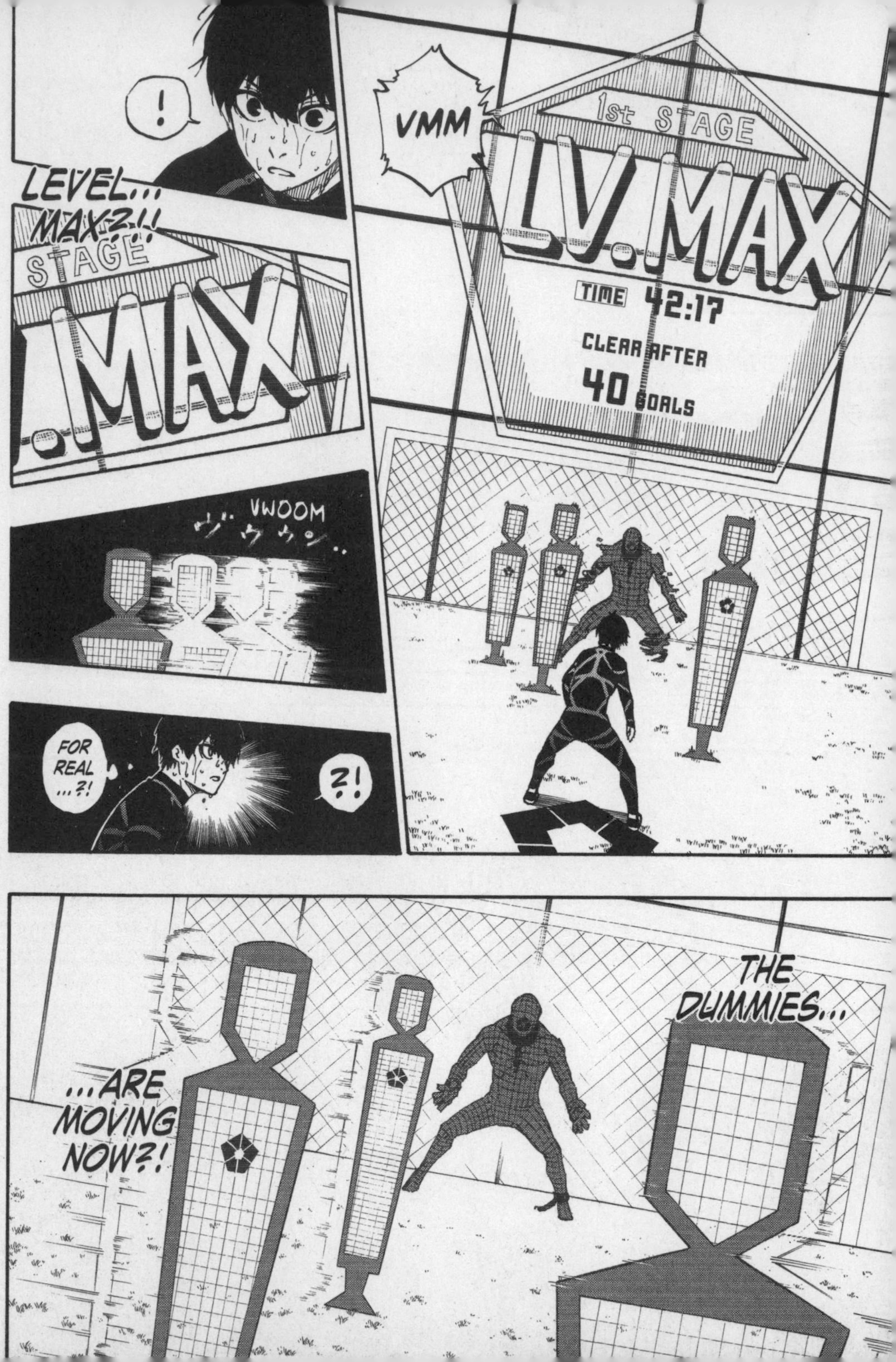
VMM
1st STAGE
LV. MAX
TIME 42:17
CLEAR AFTER
40 GOALS
!
LEVEL... MAX?!!
STAGE
.MAX
VWOOM
FOR REAL...?!
?!
THE DUMMIES...
...ARE MOVING NOW?!

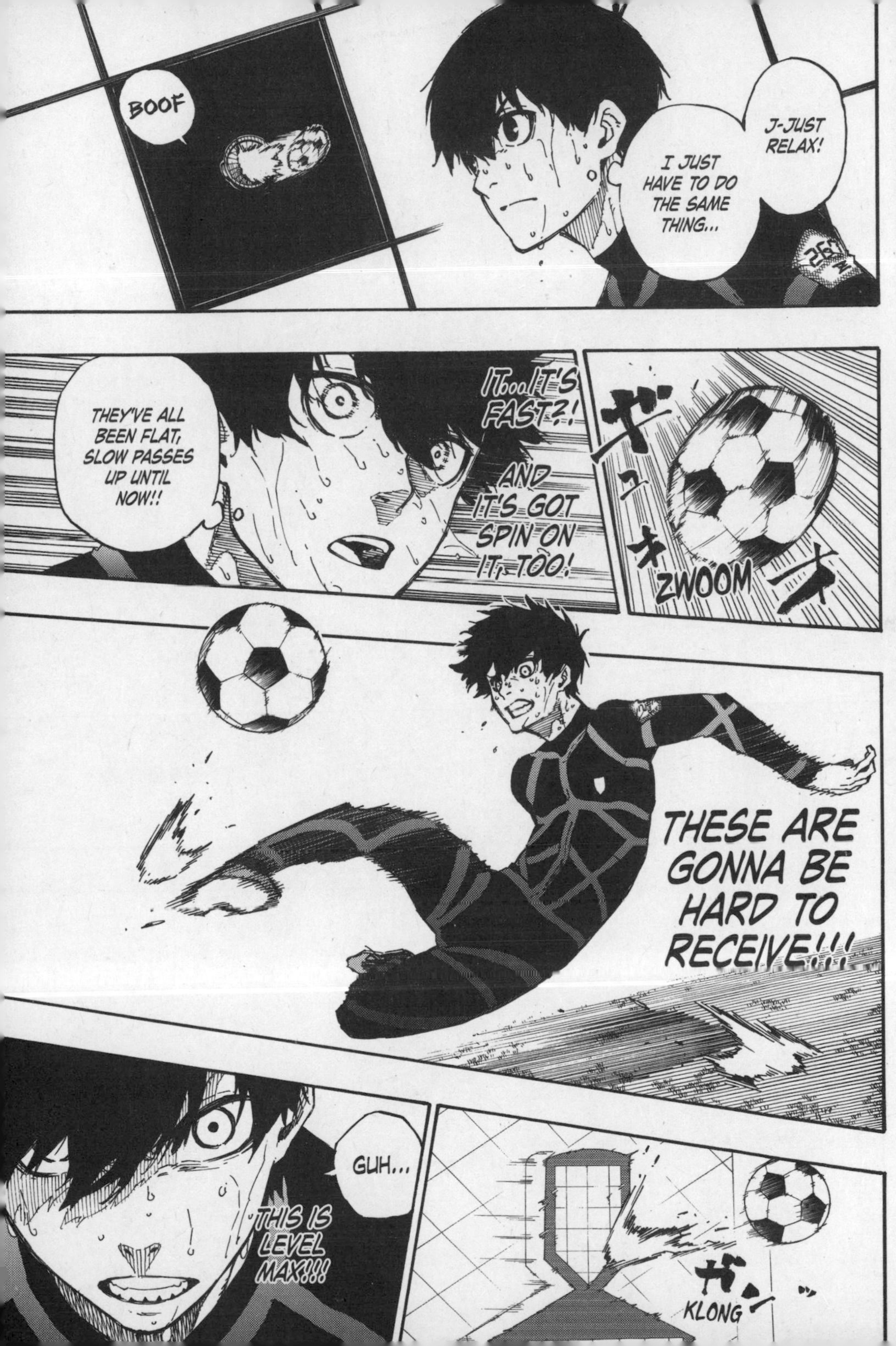
J-JUST RELAX!
I JUST HAVE TO DO THE SAME THING...
BOOF
ZWOOM
IT...IT'S FAST?!
AND IT'S GOT SPIN ON IT, TOO!
THEY'VE ALL BEEN FLAT, SLOW PASSES UP UNTIL NOW!!
THESE ARE GONNA BE HARD TO RECEIVE!!!
KLONG
GUH...
THIS IS LEVEL MAX!!!

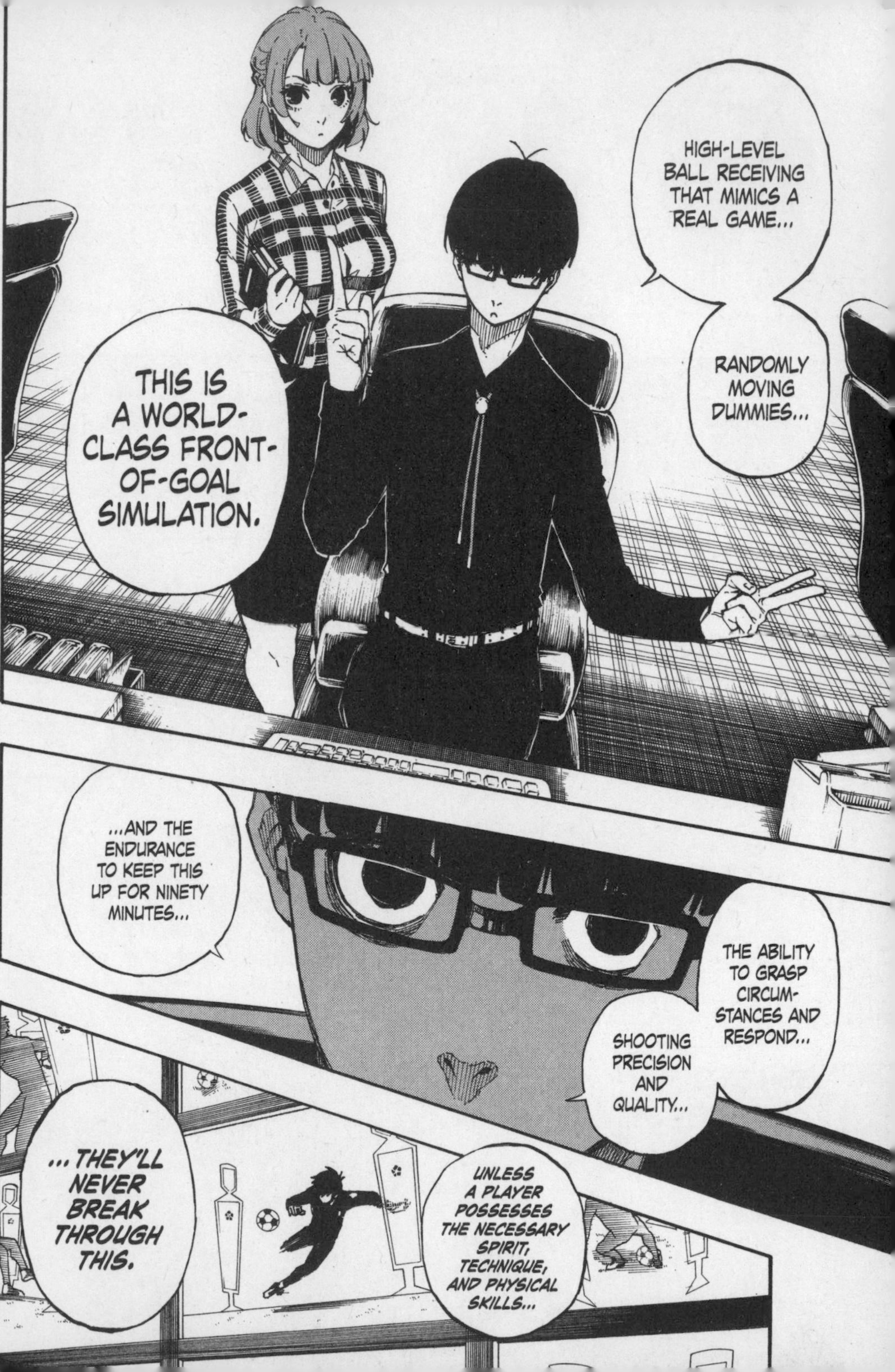
HIGH-LEVEL BALL RECEIVING THAT MIMICS A REAL GAME...
RANDOMLY MOVING DUMMIES...
THIS IS A WORLD-CLASS FRONT-OF-GOAL SIMULATION.
THE ABILITY TO GRASP CIRCUMSTANCES AND RESPOND...
SHOOTING PRECISION AND QUALITY...
...AND THE ENDURANCE TO KEEP THIS UP FOR NINETY MINUTES...
UNLESS A PLAYER POSSESSES THE NECESSARY SPIRIT, TECHNIQUE, AND PHYSICAL SKILLS...
...THEY'LL NEVER BREAK THROUGH THIS.

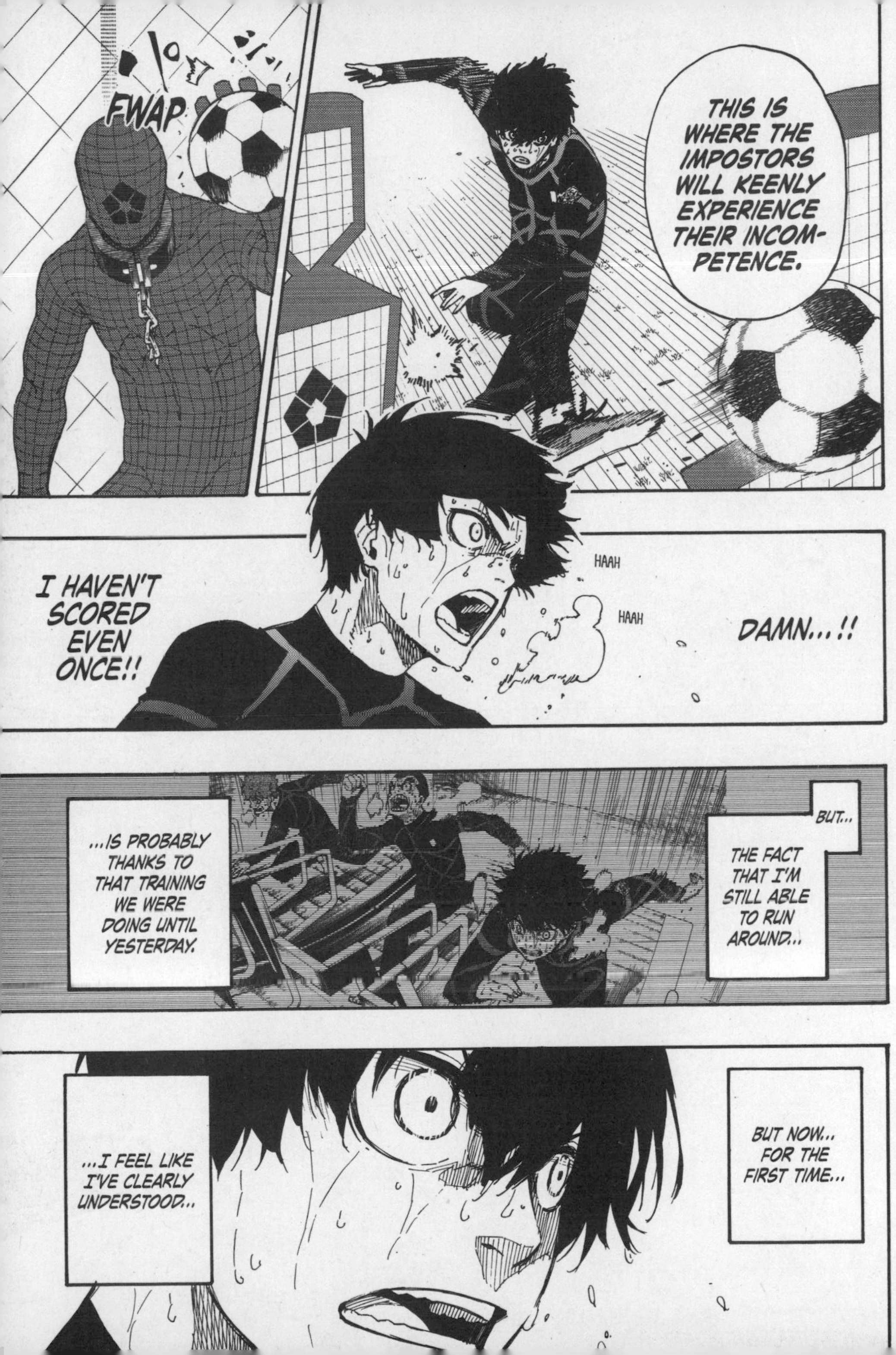
THIS IS WHERE THE IMPOSTORS WILL KEENLY EXPERIENCE THEIR INCOMPETENCE.
FWAP
DAMN...!!
HAAH
HAAH
I HAVEN'T SCORED EVEN ONCE!!
BUT...
THE FACT THAT I'M STILL ABLE TO RUN AROUND...
...IS PROBABLY THANKS TO THAT TRAINING WE WERE DOING UNTIL YESTERDAY.
BUT NOW... FOR THE FIRST TIME...
...I FEEL LIKE I'VE CLEARLY UNDERSTOOD...

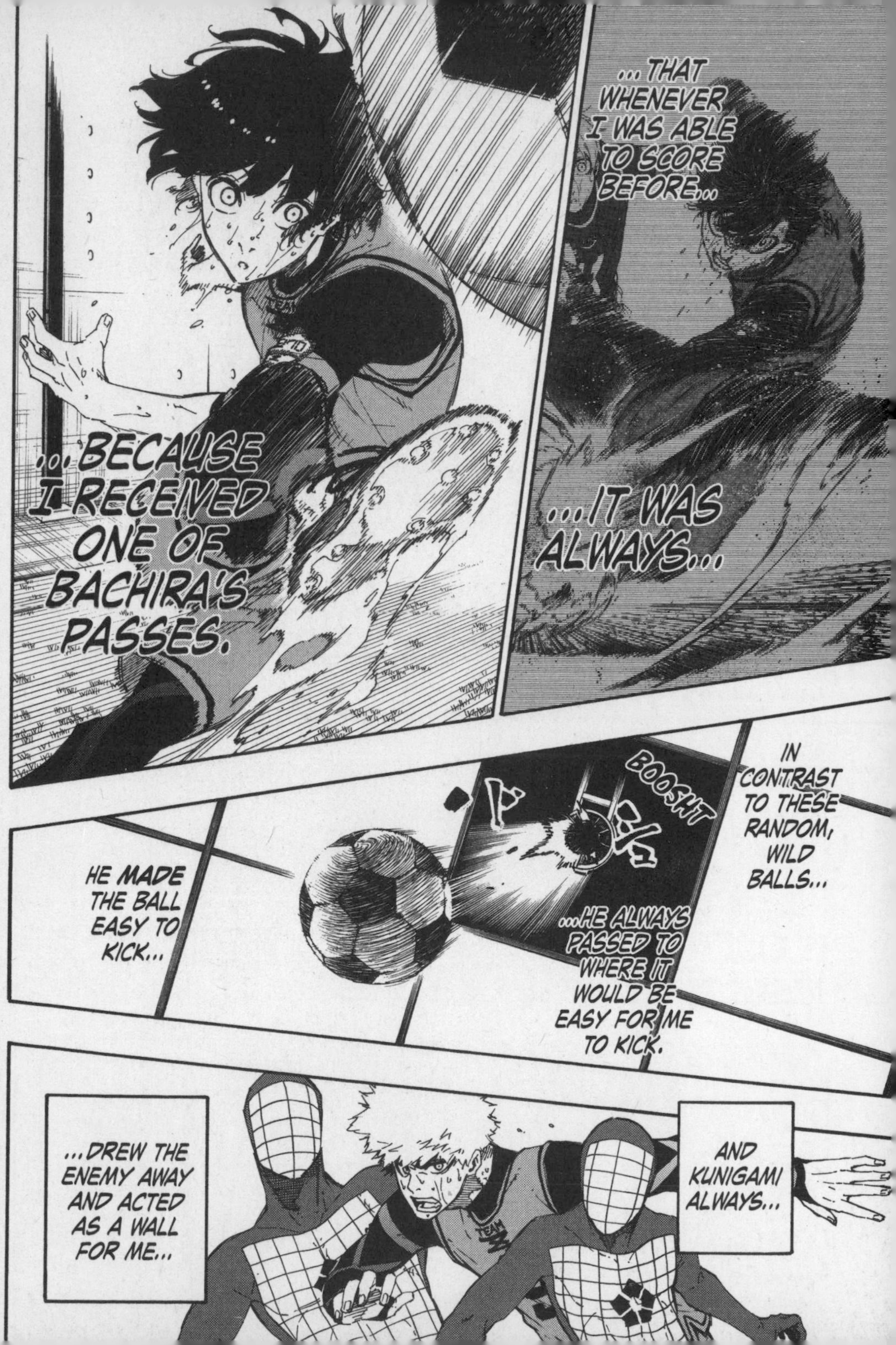
...THAT WHENEVER I WAS ABLE TO SCORE BEFORE...
...IT WAS ALWAYS...
...BECAUSE I RECEIVED ONE OF BACHIRA'S PASSES.
IN CONTRAST TO THESE RANDOM, WILD BALLS...
BOOSHT
...HE ALWAYS PASSED TO WHERE IT WOULD BE EASY FOR ME TO KICK.
HE MADE THE BALL EASY TO KICK...
AND KUNIGAMI ALWAYS...
...DREW THE ENEMY AWAY AND ACTED AS A WALL FOR ME...

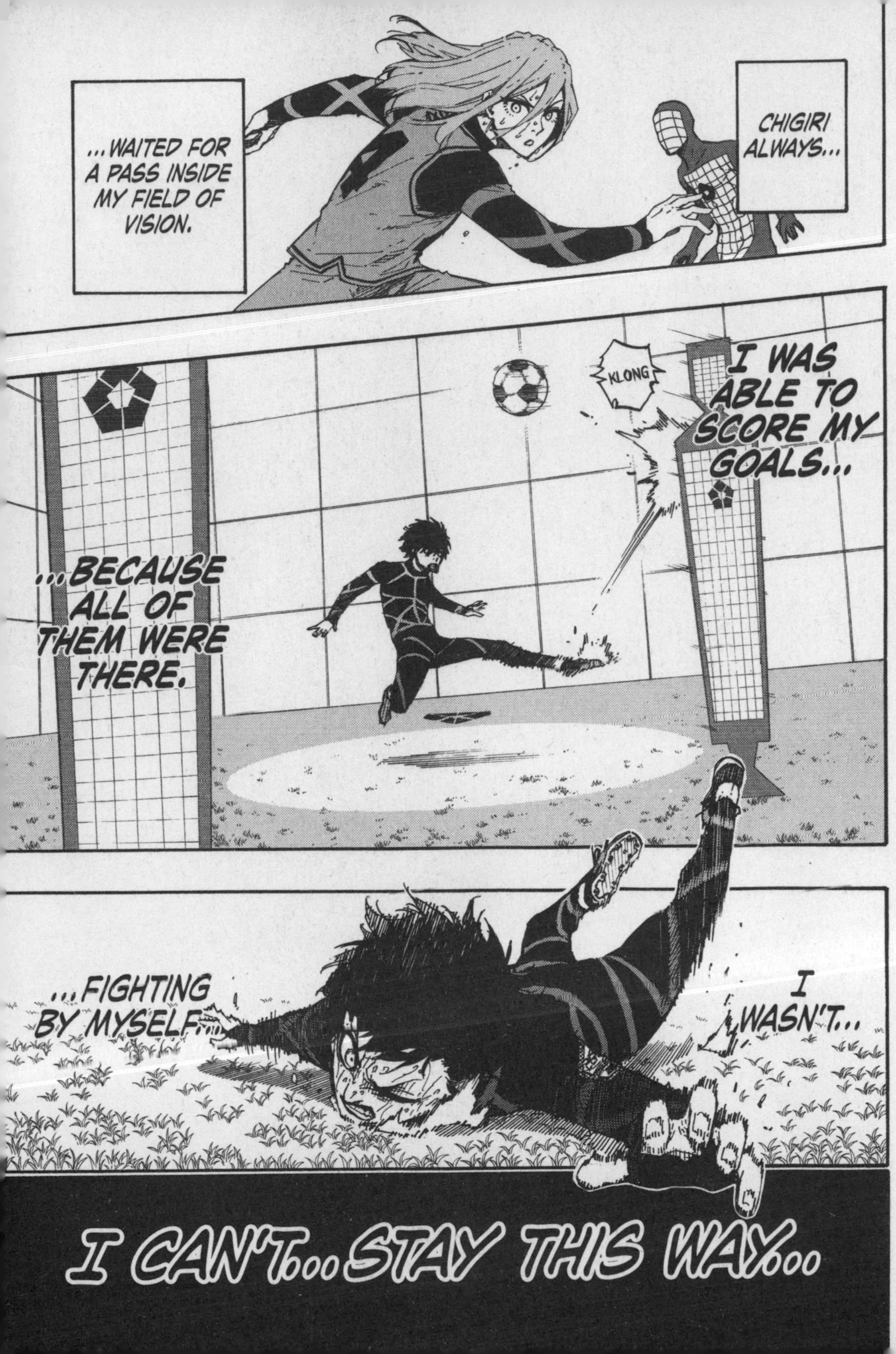
CHIGIRI ALWAYS...
...WAITED FOR A PASS INSIDE MY FIELD OF VISION.
I WAS ABLE TO SCORE MY GOALS...
KLONG
...BECAUSE ALL OF THEM WERE THERE.
I WASN'T...
...FIGHTING BY MYSELF...
I CAN'T...STAY THIS WAY...

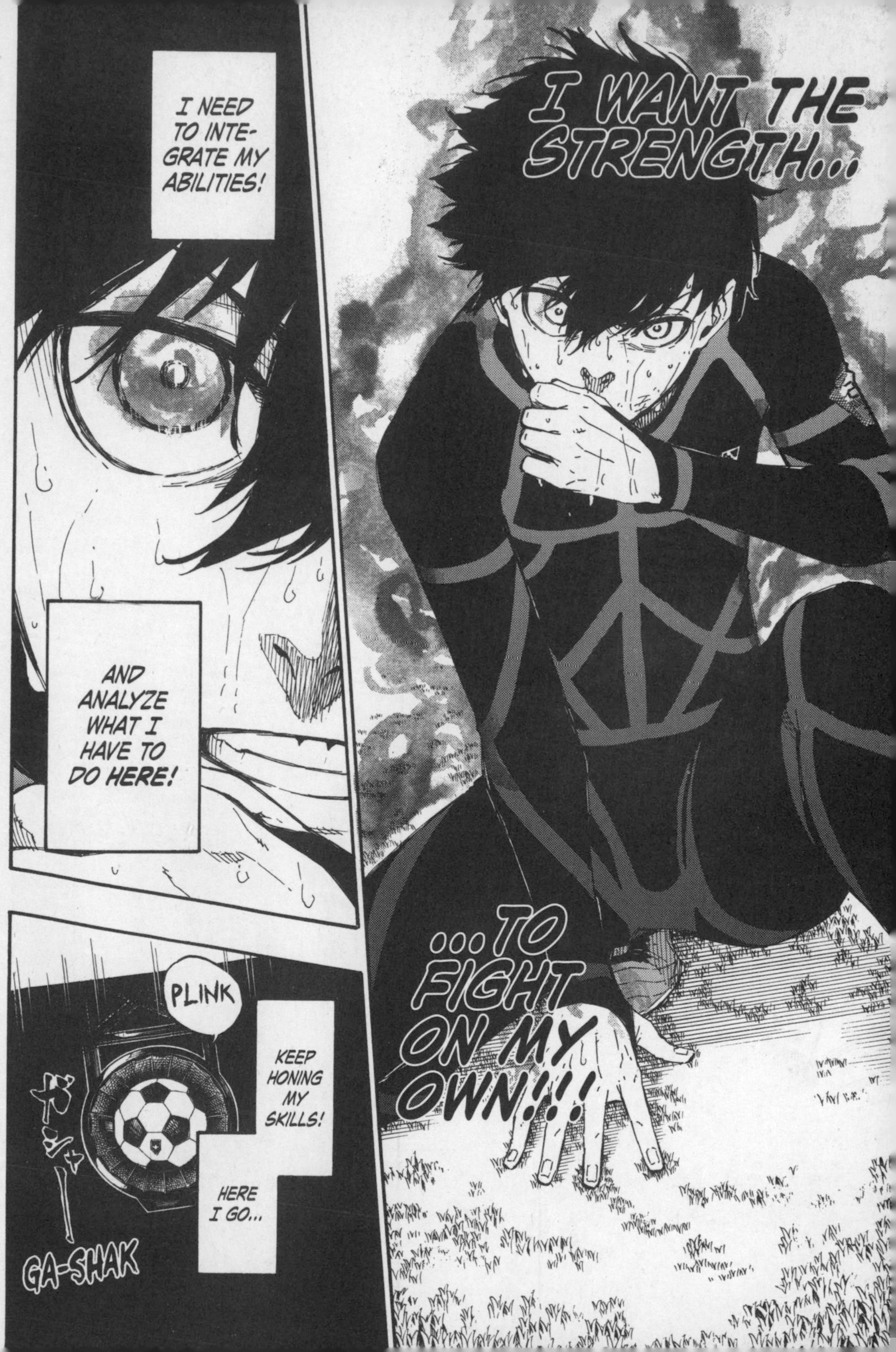
I WANT THE STRENGTH...
...TO FIGHT ON MY OWN!!!
I NEED TO INTE-GRATE MY ABILITIES!
AND ANALYZE WHAT I HAVE TO DO HERE!
PLINK
KEEP HONING MY SKILLS!
HERE I GO...
ガシャー
GA-SHAK

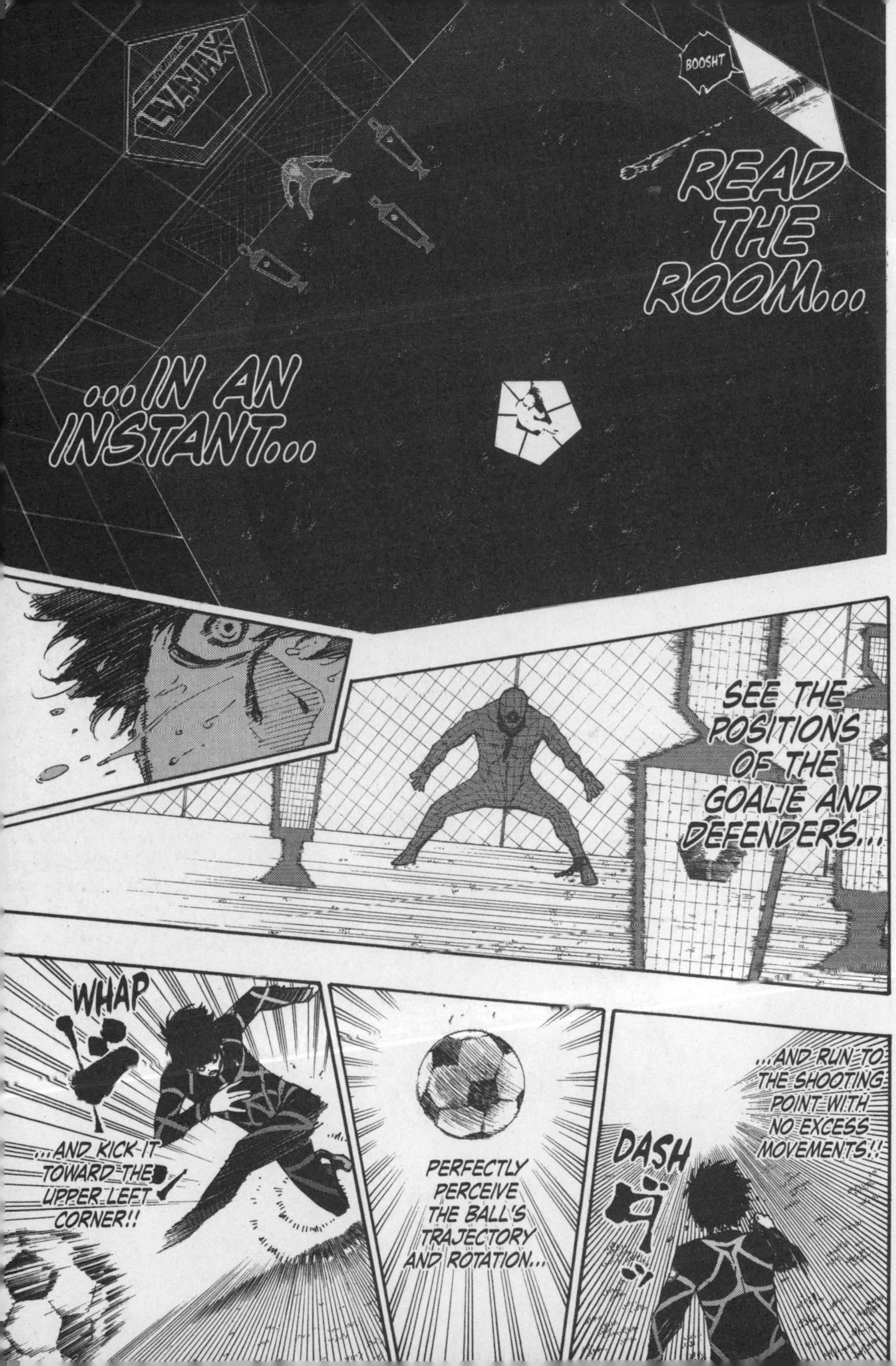
BOOSHT
READ THE ROOM...
...IN AN INSTANT...
SEE THE POSITIONS OF THE GOALIE AND DEFENDERS...
...AND RUN TO THE SHOOTING POINT WITH NO EXCESS MOVEMENTS!!
DASH
PERFECTLY PERCEIVE THE BALL'S TRAJECTORY AND ROTATION...
WHAP
...AND KICK IT TOWARD THE UPPER LEFT CORNER!!

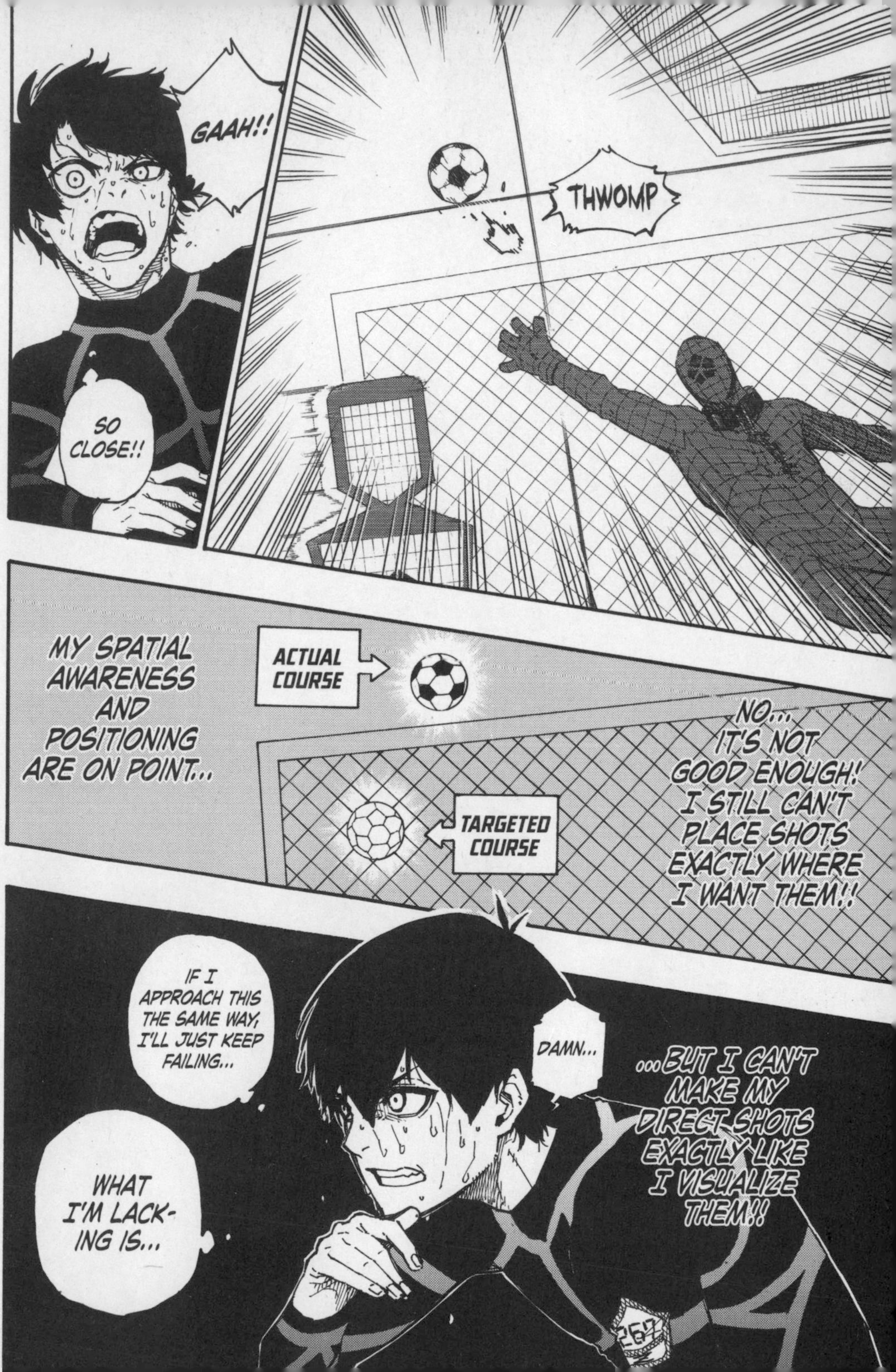
THWOMP
GAAH!!
SO CLOSE!!
MY SPATIAL AWARENESS AND POSITIONING ARE ON POINT...
ACTUAL COURSE
TARGETED COURSE
NO... IT'S NOT GOOD ENOUGH! I STILL CAN'T PLACE SHOTS EXACTLY WHERE I WANT THEM!!
...BUT I CAN'T MAKE MY DIRECT SHOTS EXACTLY LIKE I VISUALIZE THEM!!
DAMN...
IF I APPROACH THIS THE SAME WAY, I'LL JUST KEEP FAILING...
WHAT I'M LACKING IS...

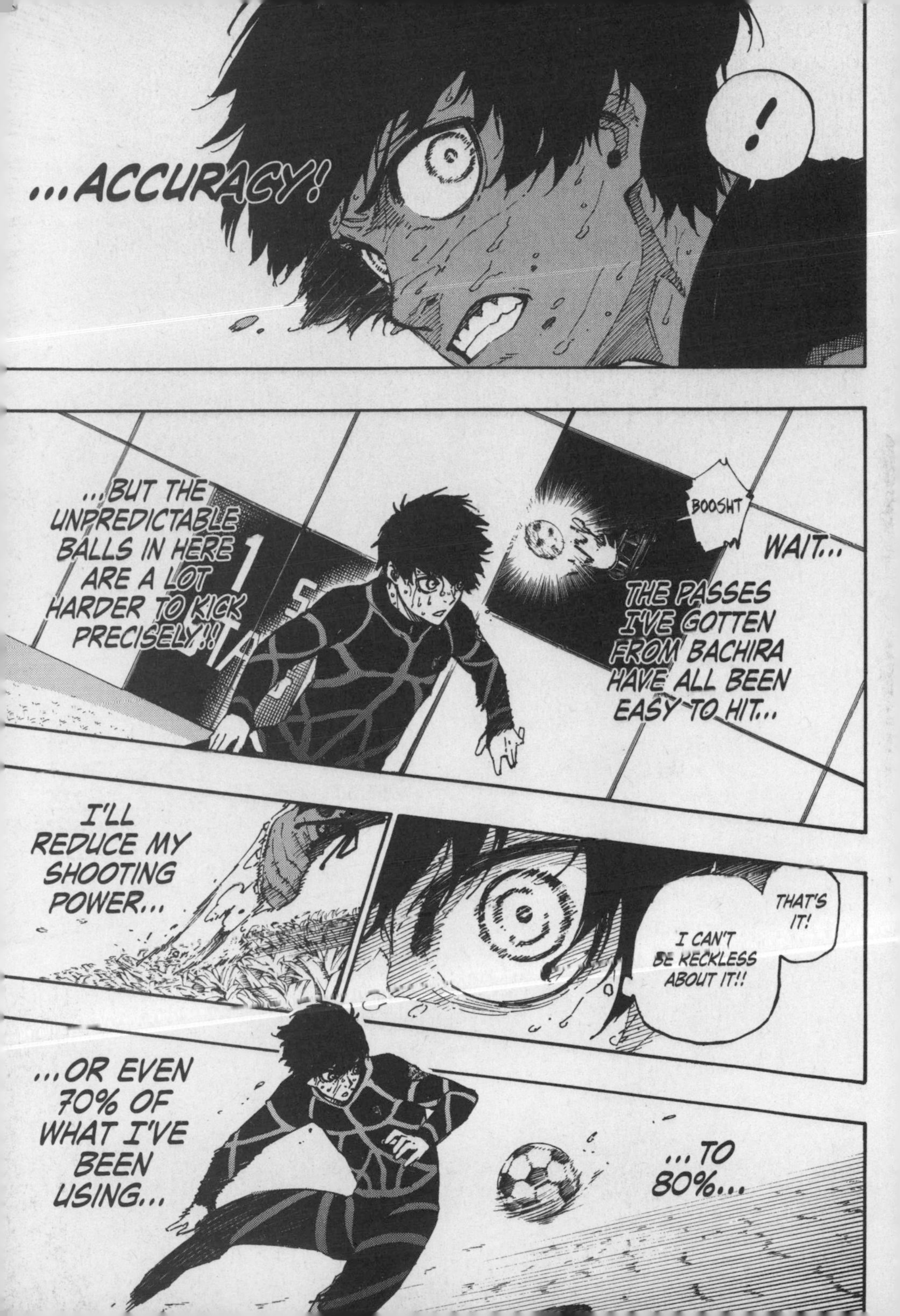
!
...ACCURACY!
BOOSHT
WAIT...
THE PASSES I'VE GOTTEN FROM BACHIRA HAVE ALL BEEN EASY TO HIT...
...BUT THE UNPREDICTABLE BALLS IN HERE ARE A LOT HARDER TO KICK PRECISELY!!
THAT'S IT!
I CAN'T BE RECKLESS ABOUT IT!!
I'LL REDUCE MY SHOOTING POWER...
...TO 80%...
...OR EVEN 70% OF WHAT I'VE BEEN USING...

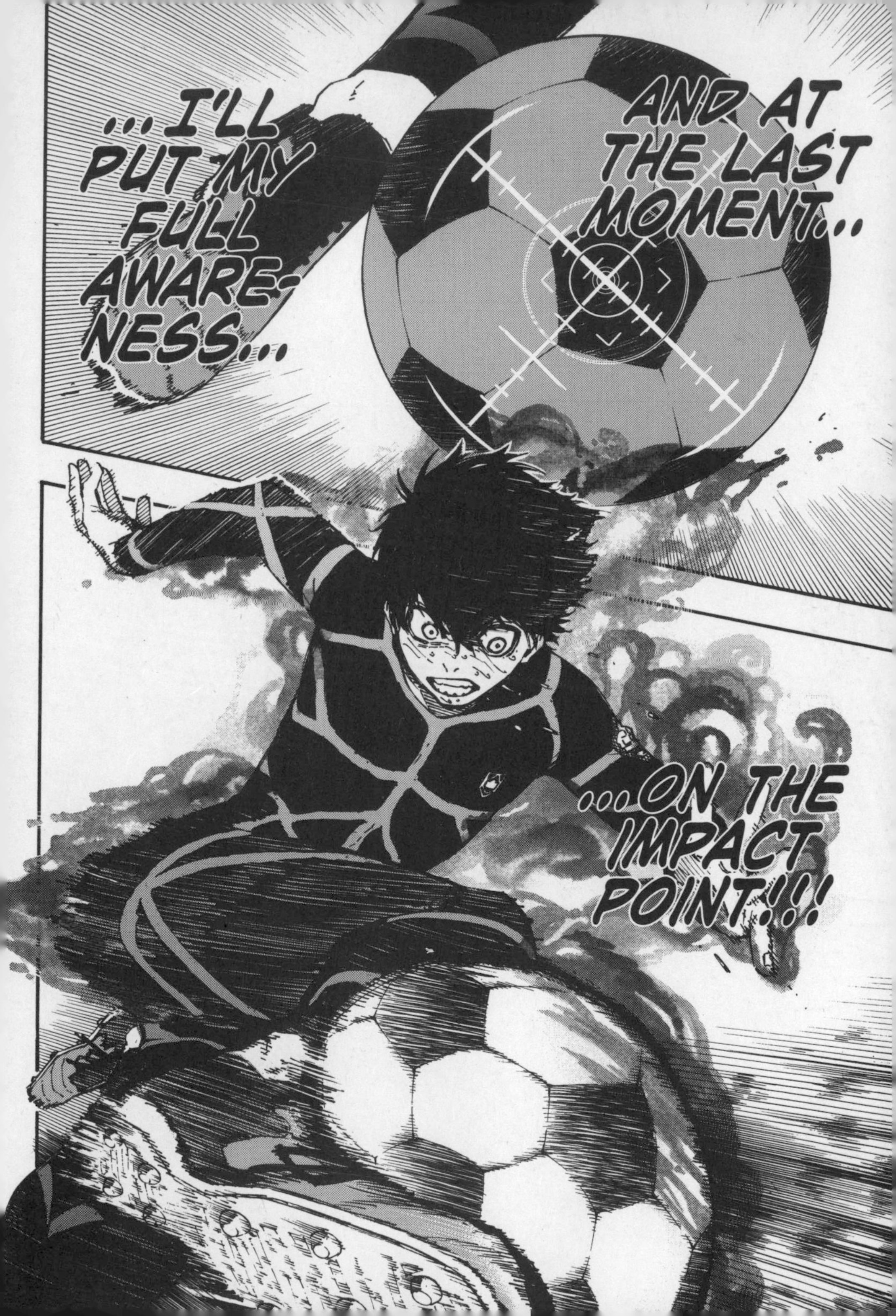
AND AT THE LAST MOMENT...
...I'LL PUT MY FULL AWARE-NESS...
...ON THE IMPACT POINT!!!

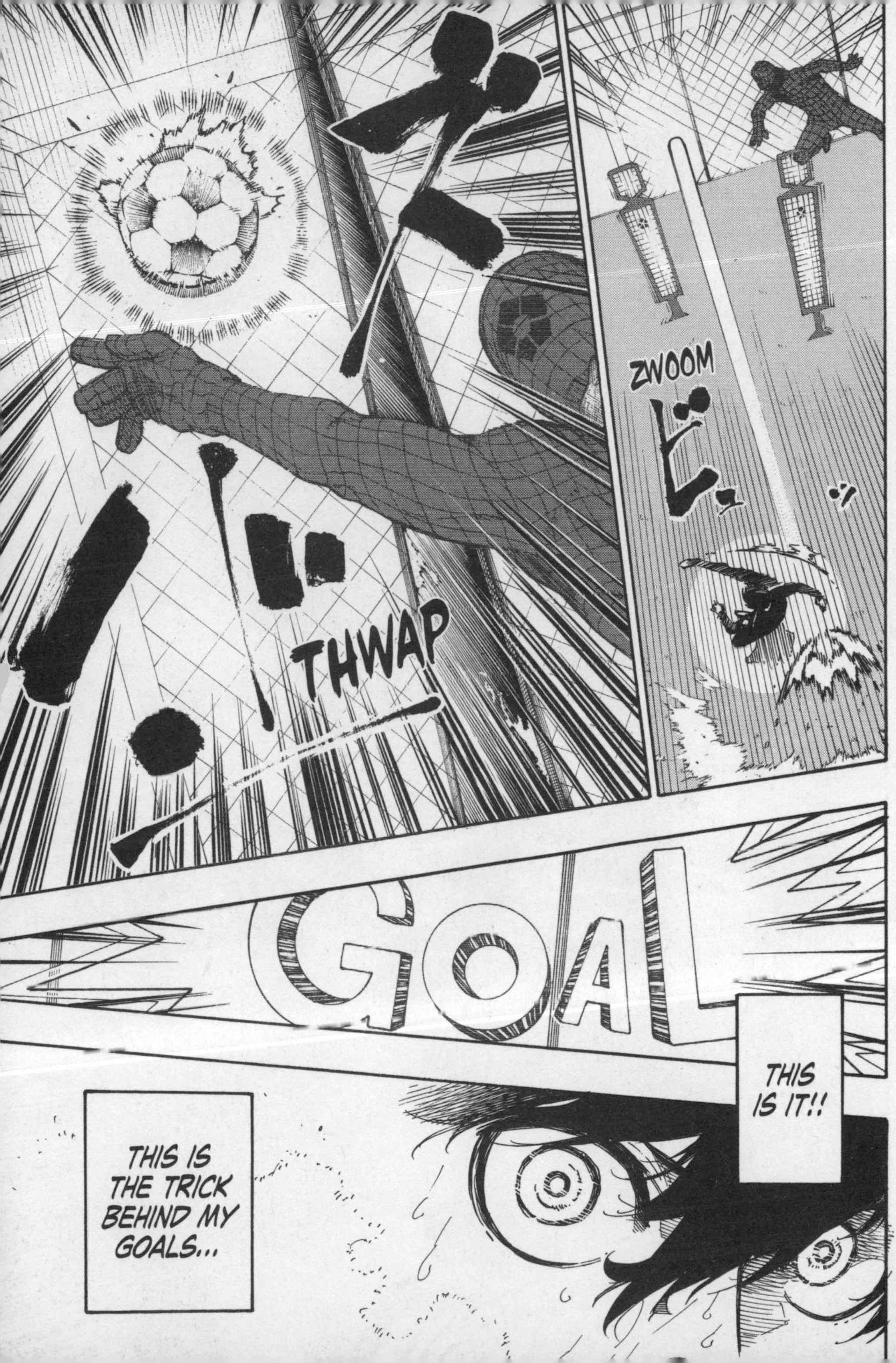
ZWOOM
THWAP
GOAL
THIS IS IT!!
THIS IS THE TRICK BEHIND MY GOALS...

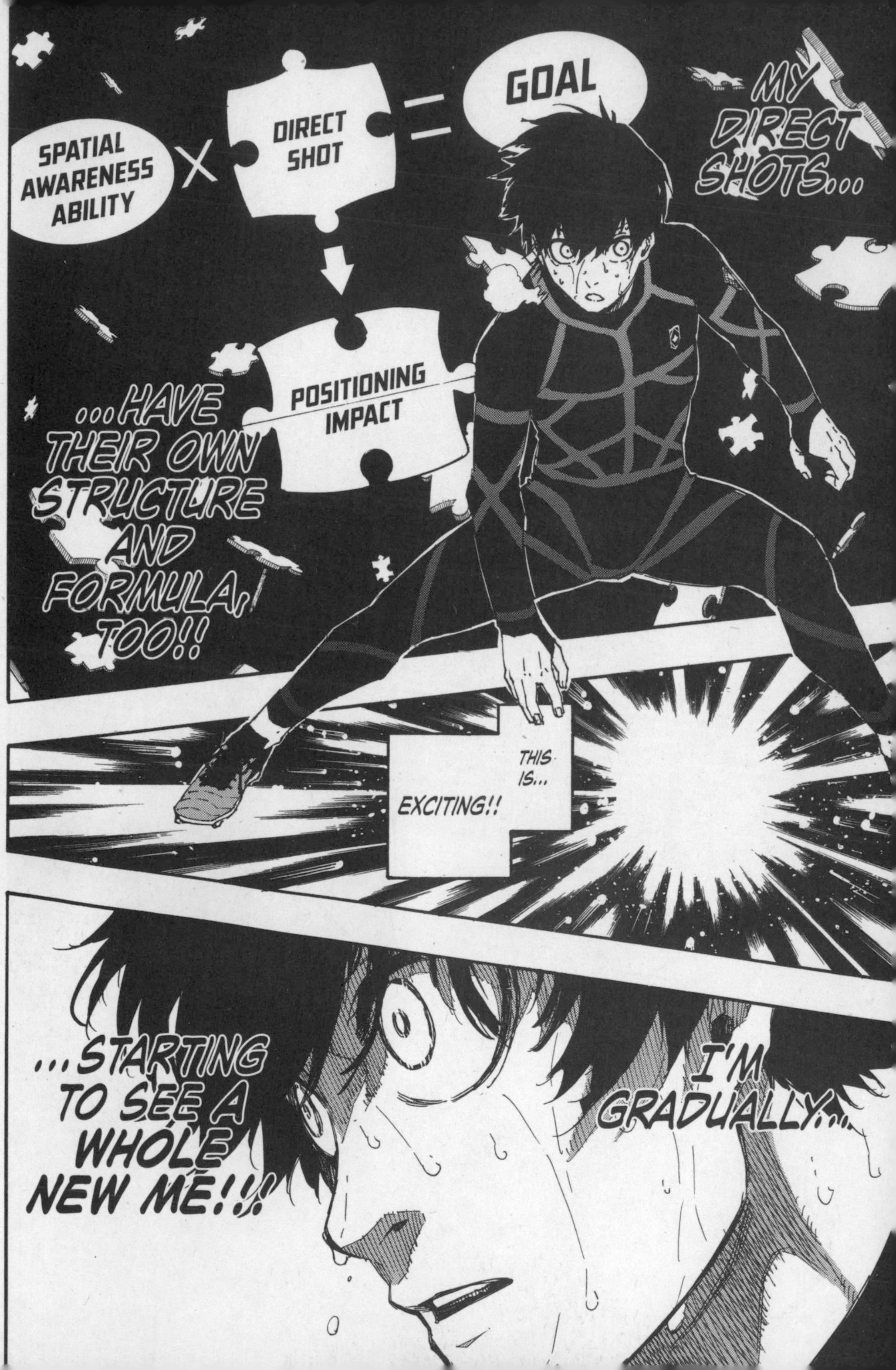

MY DIRECT SHOTS...
GOAL
DIRECT SHOT
SPATIAL AWARENESS ABILITY
POSITIONING
IMPACT
...HAVE THEIR OWN STRUCTURE AND FORMULA, TOO!!
THIS IS...
EXCITING!!
I'M GRADUALLY...
...STARTING TO SEE A WHOLE NEW ME!!!

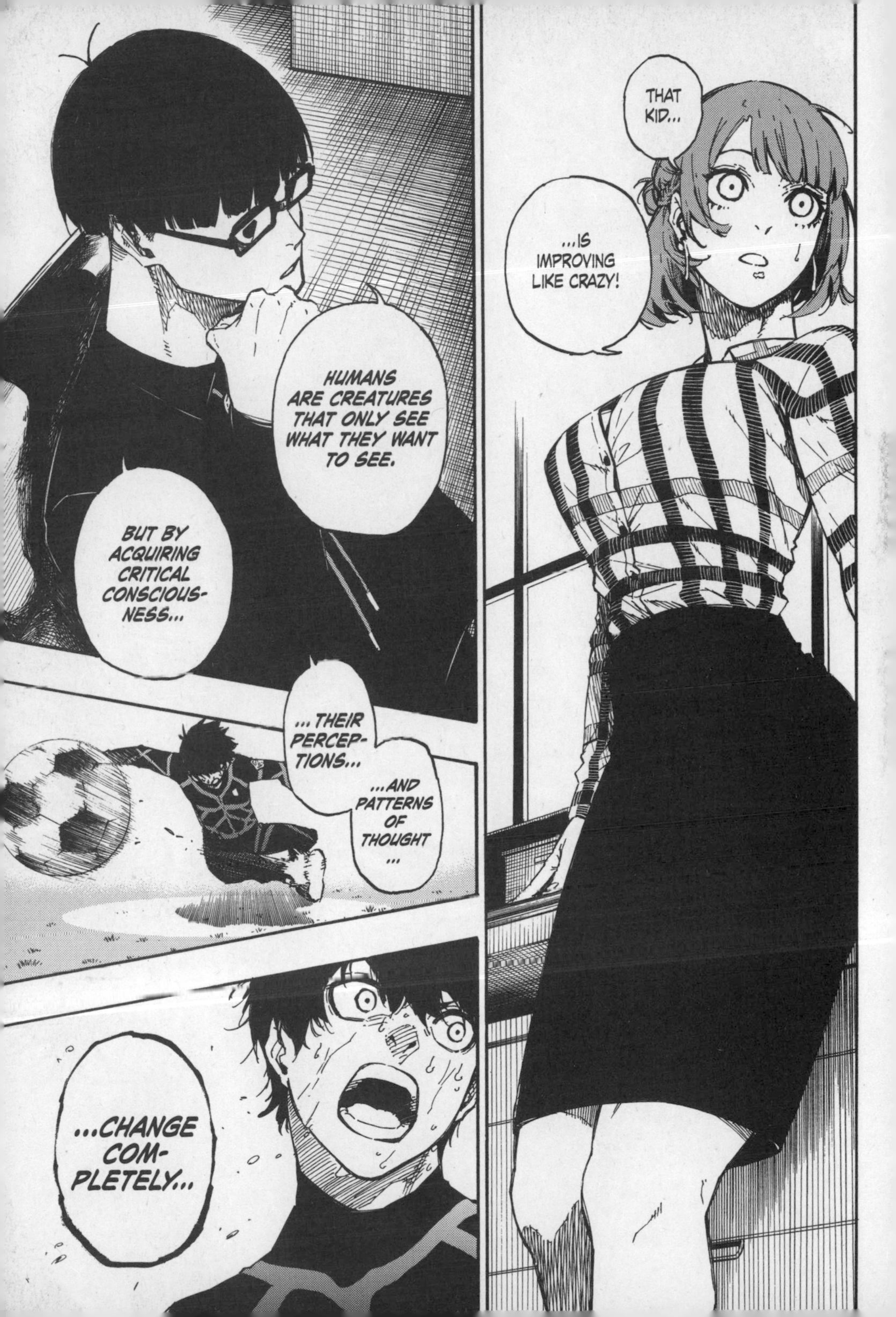
THAT KID...
...IS IMPROVING LIKE CRAZY!
HUMANS ARE CREATURES THAT ONLY SEE WHAT THEY WANT TO SEE.
BUT BY ACQUIRING CRITICAL CONSCIOUS-NESS...
...THEIR PERCEP-TIONS...
...AND PATTERNS OF THOUGHT ...
...CHANGE COM-PLETELY...

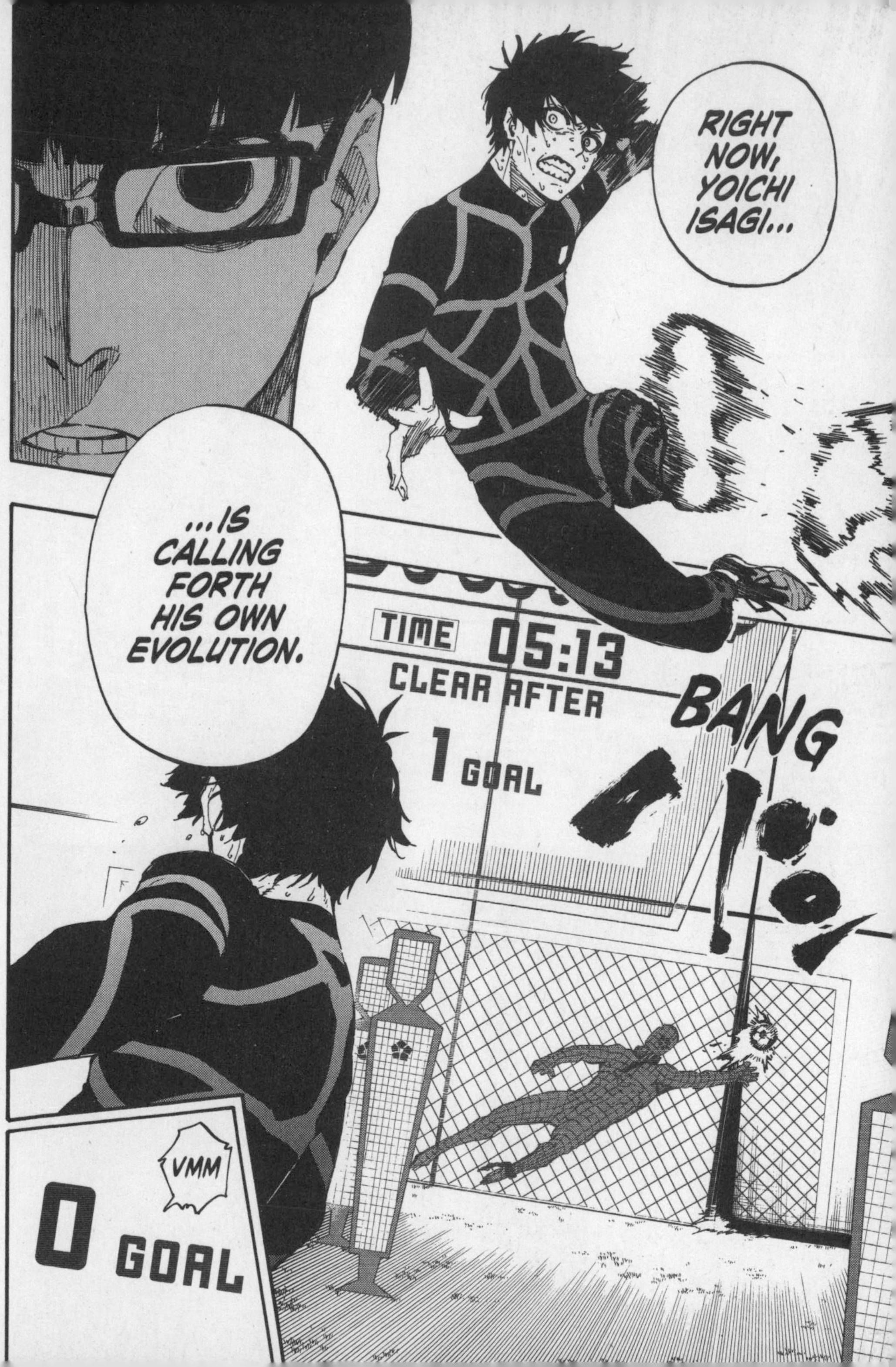
RIGHT NOW, YOICHI ISAGI...
...IS CALLING FORTH HIS OWN EVOLUTION.
TIME 05:13
CLEAR AFTER
1 GOAL
BANG
VMM
0 GOAL

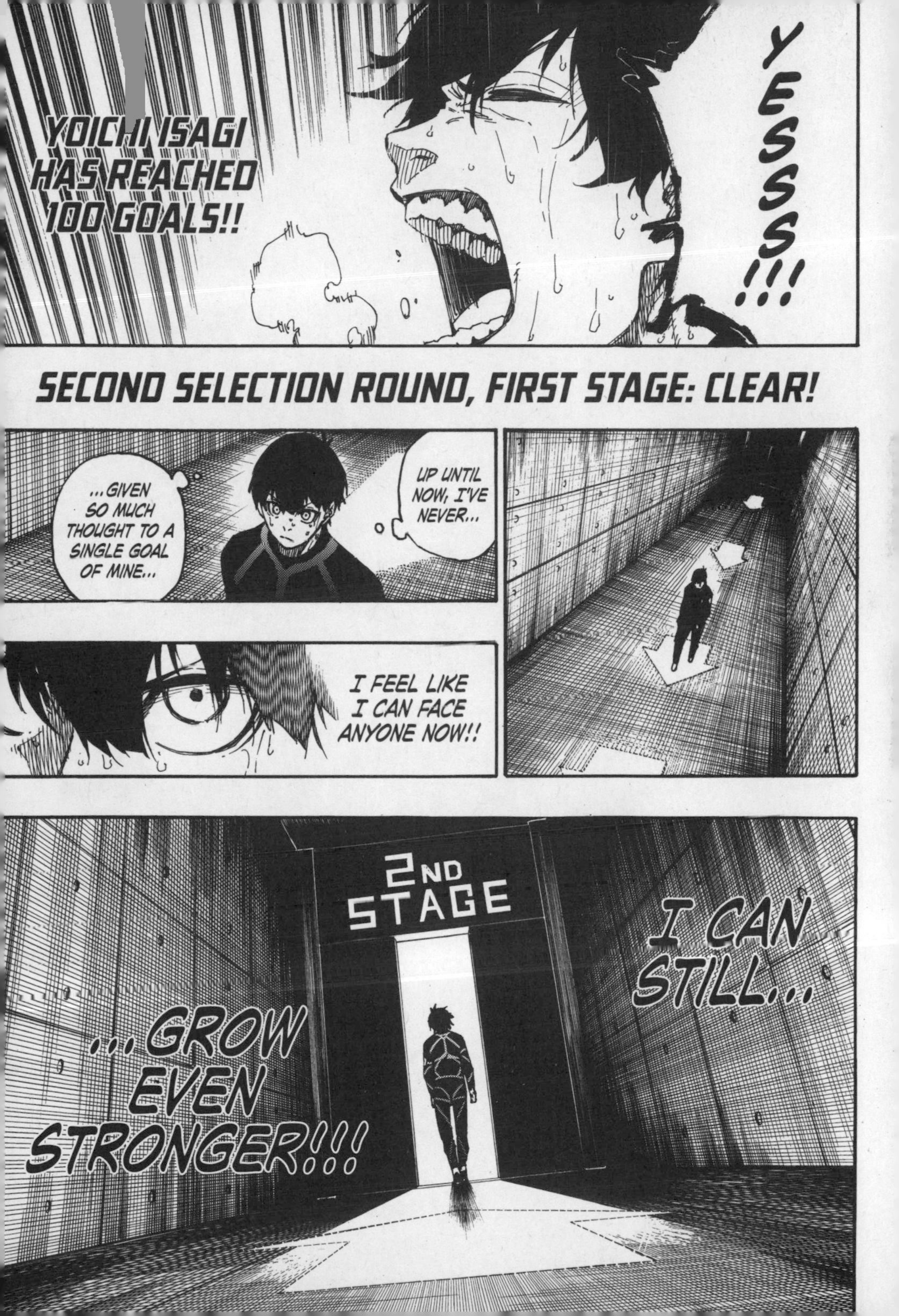
YESSS!!!
YOICHI ISAGI HAS REACHED 100 GOALS!!
SECOND SELECTION ROUND, FIRST STAGE: CLEAR!
UP UNTIL NOW, I'VE NEVER...
...GIVEN SO MUCH THOUGHT TO A SINGLE GOAL OF MINE...
I FEEL LIKE I CAN FACE ANYONE NOW!!
2ND STAGE
I CAN STILL...
...GROW EVEN STRONGER!!!

FORM THREE-
MAN TEAMS TO
ADVANCE

NEXT STAGE

THIS IS...

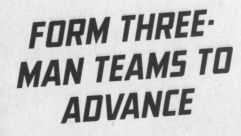

FORM THREE-
MAN TEAMS TO
ADVANCE

...THE
SECOND
STAGE?!

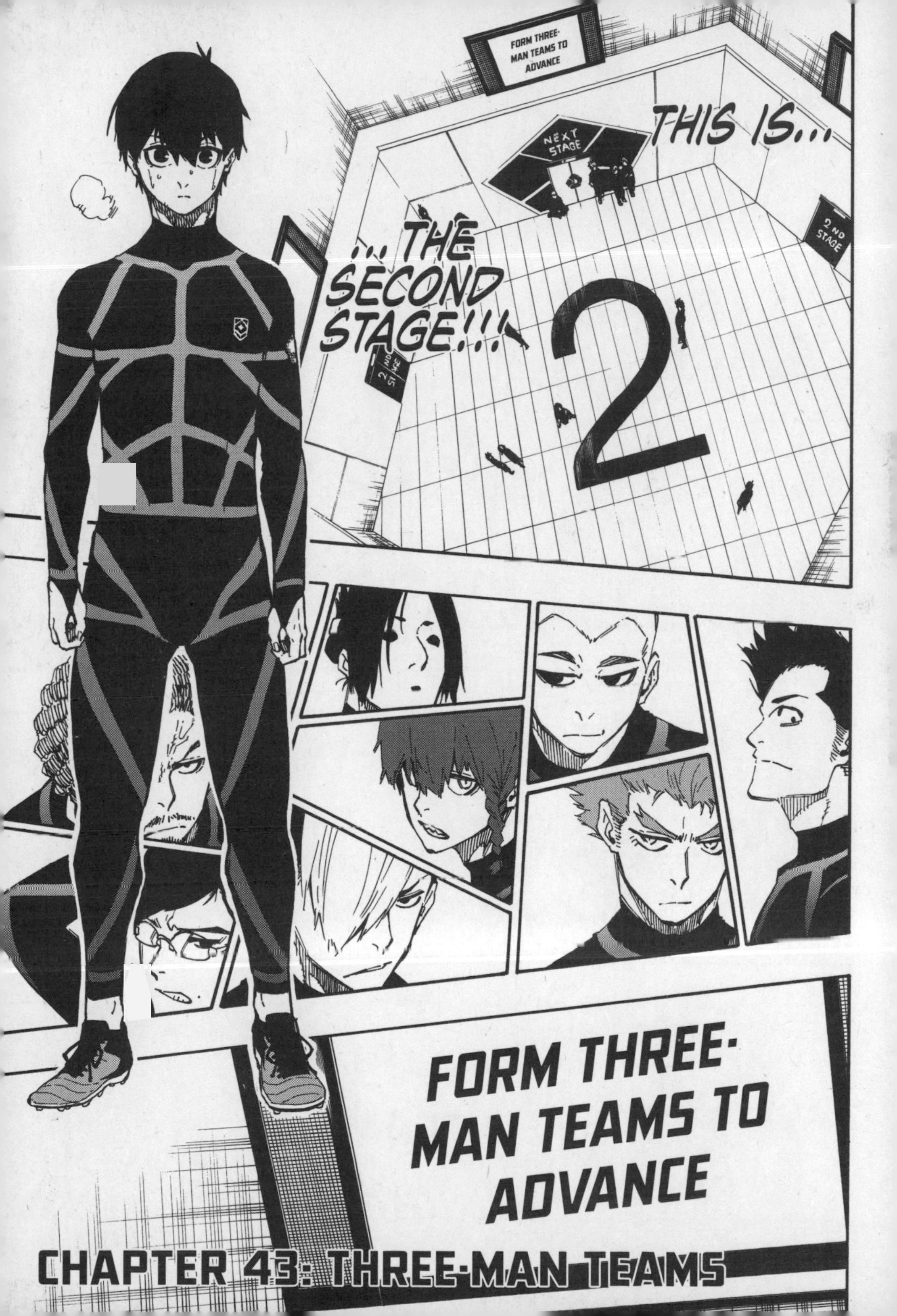
FORM THREE-MAN TEAMS TO ADVANCE
NEXT STAGE
THIS IS...
...THE SECOND STAGE!!!
2ND STAGE
2
FORM THREE-MAN TEAMS TO ADVANCE
CHAPTER 43: THREE-MAN TEAMS

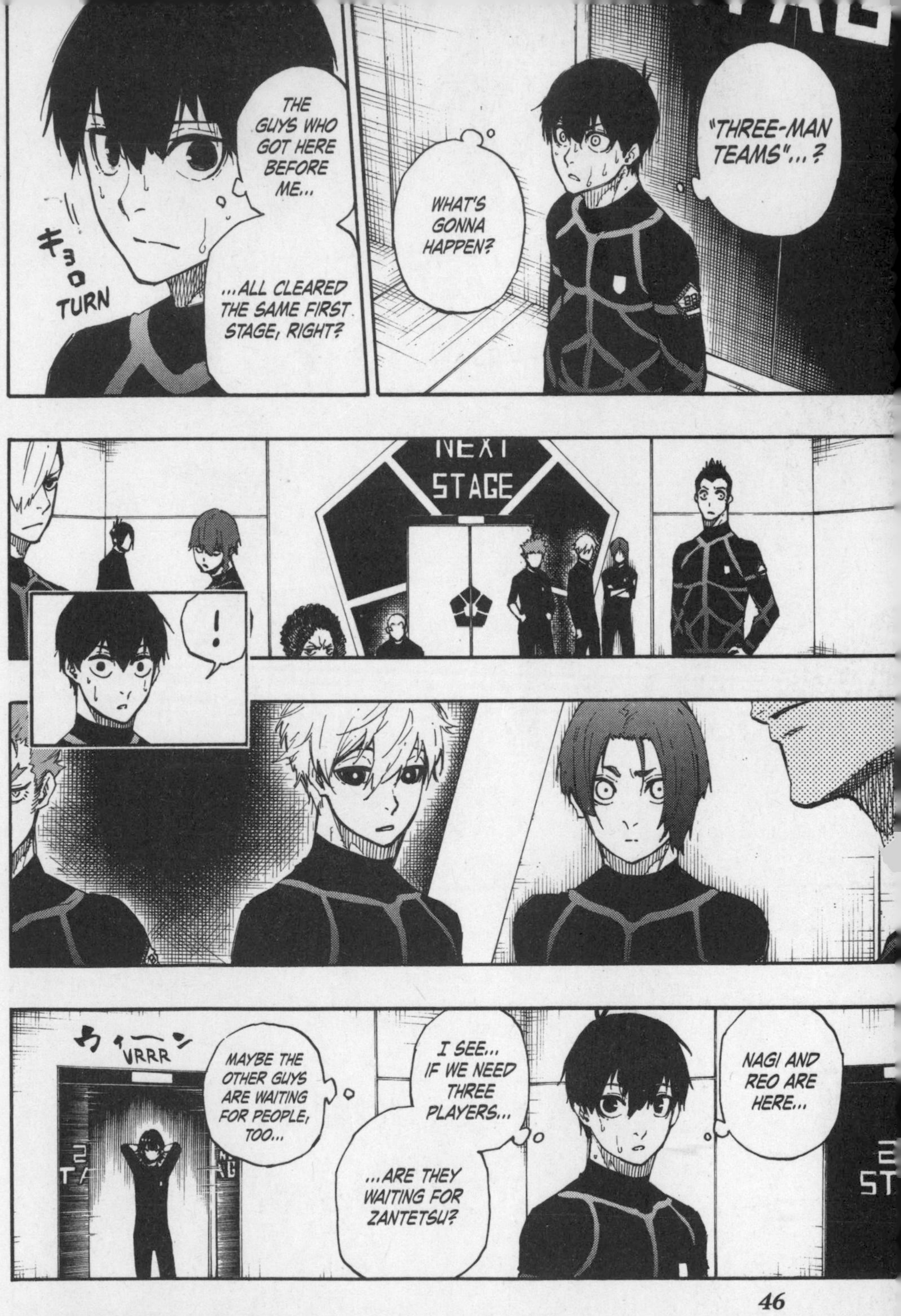
"THREE-MAN TEAMS"...?
WHAT'S GONNA HAPPEN?
THE GUYS WHO GOT HERE BEFORE ME...
...ALL CLEARED THE SAME FIRST STAGE, RIGHT?
キョロ TURN
NEXT STAGE
!
NAGI AND REO ARE HERE...
I SEE... IF WE NEED THREE PLAYERS...
...ARE THEY WAITING FOR ZANTETSU?
MAYBE THE OTHER GUYS ARE WAITING FOR PEOPLE, TOO...
ウィーン VRRR

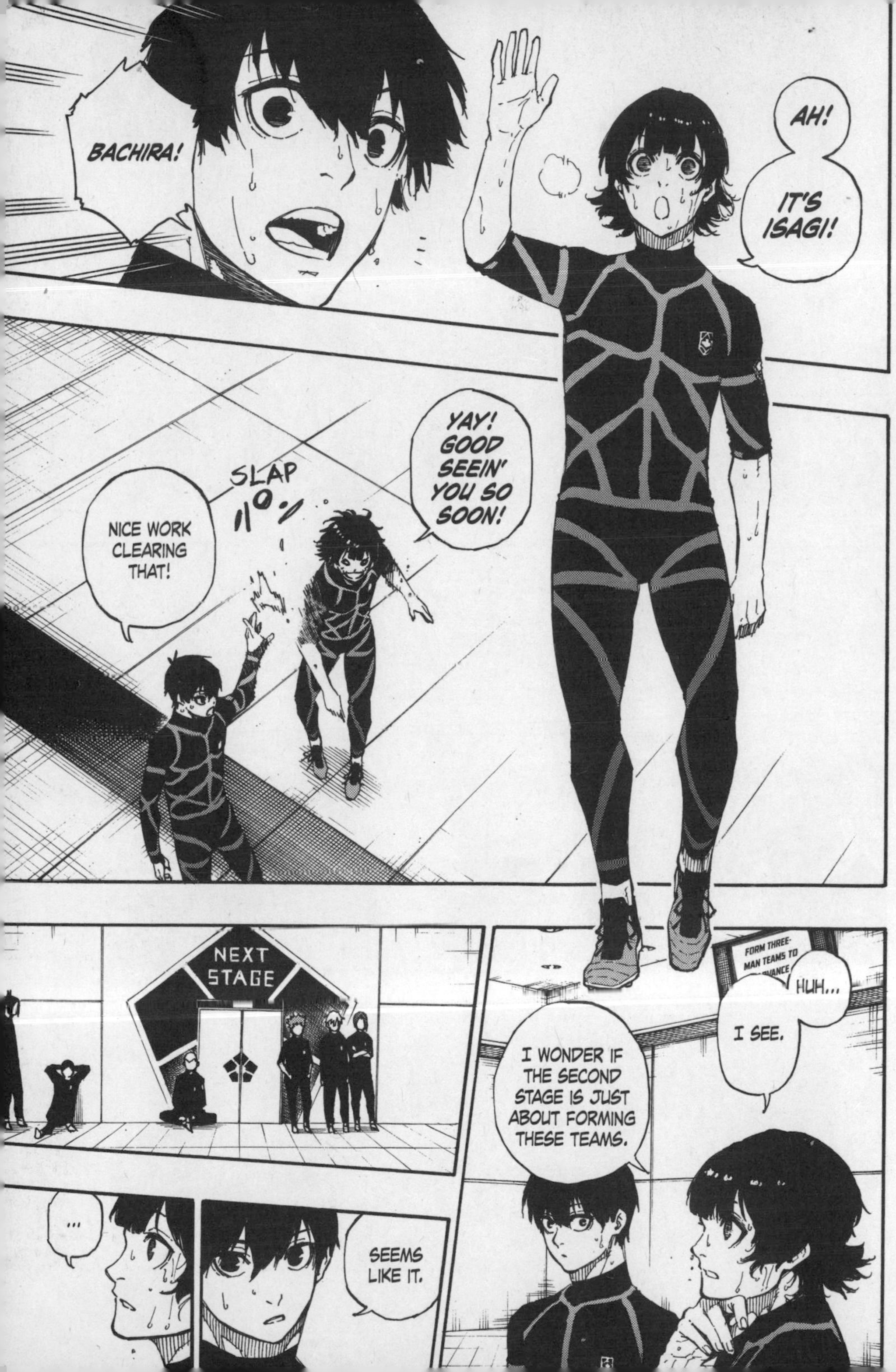
AH!
IT'S ISAGI!
BACHIRA!
YAY! GOOD SEEIN' YOU SO SOON!
SLAP
NICE WORK CLEARING THAT!
FORM THREE-MAN TEAMS TO
HUH... I SEE.
I WONDER IF THE SECOND STAGE IS JUST ABOUT FORMING THESE TEAMS.
NEXT STAGE
SEEMS LIKE IT.
...

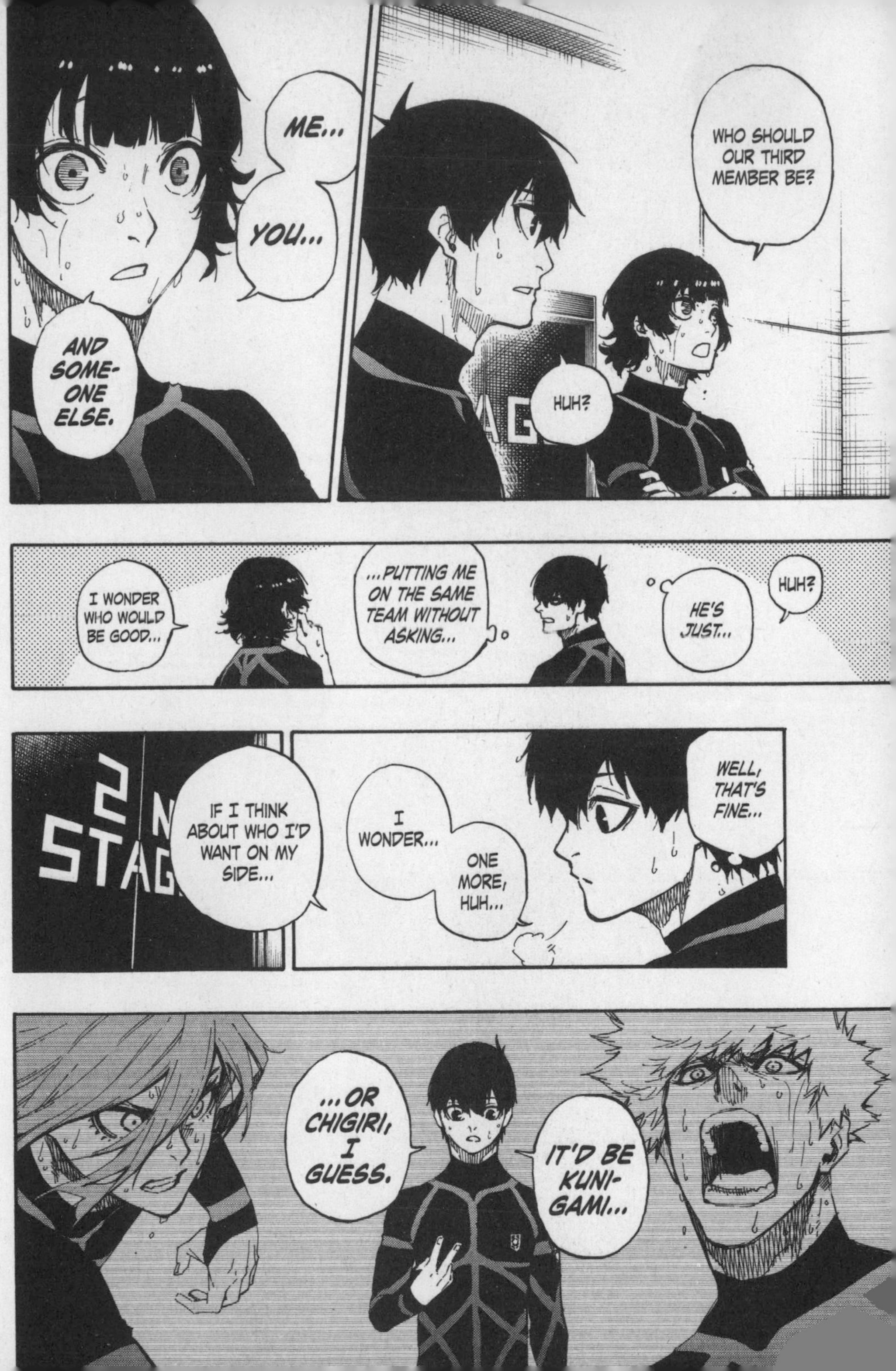
WHO SHOULD OUR THIRD MEMBER BE?
HUH?
ME...
YOU...
AND SOME-ONE ELSE.
HUH?
HE'S JUST...
...PUTTING ME ON THE SAME TEAM WITHOUT ASKING...
I WONDER WHO WOULD BE GOOD...
WELL, THAT'S FINE...
ONE MORE, HUH...
I WONDER...
IF I THINK ABOUT WHO I'D WANT ON MY SIDE...
IT'D BE KUNI-GAMI...
...OR CHIGIRI, I GUESS.

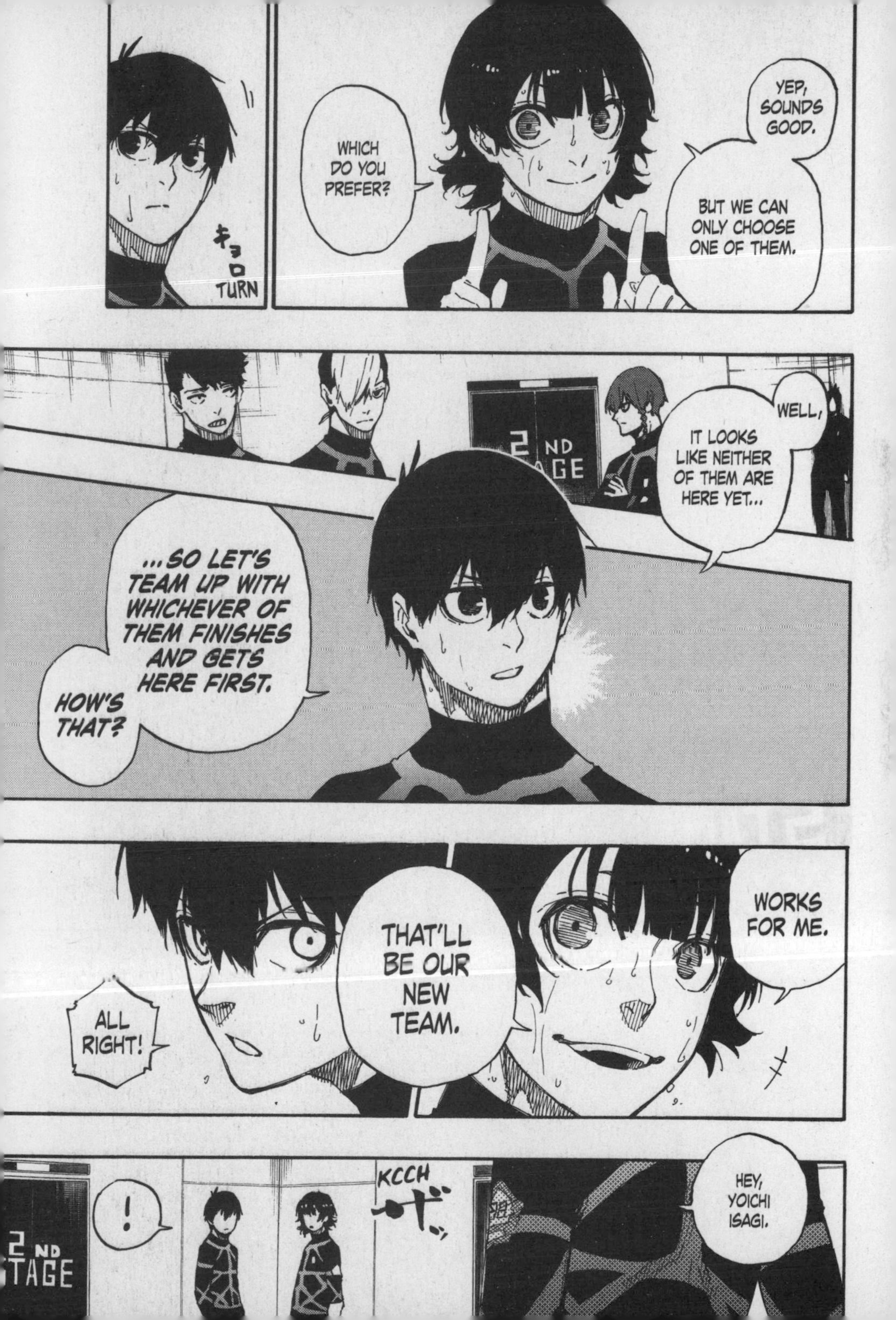
YEP, SOUNDS GOOD.
BUT WE CAN ONLY CHOOSE ONE OF THEM.
WHICH DO YOU PREFER?
キョロ TURN
WELL,
IT LOOKS LIKE NEITHER OF THEM ARE HERE YET...
...SO LET'S TEAM UP WITH WHICHEVER OF THEM FINISHES AND GETS HERE FIRST.
HOW'S THAT?
WORKS FOR ME.
THAT'LL BE OUR NEW TEAM.
ALL RIGHT!
HEY, YOICHI ISAGI.
KCCH
!

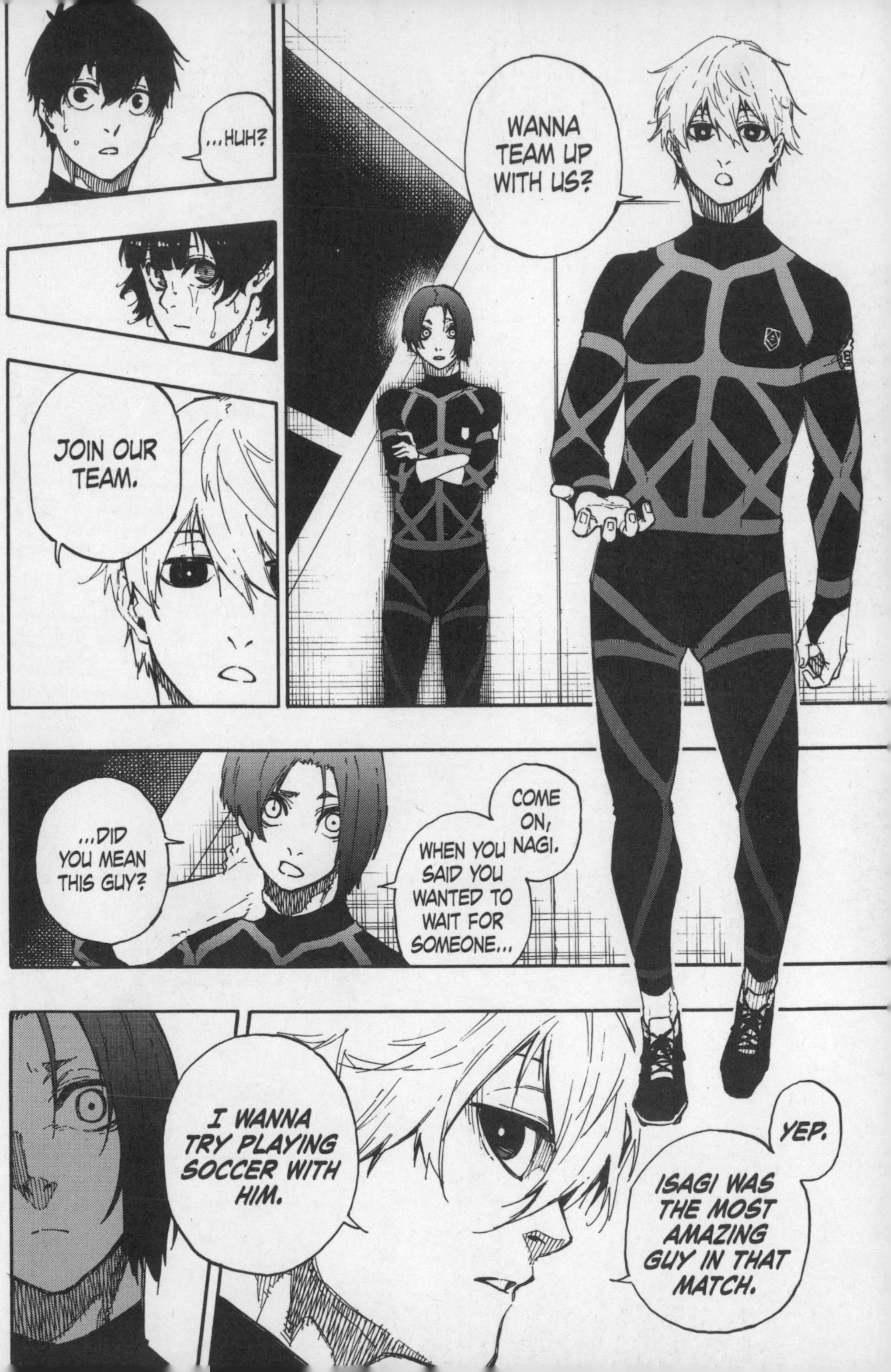
WANNA TEAM UP WITH US?
...HUH?
JOIN OUR TEAM.
COME ON, NAGI.
WHEN YOU SAID YOU WANTED TO WAIT FOR SOMEONE...
...DID YOU MEAN THIS GUY?
YEP.
ISAGI WAS THE MOST AMAZING GUY IN THAT MATCH.
I WANNA TRY PLAYING SOCCER WITH HIM.

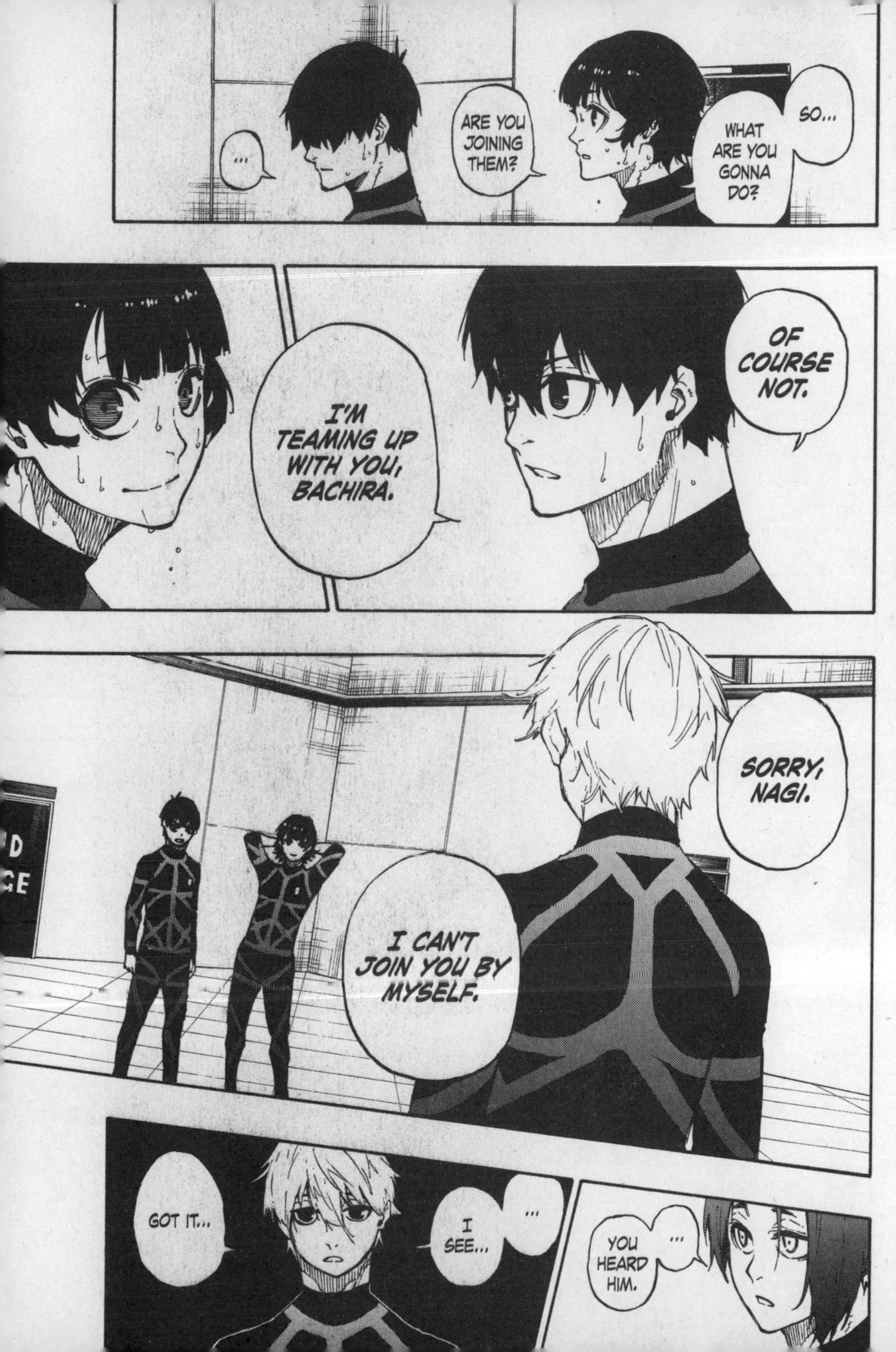
SO...
WHAT ARE YOU GONNA DO?
ARE YOU JOINING THEM?
...
OF COURSE NOT.
I'M TEAMING UP WITH YOU, BACHIRA.
SORRY, NAGI.
I CAN'T JOIN YOU BY MYSELF.
...
YOU HEARD HIM.
...
I SEE...
GOT IT...

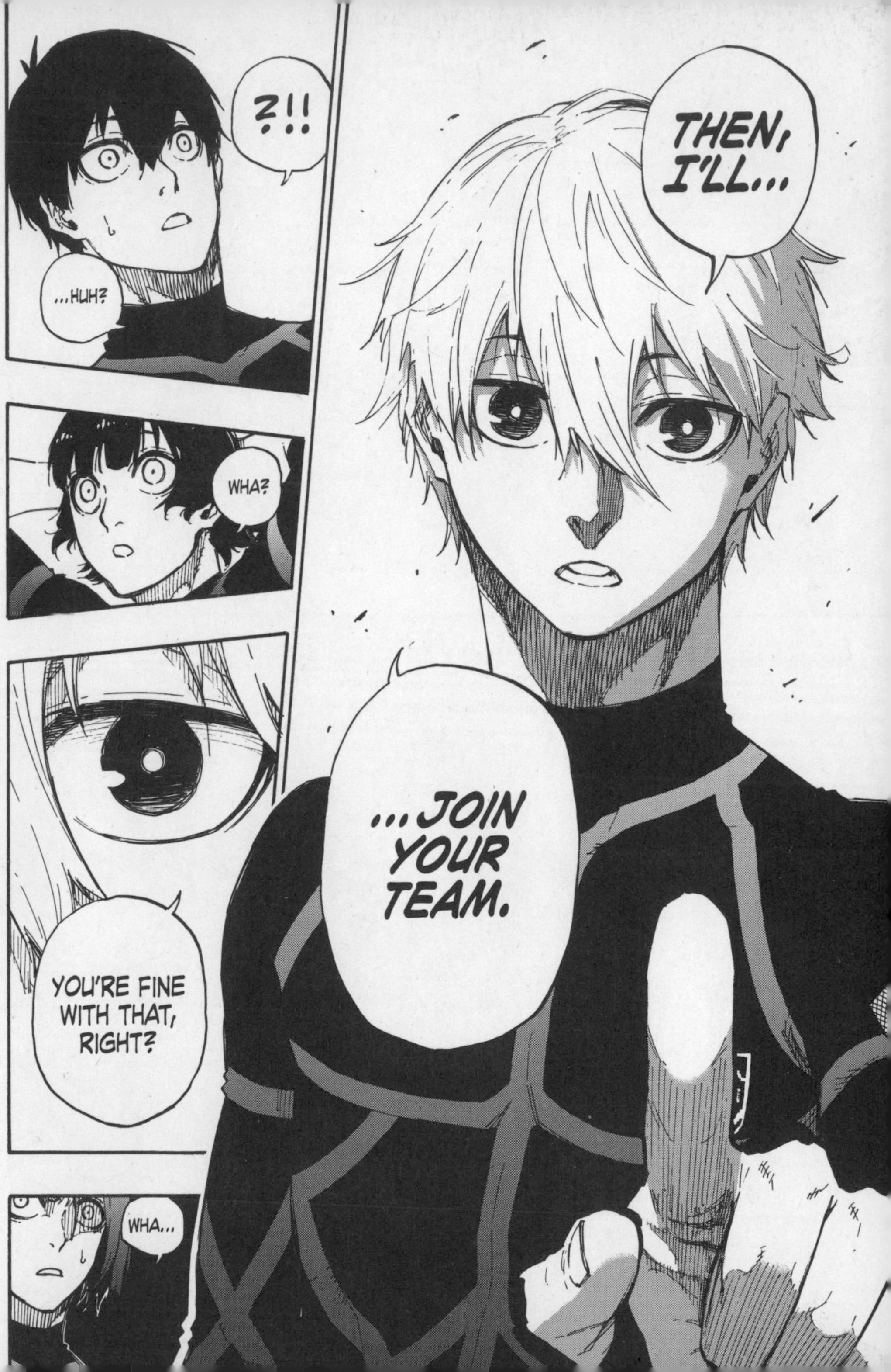
THEN, I'LL...
...JOIN YOUR TEAM.
?!!
...HUH?
WHA?
YOU'RE FINE WITH THAT, RIGHT?
WHA...

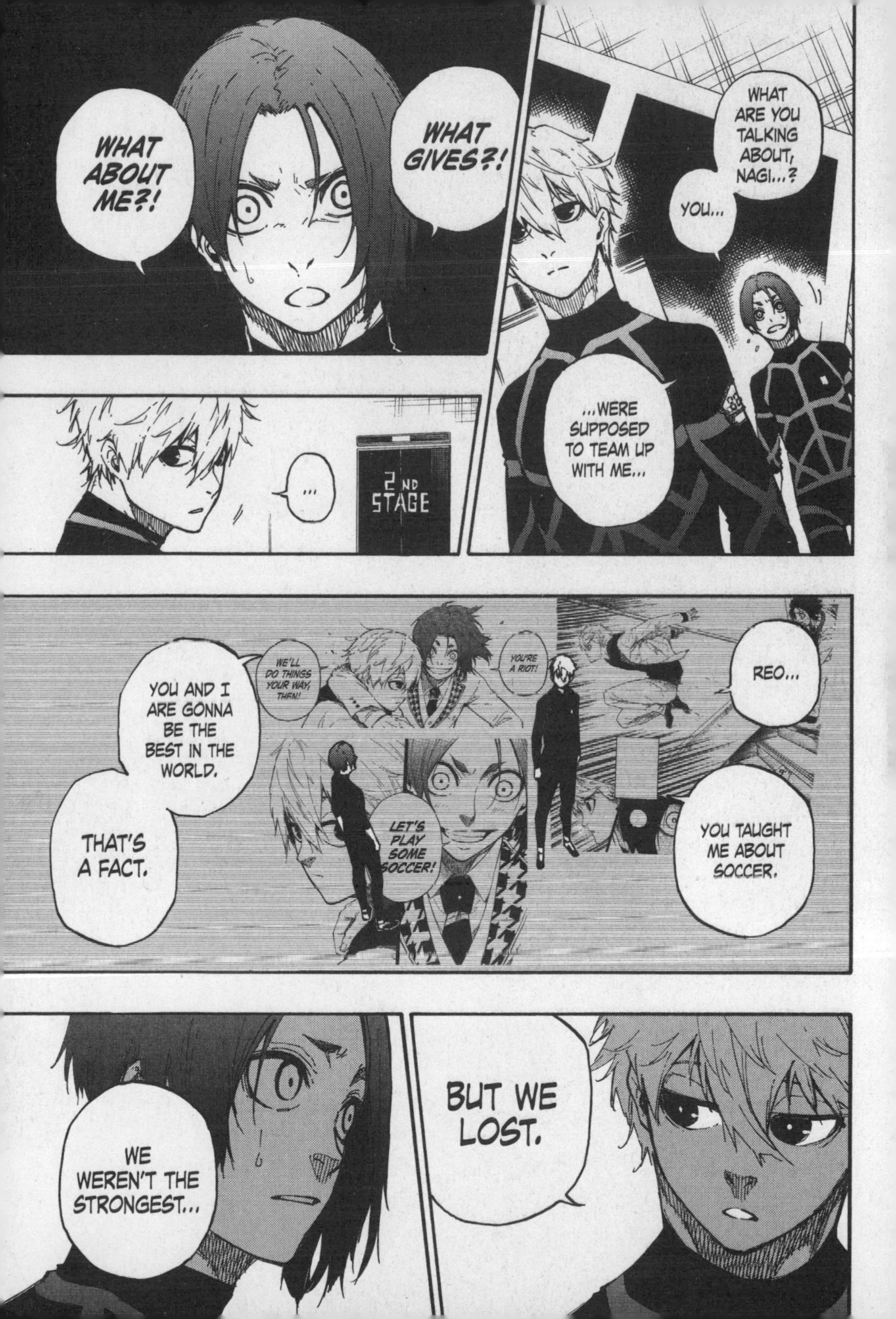
WHAT ARE YOU TALKING ABOUT, NAGI...?
YOU...
...WERE SUPPOSED TO TEAM UP WITH ME...
WHAT GIVES?!
WHAT ABOUT ME?!
...
2ND STAGE
REO...
YOU TAUGHT ME ABOUT SOCCER.
YOU'RE A RIOT!
LET'S PLAY SOME SOCCER!
WE'LL DO THINGS YOUR WAY, THEN!
YOU AND I ARE GONNA BE THE BEST IN THE WORLD.
THAT'S A FACT.
BUT WE LOST.
WE WEREN'T THE STRONGEST...

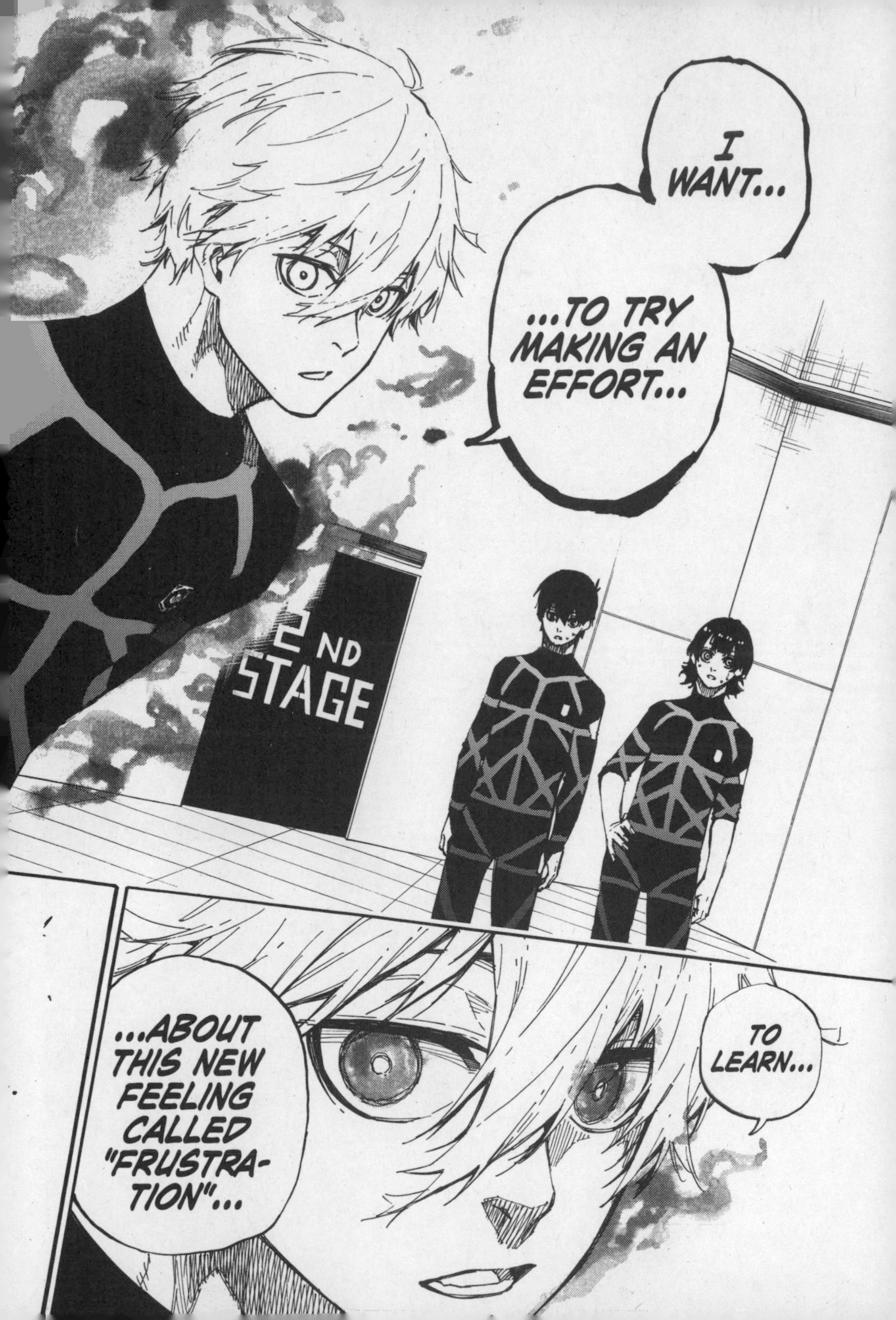
I WANT...
...TO TRY MAKING AN EFFORT...
2ND STAGE
TO LEARN...
...ABOUT THIS NEW FEELING CALLED "FRUSTRATION"...

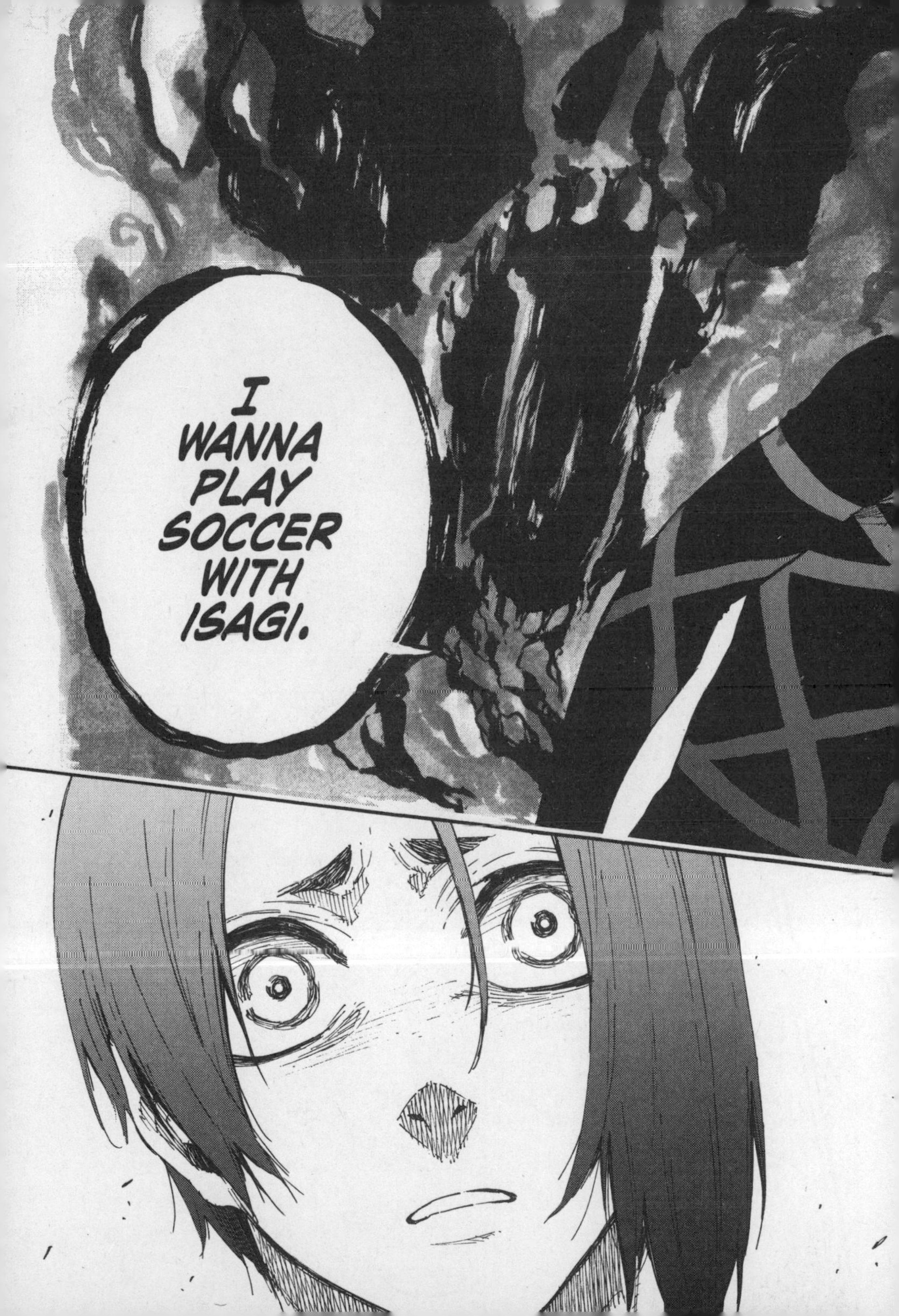
I WANNA PLAY SOCCER WITH ISAGI.

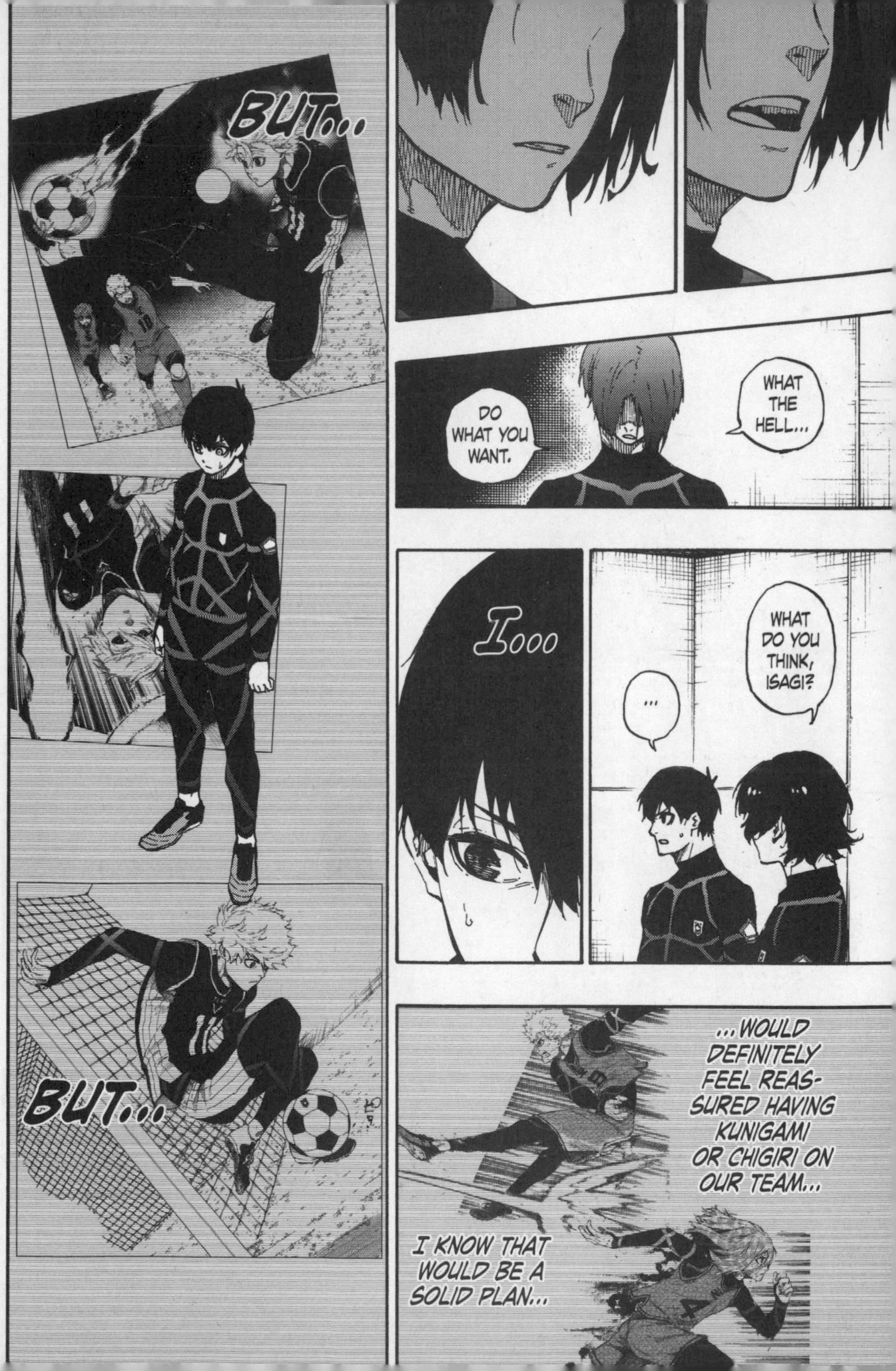
WHAT THE HELL...
DO WHAT YOU WANT.
WHAT DO YOU THINK, ISAGI?
...
Iooo
...WOULD DEFINITELY FEEL REAS-SURED HAVING KUNIGAMI OR CHIGIRI ON OUR TEAM...
I KNOW THAT WOULD BE A SOLID PLAN...
BUT...
BUT...

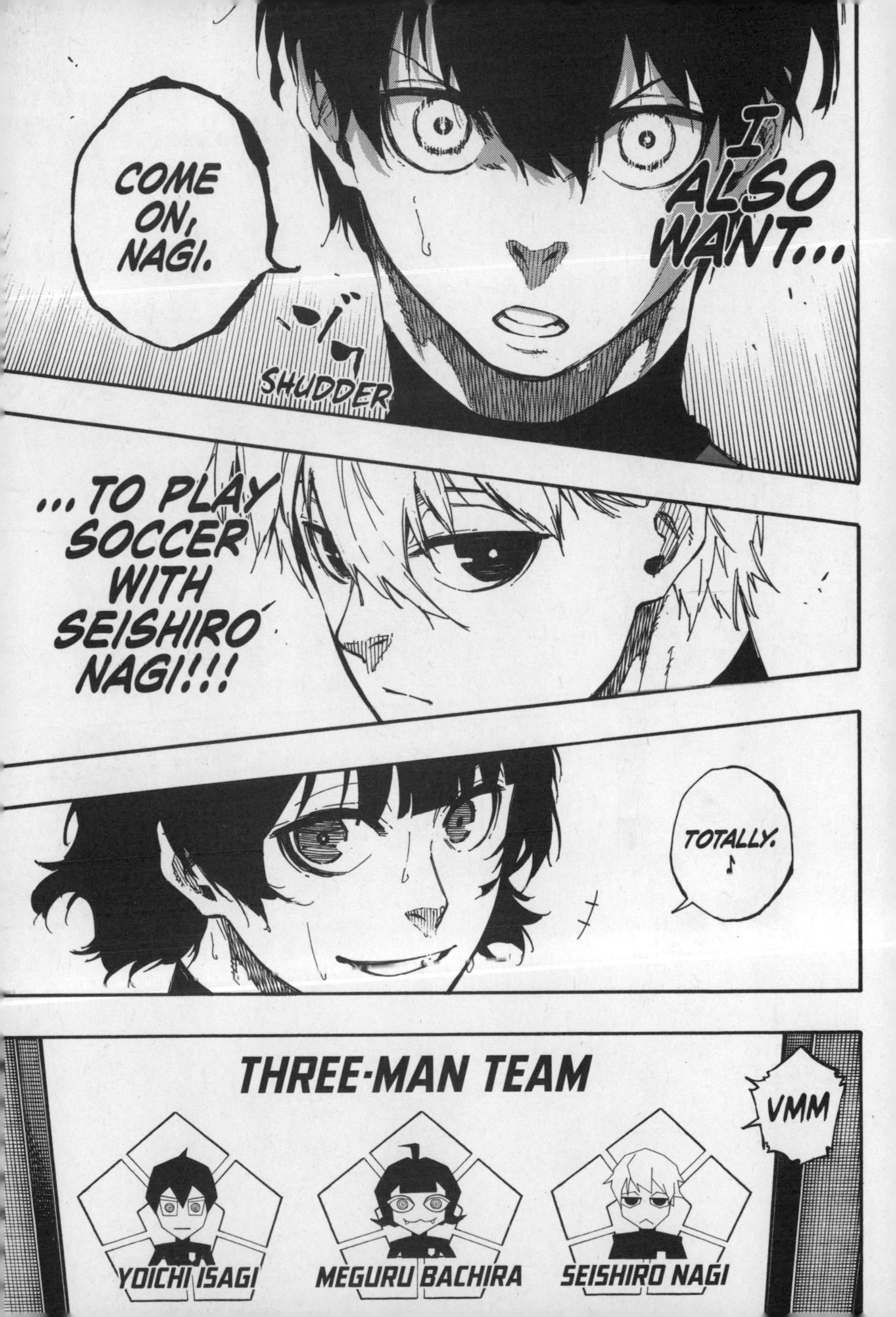
I ALSO WANT...
COME ON, NAGI.
SHUDDER
...TO PLAY SOCCER WITH SEISHIRO NAGI!!!
TOTALLY. ♪
VMM
THREE-MAN TEAM
SEISHIRO NAGI
MEGURU BACHIRA
YOICHI ISAGI

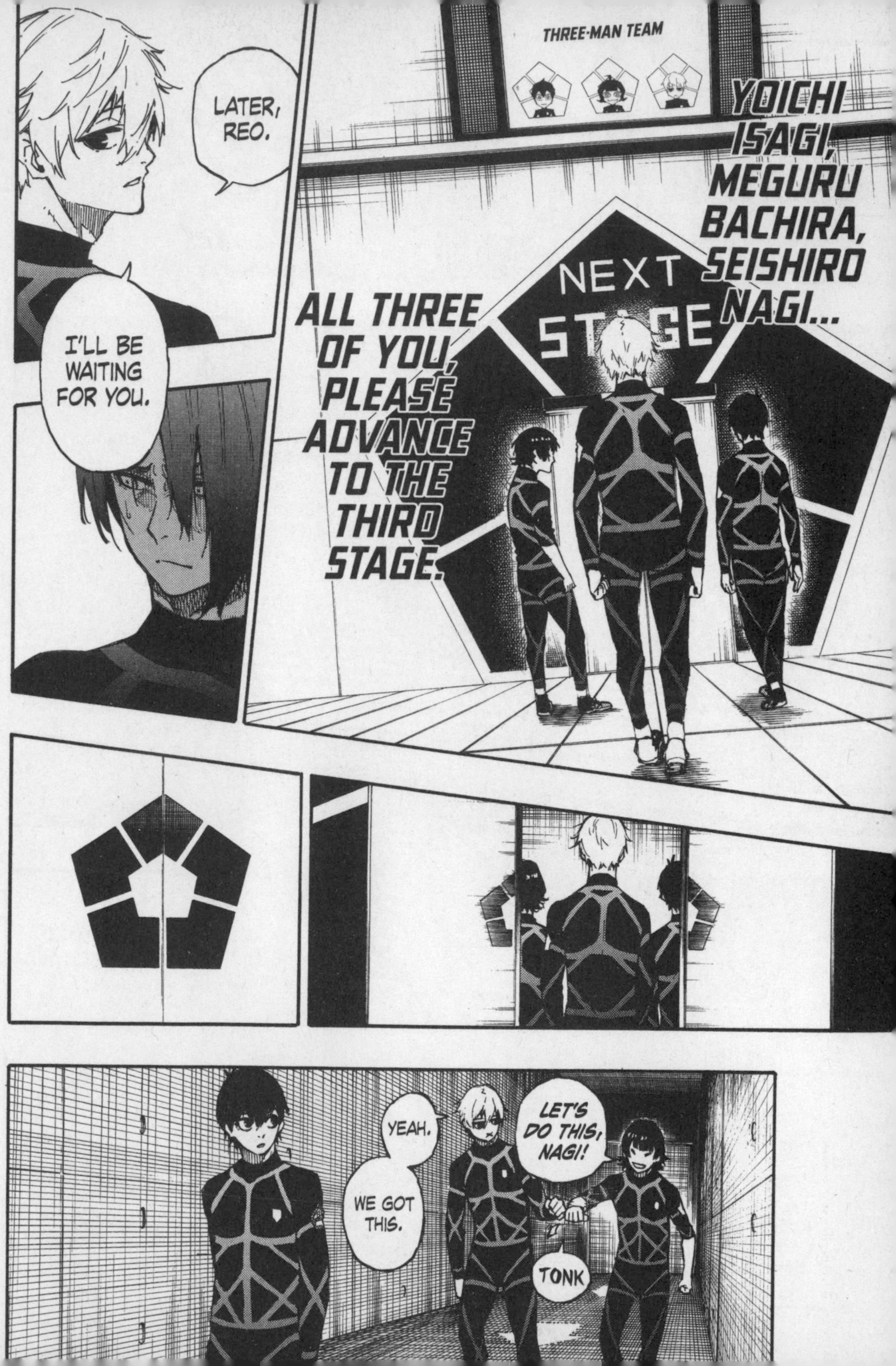
THREE-MAN TEAM
YOICHI ISAGI, MEGURU BACHIRA, SEISHIRO NAGI...
NEXT STAGE
ALL THREE OF YOU, PLEASE ADVANCE TO THE THIRD STAGE.
LATER, REO.
I'LL BE WAITING FOR YOU.
LET'S DO THIS, NAGI!
YEAH.
WE GOT THIS.
TONK

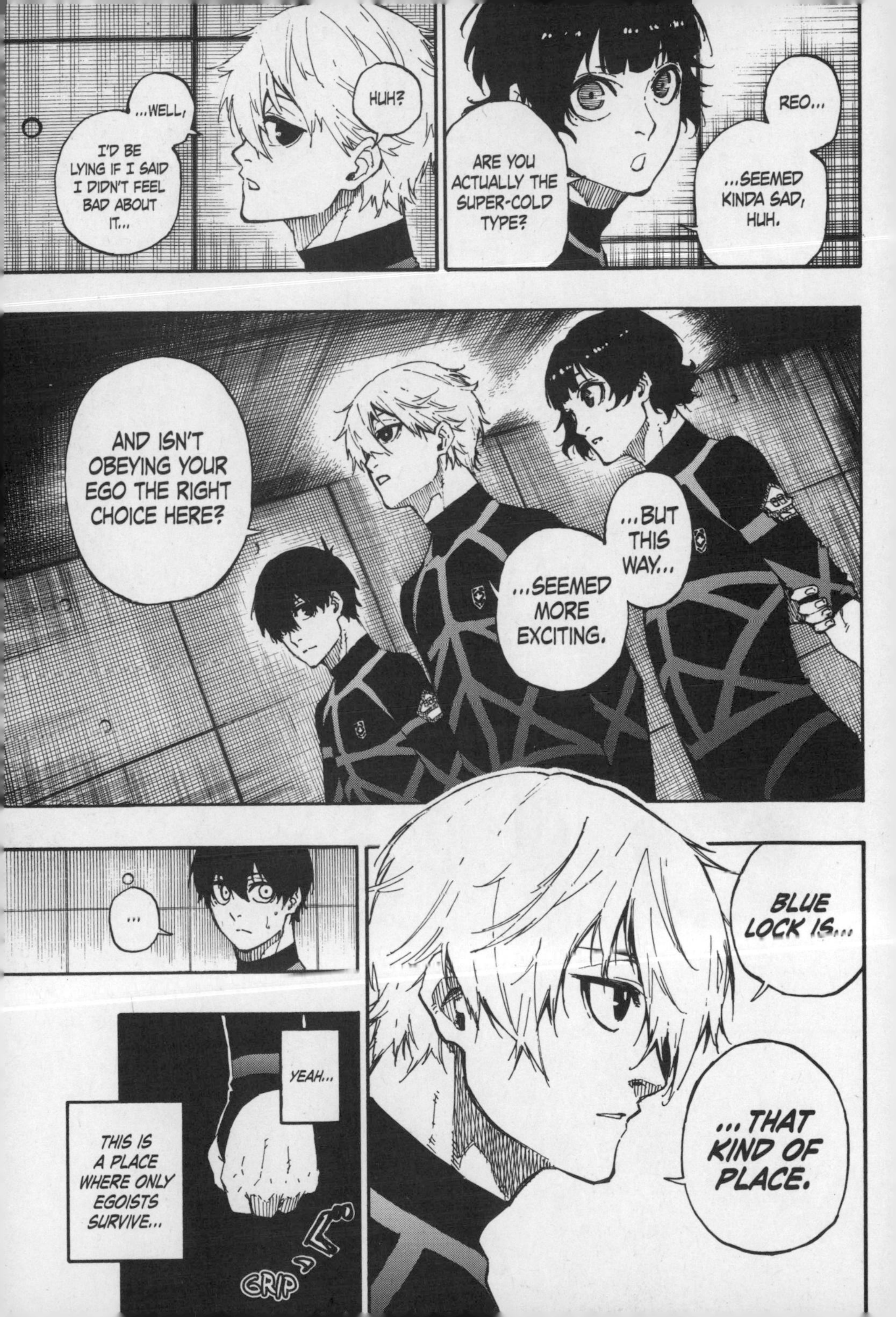
REO...
...SEEMED KINDA SAD, HUH.
ARE YOU ACTUALLY THE SUPER-COLD TYPE?
HUH?
...WELL,
I'D BE LYING IF I SAID I DIDN'T FEEL BAD ABOUT IT...
...BUT THIS WAY...
...SEEMED MORE EXCITING.
AND ISN'T OBEYING YOUR EGO THE RIGHT CHOICE HERE?
BLUE LOCK IS...
...THAT KIND OF PLACE.
...
YEAH...
THIS IS A PLACE WHERE ONLY EGOISTS SURVIVE...
GRIP

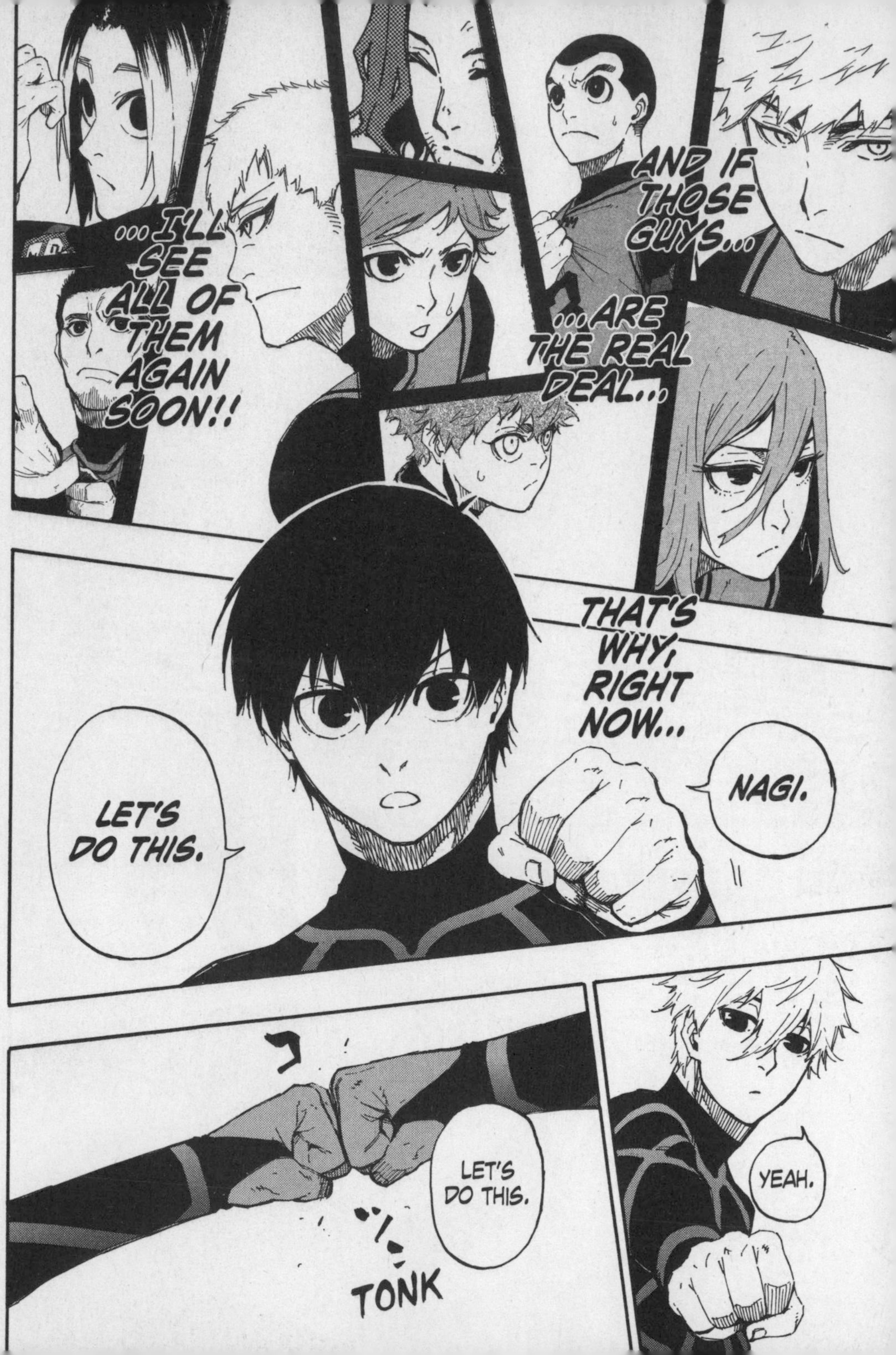
AND IF THOSE GUYS...
...ARE THE REAL DEAL...
...I'LL SEE ALL OF THEM AGAIN SOON!!
THAT'S WHY, RIGHT NOW...
NAGI.
LET'S DO THIS.
YEAH.
LET'S DO THIS.
TONK

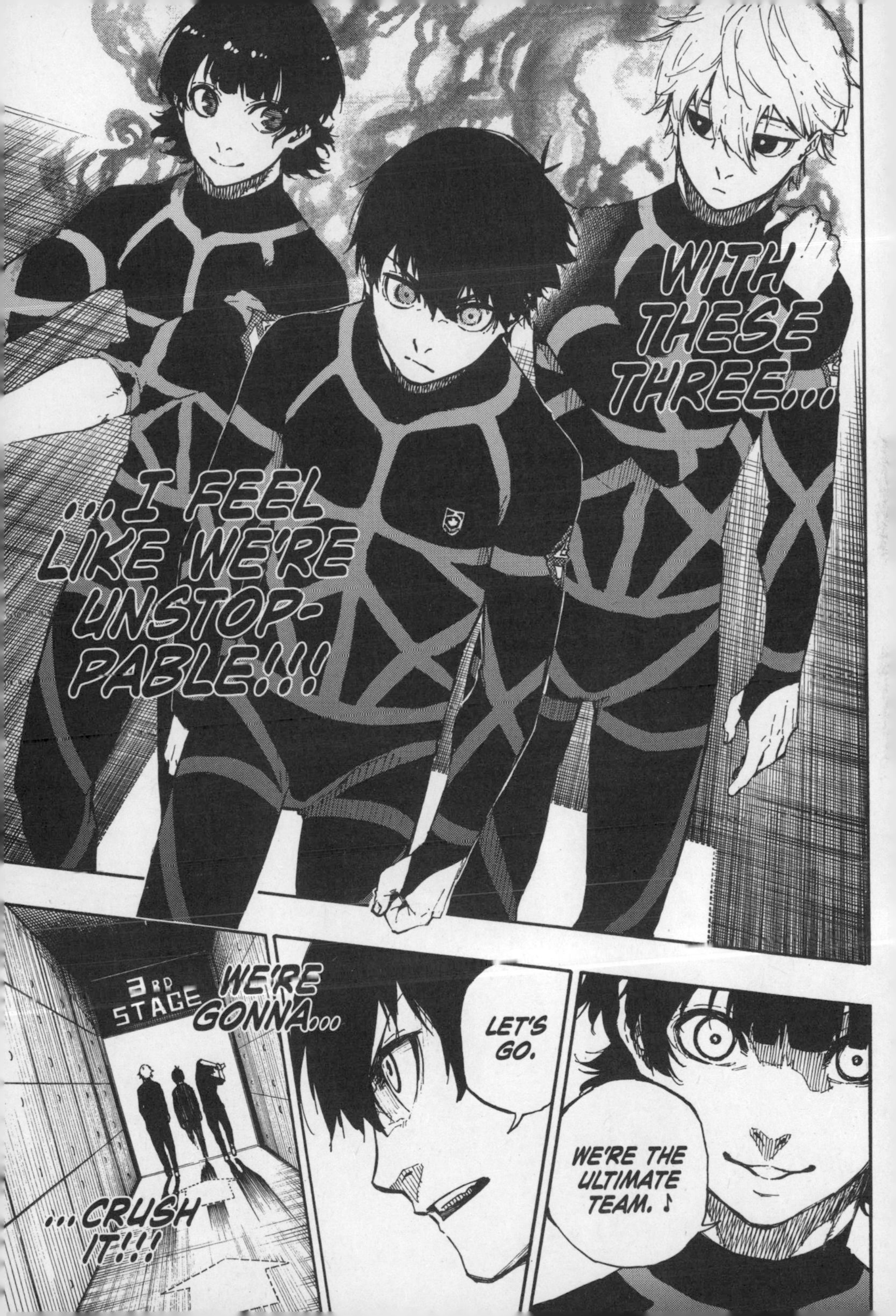
WITH THESE THREE...
...I FEEL LIKE WE'RE UNSTOP-PABLE!!!
WE'RE THE ULTIMATE TEAM. ♪
LET'S GO.
3RD STAGE
WE'RE GONNA...
...CRUSH IT!!!

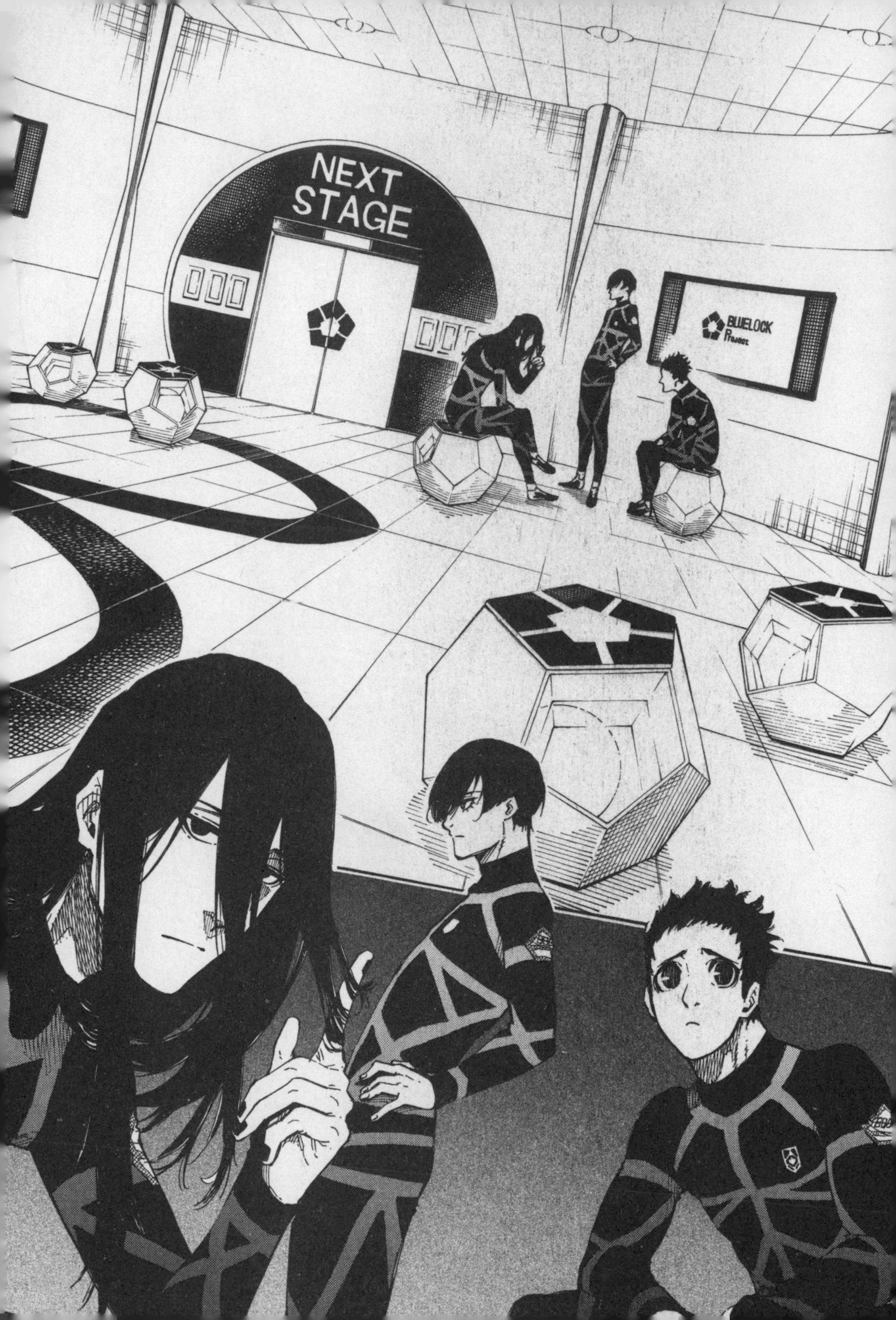
NEXT
STAGE
BLUELOCK
Project

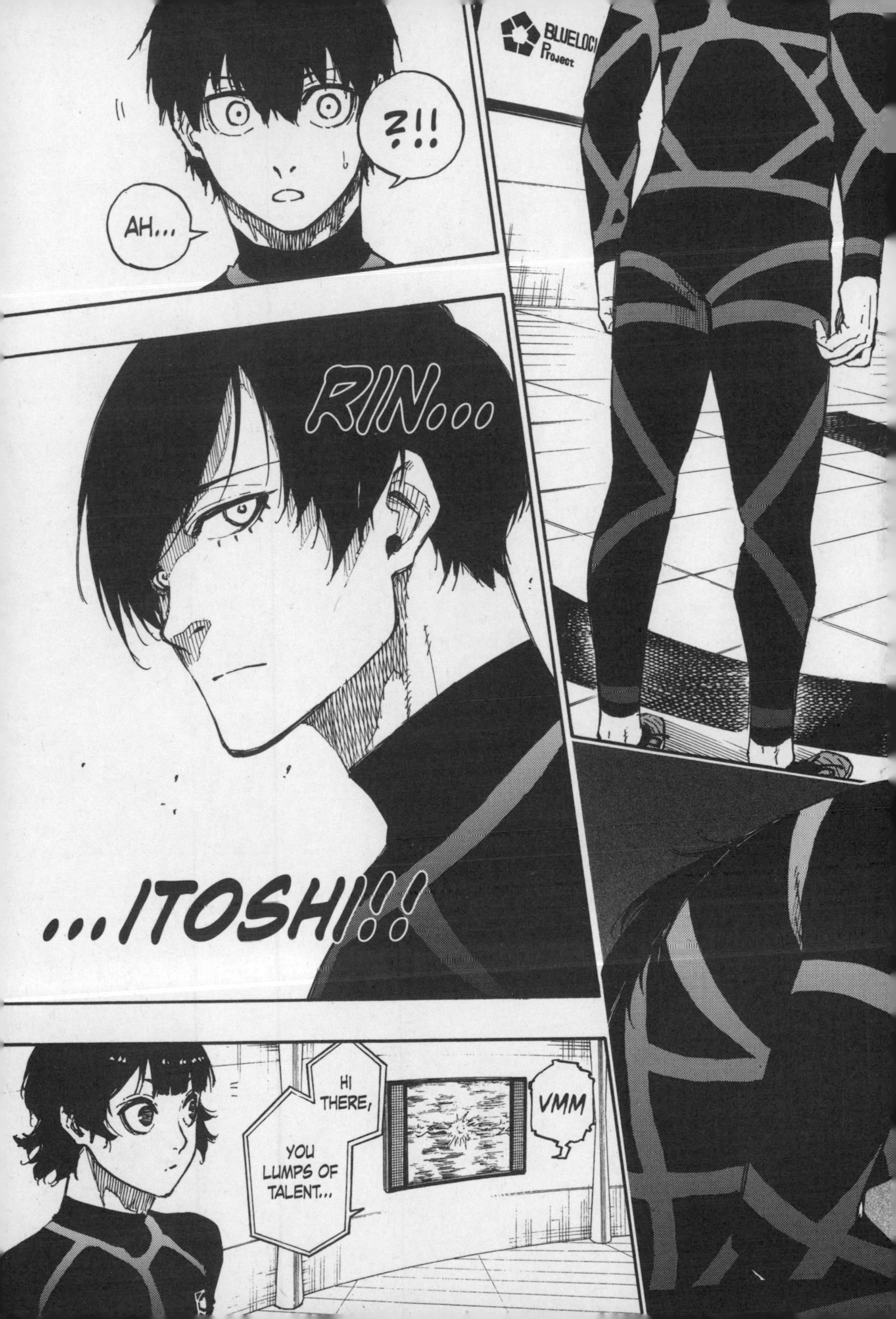

BLUELOCK Project
?!!
AH...
RIN...
...ITOSHI!!
VMM
HI THERE, YOU LUMPS OF TALENT...

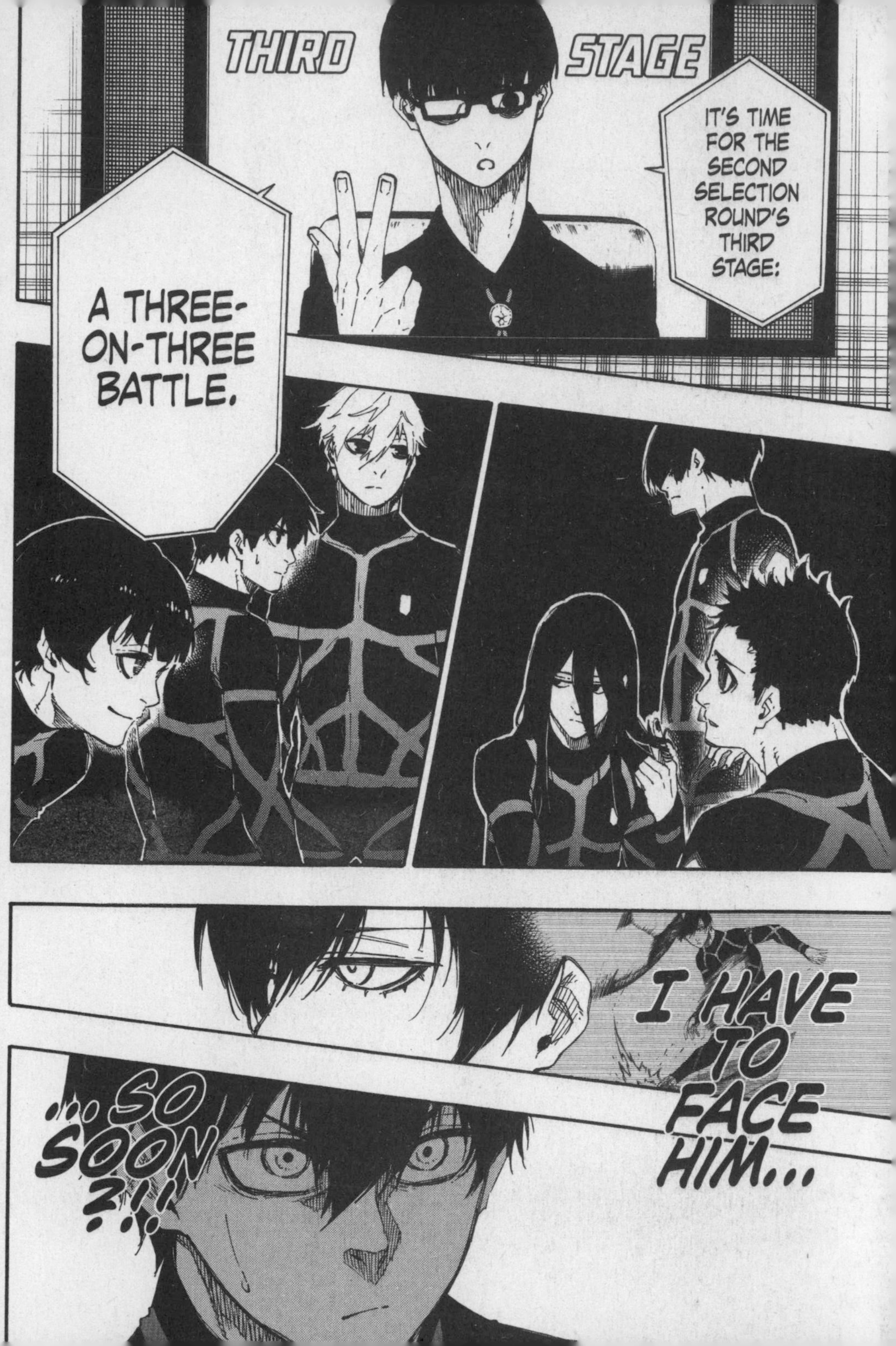
THIRD STAGE
IT'S TIME FOR THE SECOND SELECTION ROUND'S THIRD STAGE:
A THREE-ON-THREE BATTLE.
I HAVE TO FACE HIM...
...SO SOON?!!

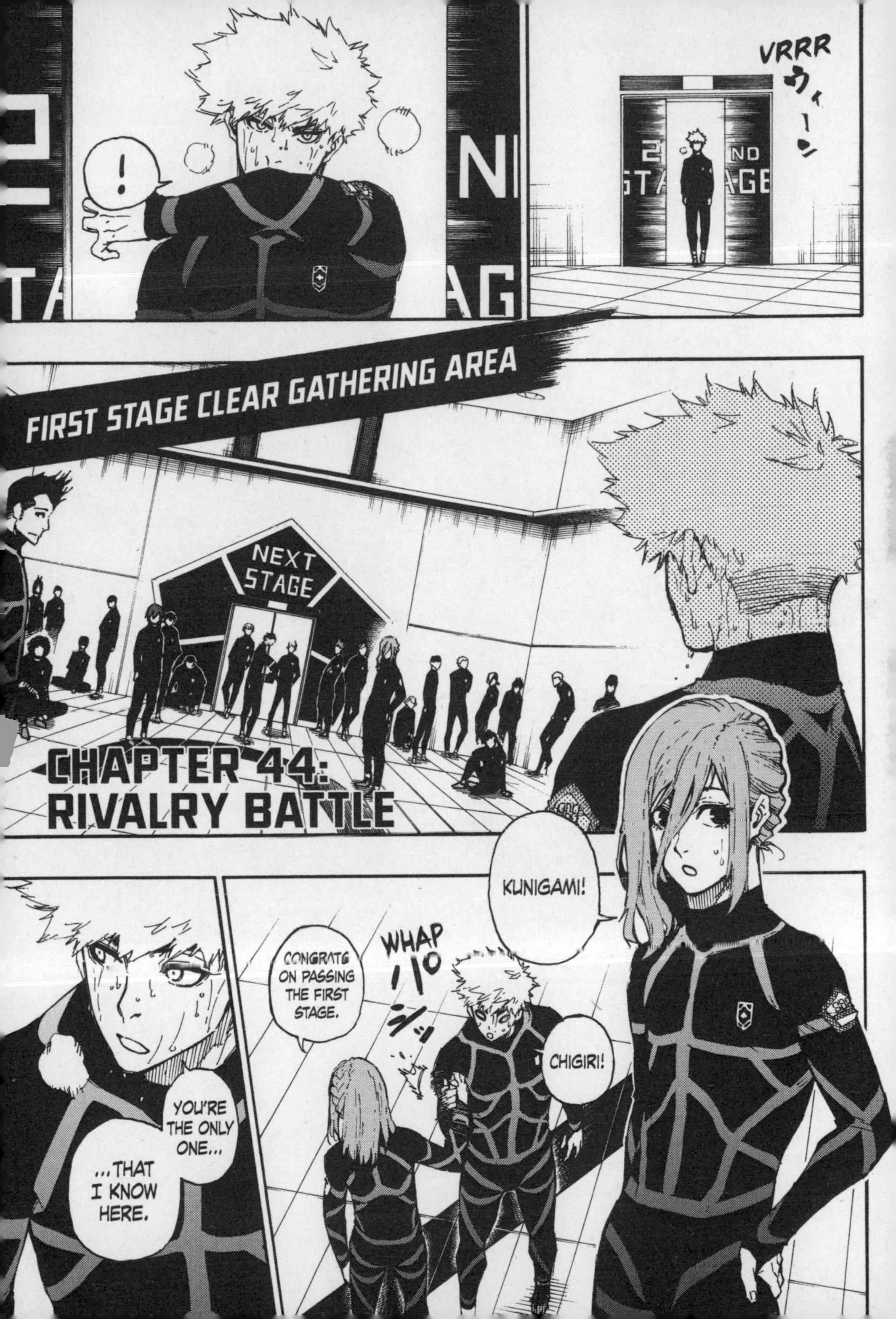
VRRR
ウィーン
2ND STAGE
!
FIRST STAGE CLEAR GATHERING AREA
NEXT STAGE
CHAPTER 44: RIVALRY BATTLE
KUNIGAMI!
WHAP
CONGRATS ON PASSING THE FIRST STAGE.
CHIGIRI!
YOU'RE THE ONLY ONE...
...THAT I KNOW HERE.

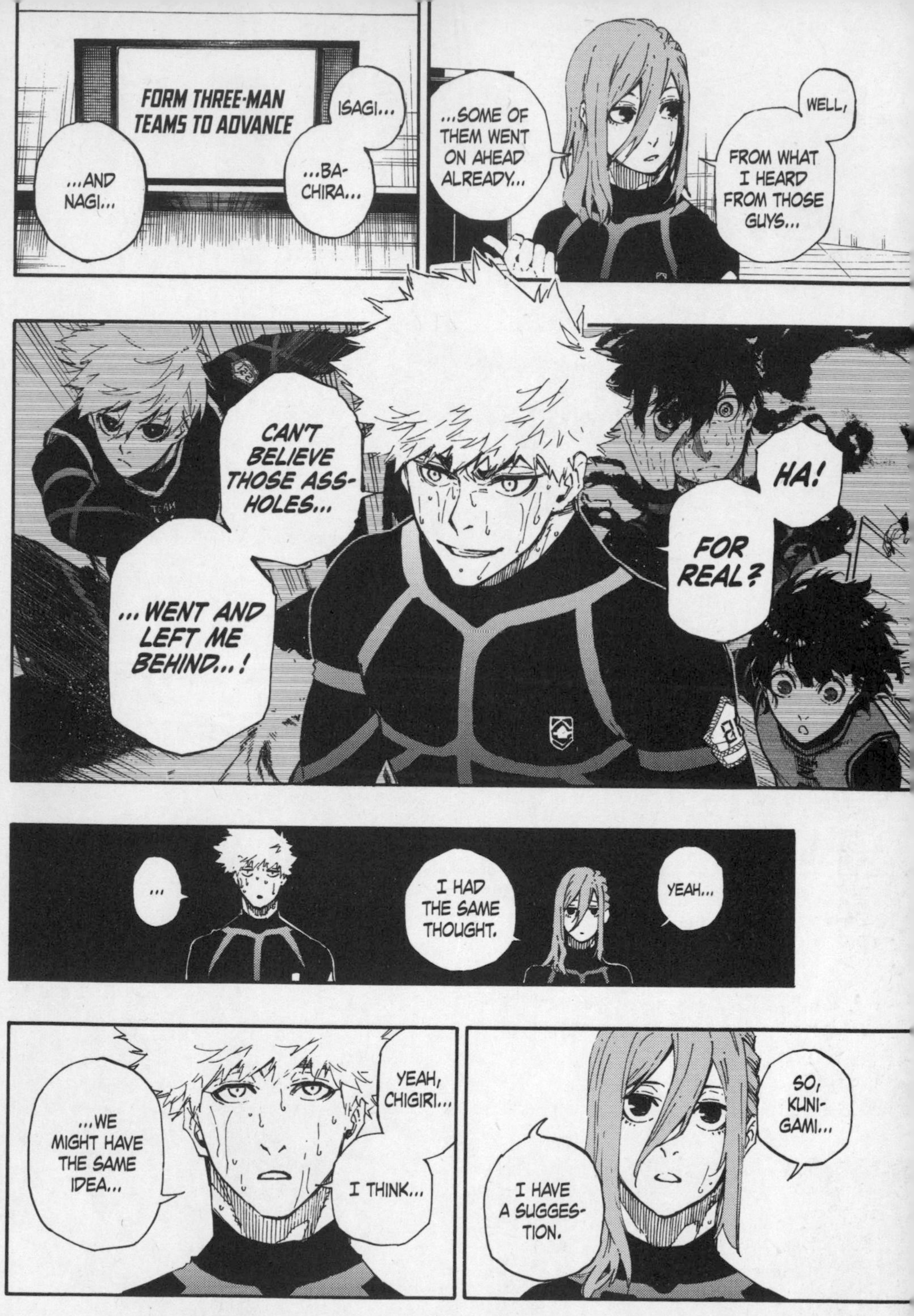
WELL,
FROM WHAT I HEARD FROM THOSE GUYS...
...SOME OF THEM WENT ON AHEAD ALREADY...
FORM THREE-MAN TEAMS TO ADVANCE
ISAGI...
...BA-CHIRA...
...AND NAGI...
HA!
FOR REAL?
CAN'T BELIEVE THOSE ASS-HOLES...
...WENT AND LEFT ME BEHIND...!
YEAH...
I HAD THE SAME THOUGHT.
...
SO, KUNI-GAMI...
I HAVE A SUGGES-TION.
YEAH, CHIGIRI...
I THINK...
...WE MIGHT HAVE THE SAME IDEA...

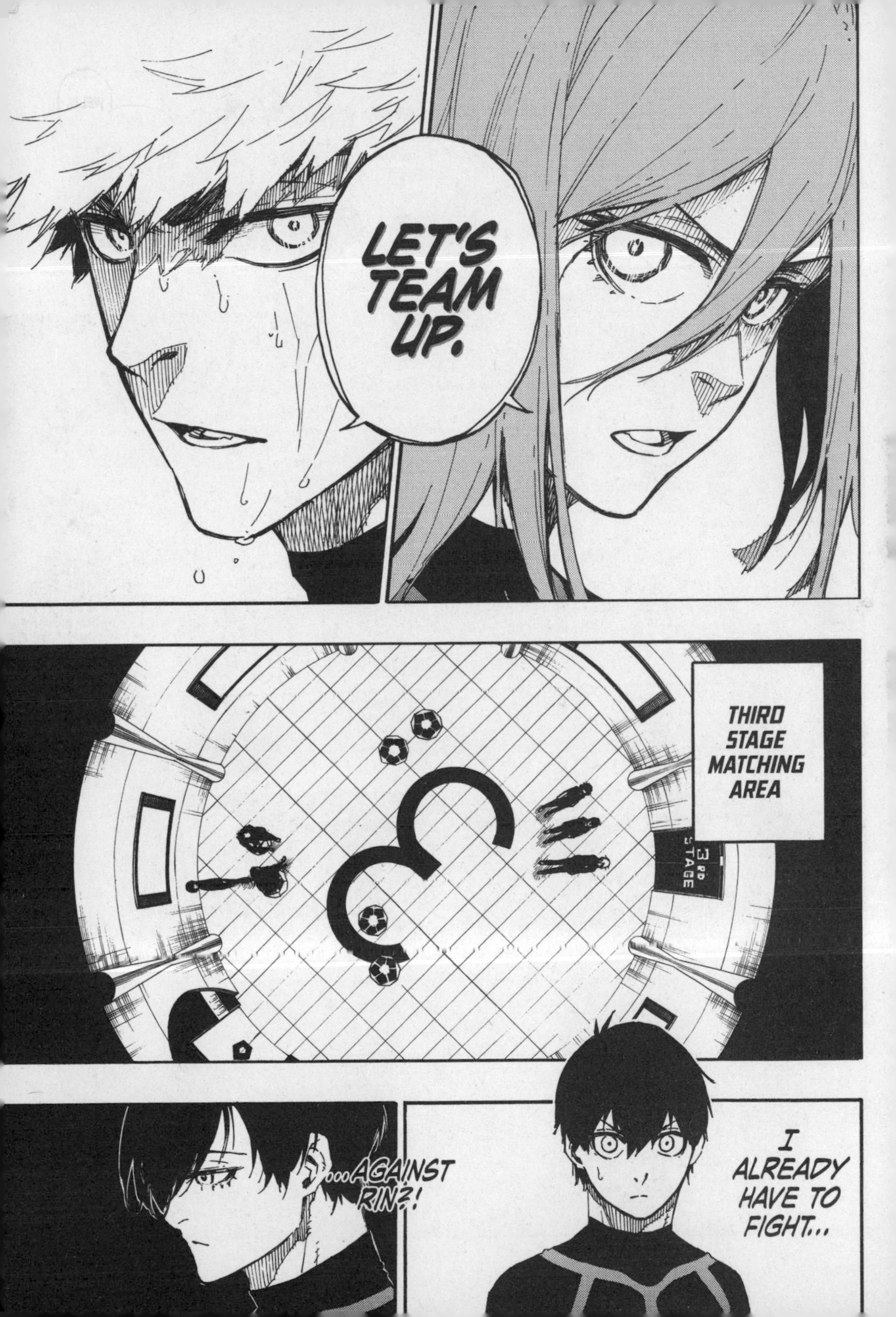
LET'S TEAM UP.
THIRD STAGE MATCHING AREA
3RD STAGE
I ALREADY HAVE TO FIGHT...
...AGAINST RIN?!

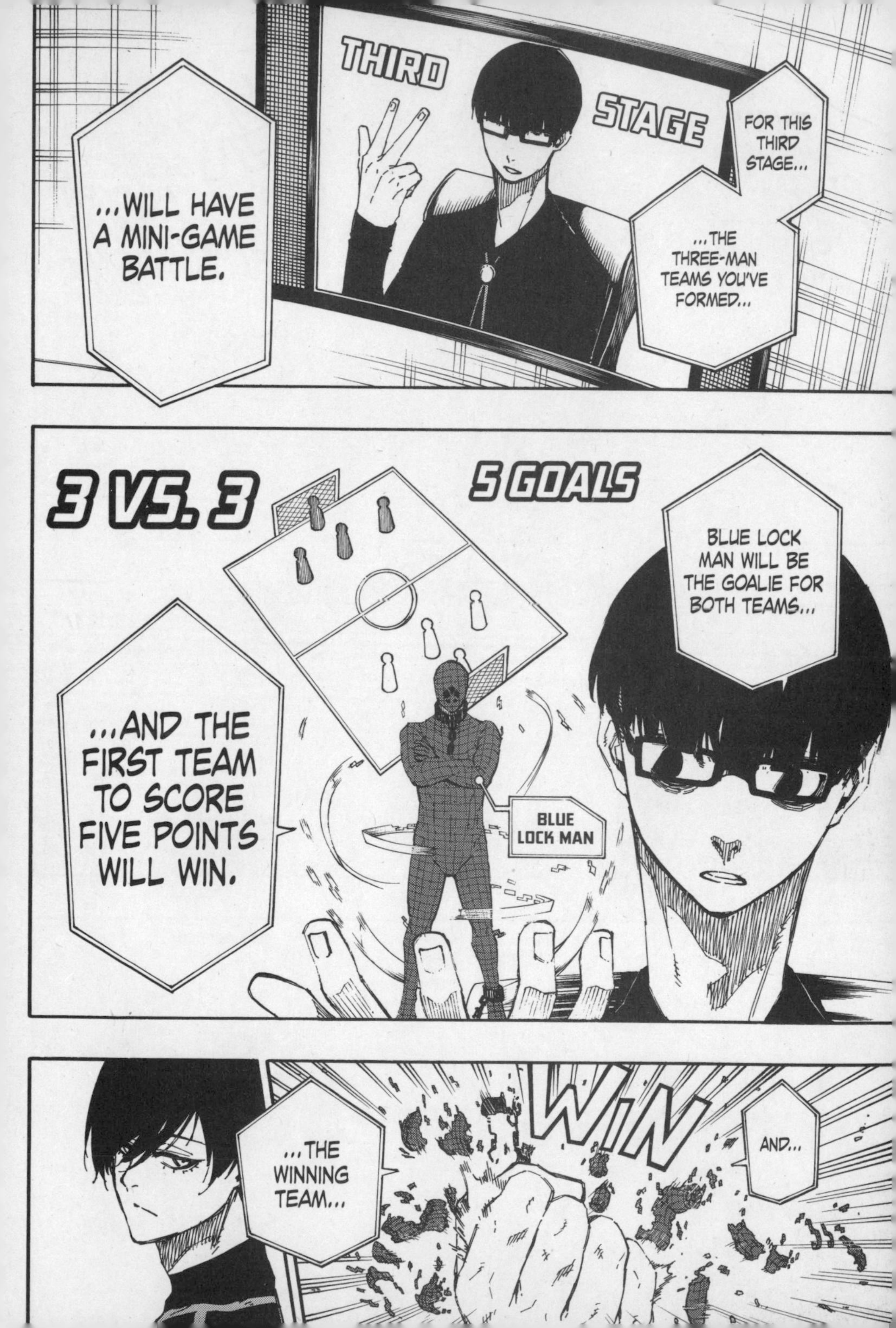
THIRD STAGE
FOR THIS THIRD STAGE...
...THE THREE-MAN TEAMS YOU'VE FORMED...
...WILL HAVE A MINI-GAME BATTLE.
5 GOALS
BLUE LOCK MAN WILL BE THE GOALIE FOR BOTH TEAMS...
3 VS. 3
BLUE LOCK MAN
...AND THE FIRST TEAM TO SCORE FIVE POINTS WILL WIN.
AND...
WIN
...THE WINNING TEAM...

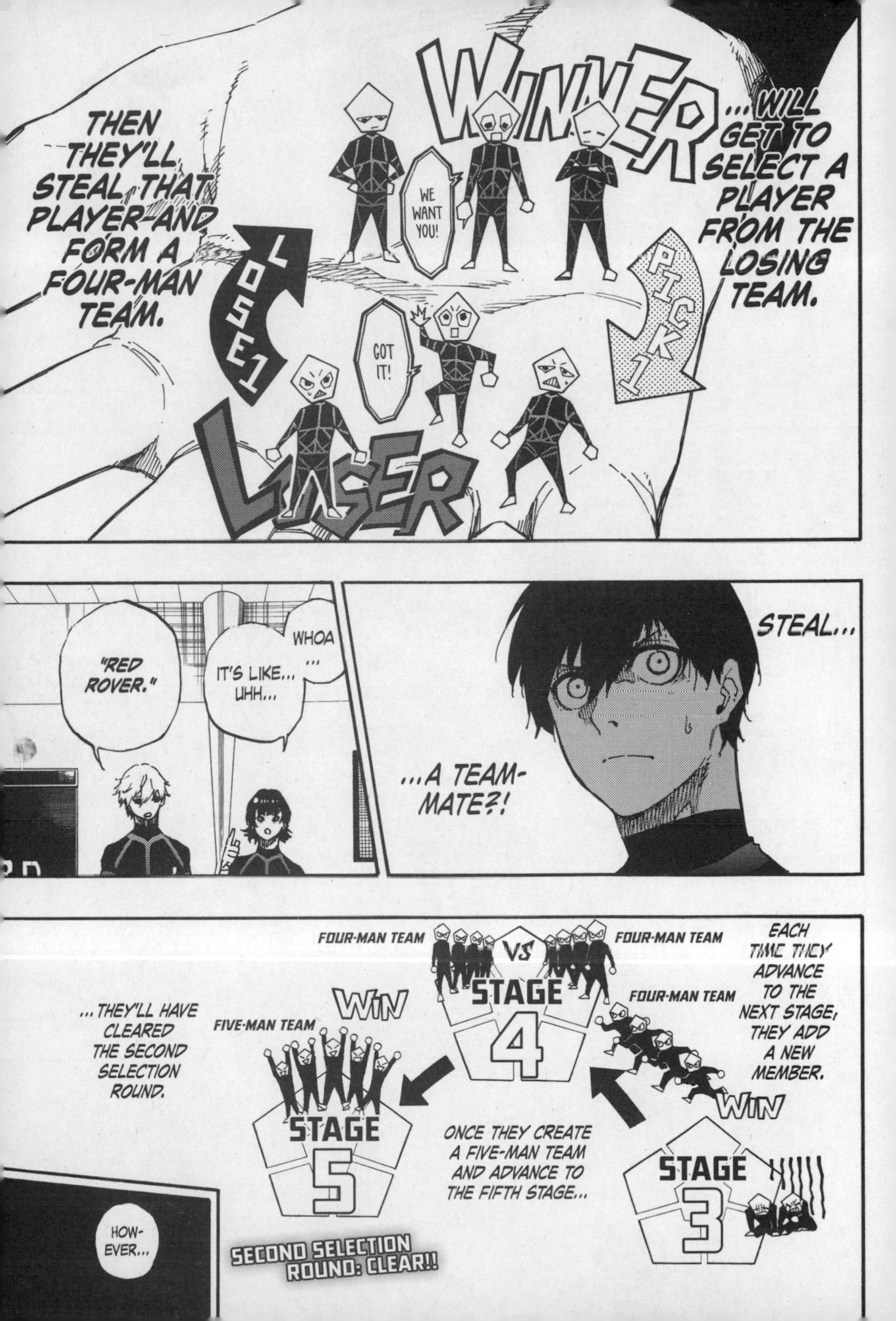
WINNER
...WILL GET TO SELECT A PLAYER FROM THE LOSING TEAM.
WE WANT YOU!
PICK 1
GOT IT!
LOSE 1
LOSER
THEN THEY'LL STEAL THAT PLAYER AND FORM A FOUR-MAN TEAM.
STEAL...
...A TEAM-MATE?!
WHOA...
IT'S LIKE... UHH...
"RED ROVER."
EACH TIME THEY ADVANCE TO THE NEXT STAGE, THEY ADD A NEW MEMBER.
FOUR-MAN TEAM
VS
FOUR-MAN TEAM
STAGE 4
FOUR-MAN TEAM
WIN
STAGE 3
WIN
FIVE-MAN TEAM
STAGE 5
ONCE THEY CREATE A FIVE-MAN TEAM AND ADVANCE TO THE FIFTH STAGE...
...THEY'LL HAVE CLEARED THE SECOND SELECTION ROUND.
SECOND SELECTION ROUND: CLEAR!!
HOW-EVER...

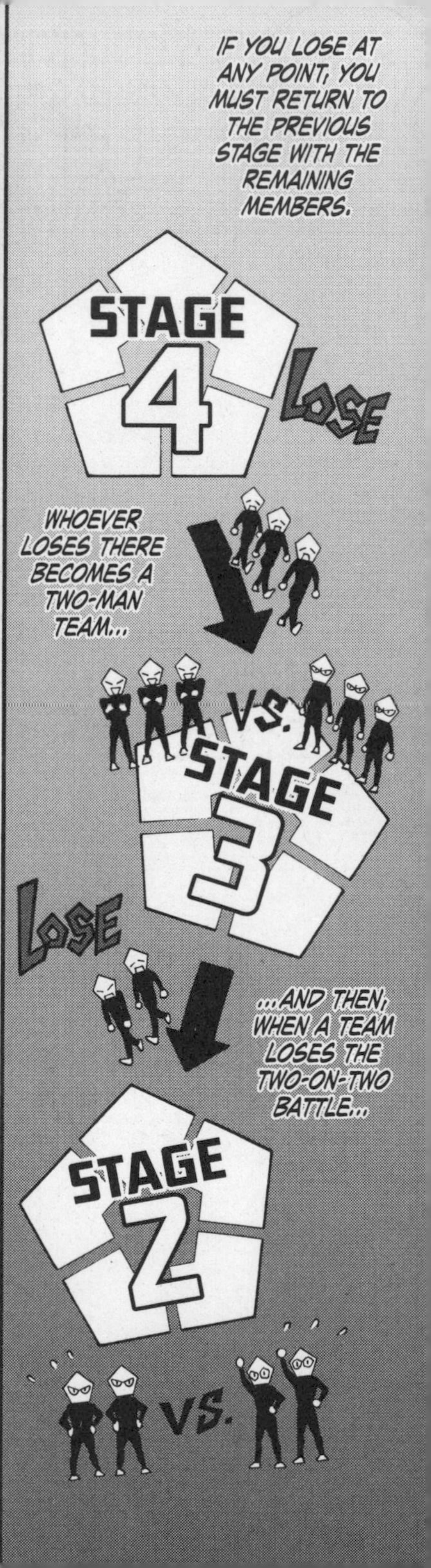
IF YOU LOSE AT ANY POINT, YOU MUST RETURN TO THE PREVIOUS STAGE WITH THE REMAINING MEMBERS.
STAGE 4
LOSE
WHOEVER LOSES THERE BECOMES A TWO-MAN TEAM...
VS.
STAGE 3
LOSE
...AND THEN, WHEN A TEAM LOSES THE TWO-ON-TWO BATTLE...
STAGE 2
VS.

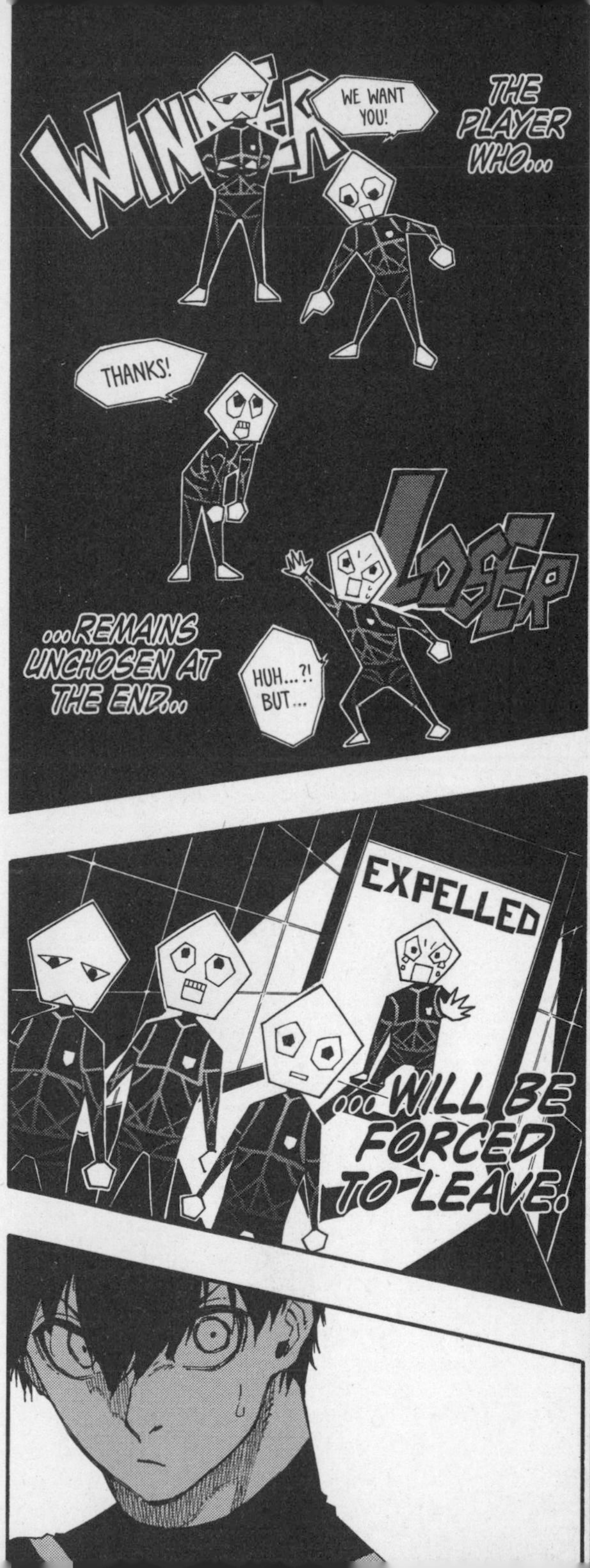
THE PLAYER WHO...
WINNER
WE WANT YOU!
THANKS!
LOSER
...REMAINS UNCHOSEN AT THE END...
HUH...?! BUT...
EXPELLED
...WILL BE FORCED TO LEAVE.

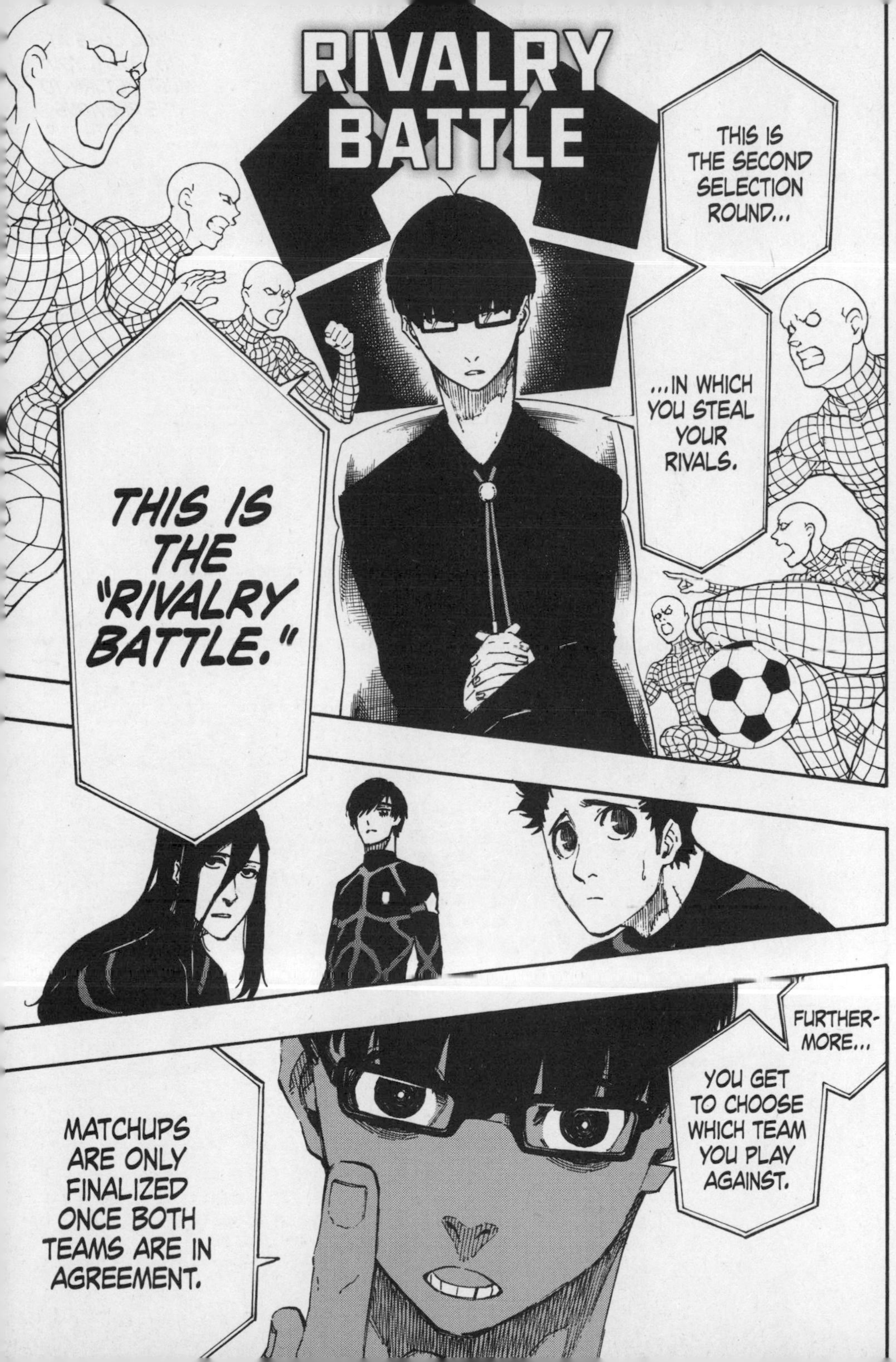
RIVALRY BATTLE
THIS IS THE SECOND SELECTION ROUND...
...IN WHICH YOU STEAL YOUR RIVALS.
THIS IS THE "RIVALRY BATTLE."
FURTHER-MORE...
YOU GET TO CHOOSE WHICH TEAM YOU PLAY AGAINST.
MATCHUPS ARE ONLY FINALIZED ONCE BOTH TEAMS ARE IN AGREEMENT.

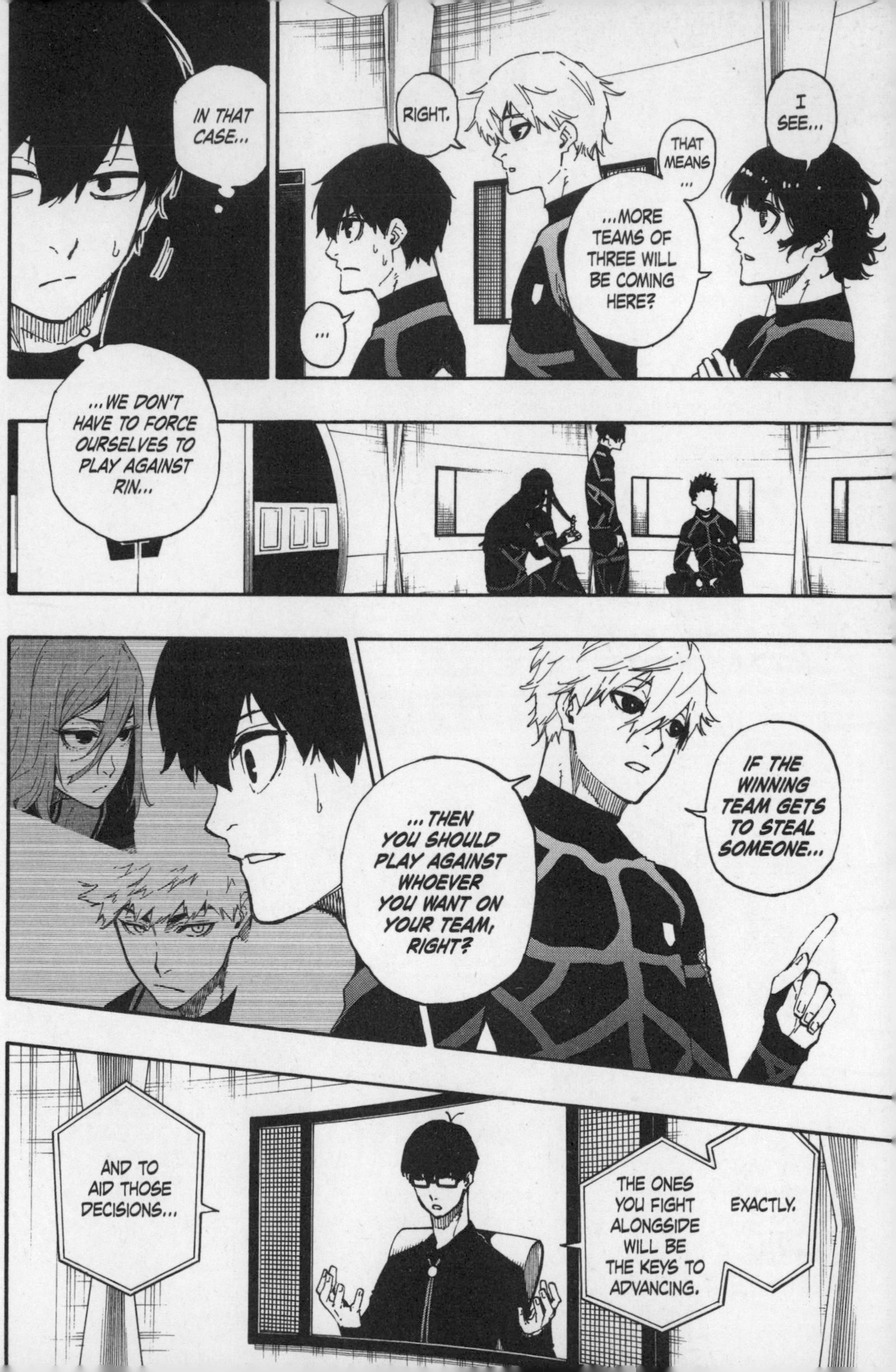
I SEE...
THAT MEANS ...
...MORE TEAMS OF THREE WILL BE COMING HERE?
RIGHT.
...
IN THAT CASE...
...WE DON'T HAVE TO FORCE OURSELVES TO PLAY AGAINST RIN...
IF THE WINNING TEAM GETS TO STEAL SOMEONE...
...THEN YOU SHOULD PLAY AGAINST WHOEVER YOU WANT ON YOUR TEAM, RIGHT?
EXACTLY.
THE ONES YOU FIGHT ALONGSIDE WILL BE THE KEYS TO ADVANCING.
AND TO AID THOSE DECISIONS...

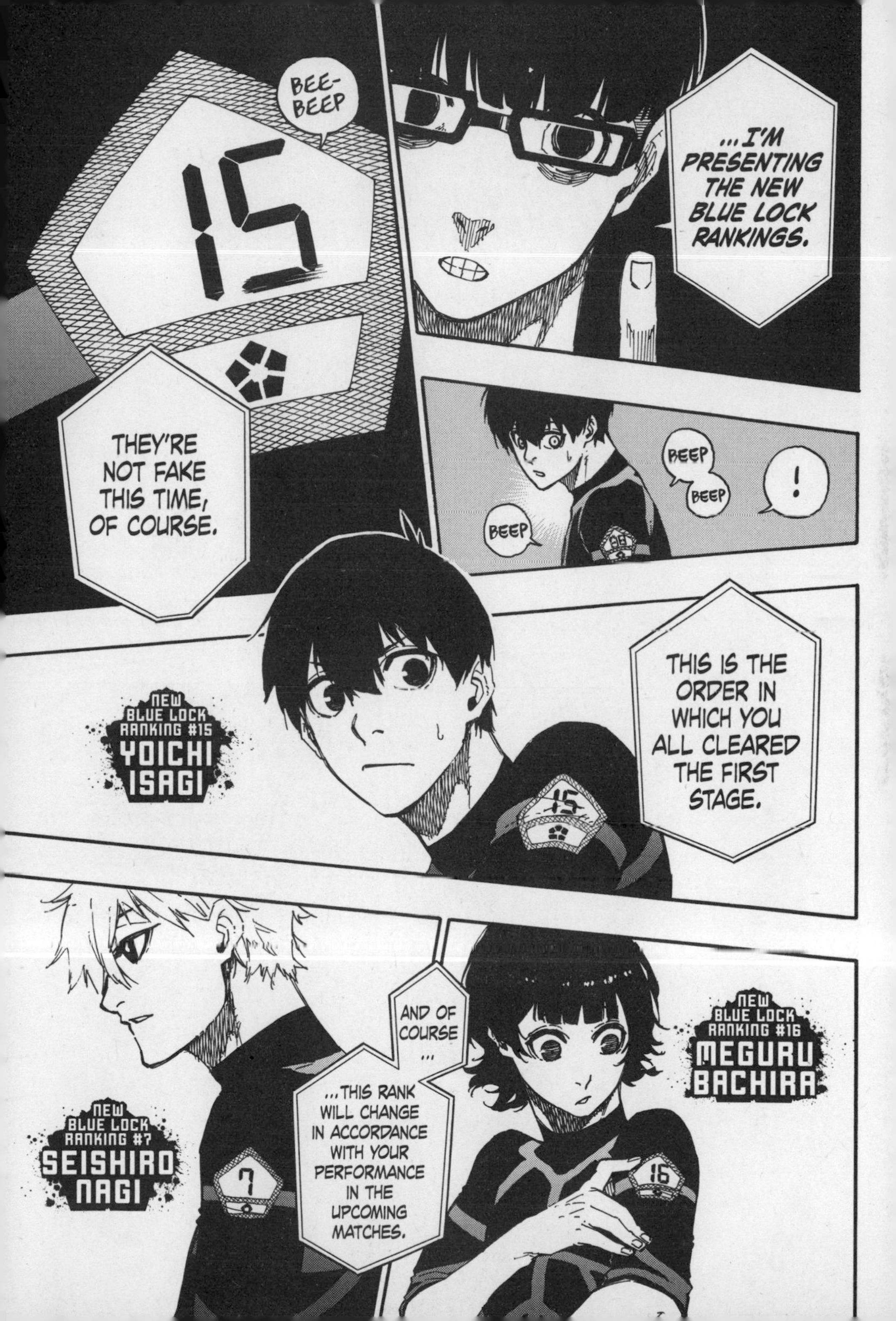
...I'M PRESENTING THE NEW BLUE LOCK RANKINGS.
BEEP
BEEP
BEEP
!
BEE-BEEP
15
THEY'RE NOT FAKE THIS TIME, OF COURSE.
THIS IS THE ORDER IN WHICH YOU ALL CLEARED THE FIRST STAGE.
NEW BLUE LOCK RANKING #15 YOICHI ISAGI
NEW BLUE LOCK RANKING #16 MEGURU BACHIRA
AND OF COURSE...
...THIS RANK WILL CHANGE IN ACCORDANCE WITH YOUR PERFORMANCE IN THE UPCOMING MATCHES.
NEW BLUE LOCK RANKING #7 SEISHIRO NAGI

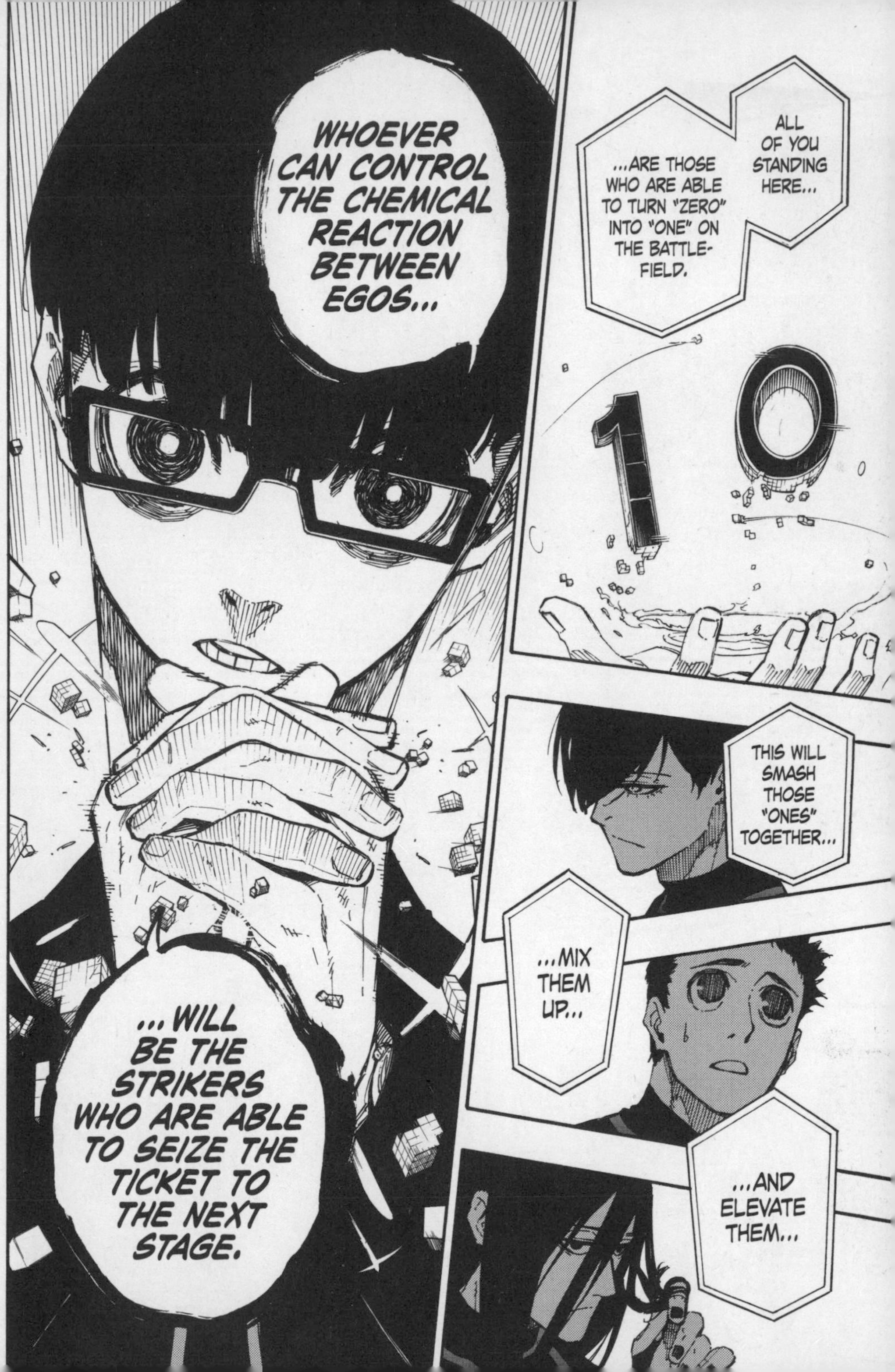
ALL OF YOU STANDING HERE...
...ARE THOSE WHO ARE ABLE TO TURN "ZERO" INTO "ONE" ON THE BATTLE-FIELD.
1 0
THIS WILL SMASH THOSE "ONES" TOGETHER...
...MIX THEM UP...
...AND ELEVATE THEM...
WHOEVER CAN CONTROL THE CHEMICAL REACTION BETWEEN EGOS...
...WILL BE THE STRIKERS WHO ARE ABLE TO SEIZE THE TICKET TO THE NEXT STAGE.

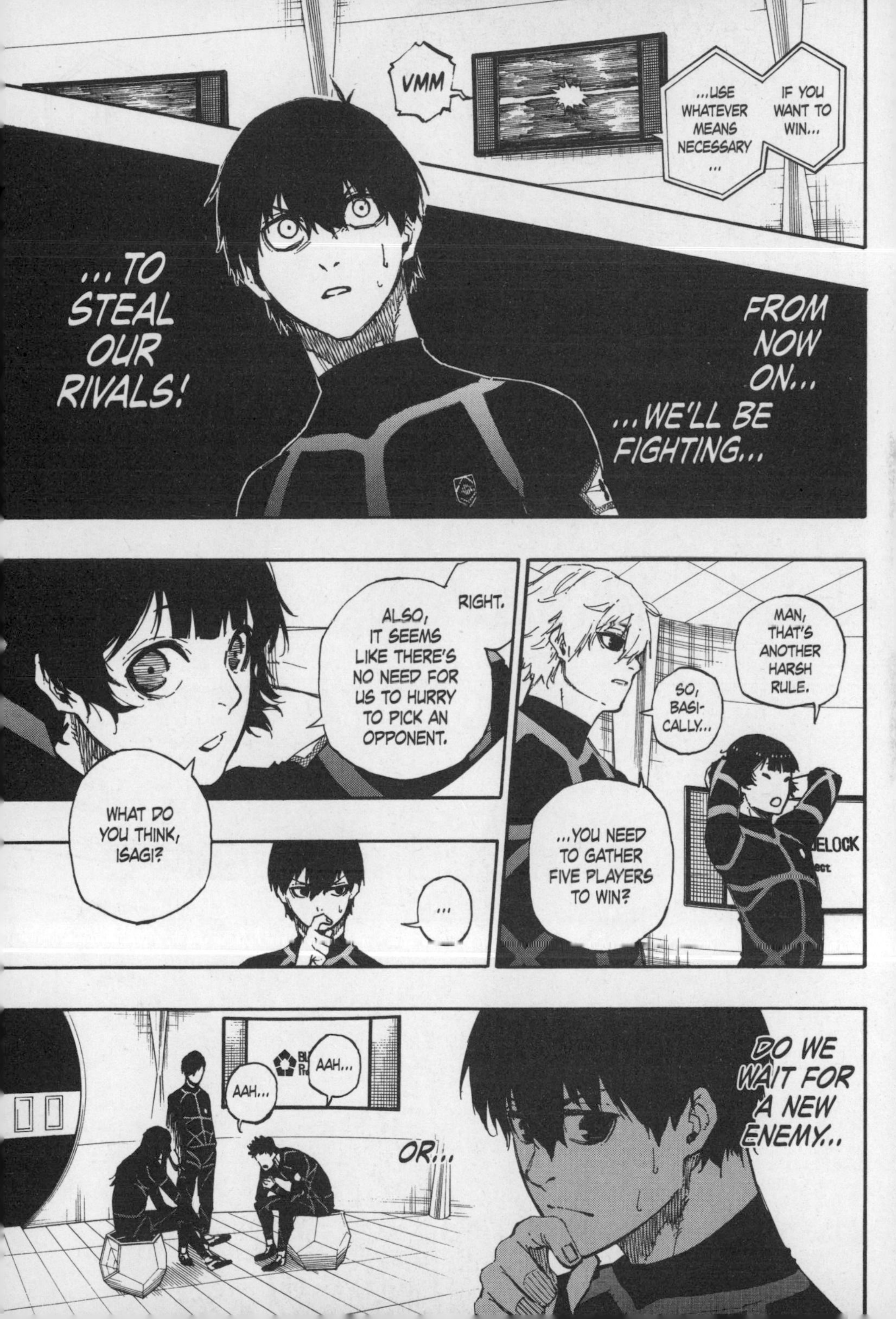
IF YOU WANT TO WIN...
...USE WHATEVER MEANS NECESSARY ...
VMM
FROM NOW ON...
...WE'LL BE FIGHTING...
...TO STEAL OUR RIVALS!
MAN, THAT'S ANOTHER HARSH RULE.
SO, BASICALLY...
...YOU NEED TO GATHER FIVE PLAYERS TO WIN?
RIGHT.
ALSO, IT SEEMS LIKE THERE'S NO NEED FOR US TO HURRY TO PICK AN OPPONENT.
WHAT DO YOU THINK, ISAGI?
...
DO WE WAIT FOR A NEW ENEMY...
OR...
AAH...
AAH...

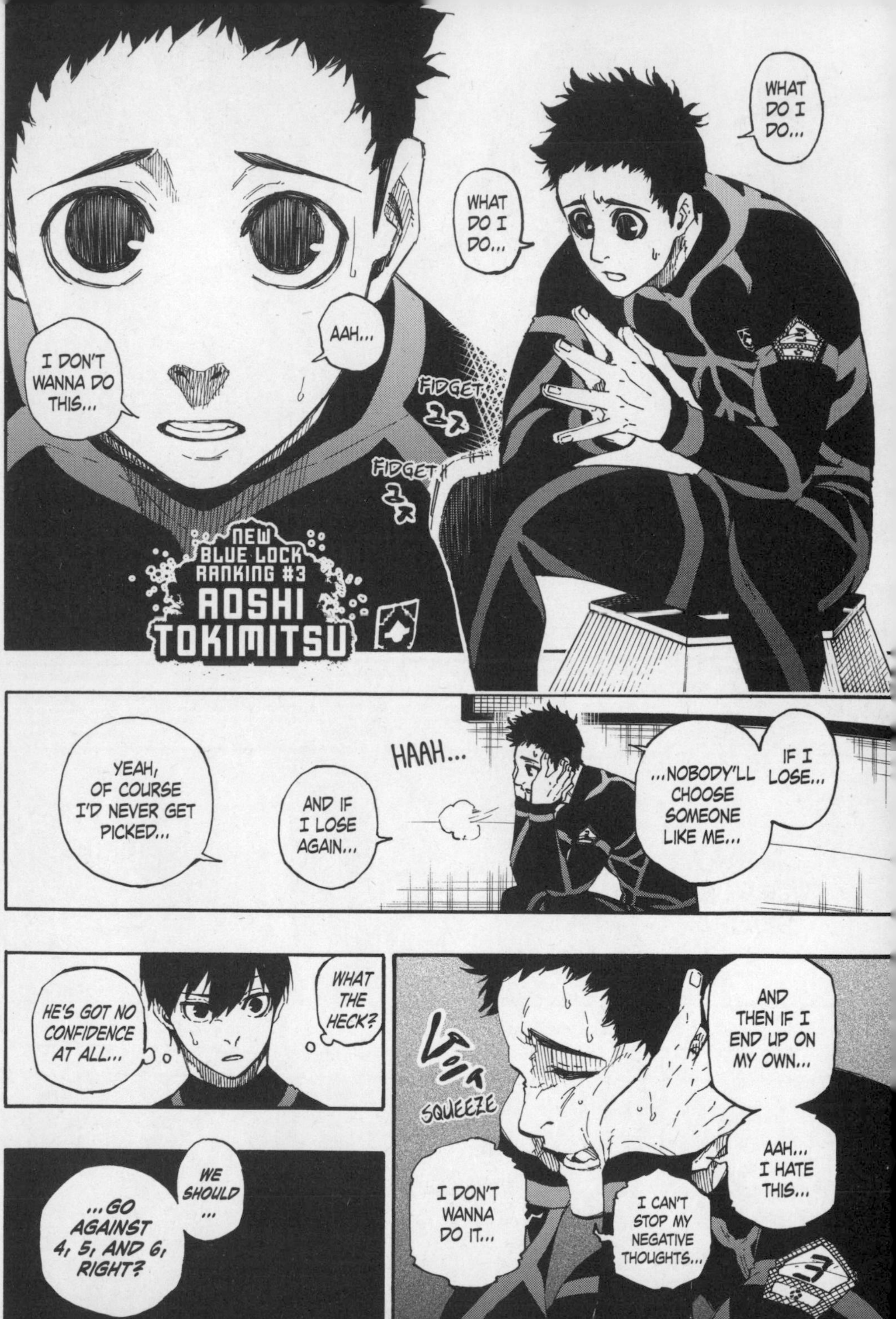
WHAT DO I DO...
WHAT DO I DO...
AAH...
I DON'T WANNA DO THIS...
FIDGET
FIDGET
NEW BLUE LOCK RANKING #3
AOSHI TOKIMITSU
IF I LOSE...
...NOBODY'LL CHOOSE SOMEONE LIKE ME...
HAAH...
AND IF I LOSE AGAIN...
YEAH, OF COURSE I'D NEVER GET PICKED...
AND THEN IF I END UP ON MY OWN...
SQUEEZE
AAH... I HATE THIS...
I CAN'T STOP MY NEGATIVE THOUGHTS...
I DON'T WANNA DO IT...
WHAT THE HECK?
HE'S GOT NO CONFIDENCE AT ALL...
WE SHOULD...
...GO AGAINST 4, 5, AND 6, RIGHT?

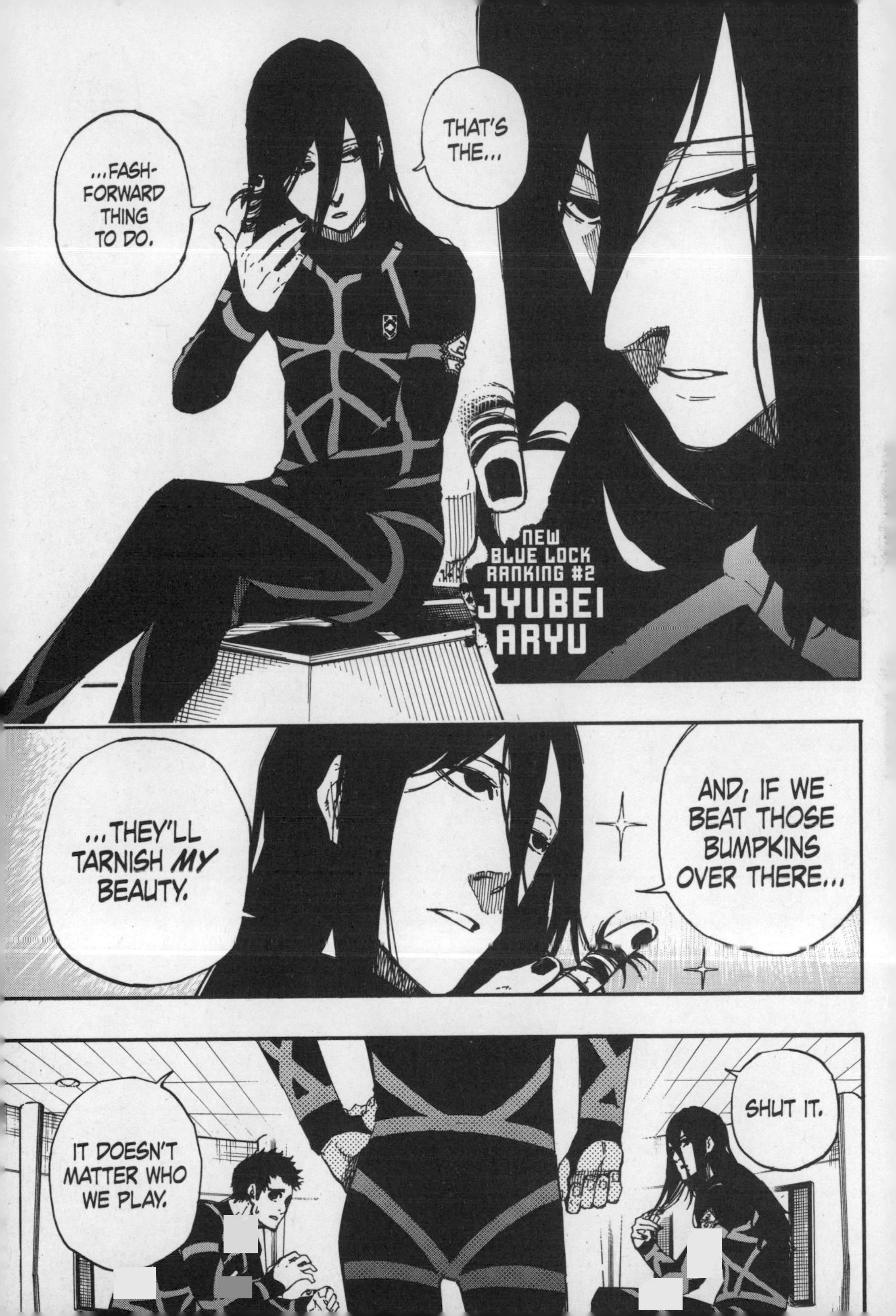
THAT'S THE...
...FASH-FORWARD THING TO DO.
NEW BLUE LOCK RANKING #2
JYUBEI ARYU
AND, IF WE BEAT THOSE BUMPKINS OVER THERE...
...THEY'LL TARNISH *MY* BEAUTY.
SHUT IT.
IT DOESN'T MATTER WHO WE PLAY.

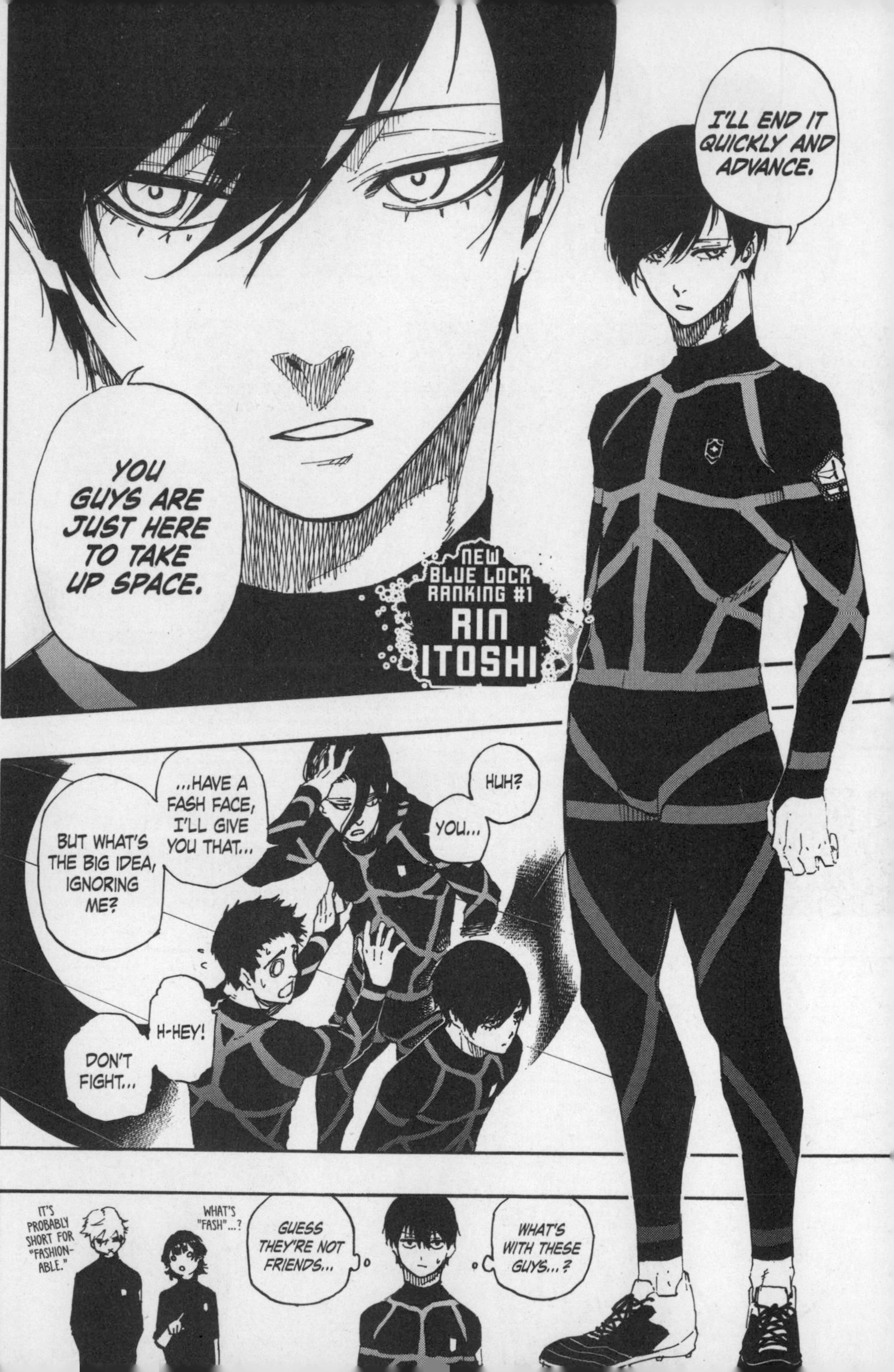
I'LL END IT QUICKLY AND ADVANCE.
NEW BLUE LOCK RANKING #1 RIN ITOSHI
YOU GUYS ARE JUST HERE TO TAKE UP SPACE.
HUH?
YOU...
...HAVE A FASH FACE, I'LL GIVE YOU THAT...
BUT WHAT'S THE BIG IDEA, IGNORING ME?
H-HEY!
DON'T FIGHT...
WHAT'S WITH THESE GUYS...?
GUESS THEY'RE NOT FRIENDS...
WHAT'S "FASH"...?
IT'S PROBABLY SHORT FOR "FASHION-ABLE."

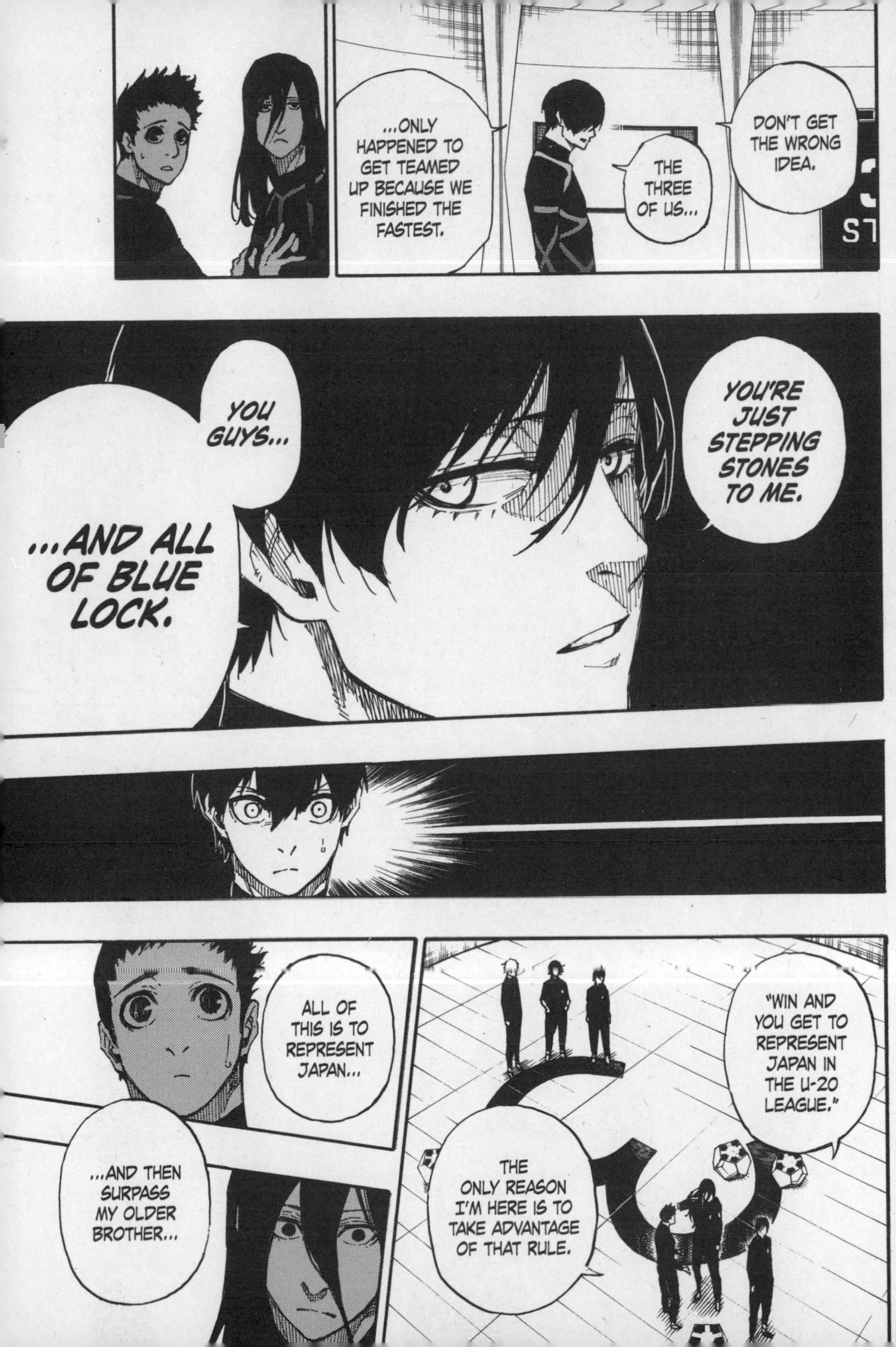
DON'T GET THE WRONG IDEA.
THE THREE OF US...
...ONLY HAPPENED TO GET TEAMED UP BECAUSE WE FINISHED THE FASTEST.
YOU'RE JUST STEPPING STONES TO ME.
YOU GUYS...
...AND ALL OF BLUE LOCK.
"WIN AND YOU GET TO REPRESENT JAPAN IN THE U-20 LEAGUE."
THE ONLY REASON I'M HERE IS TO TAKE ADVANTAGE OF THAT RULE.
ALL OF THIS IS TO REPRESENT JAPAN...
...AND THEN SURPASS MY OLDER BROTHER...

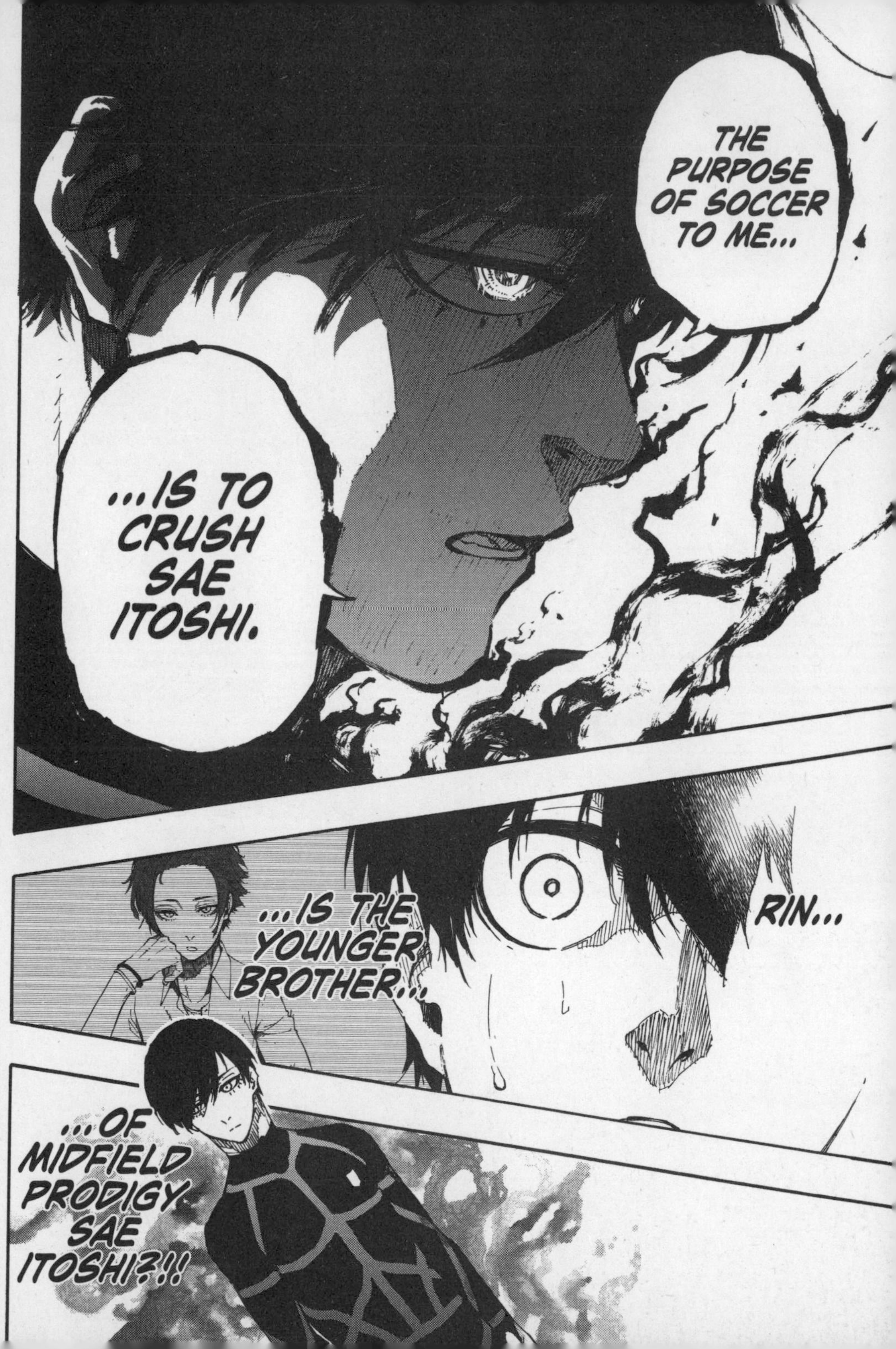
THE PURPOSE OF SOCCER TO ME...
...IS TO CRUSH SAE ITOSHI.
RIN...
...IS THE YOUNGER BROTHER...
...OF MIDFIELD PRODIGY SAE ITOSHI?!!

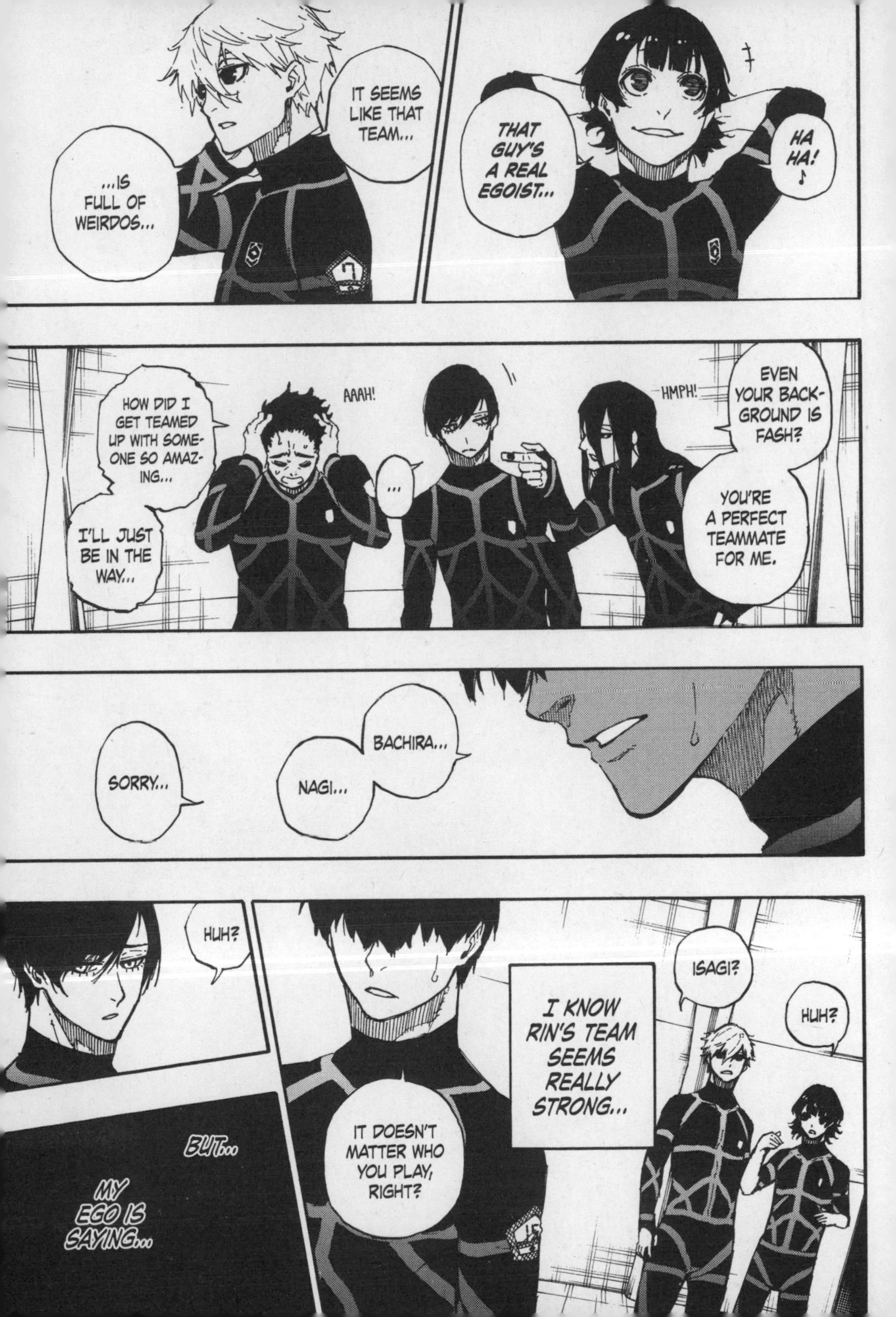
HA HA! ♪
THAT GUY'S A REAL EGOIST...
IT SEEMS LIKE THAT TEAM...
...IS FULL OF WEIRDOS...
EVEN YOUR BACK-GROUND IS FASH?
YOU'RE A PERFECT TEAMMATE FOR ME.
HMPH!
...
AAAH!
HOW DID I GET TEAMED UP WITH SOME-ONE SO AMAZ-ING...
I'LL JUST BE IN THE WAY...
BACHIRA...
NAGI...
SORRY...
ISAGI?
HUH?
I KNOW RIN'S TEAM SEEMS REALLY STRONG...
IT DOESN'T MATTER WHO YOU PLAY, RIGHT?
HUH?
BUT...
MY EGO IS SAYING...

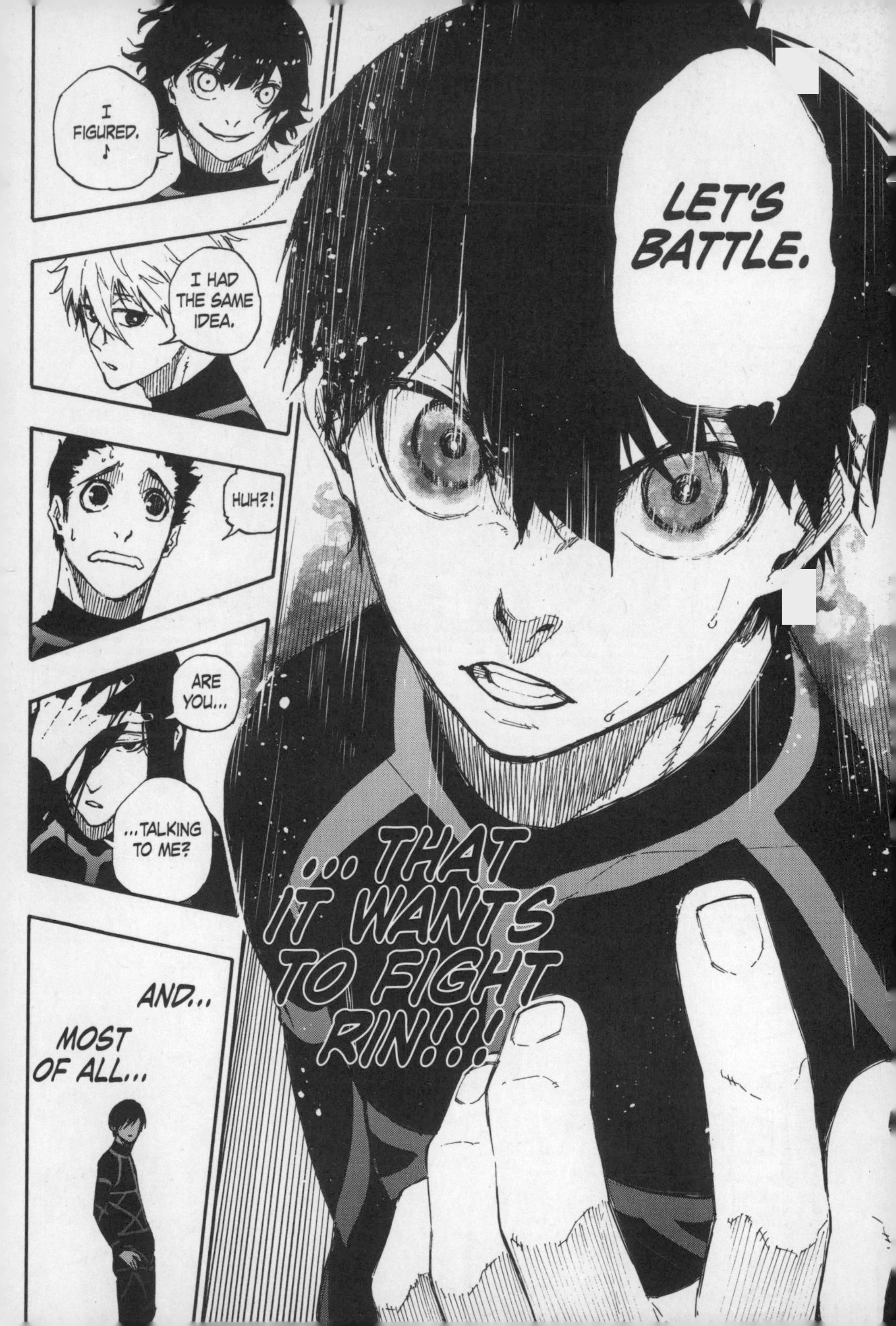
LET'S BATTLE.
...THAT IT WANTS TO FIGHT RIN!!!
I FIGURED. ♪
I HAD THE SAME IDEA.
HUH?!
ARE YOU...
...TALKING TO ME?
AND... MOST OF ALL...

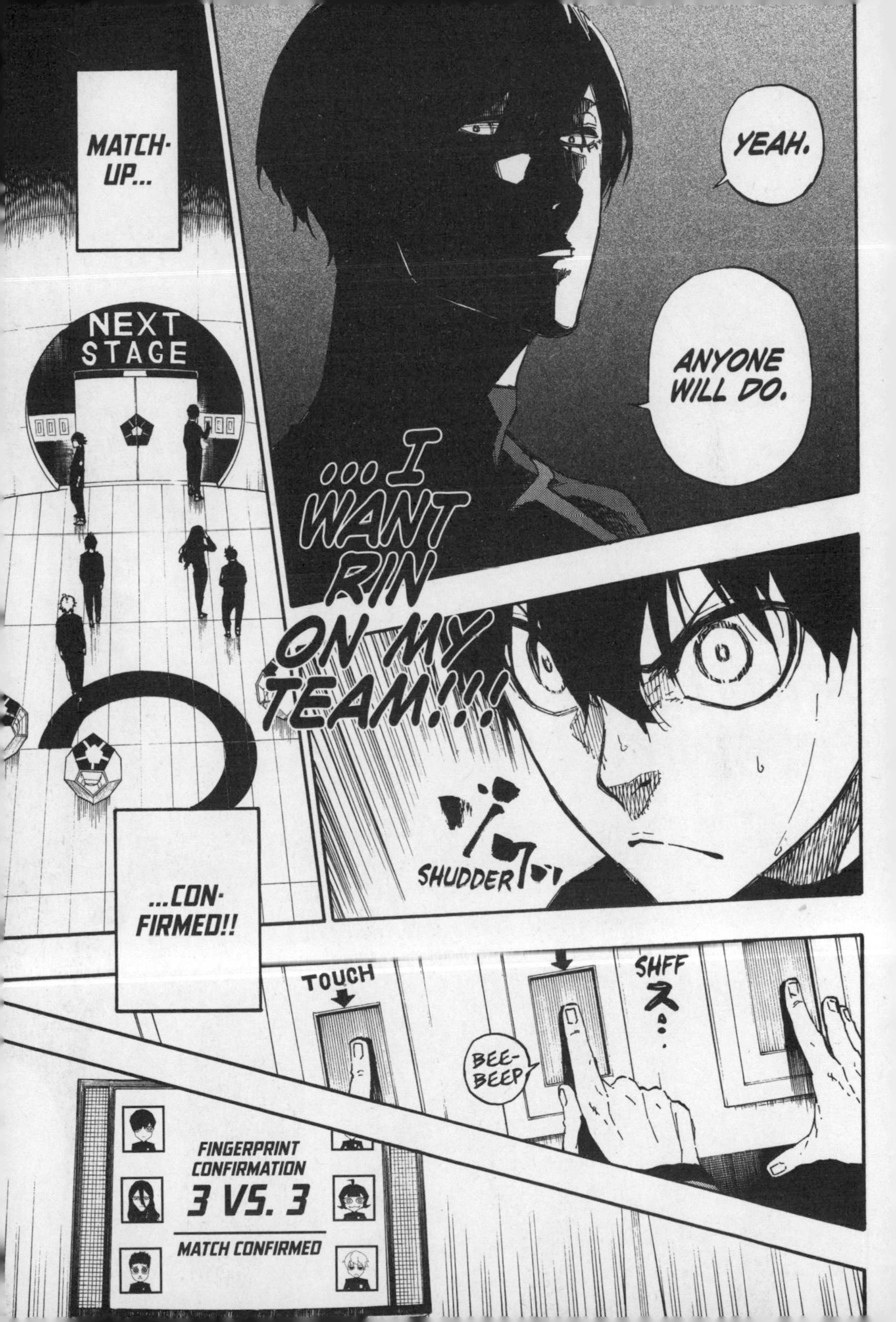
YEAH.
ANYONE WILL DO.
...I WANT RIN ON MY TEAM!!!
SHUDDER
MATCH-UP...
NEXT STAGE
...CON-FIRMED!!
SHFF
ス
BEE-BEEP
TOUCH
FINGERPRINT CONFIRMATION
3 VS. 3
MATCH CONFIRMED

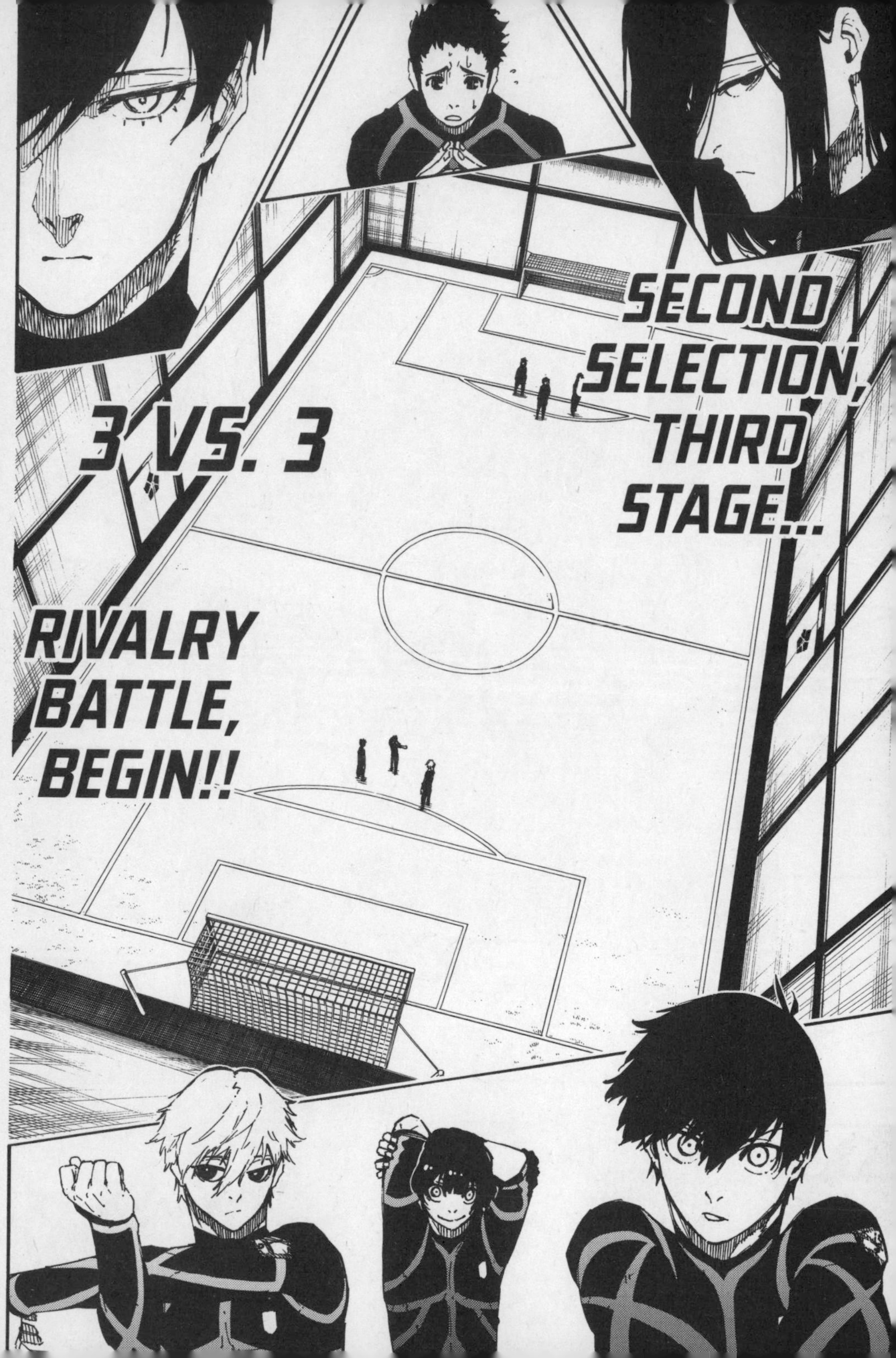
SECOND SELECTION, THIRD STAGE...
3 VS. 3
RIVALRY BATTLE, BEGIN!!

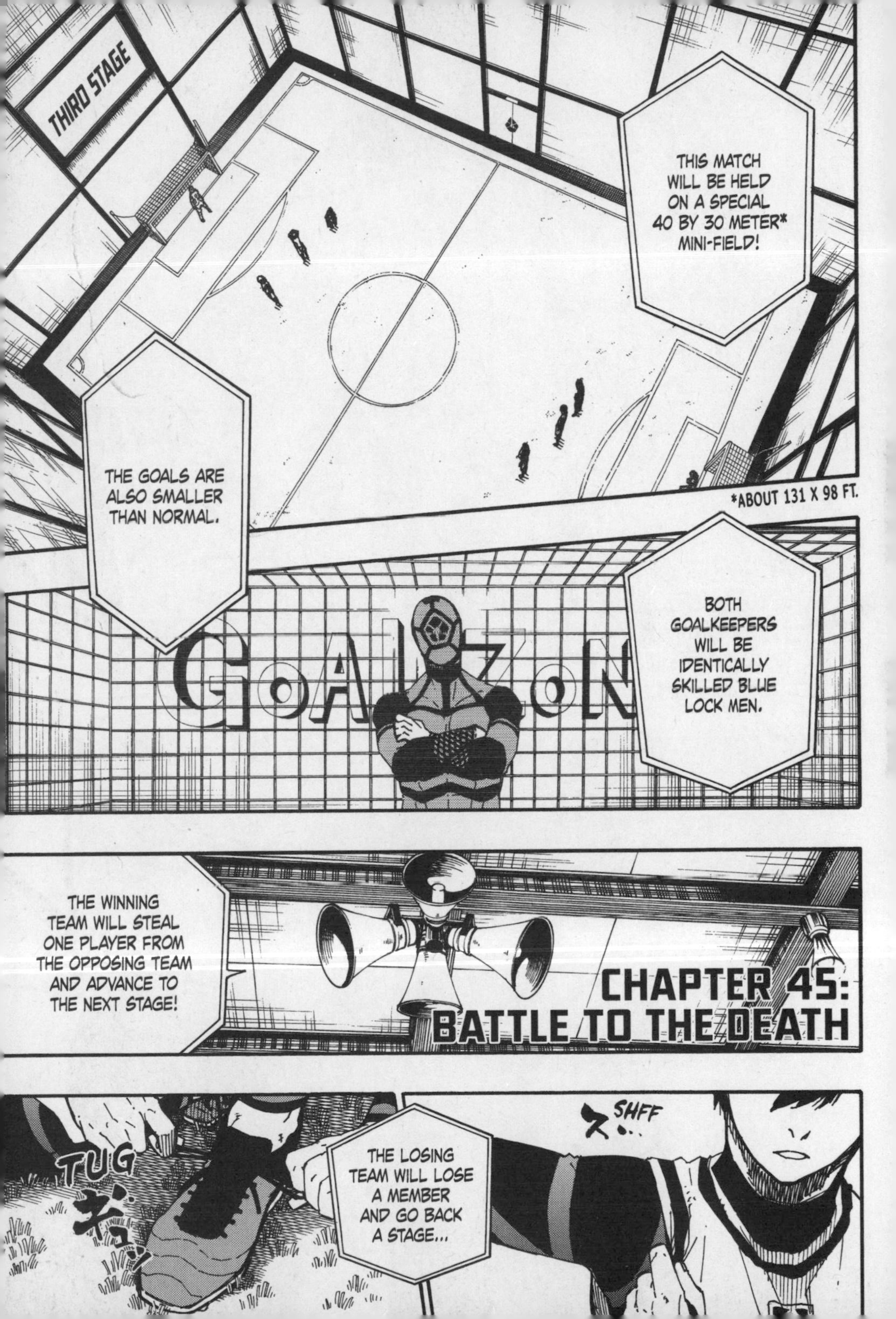
THIS MATCH WILL BE HELD ON A SPECIAL 40 BY 30 METER* MINI-FIELD!
THIRD STAGE
THE GOALS ARE ALSO SMALLER THAN NORMAL.
*ABOUT 131 X 98 FT.
BOTH GOALKEEPERS WILL BE IDENTICALLY SKILLED BLUE LOCK MEN.
THE WINNING TEAM WILL STEAL ONE PLAYER FROM THE OPPOSING TEAM AND ADVANCE TO THE NEXT STAGE!
CHAPTER 45: BATTLE TO THE DEATH
SHFF
THE LOSING TEAM WILL LOSE A MEMBER AND GO BACK A STAGE...
TUG

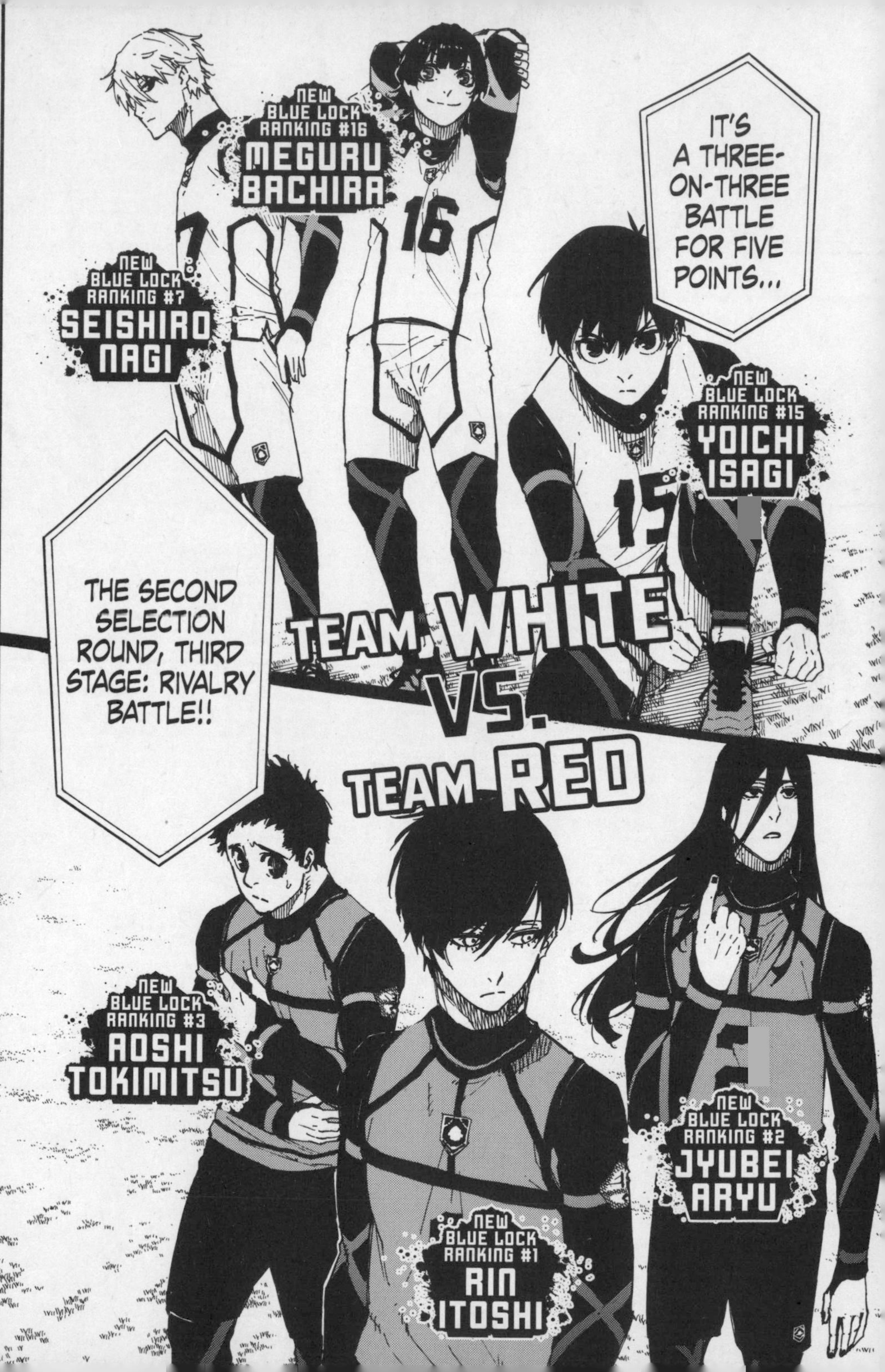
IT'S A THREE-ON-THREE BATTLE FOR FIVE POINTS...
NEW BLUE LOCK RANKING #16
MEGURU BACHIRA
NEW BLUE LOCK RANKING #7
SEISHIRO NAGI
NEW BLUE LOCK RANKING #15
YOICHI ISAGI
THE SECOND SELECTION ROUND, THIRD STAGE: RIVALRY BATTLE!!
TEAM WHITE
VS.
TEAM RED
NEW BLUE LOCK RANKING #2
JYUBEI ARYU
NEW BLUE LOCK RANKING #3
AOSHI TOKIMITSU
NEW BLUE LOCK RANKING #1
RIN ITOSHI

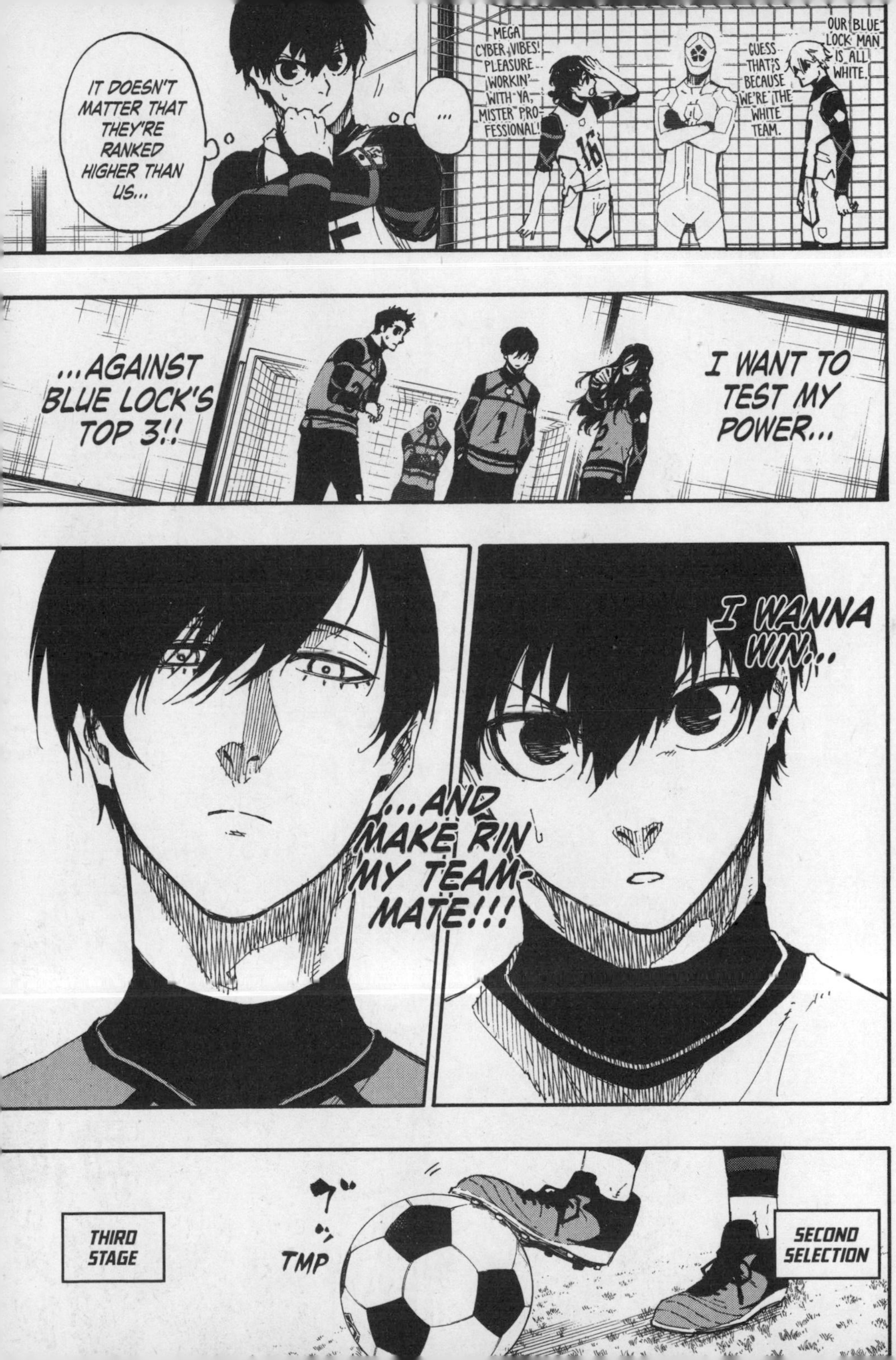
OUR BLUE LOCK MAN IS ALL WHITE.
GUESS THAT'S BECAUSE WE'RE THE WHITE TEAM.
MEGA CYBER VIBES! PLEASURE WORKIN' WITH YA, MISTER PRO-FESSIONAL!
...
IT DOESN'T MATTER THAT THEY'RE RANKED HIGHER THAN US...
I WANT TO TEST MY POWER...
...AGAINST BLUE LOCK'S TOP 3!!
I WANNA WIN...
...AND MAKE RIN MY TEAM-MATE!!!
SECOND SELECTION
TMP
THIRD STAGE

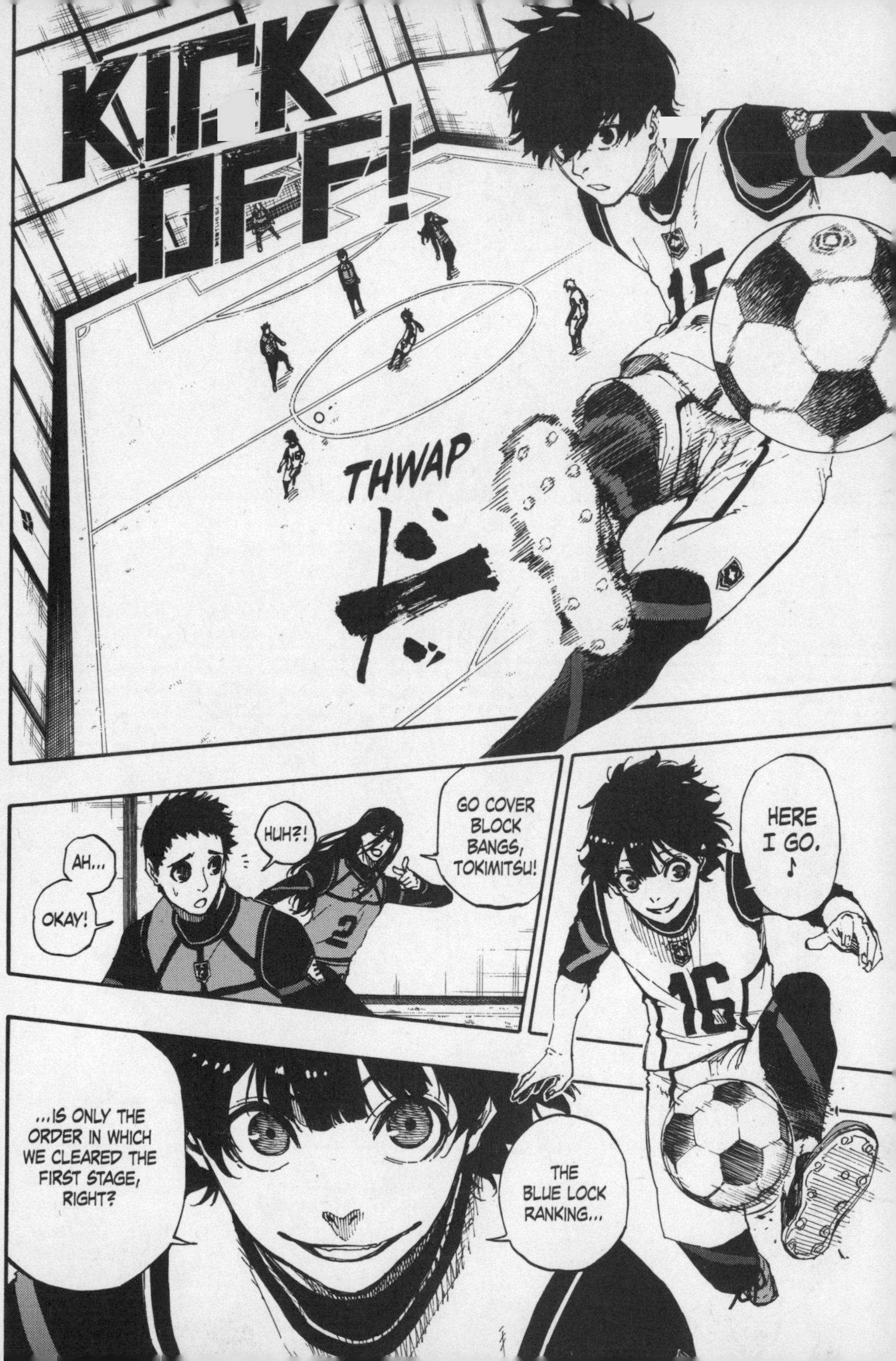
KICK OFF!
THWAP
HERE I GO. ♪
GO COVER BLOCK BANGS, TOKIMITSU!
HUH?!
AH... OKAY!
THE BLUE LOCK RANKING...
...IS ONLY THE ORDER IN WHICH WE CLEARED THE FIRST STAGE, RIGHT?

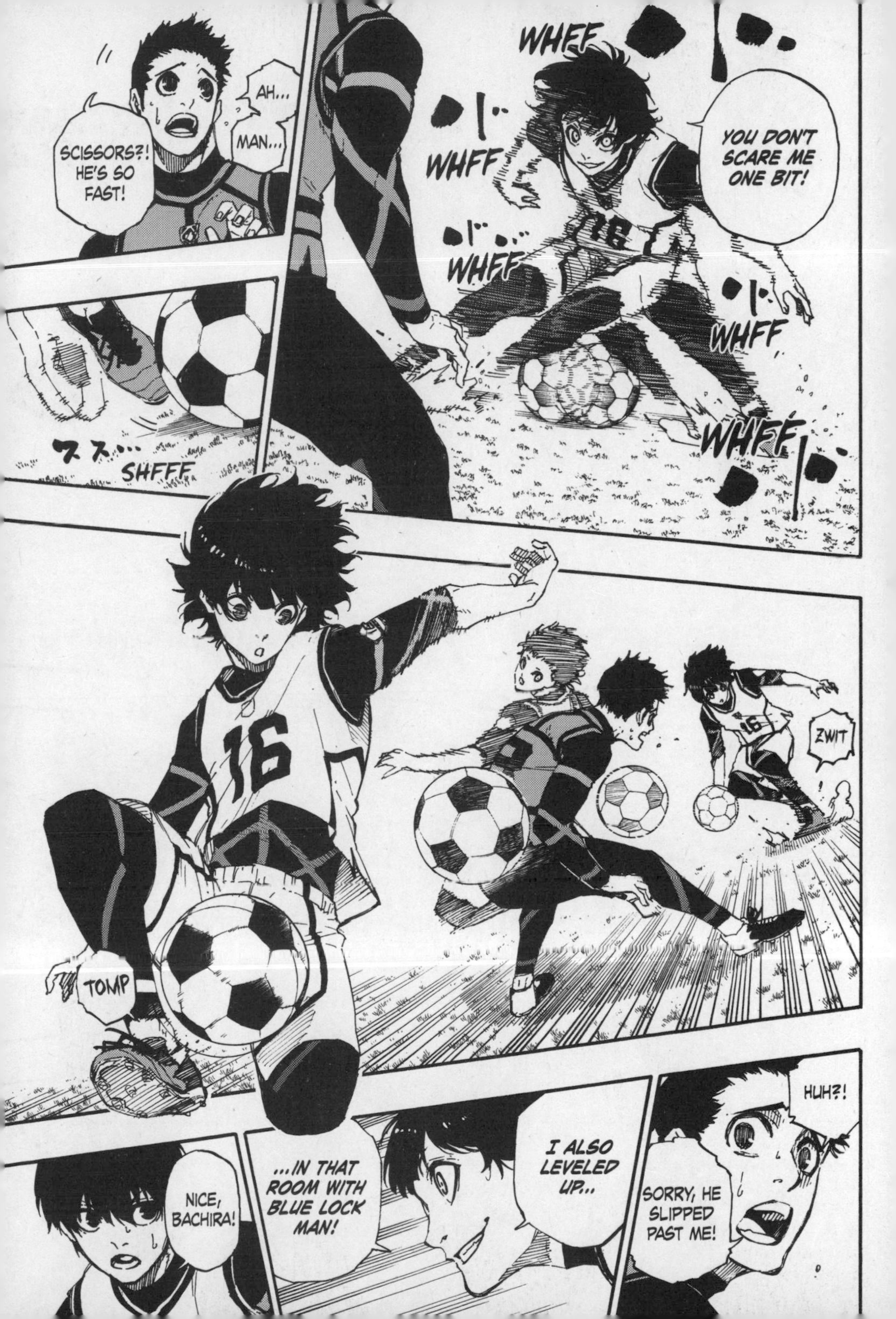

WHFF
WHFF
WHFF
WHFF
WHFF
YOU DON'T SCARE ME ONE BIT!
AH... MAN...
SCISSORS?! HE'S SO FAST!
SHFFF
ZWIT
TOMP
HUH?!
SORRY, HE SLIPPED PAST ME!
I ALSO LEVELED UP...
...IN THAT ROOM WITH BLUE LOCK MAN!
NICE, BACHIRA!

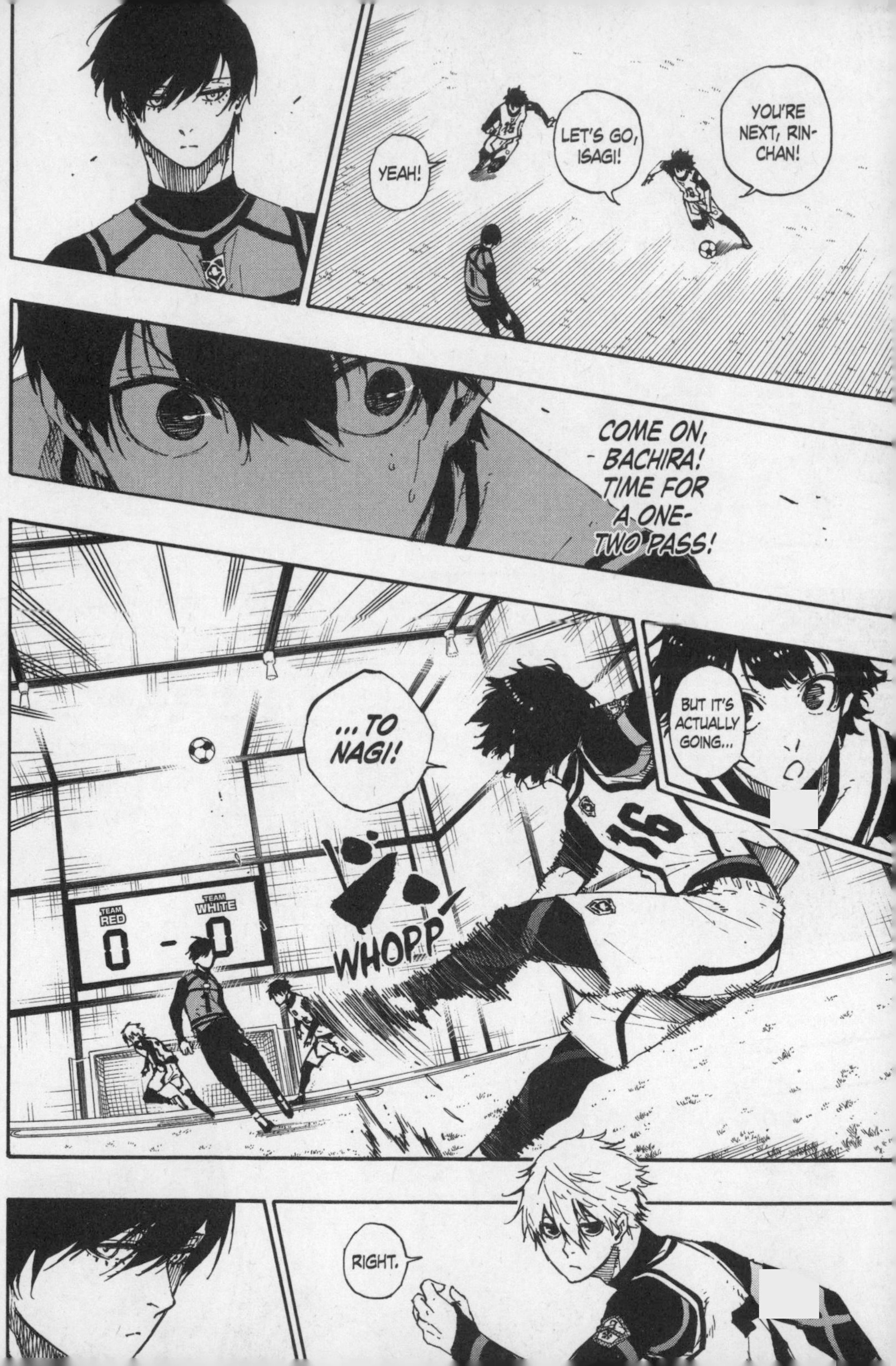
YOU'RE NEXT, RIN-CHAN!
LET'S GO, ISAGI!
YEAH!
COME ON, BACHIRA! TIME FOR A ONE-TWO PASS!
BUT IT'S ACTUALLY GOING...
...TO NAGI!
WHOPP
TEAM RED
TEAM WHITE
0 - 0
RIGHT.

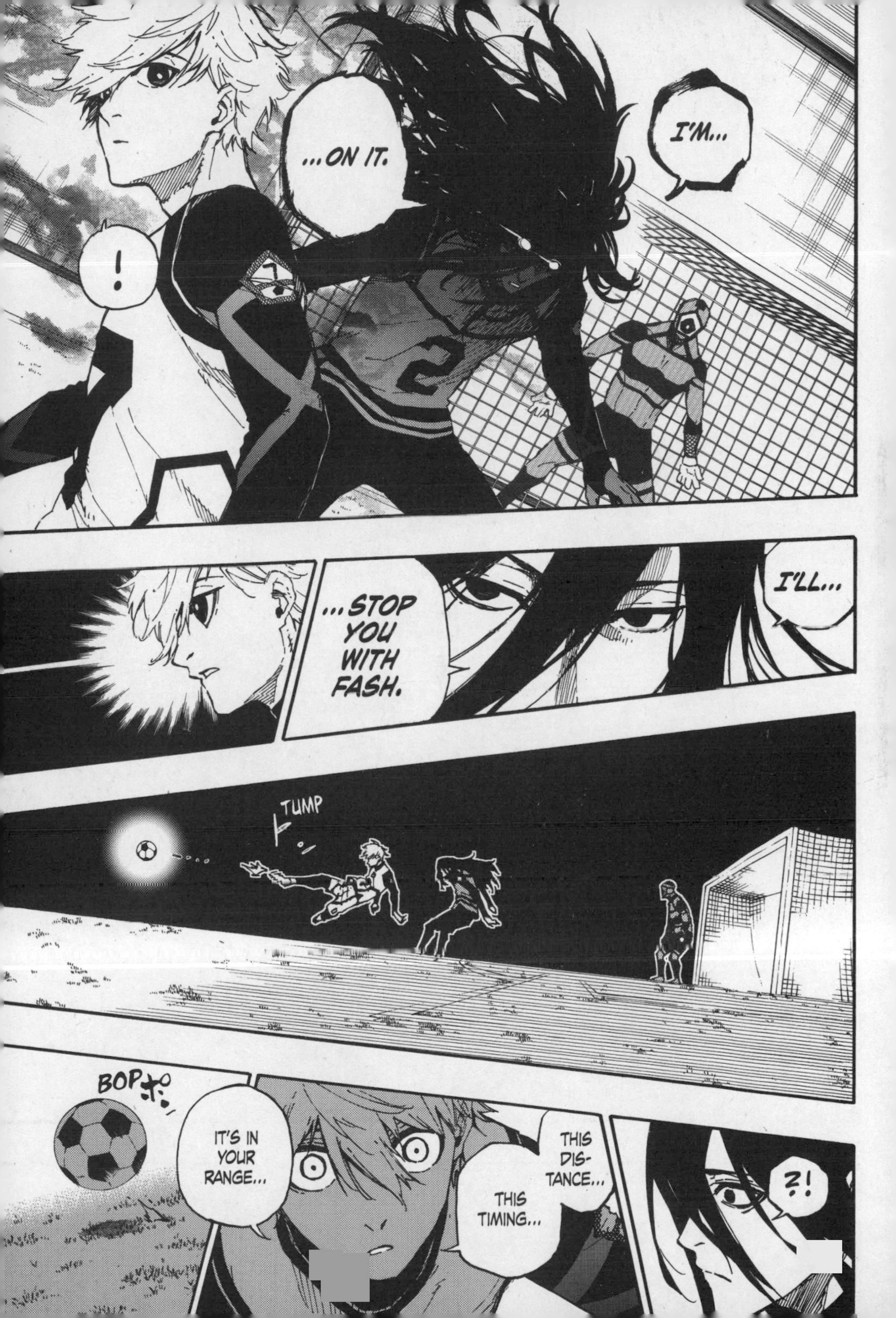
I'M...
...ON IT.
!
I'LL...
...STOP YOU WITH FASH.
TUMP
?!
THIS DIS-TANCE...
THIS TIMING...
IT'S IN YOUR RANGE...
BOP

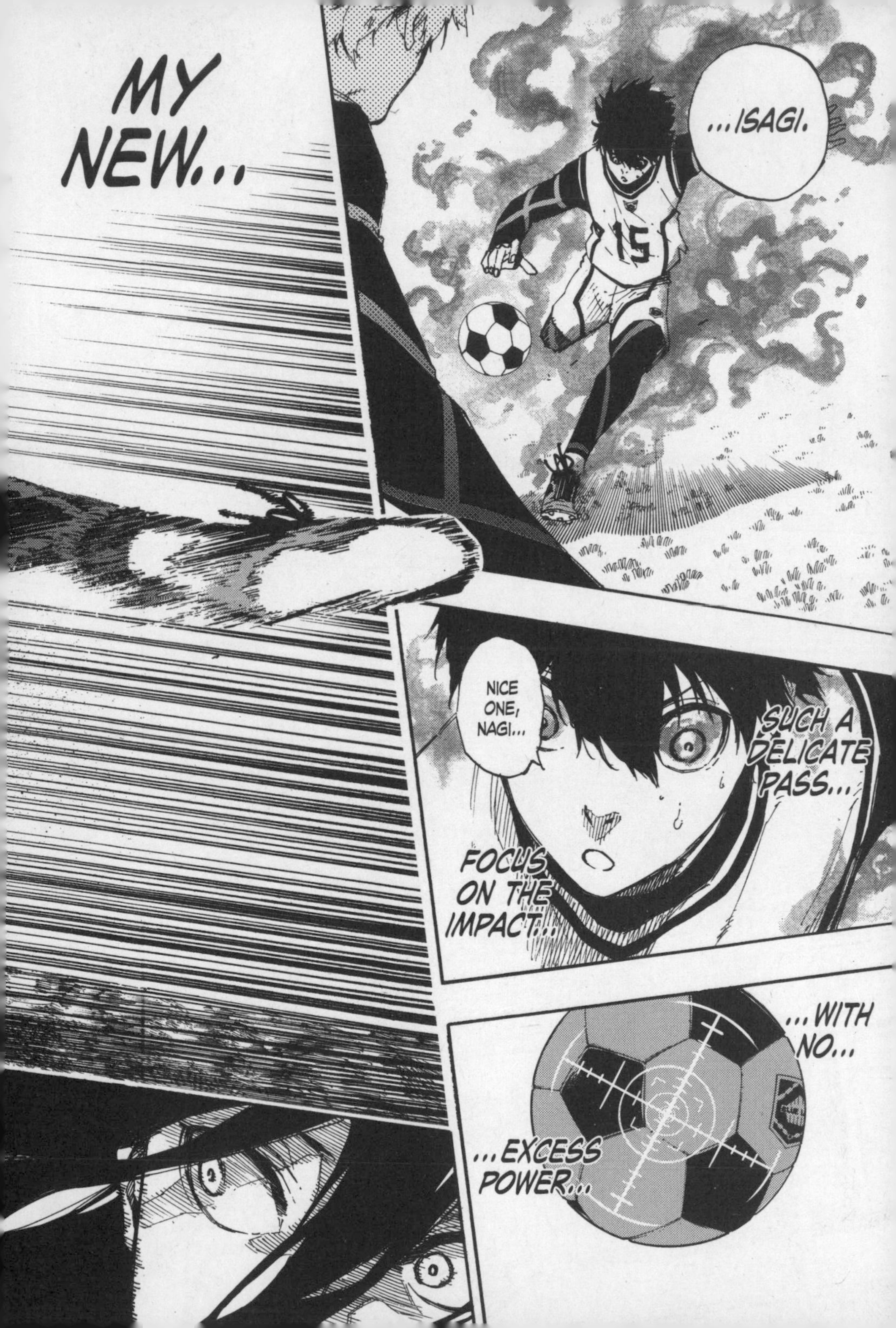
...ISAGI.
NICE ONE, NAGI...
SUCH A DELICATE PASS...
FOCUS ON THE IMPACT...
...WITH NO...
...EXCESS POWER...
MY NEW...

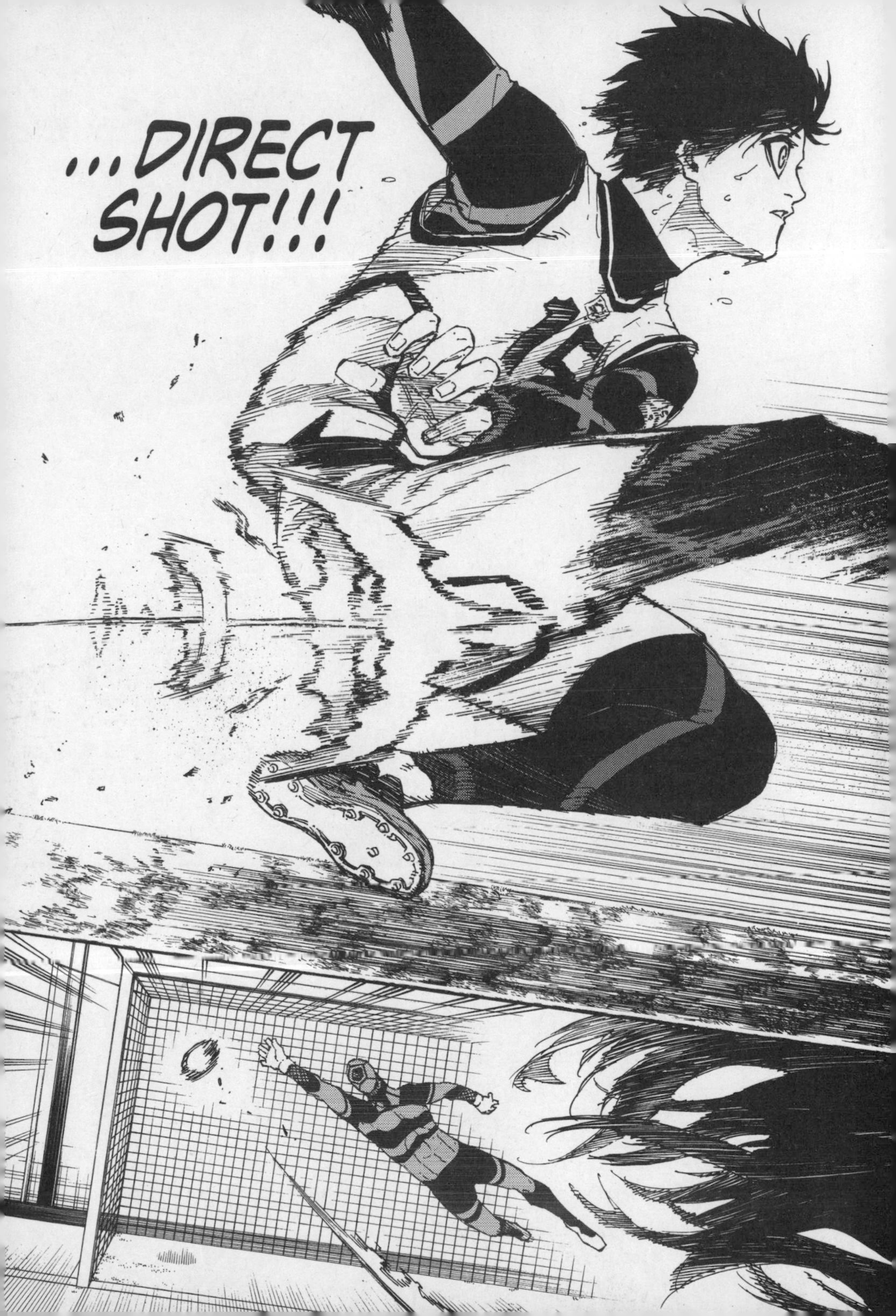
...DIRECT SHOT!!!

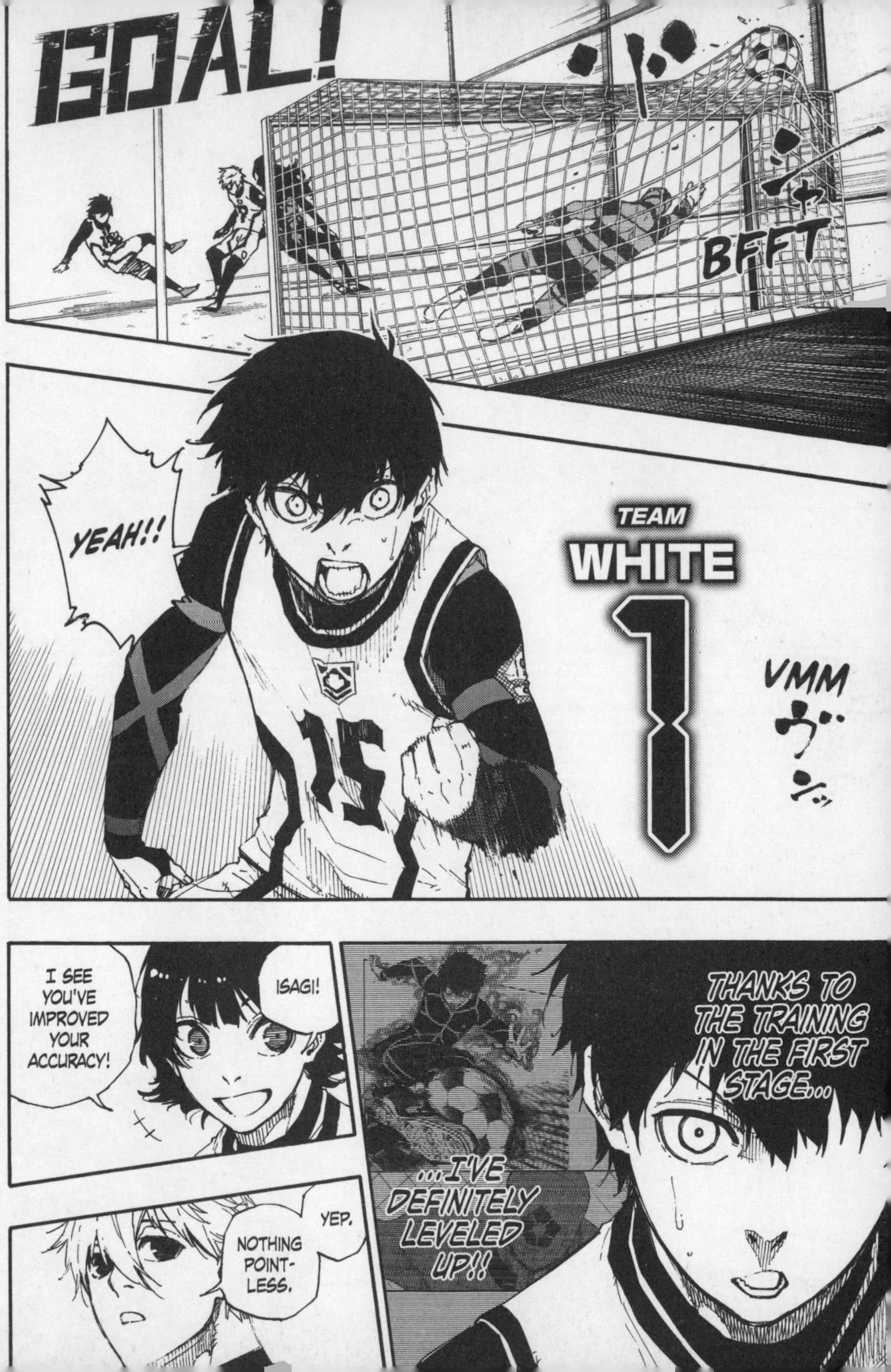
GOAL!
BFFT
YEAH!!
TEAM
WHITE
1
VMM
THANKS TO THE TRAINING IN THE FIRST STAGE...
...I'VE DEFINITELY LEVELED UP!!
ISAGI!
I SEE YOU'VE IMPROVED YOUR ACCURACY!
YEP.
NOTHING POINT-LESS.

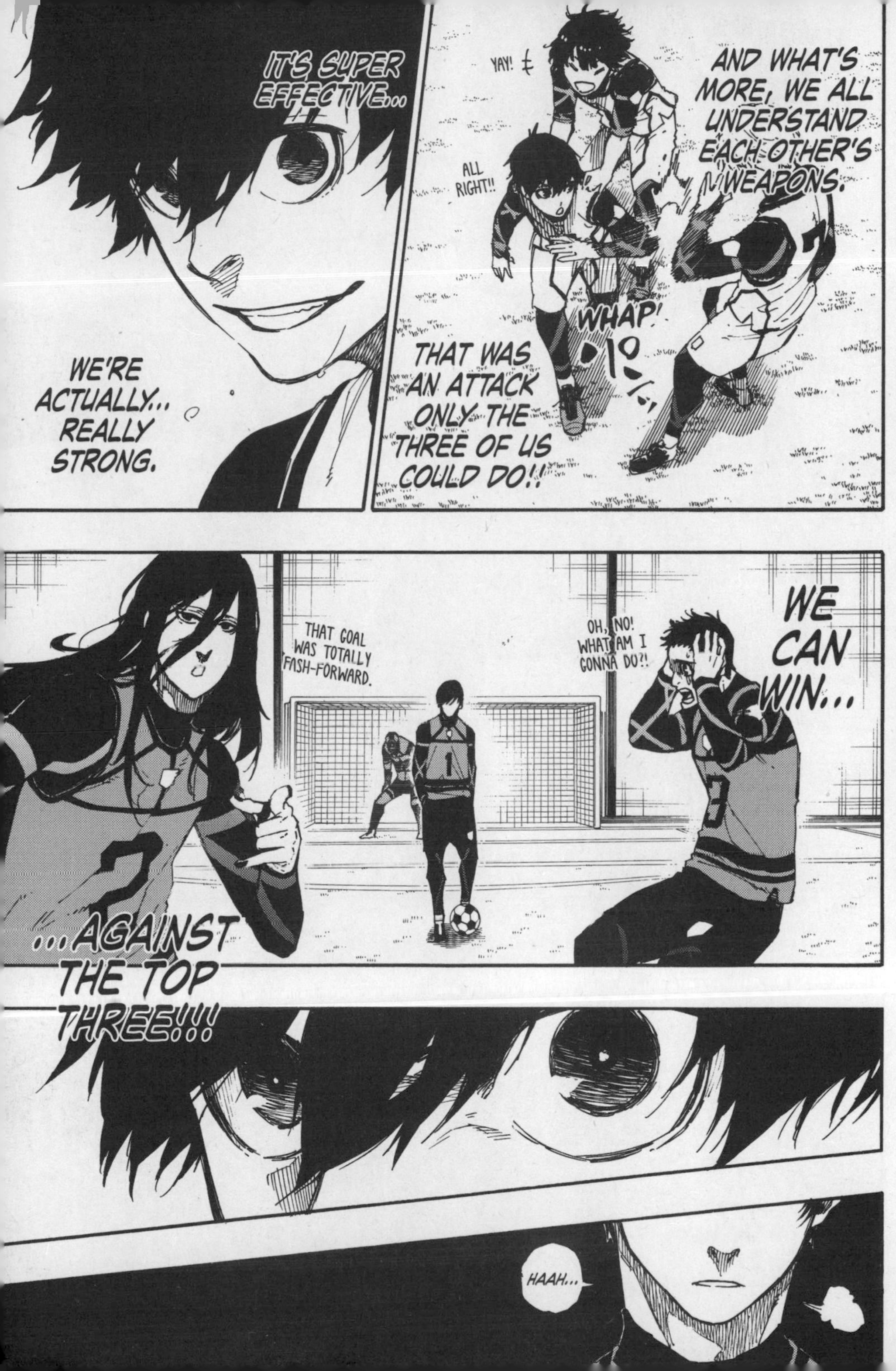
AND WHAT'S MORE, WE ALL UNDERSTAND EACH OTHER'S WEAPONS.
YAY!
ALL RIGHT!!
WHAP!
THAT WAS AN ATTACK ONLY THE THREE OF US COULD DO!!
IT'S SUPER EFFECTIVE...
WE'RE ACTUALLY... REALLY STRONG.
WE CAN WIN...
OH, NO! WHAT AM I GONNA DO?!
THAT GOAL WAS TOTALLY FASH-FORWARD.
...AGAINST THE TOP THREE!!!
HAAH...

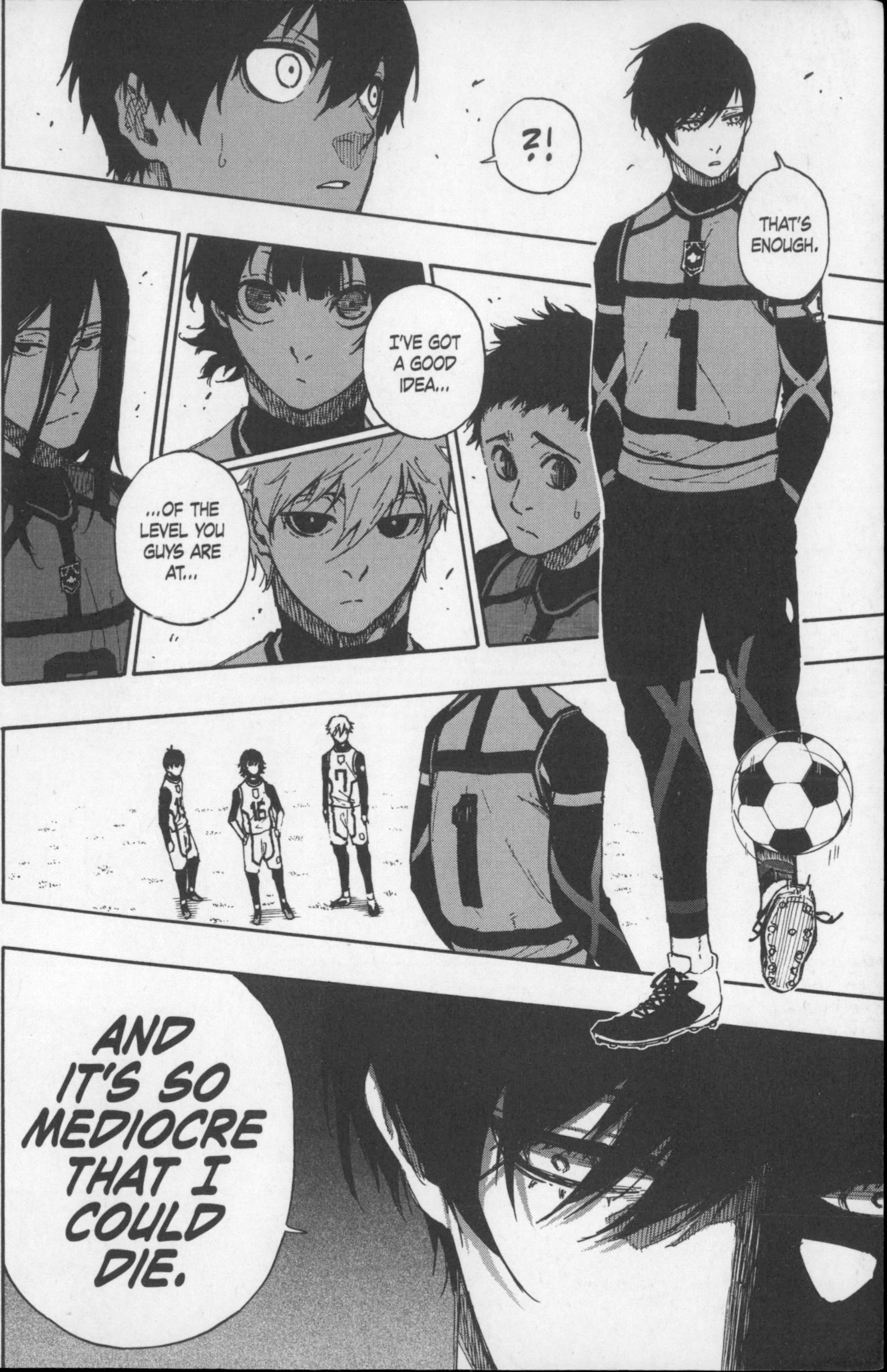
THAT'S ENOUGH.
?!
I'VE GOT A GOOD IDEA...
...OF THE LEVEL YOU GUYS ARE AT...
AND IT'S SO MEDIOCRE THAT I COULD DIE.

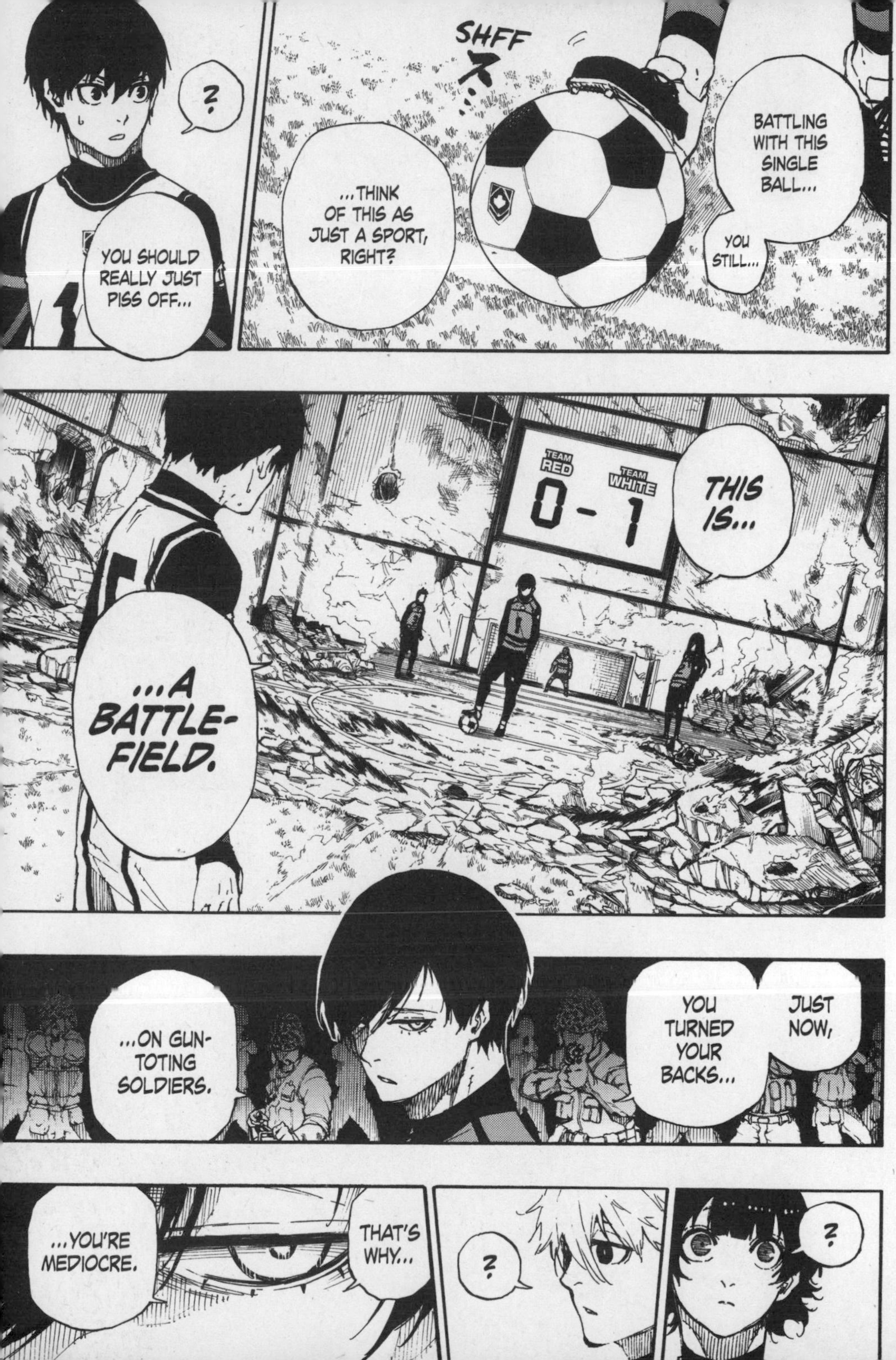
SHFF
BATTLING WITH THIS SINGLE BALL...
YOU STILL...
...THINK OF THIS AS JUST A SPORT, RIGHT?
?
YOU SHOULD REALLY JUST PISS OFF...
TEAM RED
TEAM WHITE
0 - 1
THIS IS...
...A BATTLE-FIELD.
JUST NOW,
YOU TURNED YOUR BACKS...
...ON GUN-TOTING SOLDIERS.
?
?
THAT'S WHY...
...YOU'RE MEDIOCRE.

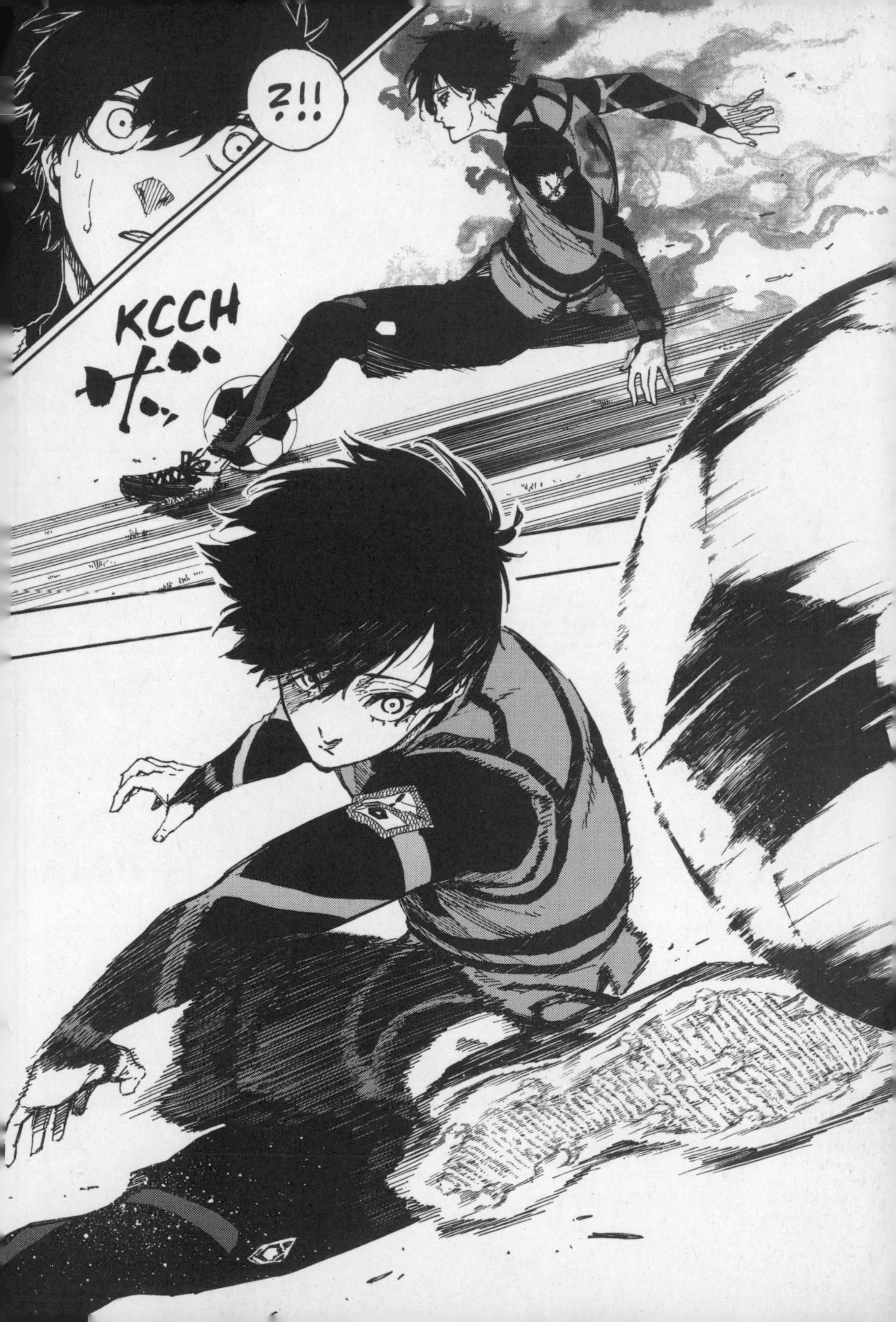
?!!
KCCH

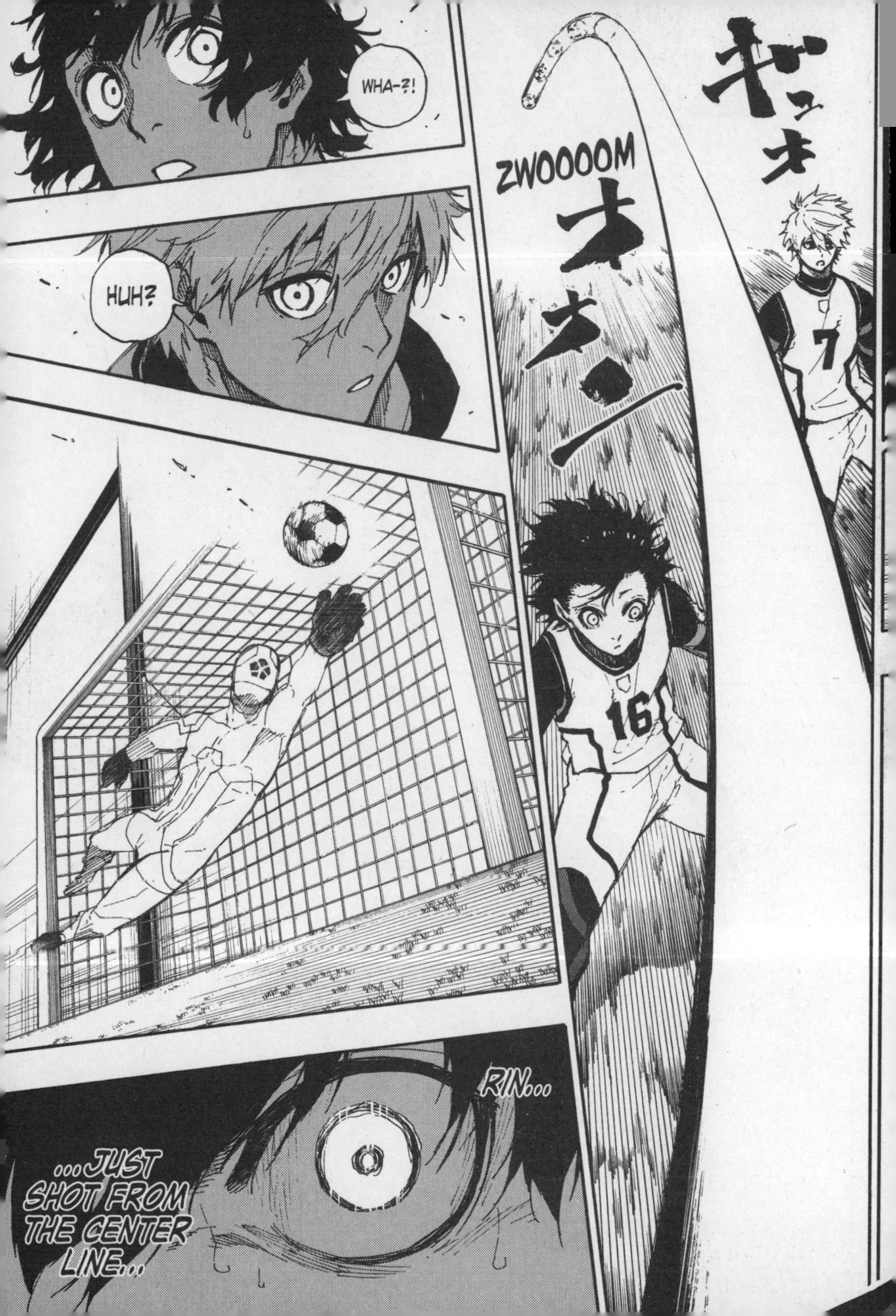
ギュオ
ZWOOOOM
オォンー
WHA-?!
HUH?
RIN...
...JUST SHOT FROM THE CENTER LINE...

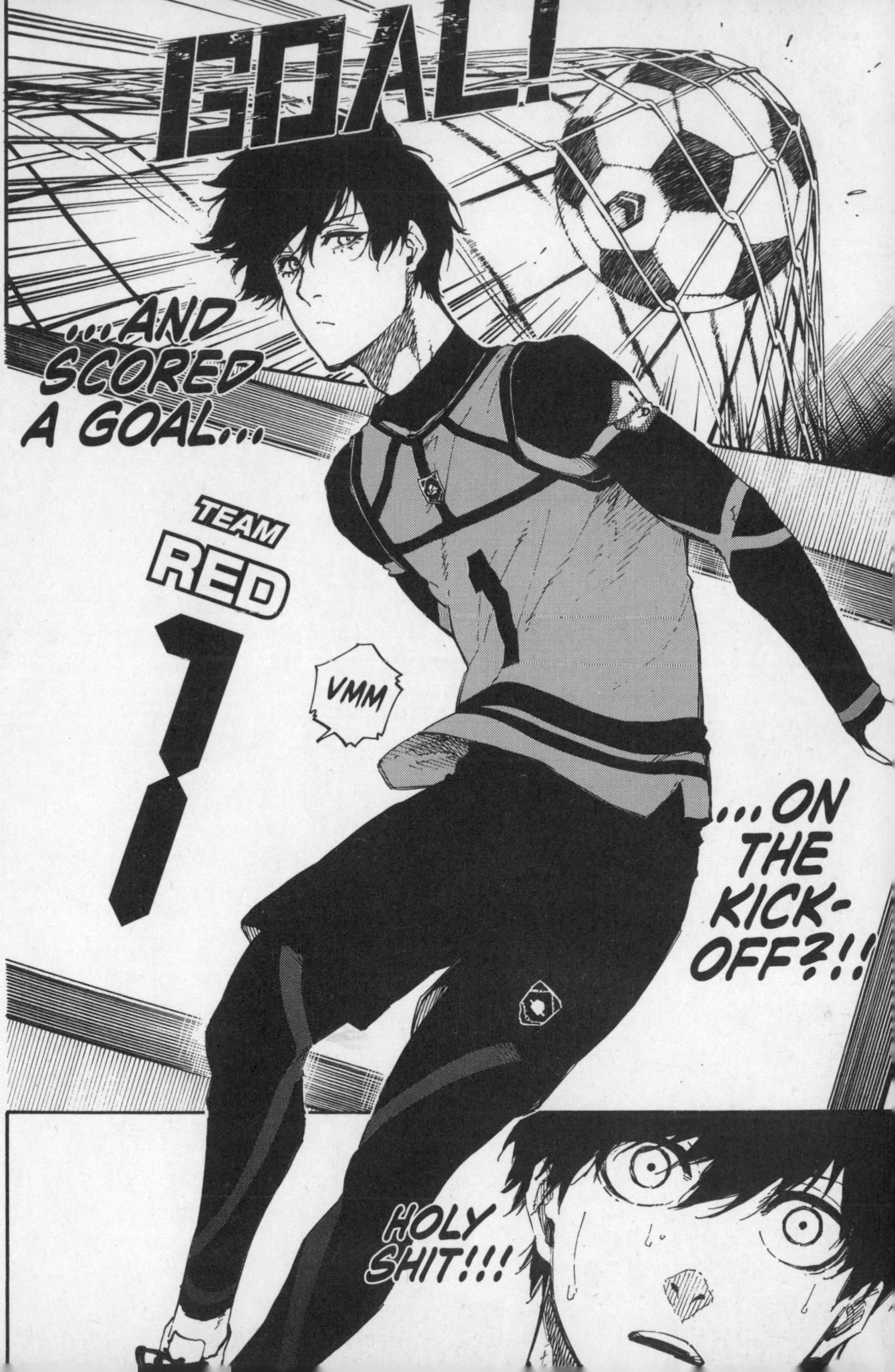
GOAL!
...AND SCORED A GOAL...
TEAM RED 1
VMM
...ON THE KICK-OFF?!!
HOLY SHIT!!!

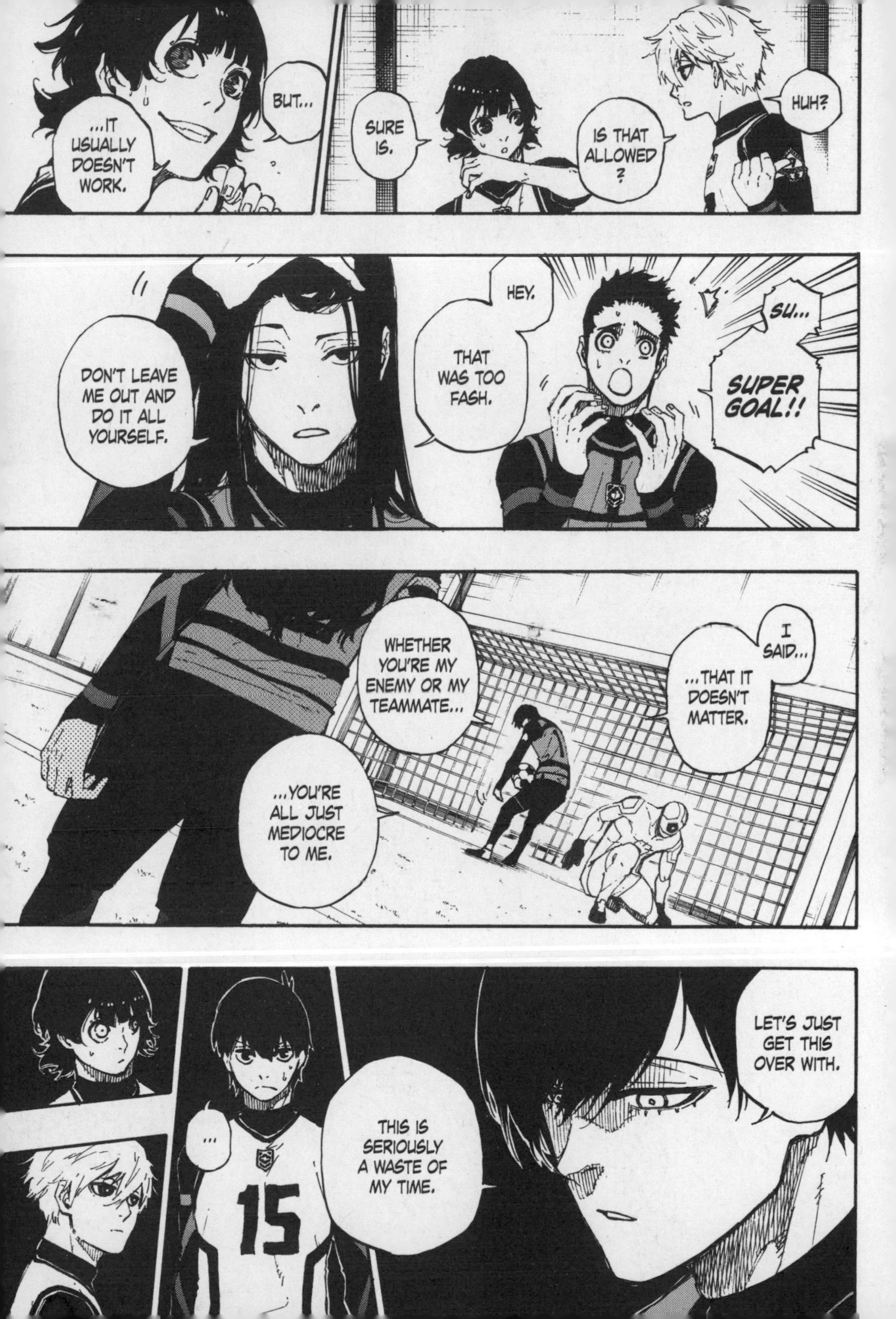
HUH?
IS THAT ALLOWED?
SURE IS.
BUT...
...IT USUALLY DOESN'T WORK.
SU...
SUPER GOAL!!
HEY.
THAT WAS TOO FASH.
DON'T LEAVE ME OUT AND DO IT ALL YOURSELF.
I SAID...
...THAT IT DOESN'T MATTER.
WHETHER YOU'RE MY ENEMY OR MY TEAMMATE...
...YOU'RE ALL JUST MEDIOCRE TO ME.
LET'S JUST GET THIS OVER WITH.
THIS IS SERIOUSLY A WASTE OF MY TIME.
...

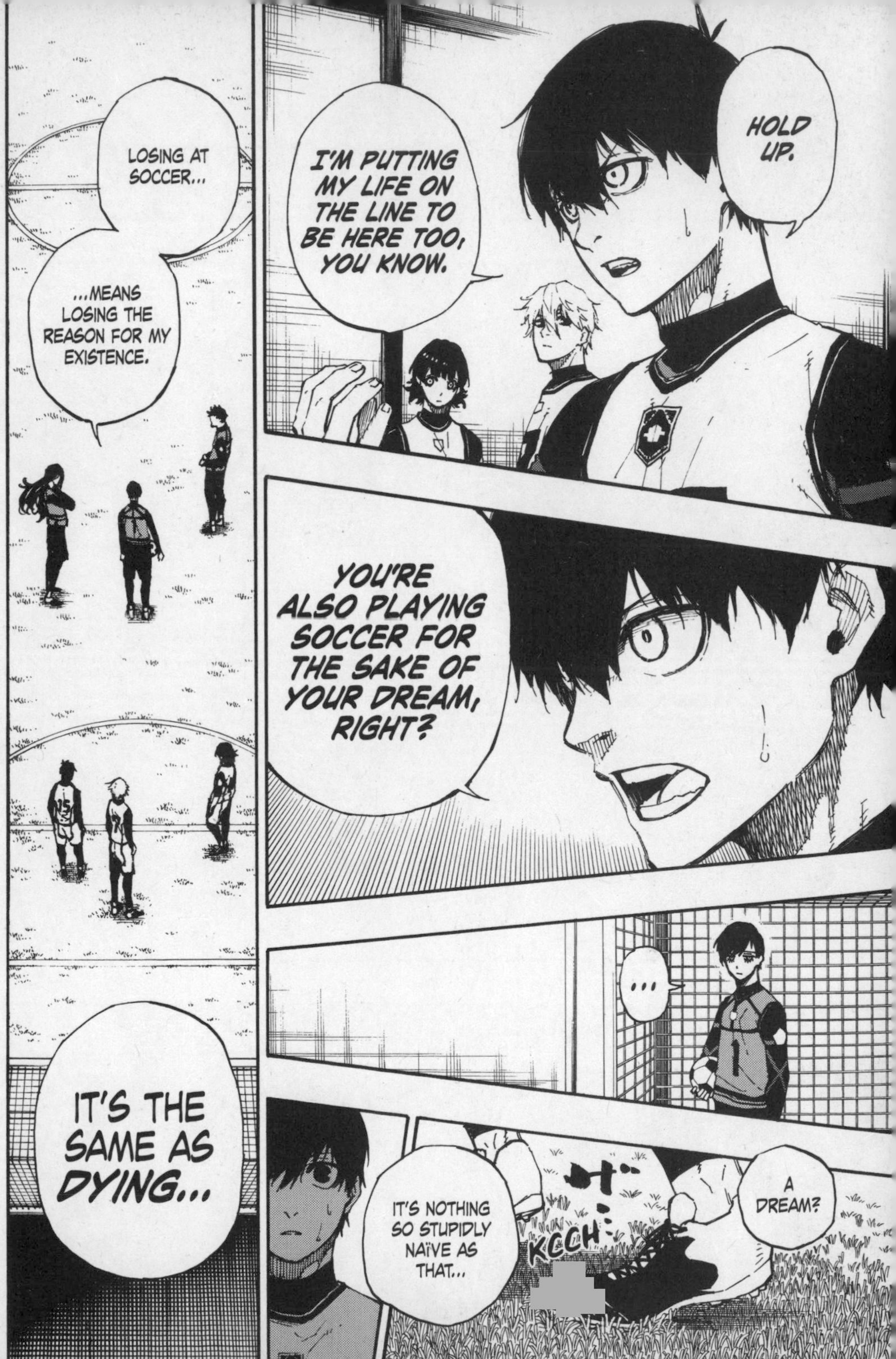
HOLD UP.
I'M PUTTING MY LIFE ON THE LINE TO BE HERE TOO, YOU KNOW.
YOU'RE ALSO PLAYING SOCCER FOR THE SAKE OF YOUR DREAM, RIGHT?
...
A DREAM?
KCCH
IT'S NOTHING SO STUPIDLY NAÏVE AS THAT...
LOSING AT SOCCER...
...MEANS LOSING THE REASON FOR MY EXISTENCE.
IT'S THE SAME AS DYING...

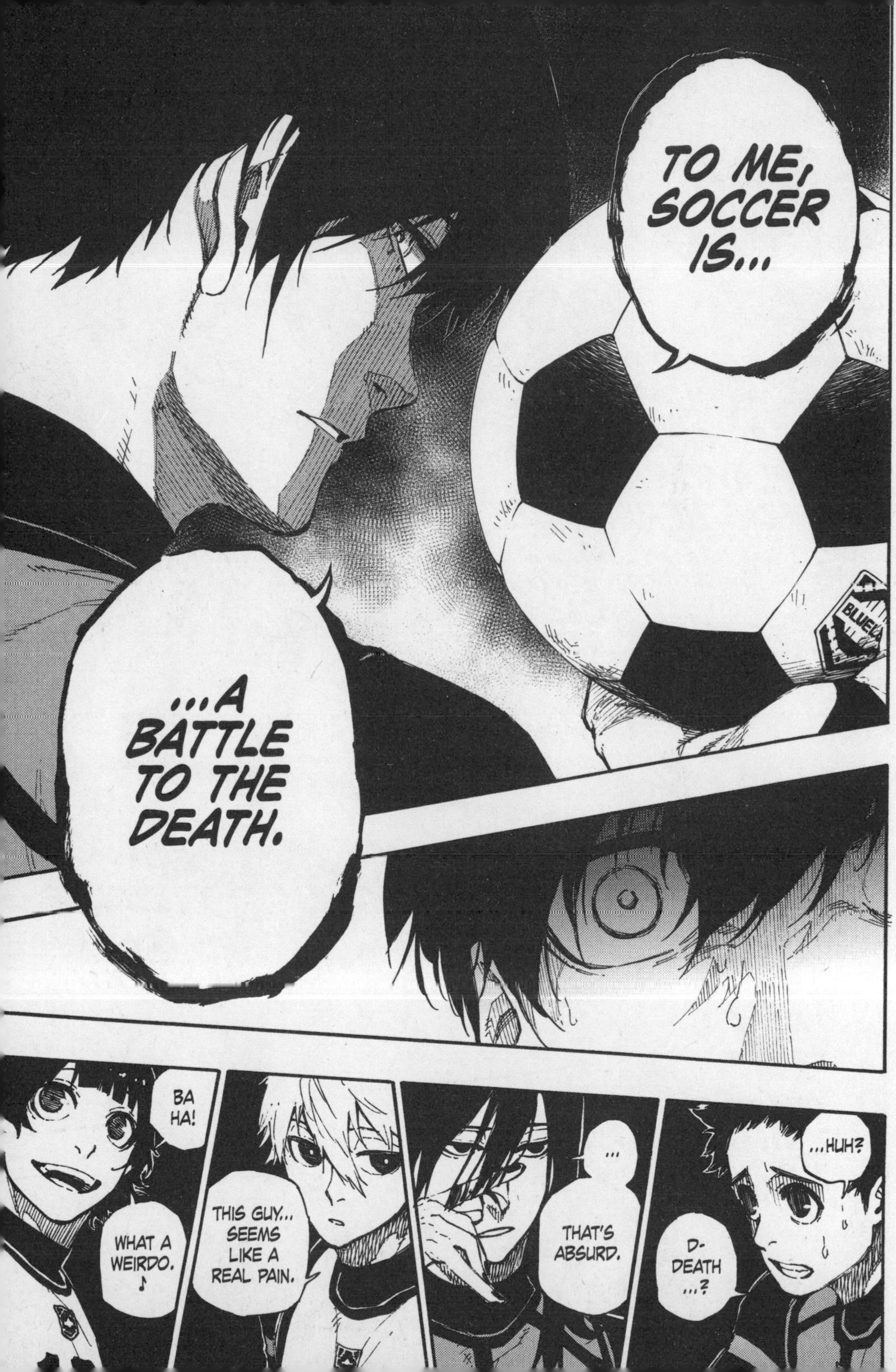
TO ME, SOCCER IS...
...A BATTLE TO THE DEATH.
...HUH?
D- DEATH ...?
...
THAT'S ABSURD.
THIS GUY... SEEMS LIKE A REAL PAIN.
BA HA!
WHAT A WEIRDO. ♪

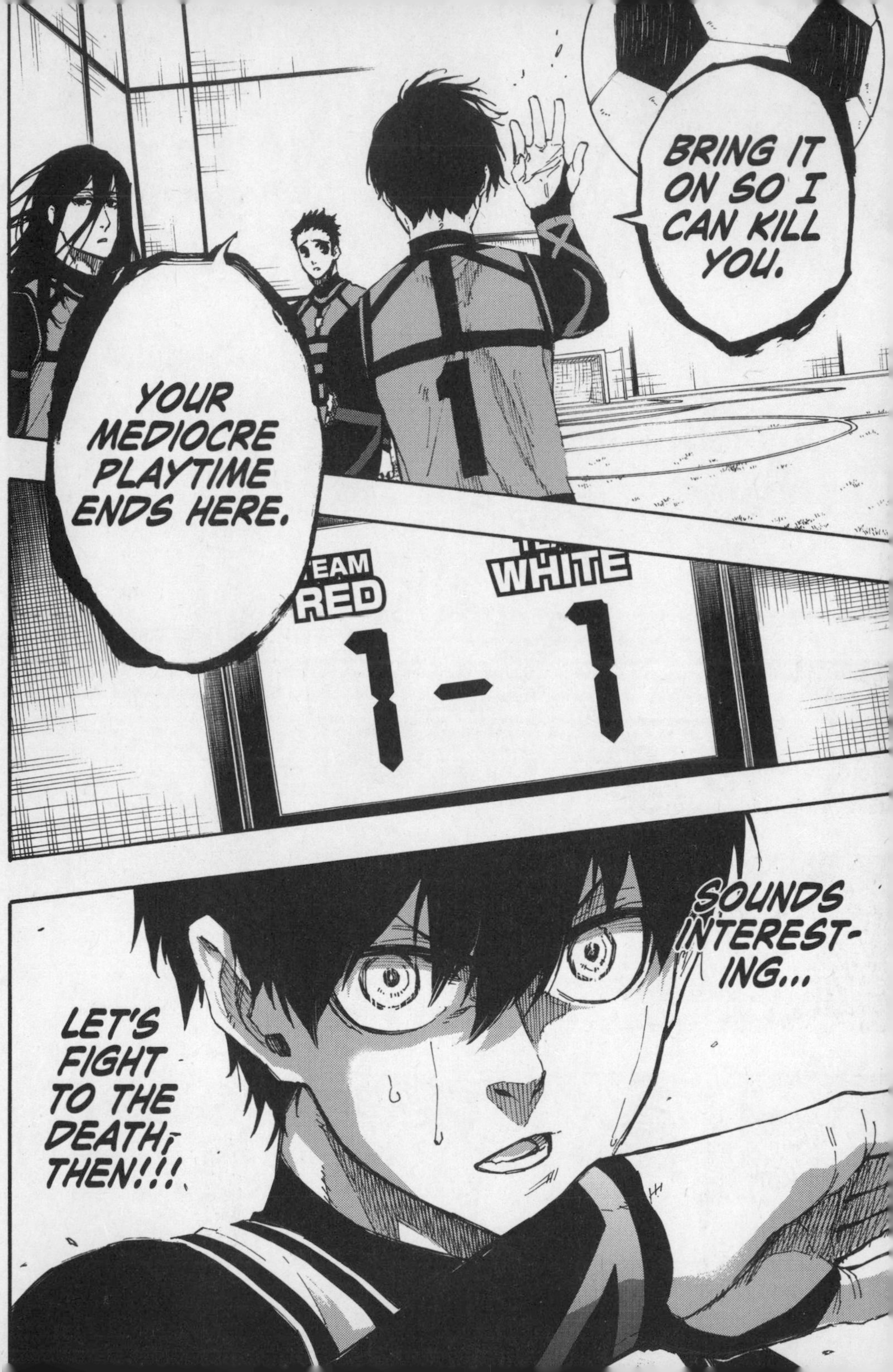
BRING IT ON SO I CAN KILL YOU.
YOUR MEDIOCRE PLAYTIME ENDS HERE.
WHITE
TEAM RED
1 - 1
SOUNDS INTEREST-ING...
LET'S FIGHT TO THE DEATH, THEN!!!

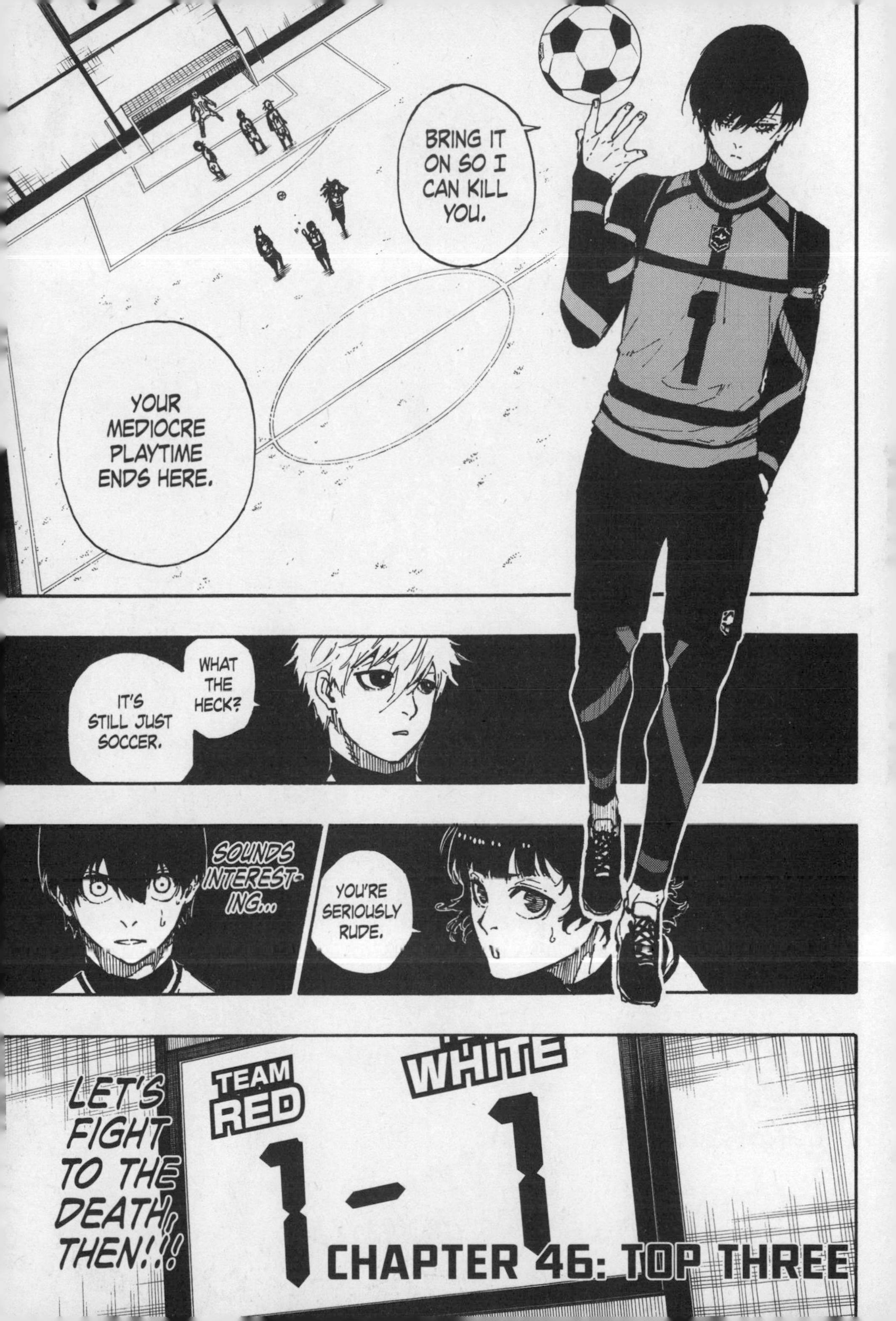
BRING IT ON SO I CAN KILL YOU.
YOUR MEDIOCRE PLAYTIME ENDS HERE.
WHAT THE HECK?
IT'S STILL JUST SOCCER.
YOU'RE SERIOUSLY RUDE.
SOUNDS INTERESTING...
WHITE
TEAM RED
1 - 1
LET'S FIGHT TO THE DEATH, THEN!!!
CHAPTER 46: TOP THREE

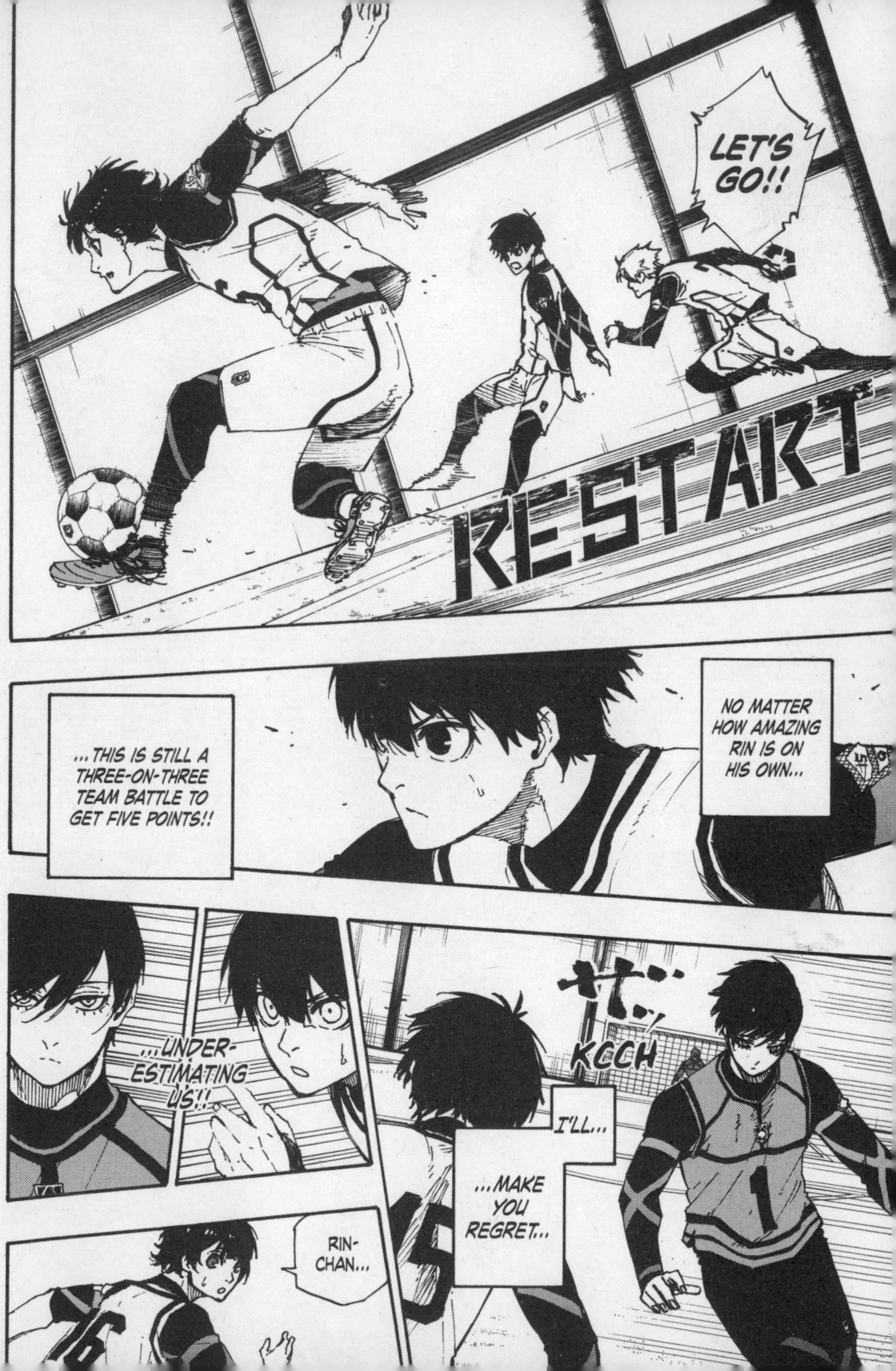
LET'S GO!!
RESTART
NO MATTER HOW AMAZING RIN IS ON HIS OWN...
...THIS IS STILL A THREE-ON-THREE TEAM BATTLE TO GET FIVE POINTS!!
KCCH
I'LL...
...MAKE YOU REGRET...
...UNDER-ESTIMATING US!!
RIN-CHAN...

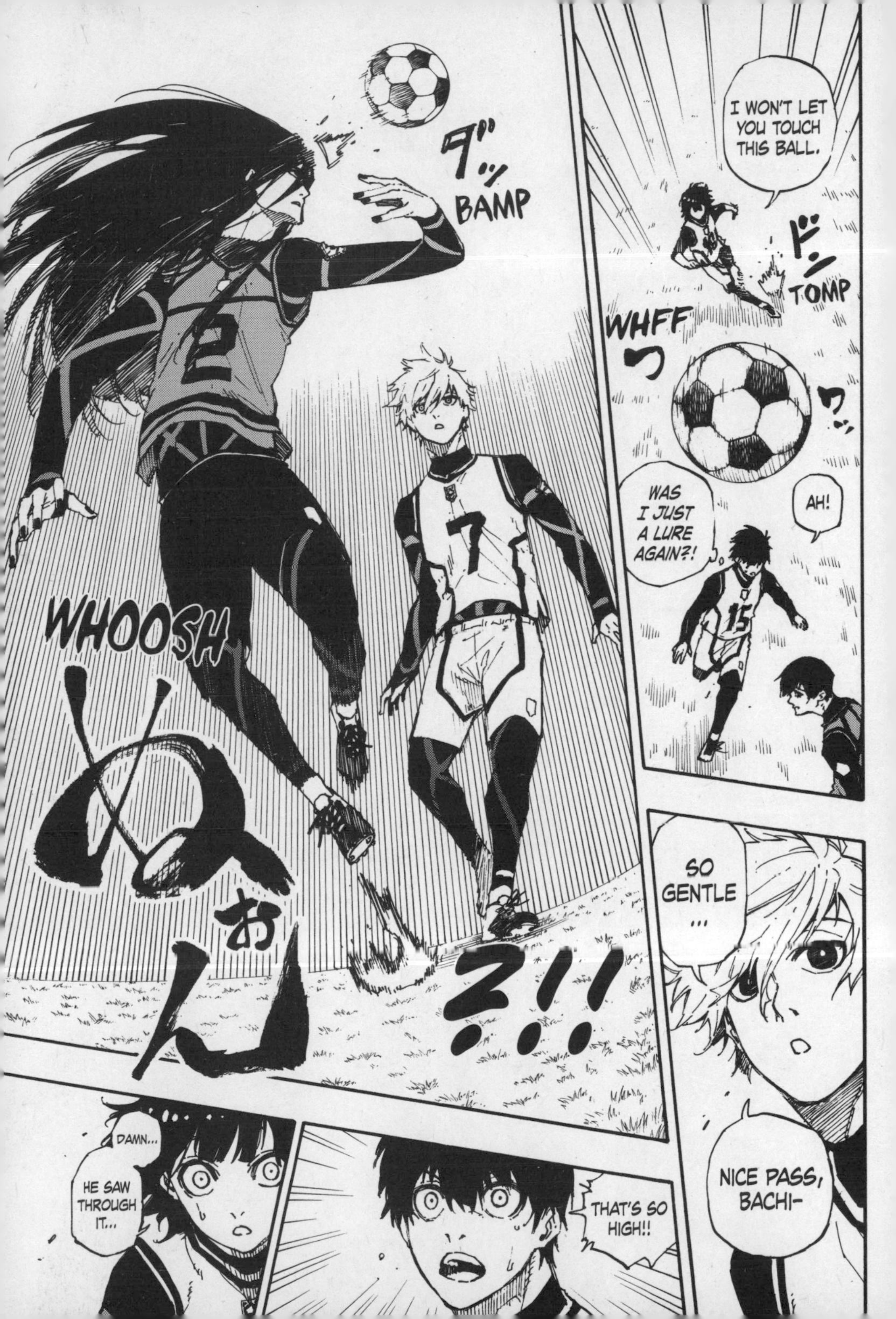
I WON'T LET YOU TOUCH THIS BALL.
ドン
TOMP
WHFF
つ
ワッ
AH!
WAS I JUST A LURE AGAIN?!
SO GENTLE …
NICE PASS, BACHI-
ダッ
BAMP
WHOOSH
?!!
THAT'S SO HIGH!!
DAMN…
HE SAW THROUGH IT…

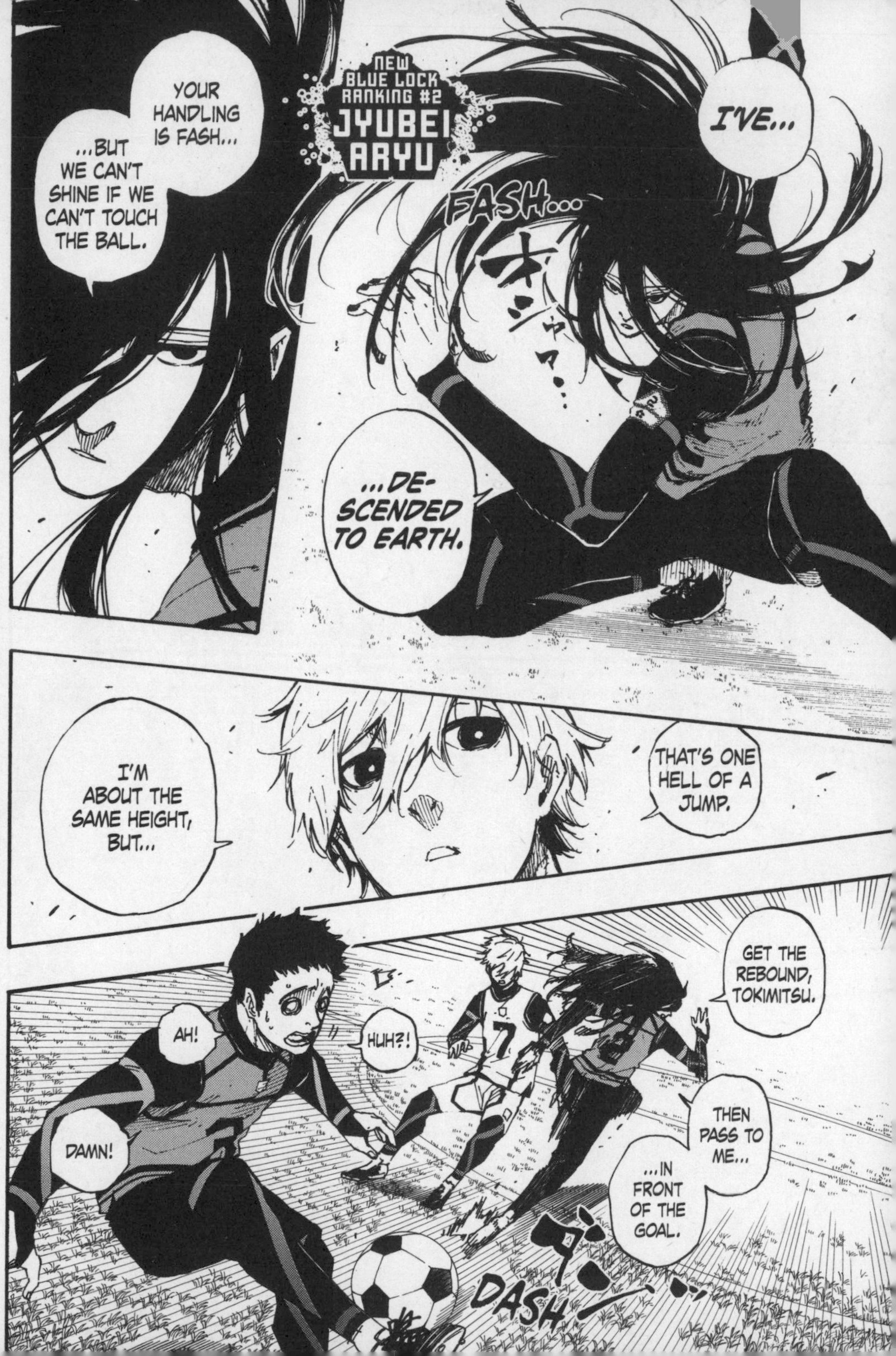
I'VE...
FASH...
...DE-SCENDED TO EARTH.
NEW BLUE LOCK RANKING #2 JYUBEI ARYU
YOUR HANDLING IS FASH...
...BUT WE CAN'T SHINE IF WE CAN'T TOUCH THE BALL.
THAT'S ONE HELL OF A JUMP.
I'M ABOUT THE SAME HEIGHT, BUT...
GET THE REBOUND, TOKIMITSU.
THEN PASS TO ME...
...IN FRONT OF THE GOAL.
DASH
HUH?!
AH!
DAMN!

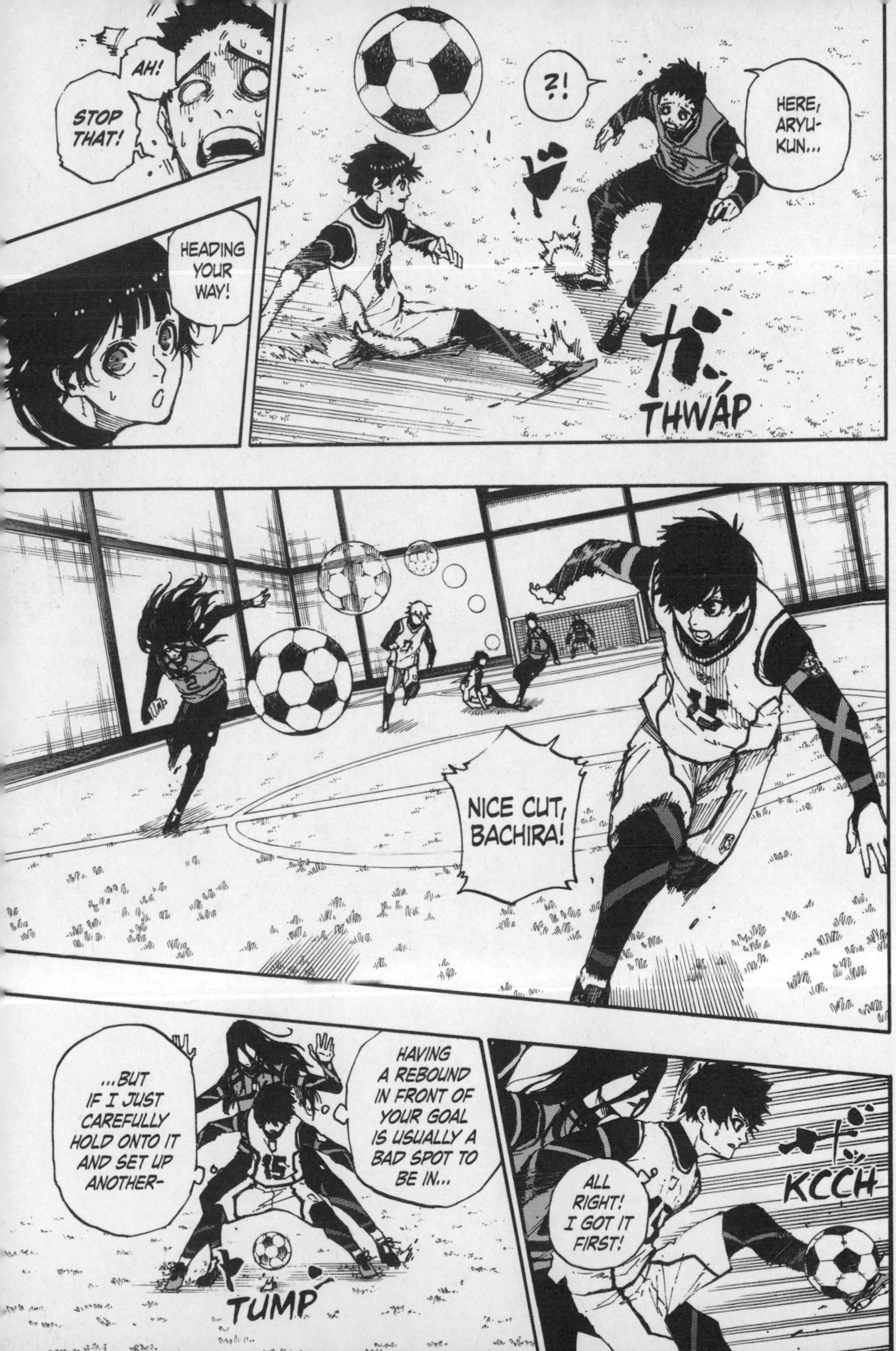
HERE, ARYU-KUN...
?!
THWAP
AH!
STOP THAT!
HEADING YOUR WAY!
NICE CUT, BACHIRA!
KCCH
ALL RIGHT! I GOT IT FIRST!
HAVING A REBOUND IN FRONT OF YOUR GOAL IS USUALLY A BAD SPOT TO BE IN...
...BUT IF I JUST CAREFULLY HOLD ONTO IT AND SET UP ANOTHER-
TUMP

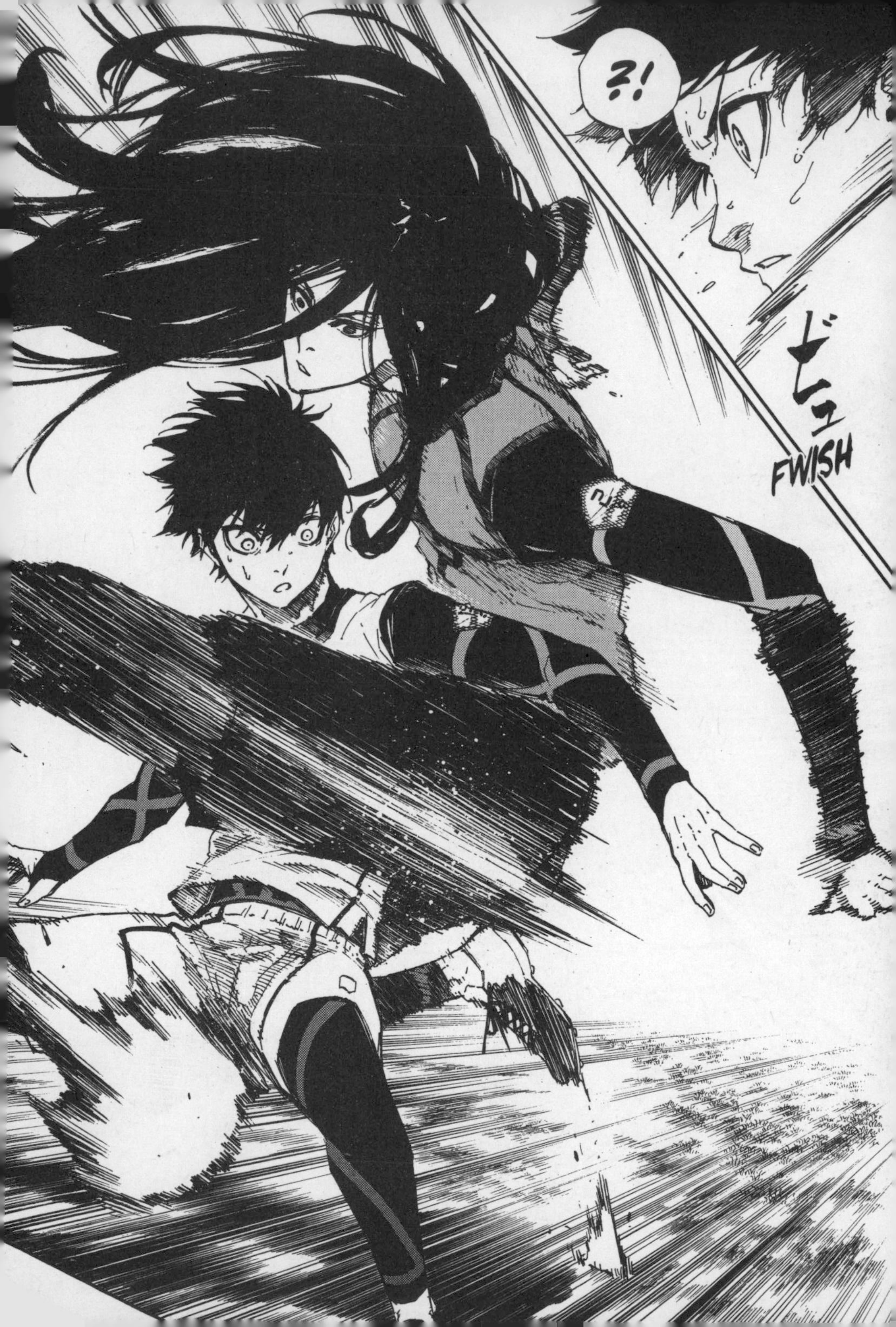
?!
ドヒュ
FWISH

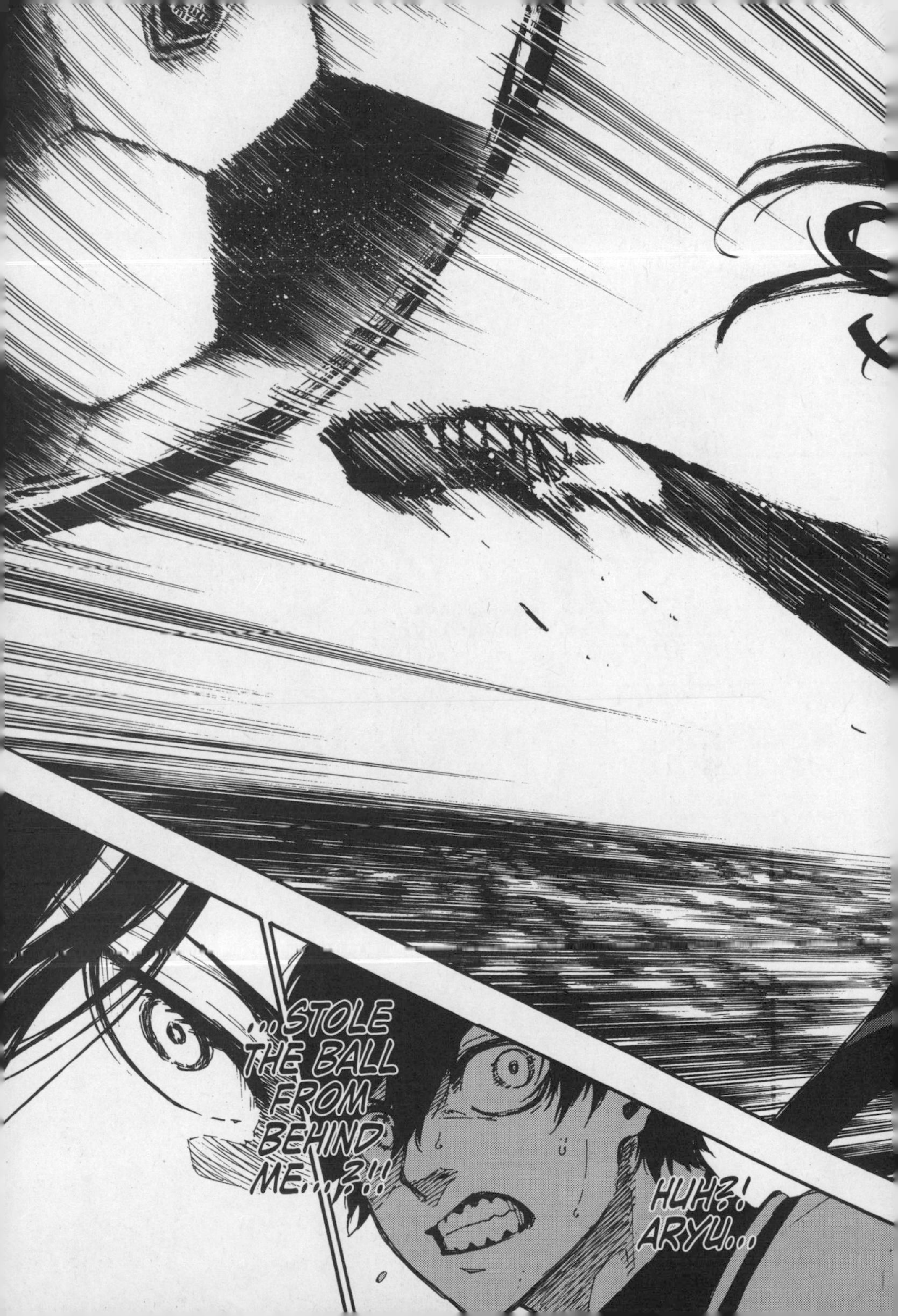
HUH?! ARYU...
...STOLE THE BALL FROM BEHIND ME...?!!

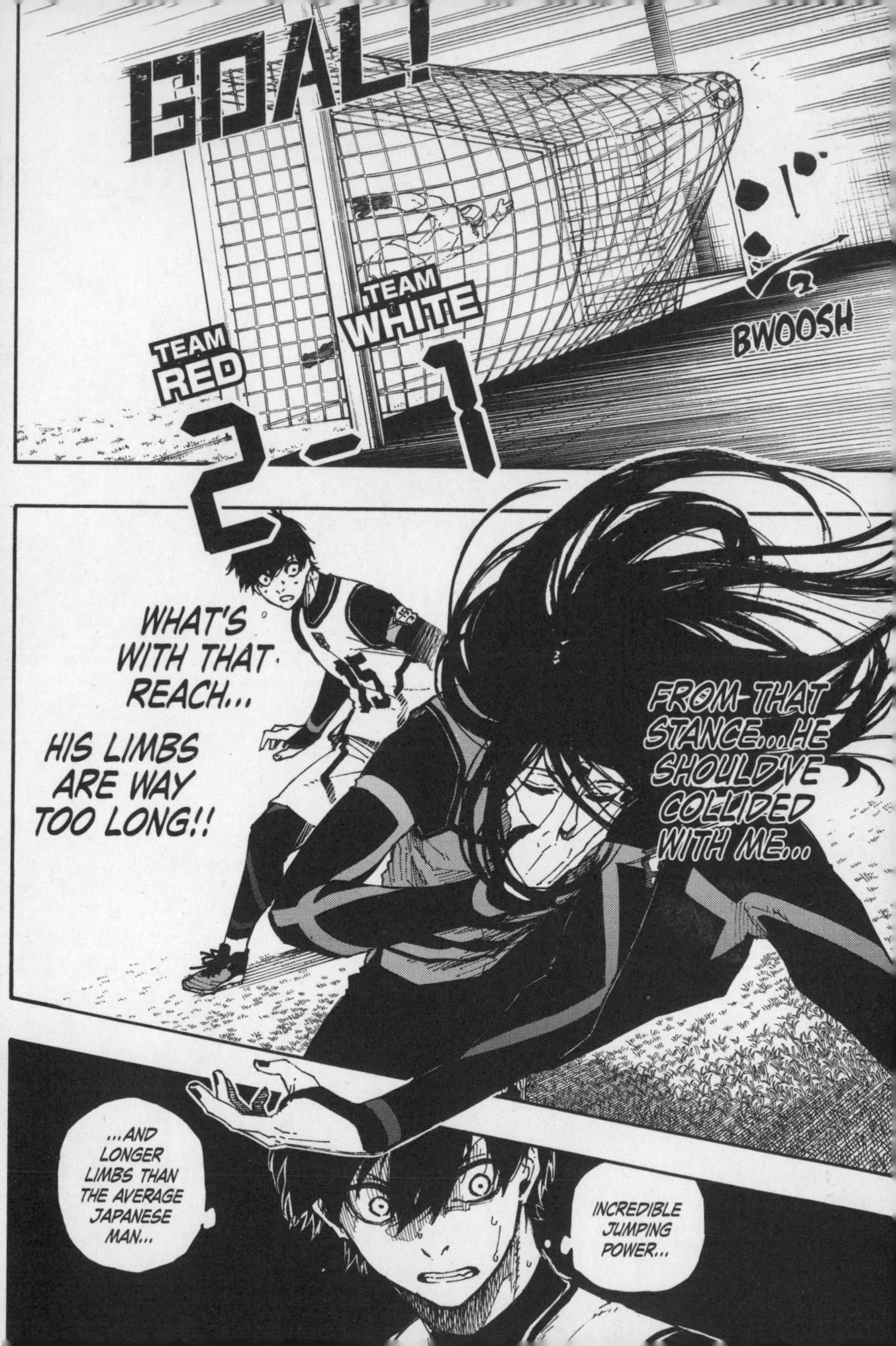

GOAL!
TEAM RED 2 - 1 TEAM WHITE
BWOOSH
FROM THAT STANCE...HE SHOULD'VE COLLIDED WITH ME...
WHAT'S WITH THAT REACH...
HIS LIMBS ARE WAY TOO LONG!!
INCREDIBLE JUMPING POWER...
...AND LONGER LIMBS THAN THE AVERAGE JAPANESE MAN...

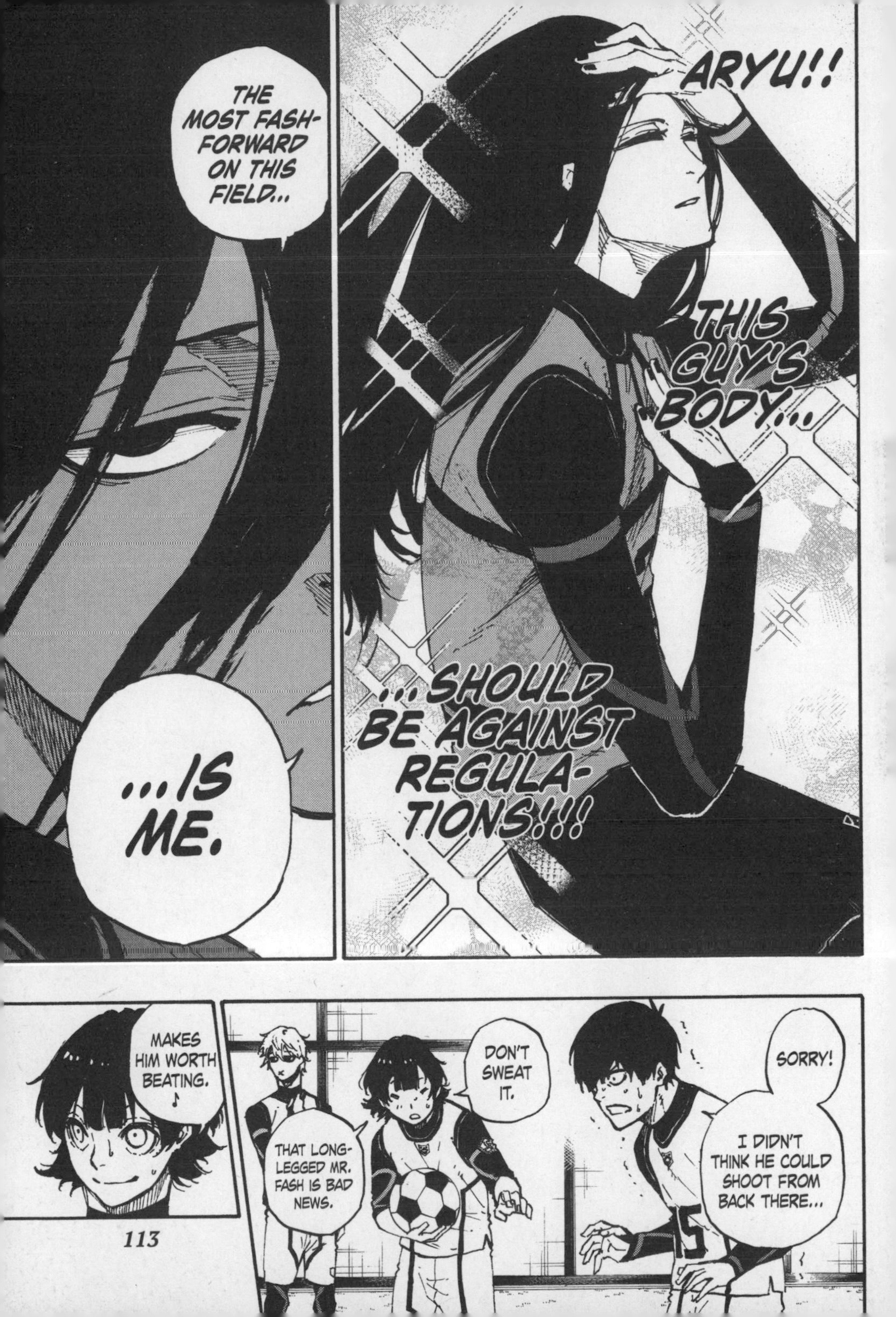
ARYU!!
THIS GUY'S BODY...
...SHOULD BE AGAINST REGULATIONS!!!
THE MOST FASH-FORWARD ON THIS FIELD...
...IS ME.
SORRY!
I DIDN'T THINK HE COULD SHOOT FROM BACK THERE...
DON'T SWEAT IT.
THAT LONG-LEGGED MR. FASH IS BAD NEWS.
MAKES HIM WORTH BEATING. ♪

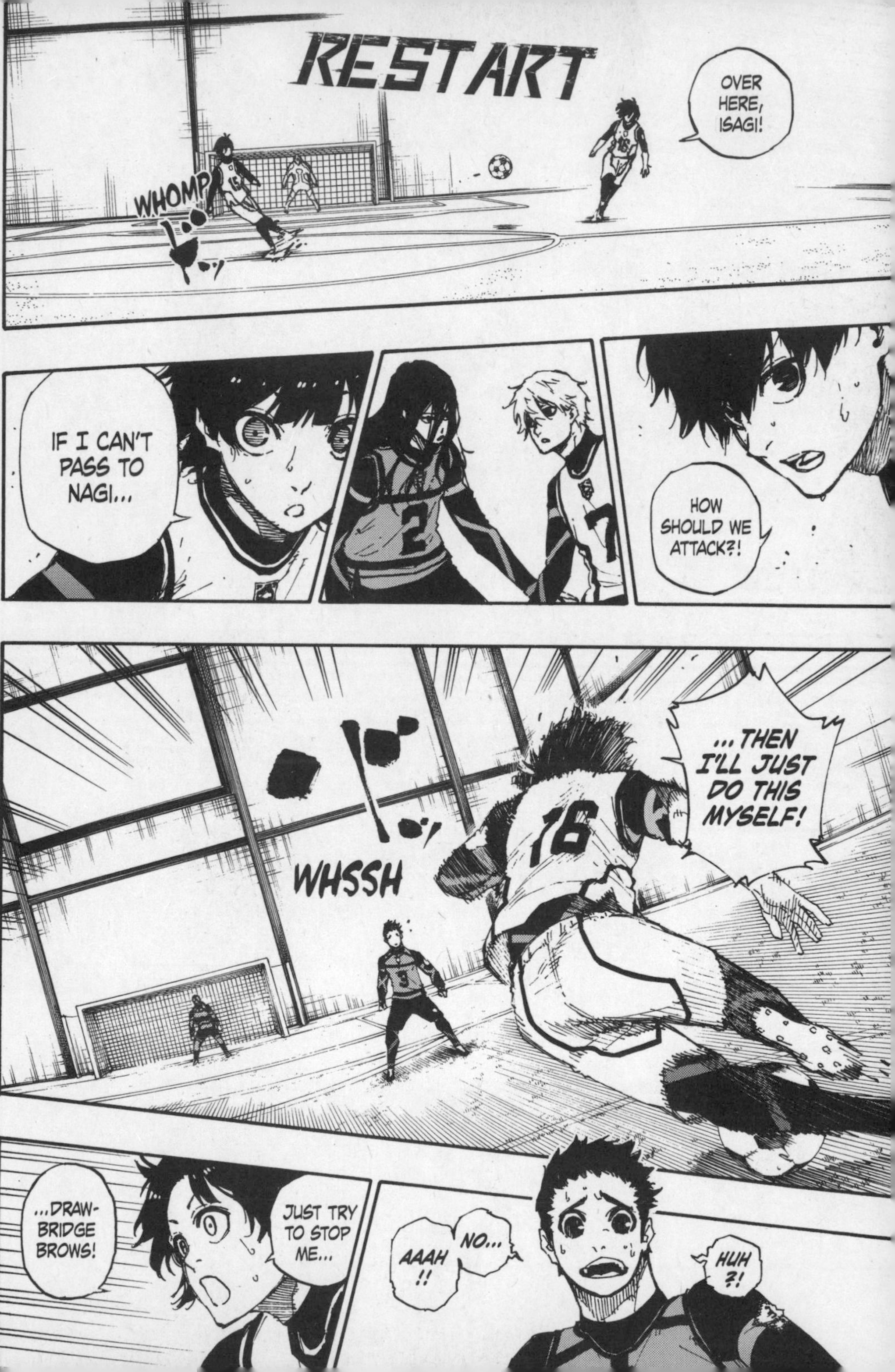
OVER HERE, ISAGI!
RESTART
WHOMP
HOW SHOULD WE ATTACK?!
IF I CAN'T PASS TO NAGI...
...THEN I'LL JUST DO THIS MYSELF!
WHSSH
HUH ?!
NO...
AAAH !!
JUST TRY TO STOP ME...
...DRAW-BRIDGE BROWS!

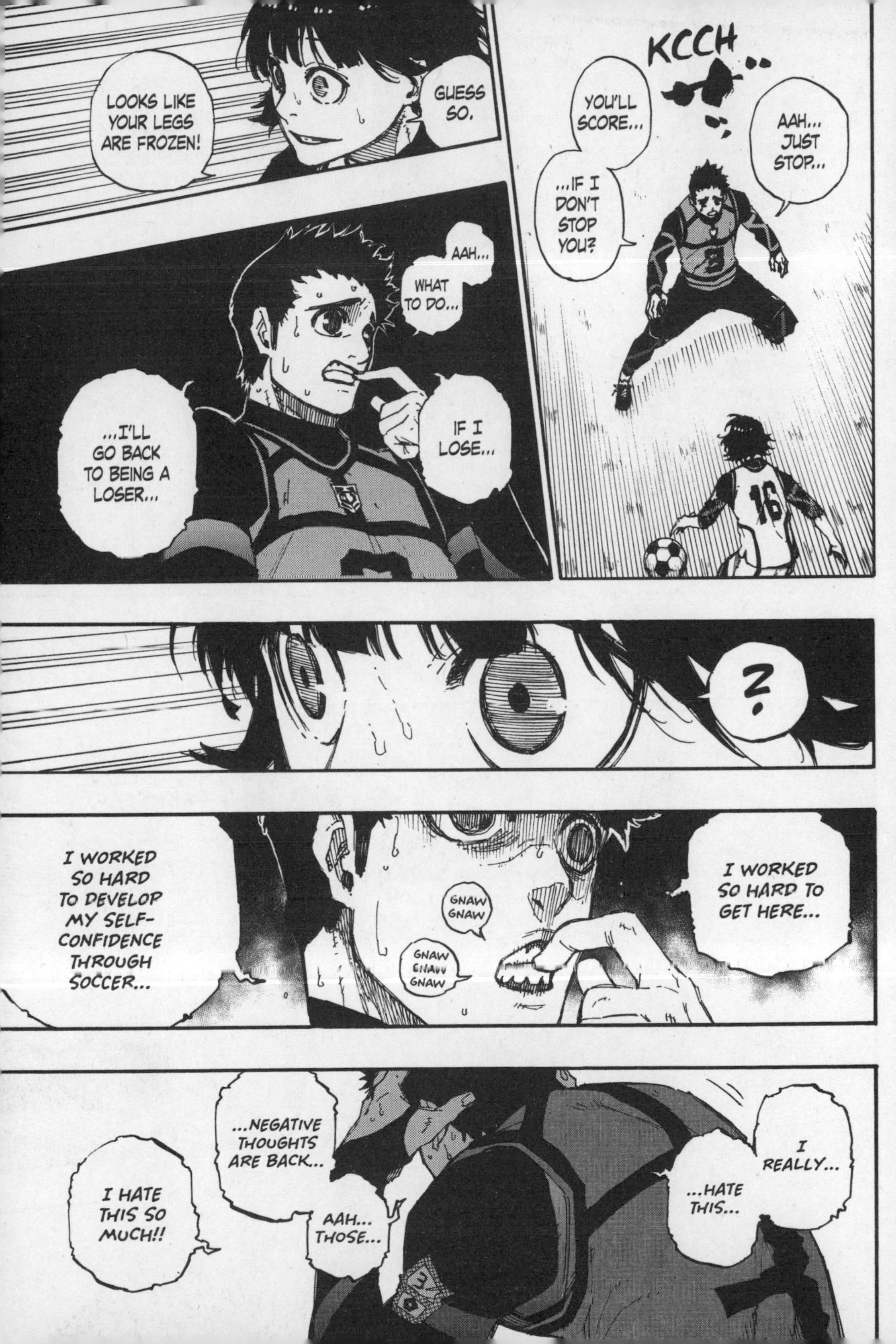
KCCH
AAH... JUST STOP...
YOU'LL SCORE...
...IF I DON'T STOP YOU?
GUESS SO.
LOOKS LIKE YOUR LEGS ARE FROZEN!
AAH... WHAT TO DO...
IF I LOSE...
...I'LL GO BACK TO BEING A LOSER...
?
I WORKED SO HARD TO GET HERE...
GNAW GNAW
GNAW GNAW GNAW
I WORKED SO HARD TO DEVELOP MY SELF-CONFIDENCE THROUGH SOCCER...
I REALLY...
...HATE THIS...
AAH... THOSE...
...NEGATIVE THOUGHTS ARE BACK...
I HATE THIS SO MUCH!!

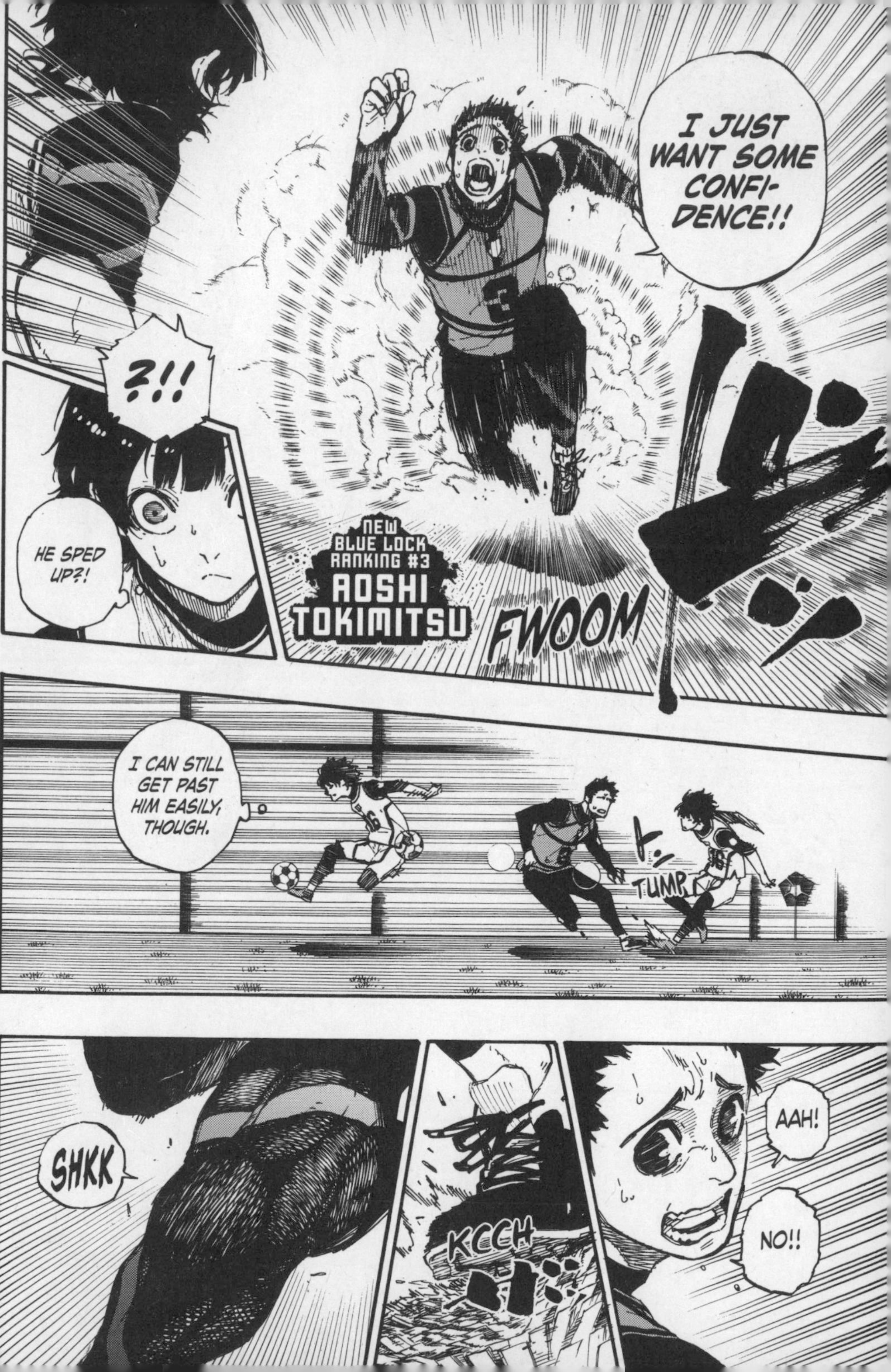
I JUST WANT SOME CONFI-DENCE!!
FWOOM
NEW BLUE LOCK RANKING #3
AOSHI TOKIMITSU
?!!
HE SPED UP?!
TUMP
I CAN STILL GET PAST HIM EASILY, THOUGH.
AAH!
NO!!
KCCH
SHKK

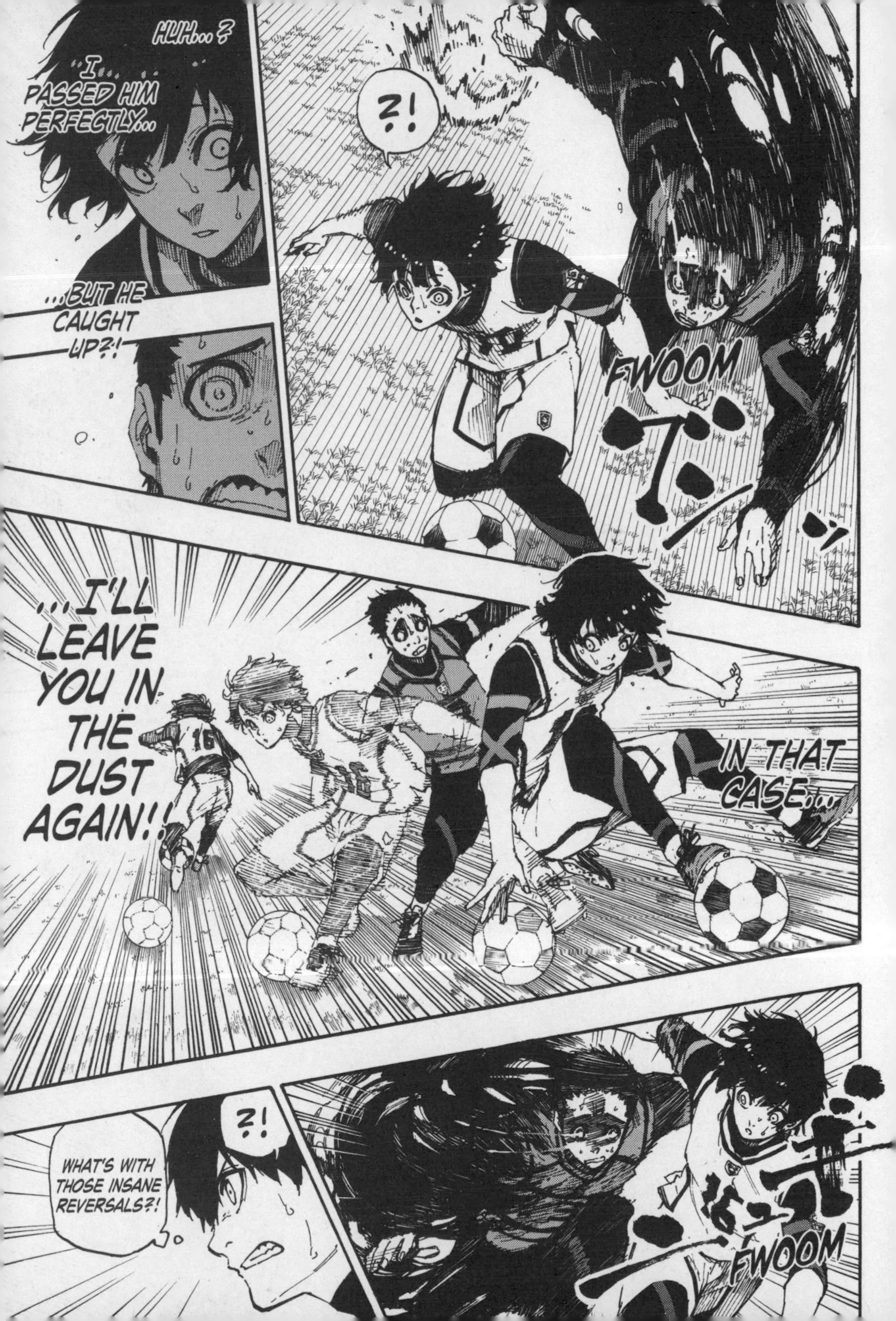

?!
FWOOM
HUH...?
...I PASSED HIM PERFECTLY...
...BUT HE CAUGHT UP?!
IN THAT CASE...
...I'LL LEAVE YOU IN THE DUST AGAIN!!
FWOOM
?!
WHAT'S WITH THOSE INSANE REVERSALS?!

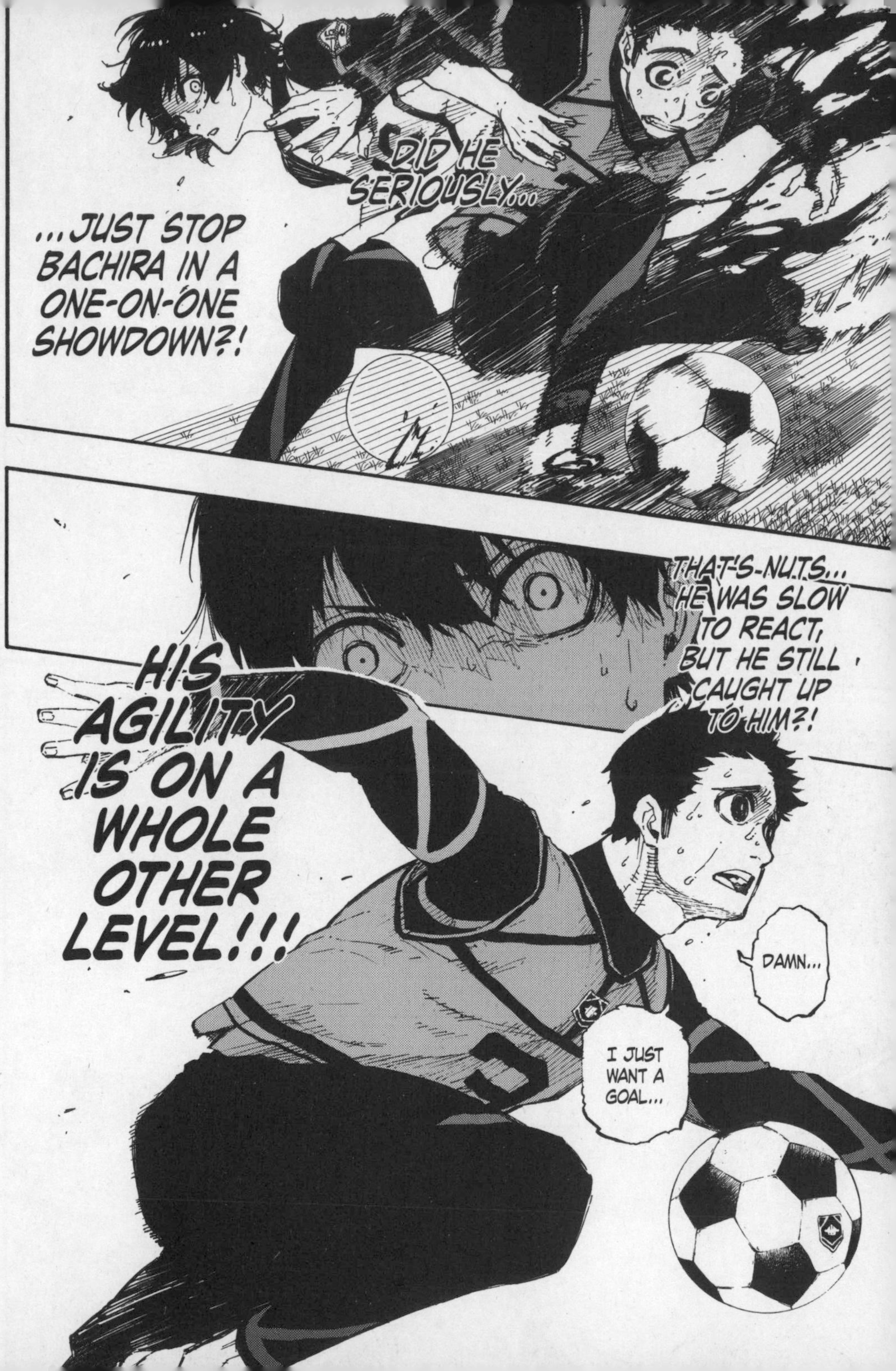
DID HE SERIOUSLY...
...JUST STOP BACHIRA IN A ONE-ON-ONE SHOWDOWN?!
THAT'S NUTS... HE WAS SLOW TO REACT, BUT HE STILL CAUGHT UP TO HIM?!
DAMN...
I JUST WANT A GOAL...
HIS AGILITY IS ON A WHOLE OTHER LEVEL!!!

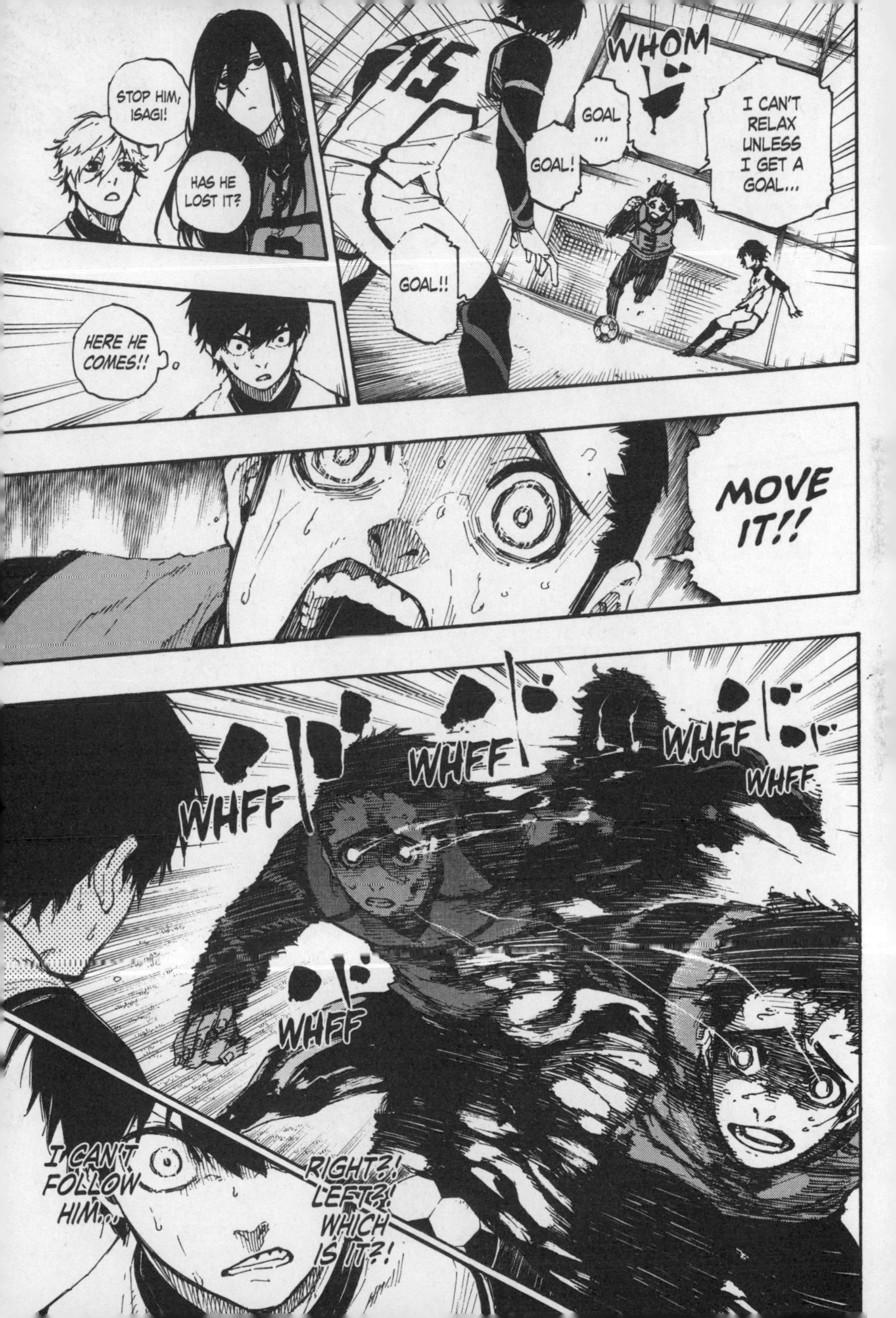
WHOM
I CAN'T RELAX UNLESS I GET A GOAL...
GOAL ...
GOAL!
GOAL!!
STOP HIM, ISAGI!
HAS HE LOST IT?
HERE HE COMES!!
MOVE IT!!
WHFF
WHFF
WHFF
WHFF
WHFF
RIGHT?! LEFT?! WHICH IS IT?!
I CAN'T FOLLOW HIM...

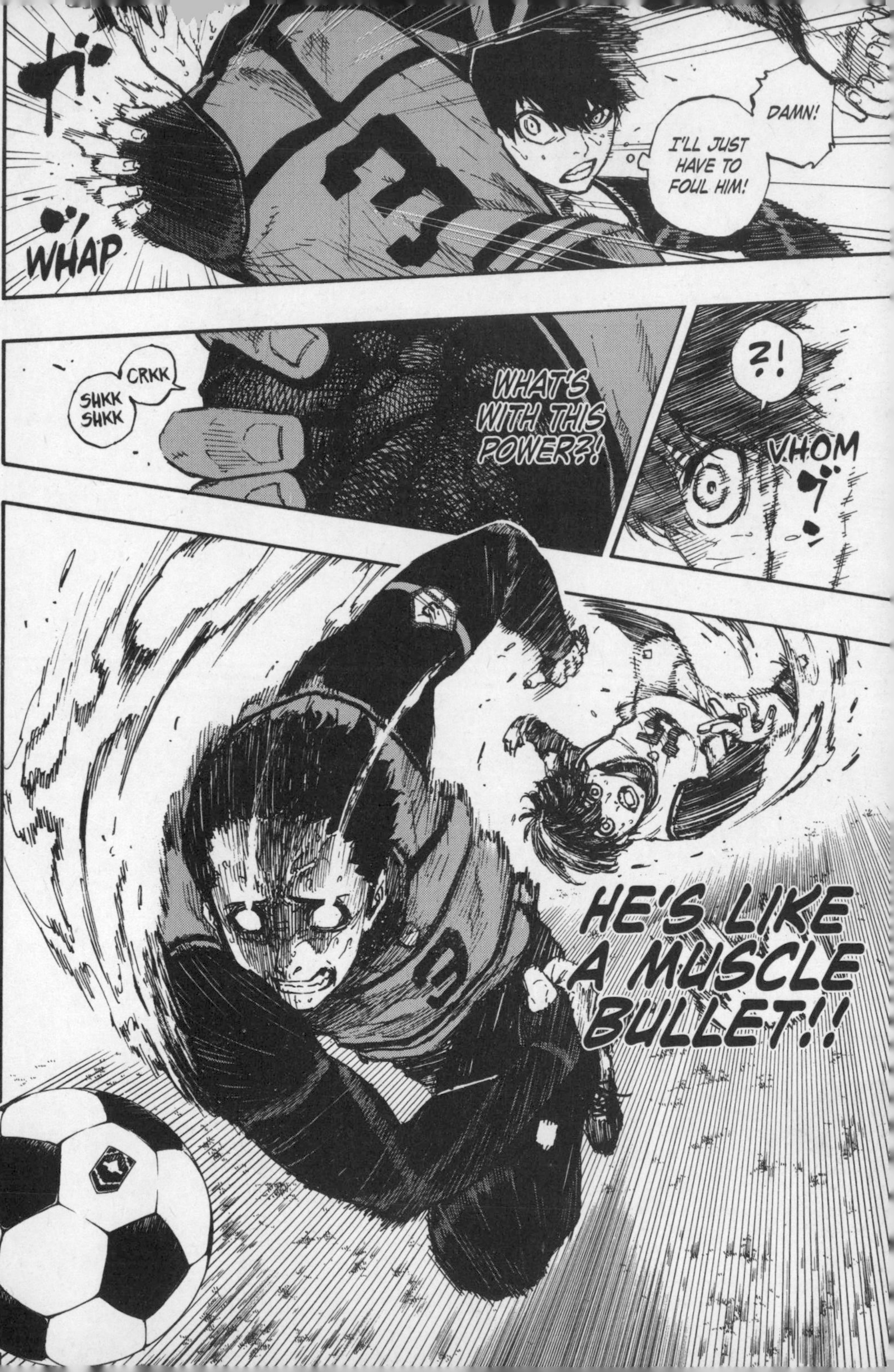
DAMN!
I'LL JUST HAVE TO FOUL HIM!
WHAP
?!
VHOM
CRKK
SHKK SHKK
WHAT'S WITH THIS POWER?!
HE'S LIKE A MUSCLE BULLET!!

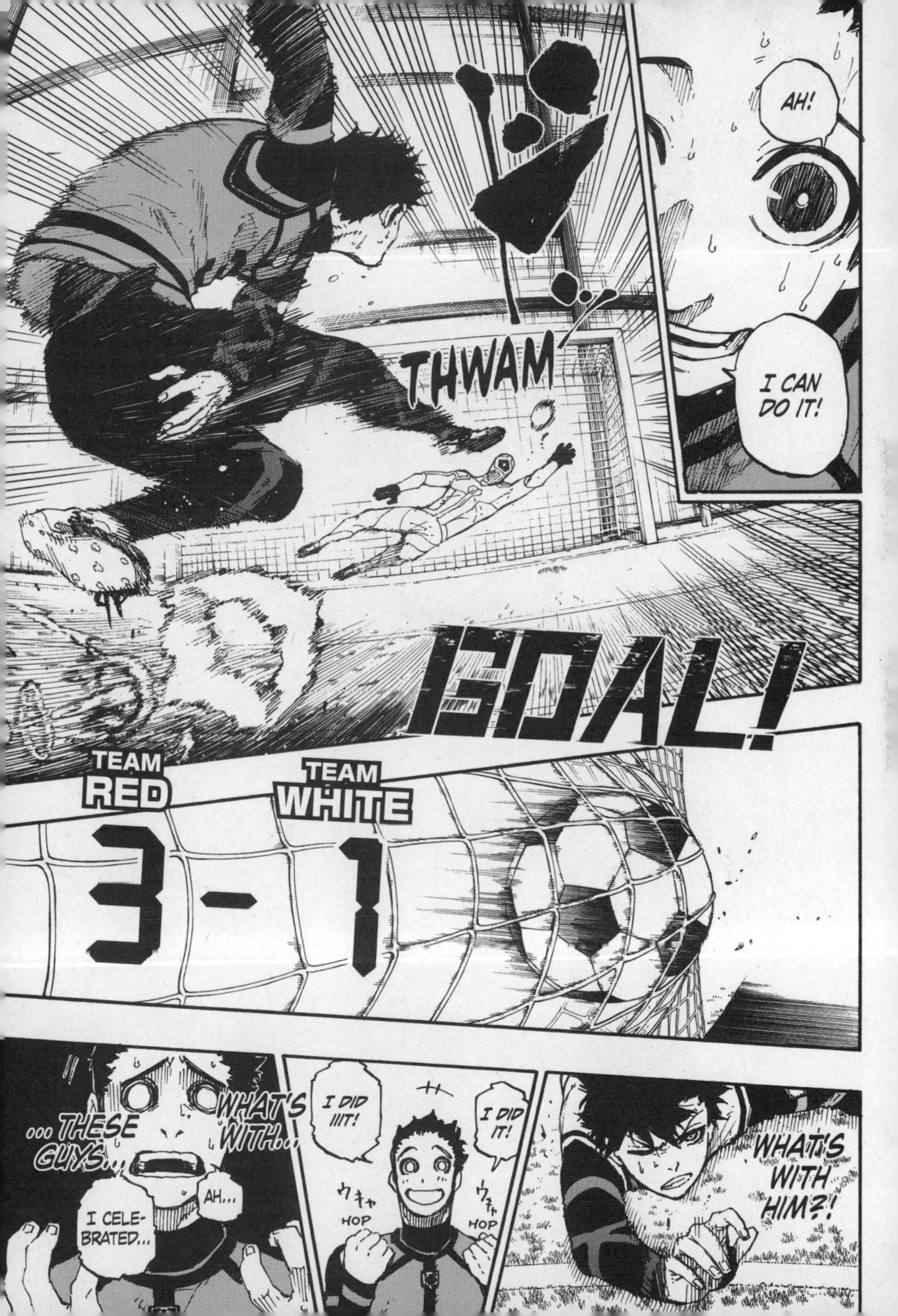
AH!
I CAN DO IT!
THWAM
GOAL!
TEAM RED
TEAM WHITE
3-1
WHAT'S WITH HIM?!
I DID IT!
I DID IIIT!
ウキャ HOP
ウキャ HOP
WHAT'S WITH...
...THESE GUYS...
AH...
I CELE-BRATED...

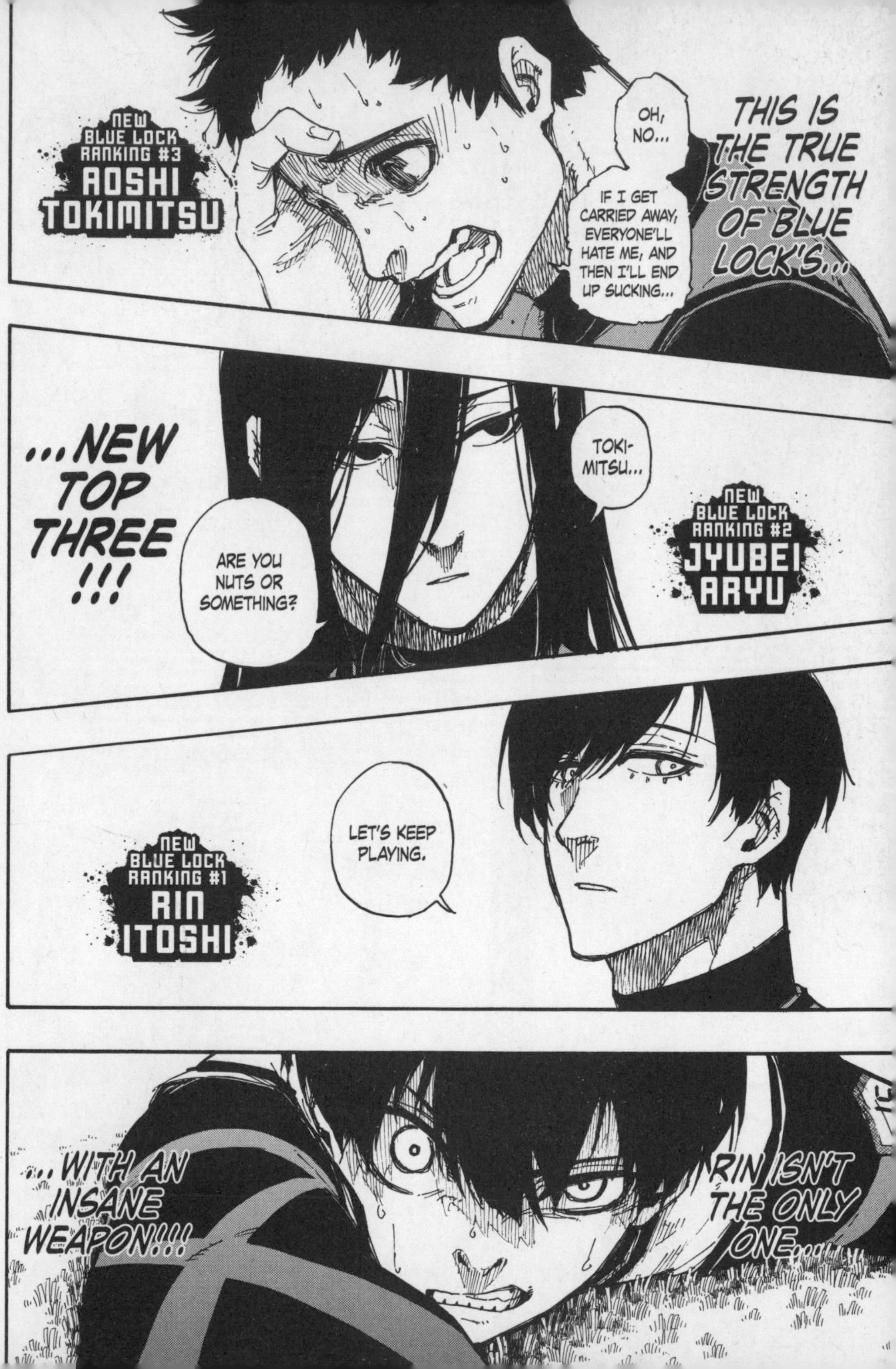
THIS IS THE TRUE STRENGTH OF BLUE LOCK'S...
OH, NO...
IF I GET CARRIED AWAY, EVERYONE'LL HATE ME, AND THEN I'LL END UP SUCKING...
NEW BLUE LOCK RANKING #3 AOSHI TOKIMITSU
NEW BLUE LOCK RANKING #2 JYUBEI ARYU
TOKI-MITSU...
ARE YOU NUTS OR SOMETHING?
...NEW TOP THREE!!!
LET'S KEEP PLAYING.
NEW BLUE LOCK RANKING #1 RIN ITOSHI
RIN ISN'T THE ONLY ONE...
...WITH AN INSANE WEAPON!!!

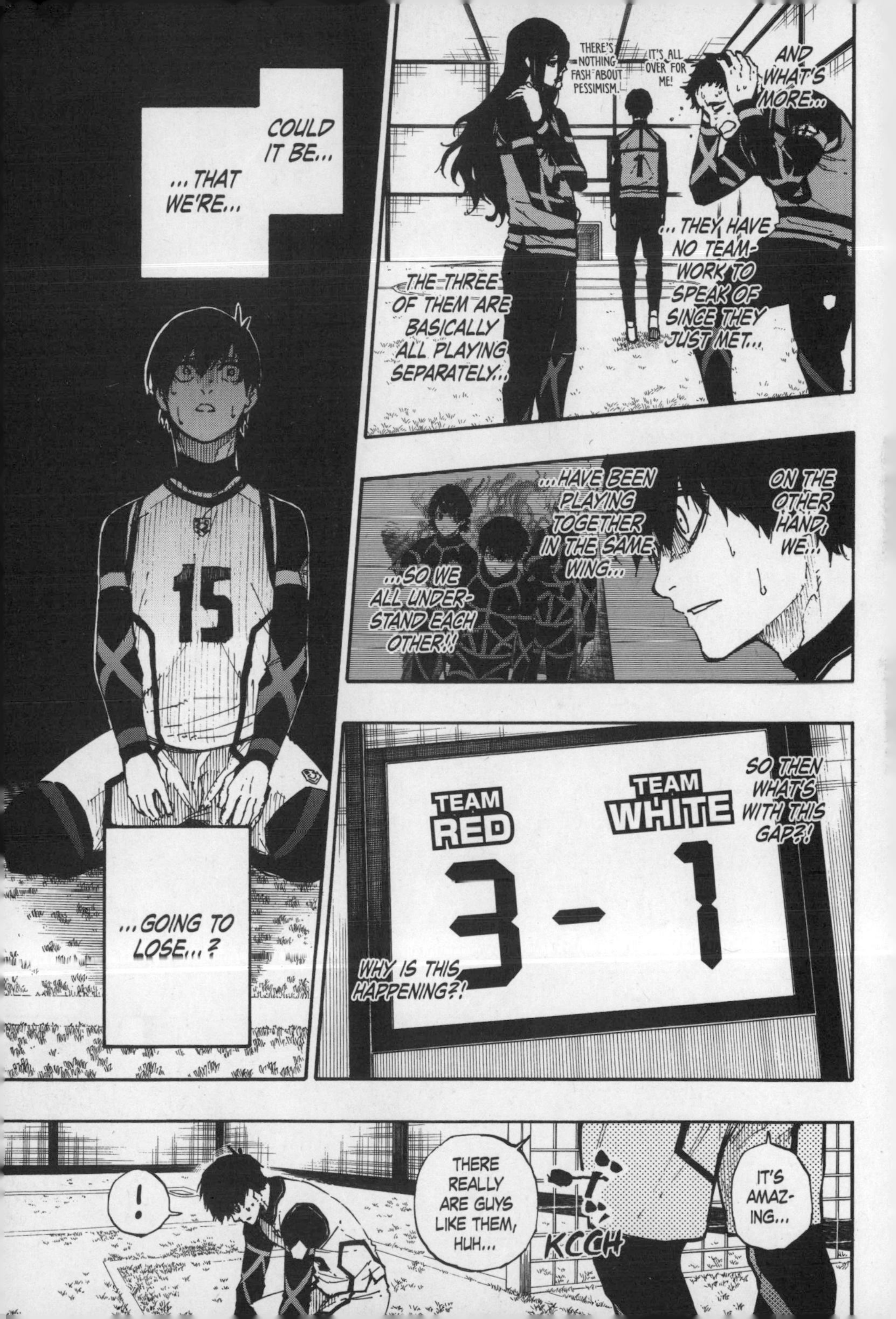
AND WHAT'S MORE...
IT'S ALL OVER FOR ME!
THERE'S NOTHING FASH ABOUT PESSIMISM.
...THEY HAVE NO TEAM-WORK TO SPEAK OF SINCE THEY JUST MET...
THE THREE OF THEM ARE BASICALLY ALL PLAYING SEPARATELY...
ON THE OTHER HAND, WE...
...HAVE BEEN PLAYING TOGETHER IN THE SAME WING...
...SO WE ALL UNDER-STAND EACH OTHER!!
SO THEN WHAT'S WITH THIS GAP?!
TEAM WHITE
TEAM RED
3 - 1
WHY IS THIS HAPPENING?!
COULD IT BE...
...THAT WE'RE...
...GOING TO LOSE...?
IT'S AMAZ-ING...
KCCH
THERE REALLY ARE GUYS LIKE THEM, HUH...
!

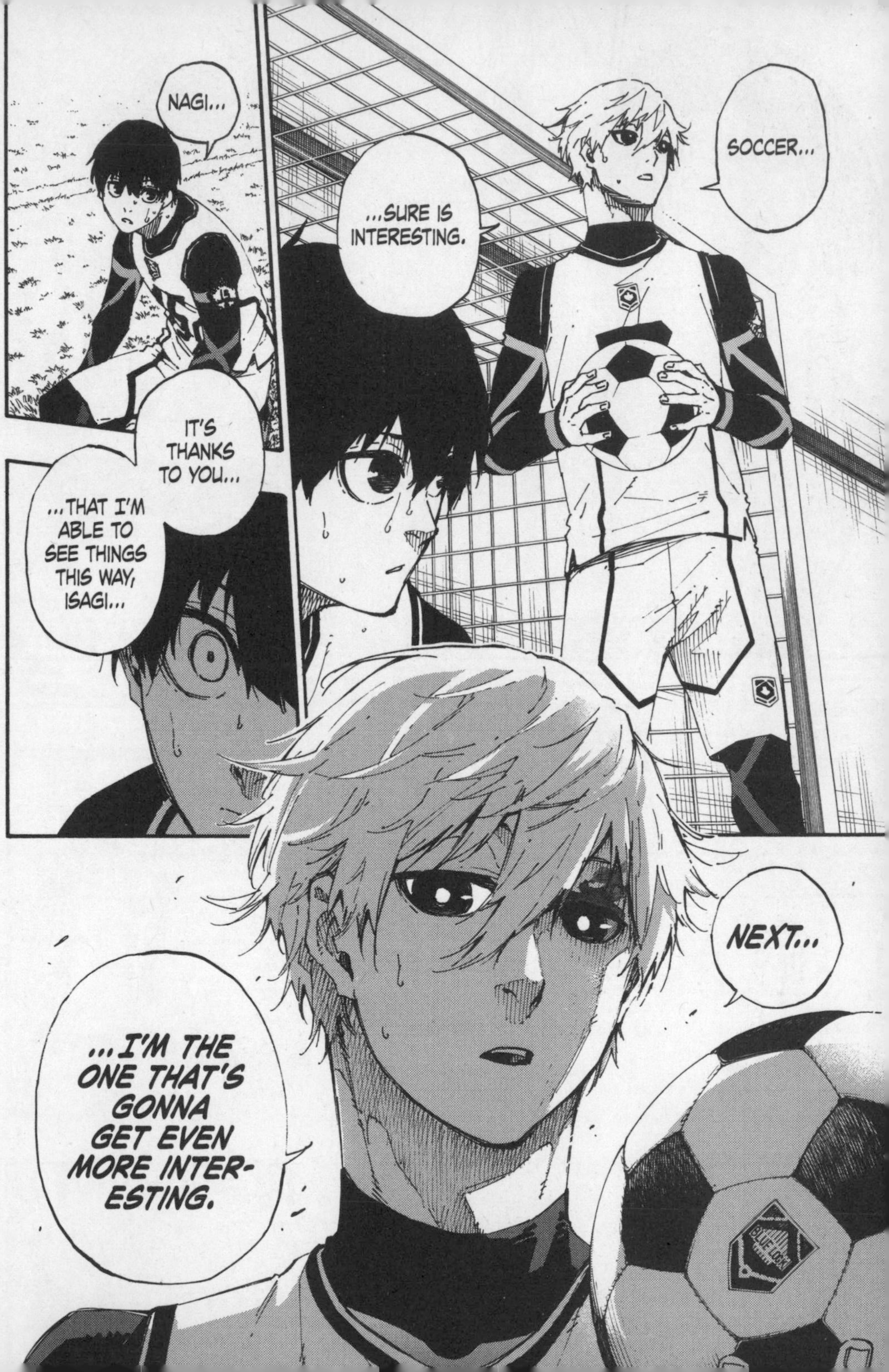
SOCCER...
...SURE IS INTERESTING.
NAGI...
IT'S THANKS TO YOU...
...THAT I'M ABLE TO SEE THINGS THIS WAY, ISAGI...
NEXT...
...I'M THE ONE THAT'S GONNA GET EVEN MORE INTER-ESTING.

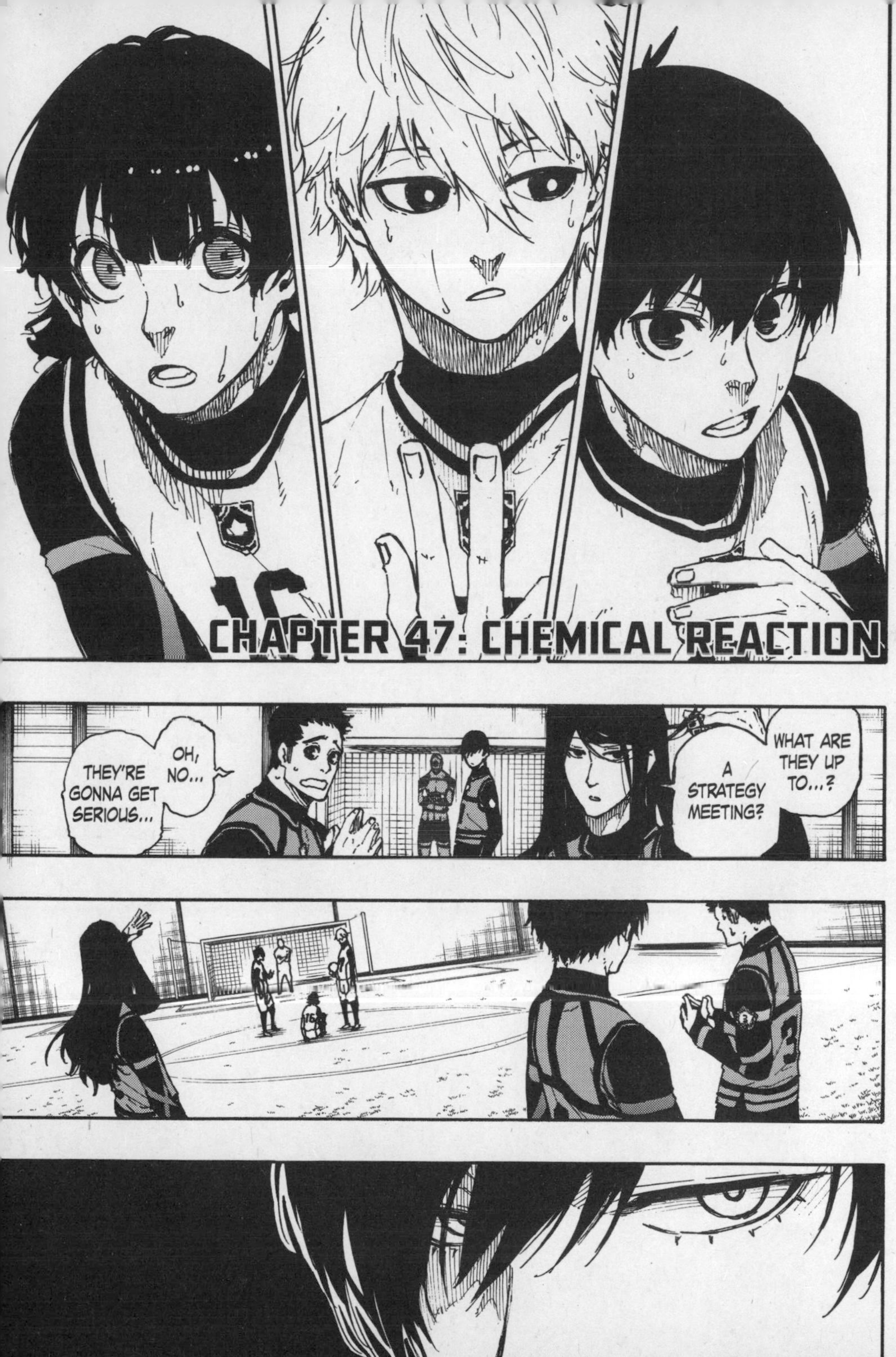
CHAPTER 47: CHEMICAL REACTION
WHAT ARE THEY UP TO...?
A STRATEGY MEETING?
OH, NO...
THEY'RE GONNA GET SERIOUS...

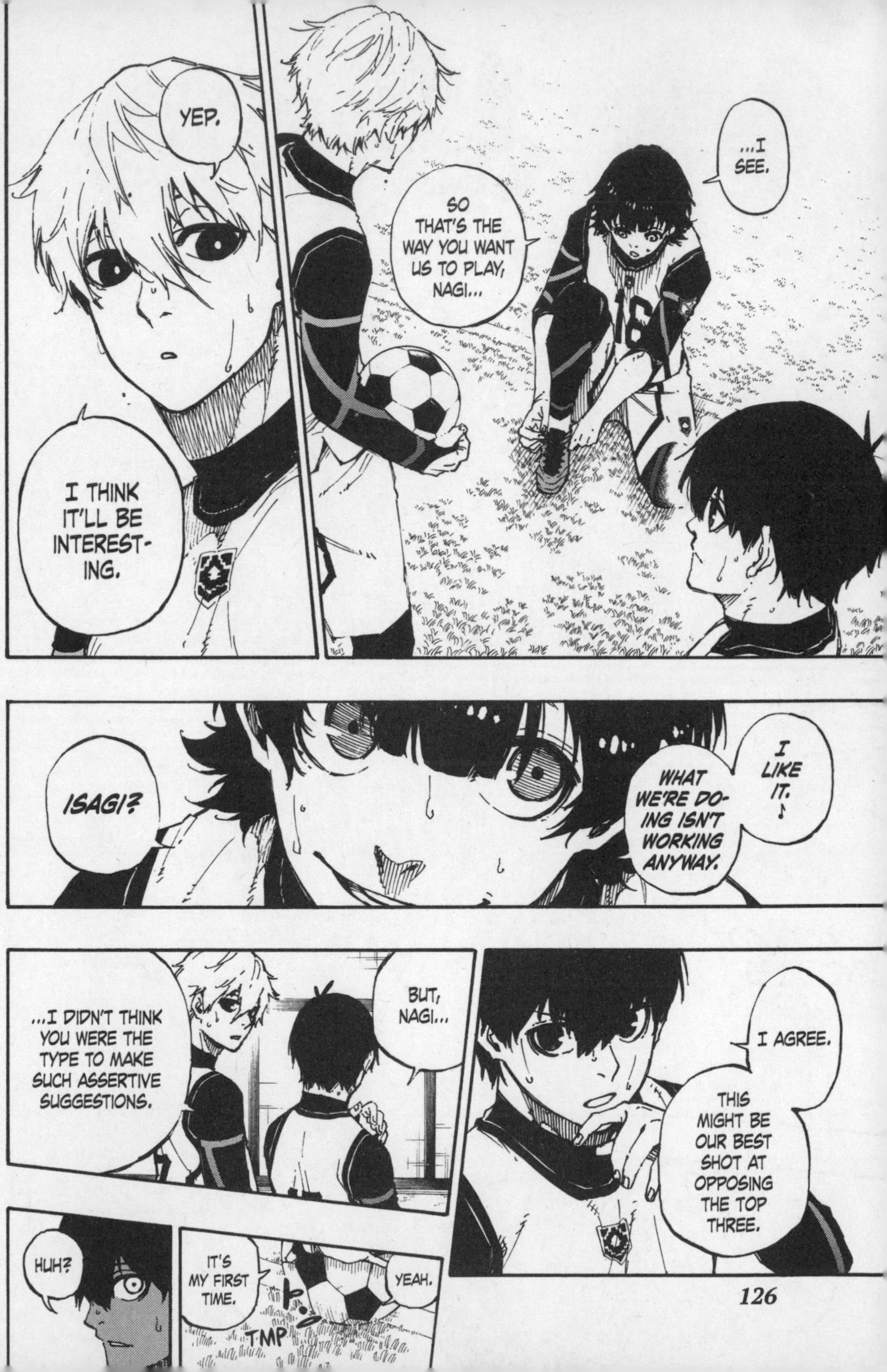
...I SEE.
SO THAT'S THE WAY YOU WANT US TO PLAY, NAGI...
YEP.
I THINK IT'LL BE INTEREST-ING.
I LIKE IT. ♪
WHAT WE'RE DO-ING ISN'T WORKING ANYWAY.
ISAGI?
I AGREE.
THIS MIGHT BE OUR BEST SHOT AT OPPOSING THE TOP THREE.
BUT, NAGI...
...I DIDN'T THINK YOU WERE THE TYPE TO MAKE SUCH ASSERTIVE SUGGESTIONS.
YEAH.
IT'S MY FIRST TIME.
TMP
HUH?

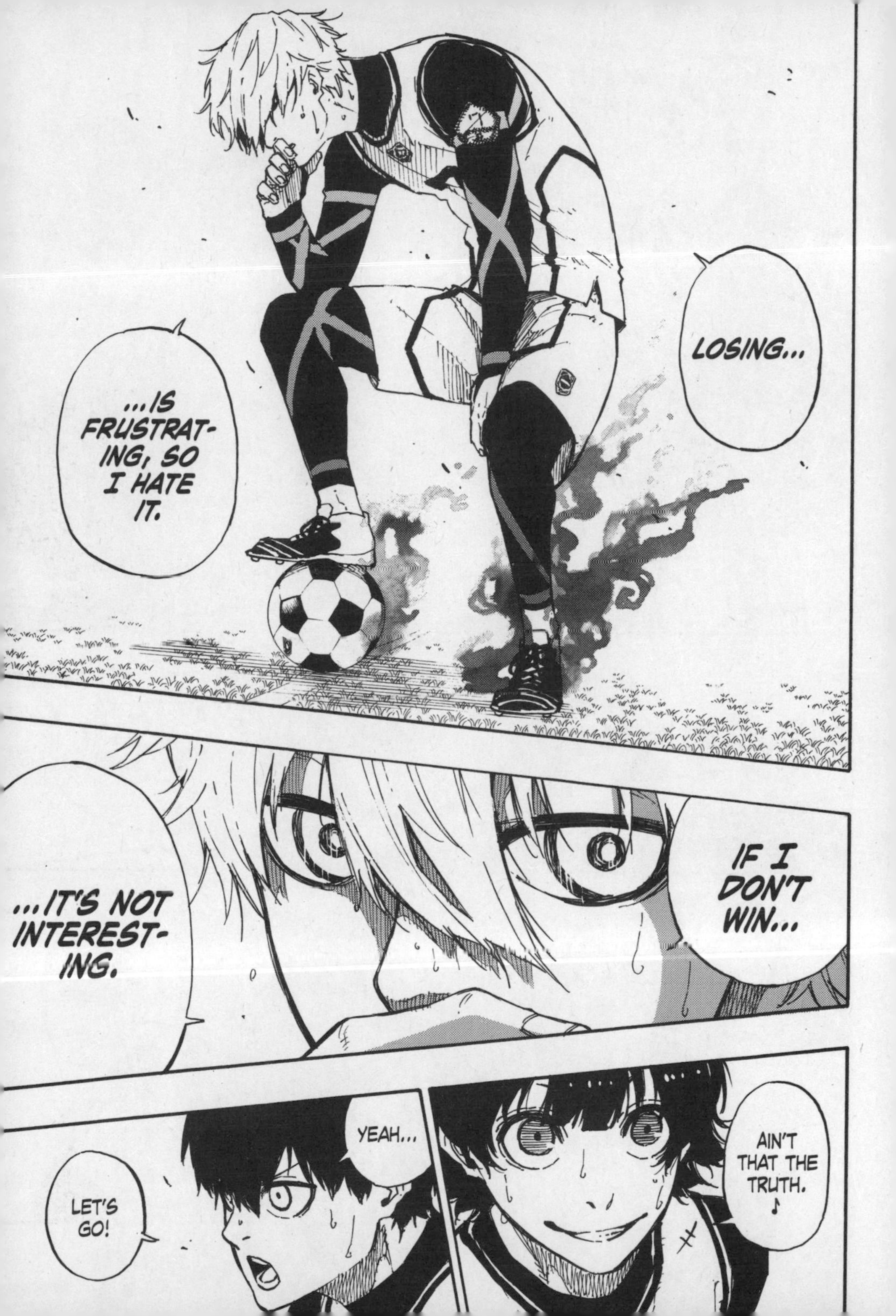
LOSING...
...IS FRUSTRATING, SO I HATE IT.
IF I DON'T WIN...
...IT'S NOT INTERESTING.
AIN'T THAT THE TRUTH. ♪
YEAH...
LET'S GO!

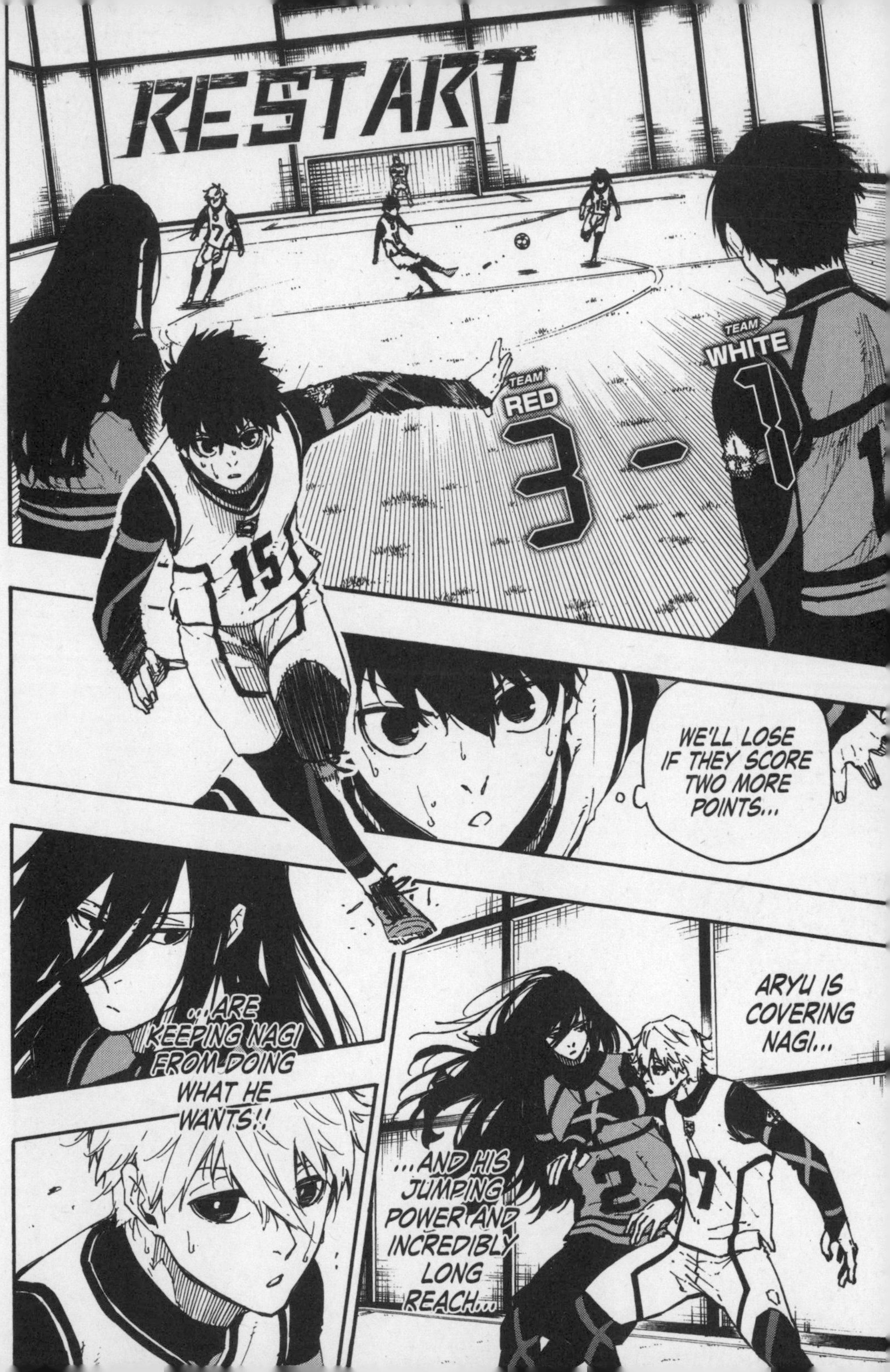
RESTART
TEAM WHITE 1
TEAM RED 3 -
WE'LL LOSE IF THEY SCORE TWO MORE POINTS...
ARYU IS COVERING NAGI...
...AND HIS JUMPING POWER AND INCREDIBLY LONG REACH...
...ARE KEEPING NAGI FROM DOING WHAT HE WANTS!!

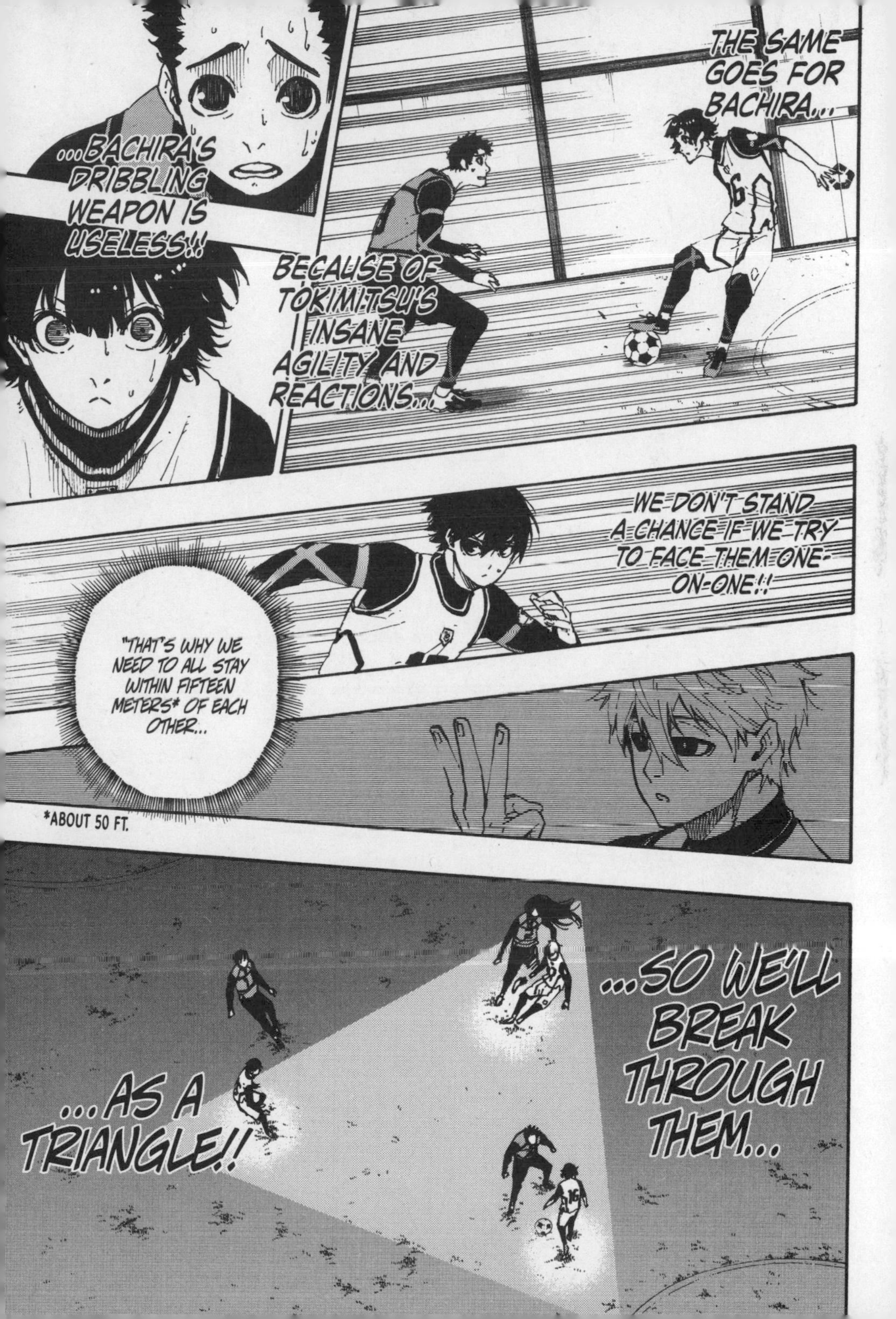
THE SAME GOES FOR BACHIRA...
BECAUSE OF TOKIMITSU'S INSANE AGILITY AND REACTIONS...
...BACHIRA'S DRIBBLING WEAPON IS USELESS!!
WE DON'T STAND A CHANCE IF WE TRY TO FACE THEM ONE-ON-ONE!!
"THAT'S WHY WE NEED TO ALL STAY WITHIN FIFTEEN METERS* OF EACH OTHER...
...SO WE'LL BREAK THROUGH THEM...
...AS A TRIANGLE!!
*ABOUT 50 FT.

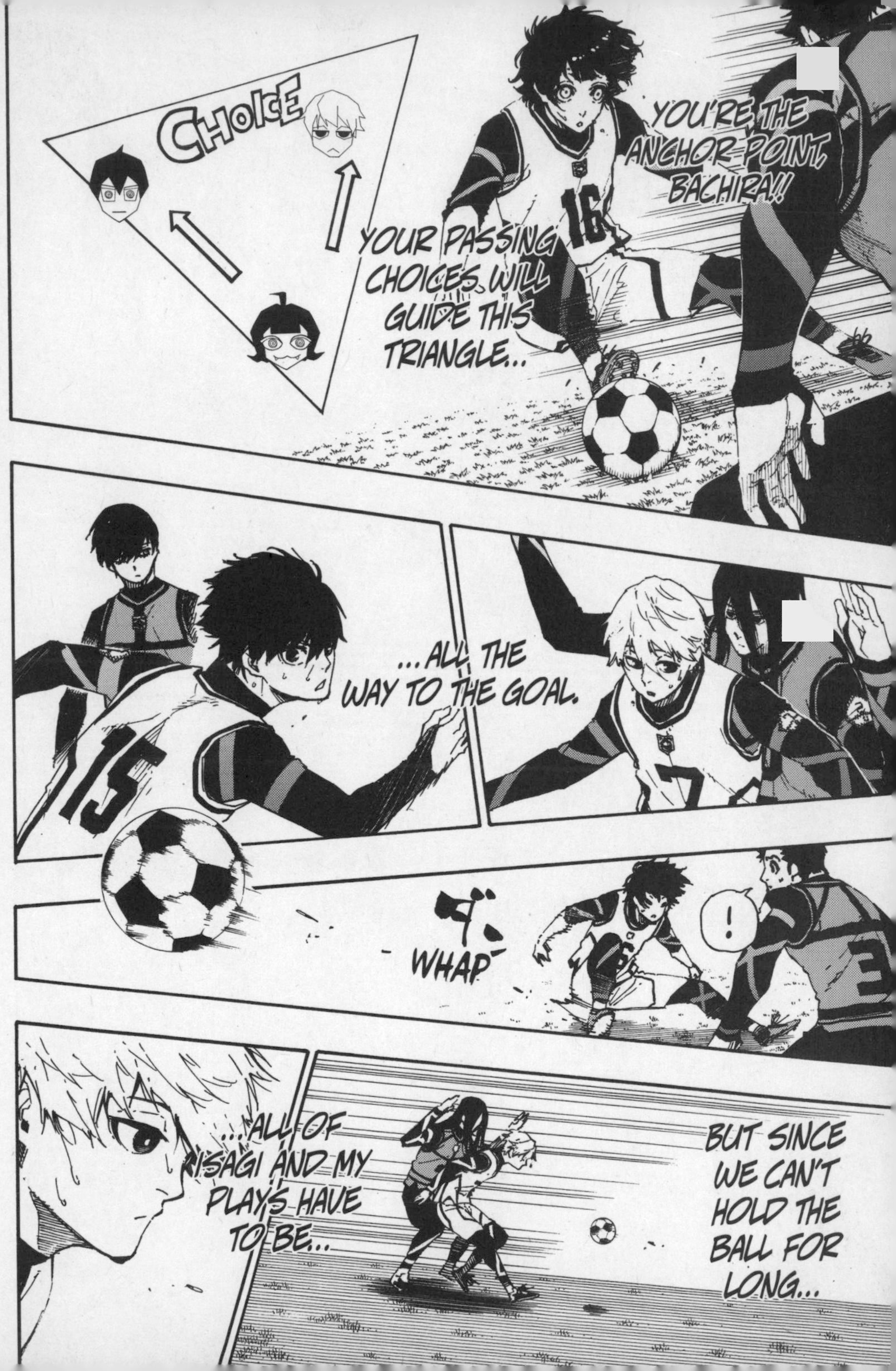
YOU'RE THE ANCHOR POINT, BACHIRA!!
CHOICE
YOUR PASSING CHOICES WILL GUIDE THIS TRIANGLE...
...ALL THE WAY TO THE GOAL.
!
WHAP
BUT SINCE WE CAN'T HOLD THE BALL FOR LONG...
...ALL OF ISAGI AND MY PLAYS HAVE TO BE...

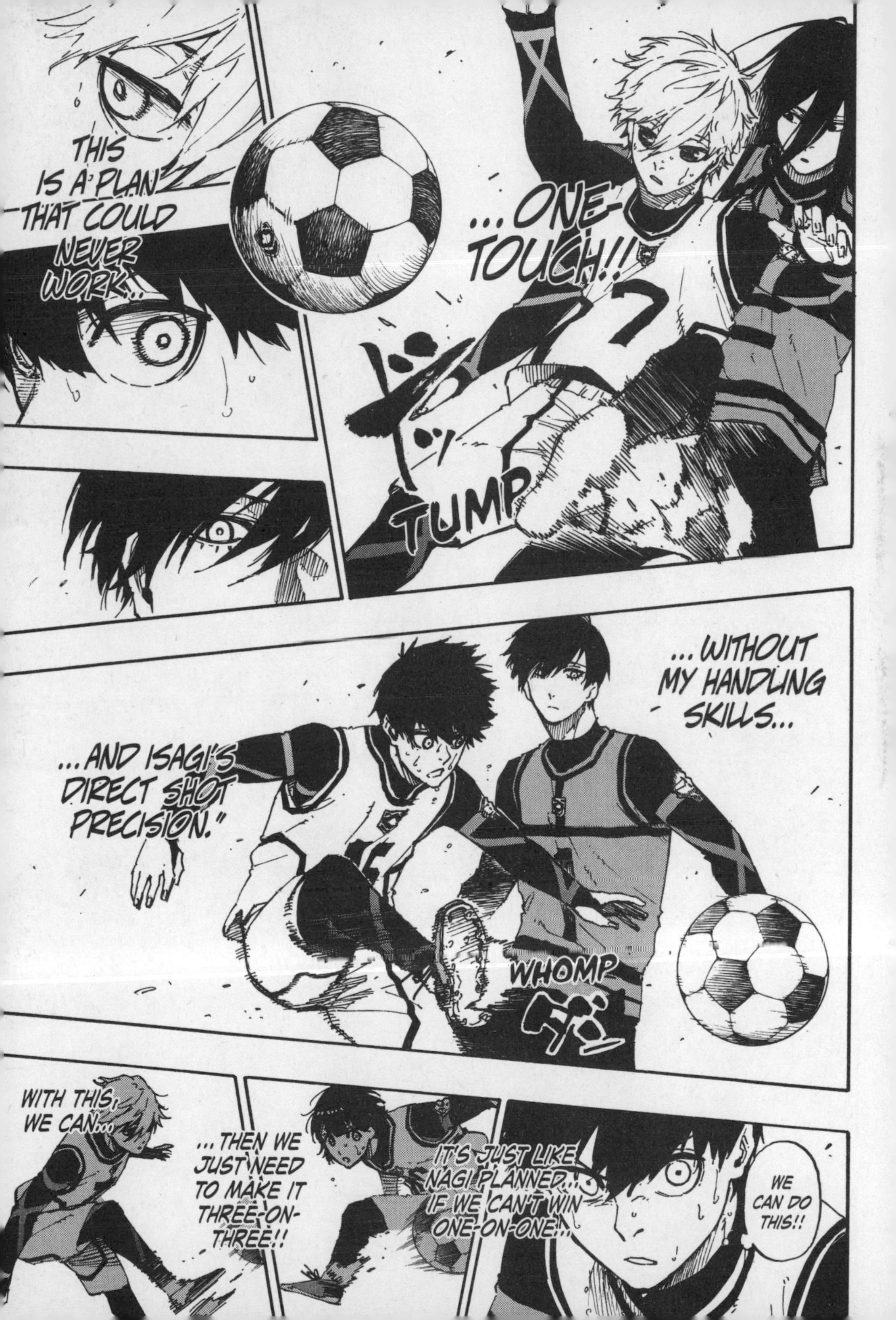
...ONE-TOUCH!!
TUMP
THIS IS A PLAN THAT COULD NEVER WORK...
...WITHOUT MY HANDLING SKILLS...
...AND ISAGI'S DIRECT SHOT PRECISION."
WHOMP
WE CAN DO THIS!!
IT'S JUST LIKE NAGI PLANNED... IF WE CAN'T WIN ONE-ON-ONE...
...THEN WE JUST NEED TO MAKE IT THREE-ON-THREE!!
WITH THIS, WE CAN...

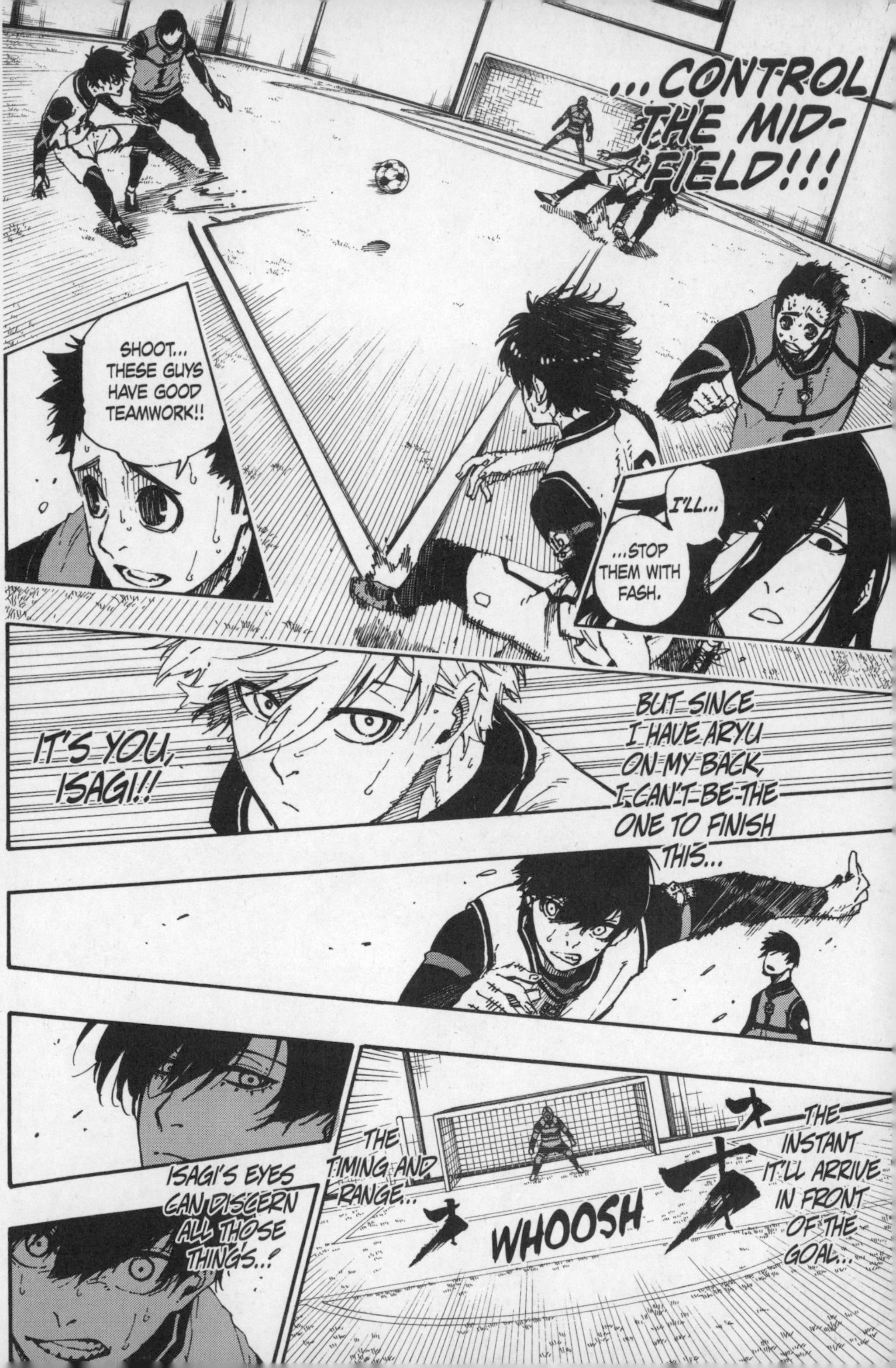
...CONTROL THE MID-FIELD!!!
I'LL...
...STOP THEM WITH FASH.
SHOOT... THESE GUYS HAVE GOOD TEAMWORK!!
BUT SINCE I HAVE ARYU ON MY BACK, I CAN'T BE THE ONE TO FINISH THIS...
IT'S YOU, ISAGI!!
THE INSTANT IT'LL ARRIVE IN FRONT OF THE GOAL...
WHOOSH
THE TIMING AND RANGE...
ISAGI'S EYES CAN DISCERN ALL THOSE THINGS...!

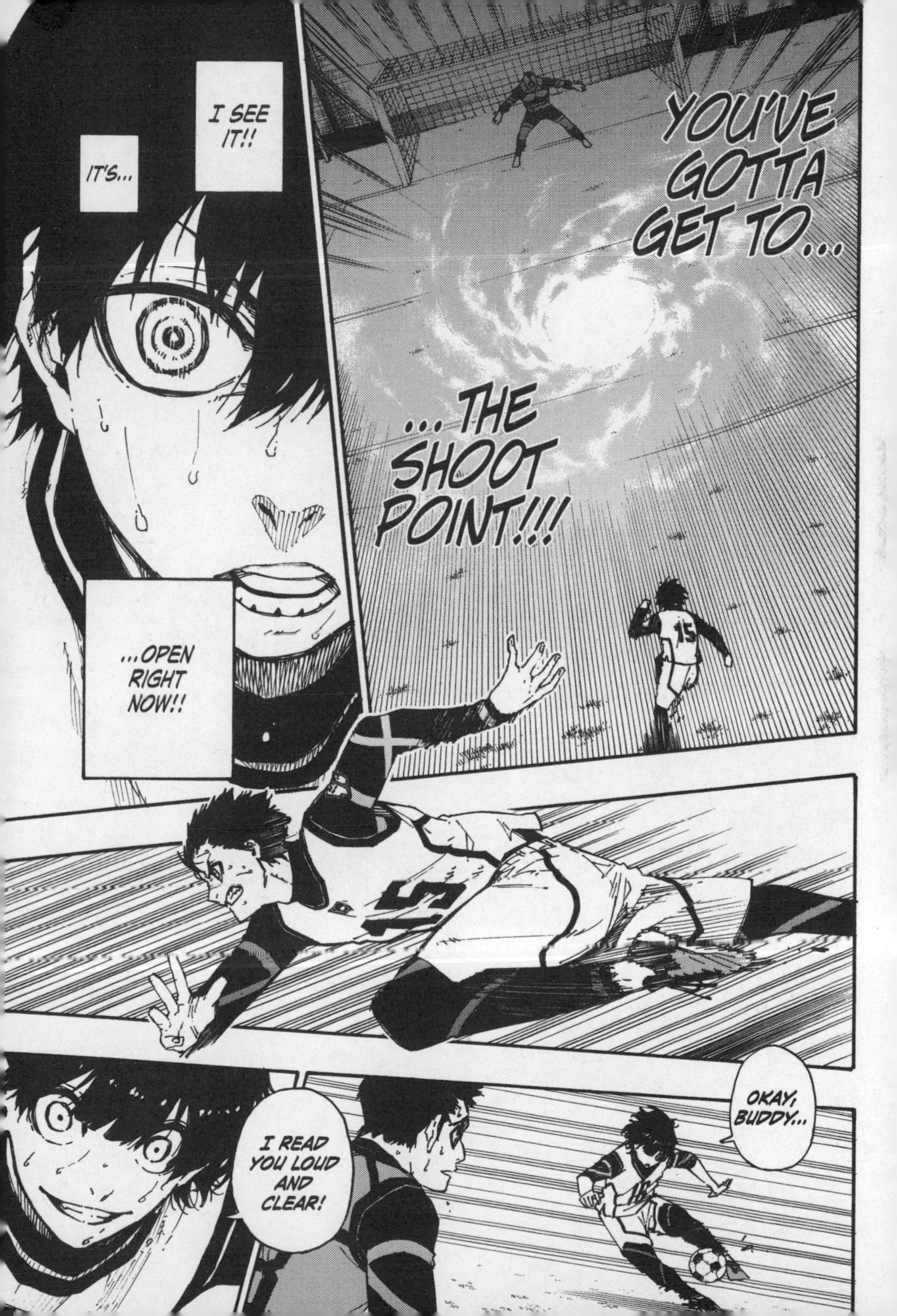
YOU'VE GOTTA GET TO...
... THE SHOOT POINT!!!
I SEE IT!!
IT'S...
...OPEN RIGHT NOW!!
OKAY, BUDDY...
I READ YOU LOUD AND CLEAR!

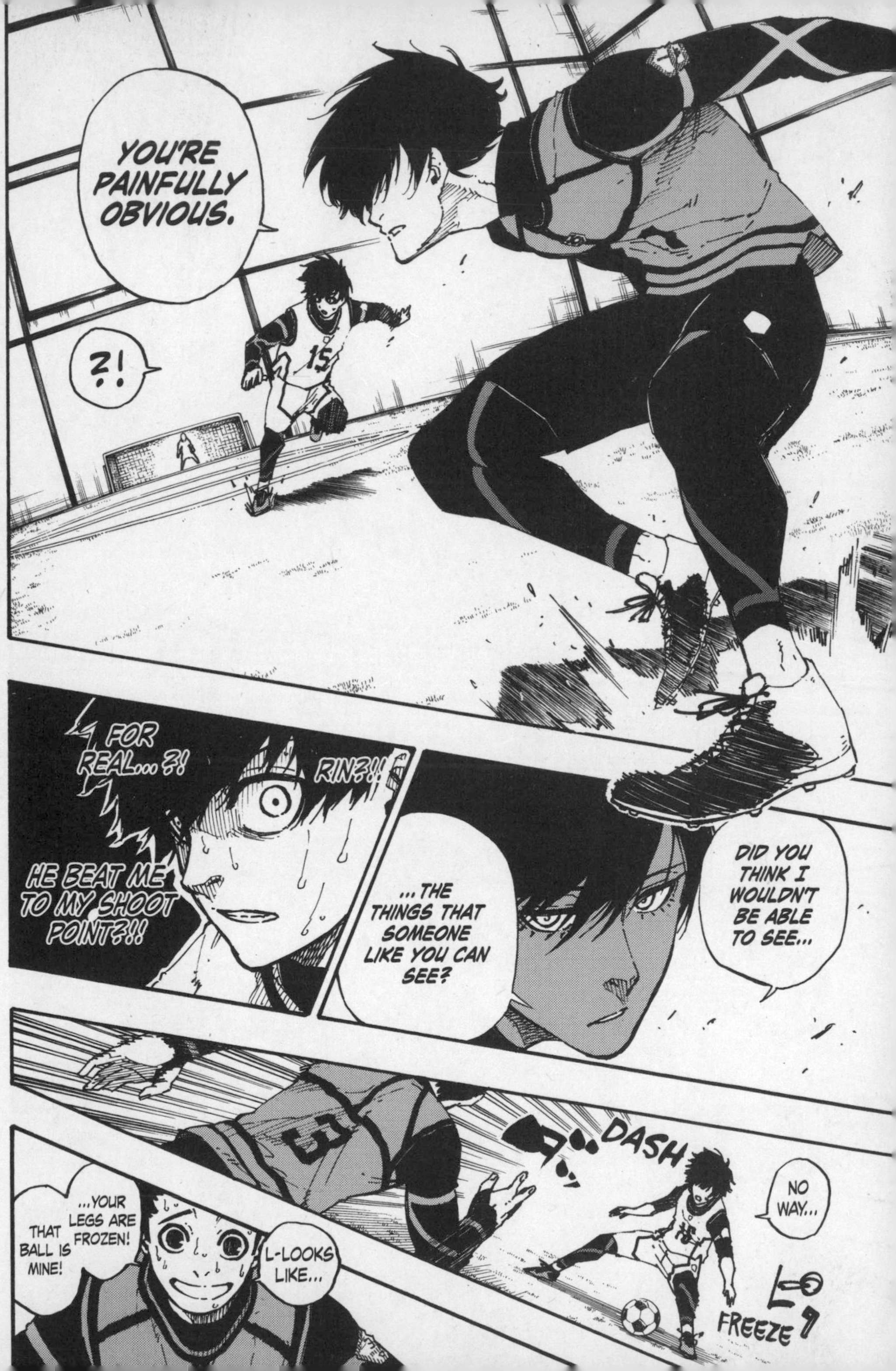
YOU'RE PAINFULLY OBVIOUS.
?!
DID YOU THINK I WOULDN'T BE ABLE TO SEE...
...THE THINGS THAT SOMEONE LIKE YOU CAN SEE?
RIN?!!
FOR REAL...?!
HE BEAT ME TO MY SHOOT POINT?!!
DASH
NO WAY...
FREEZE
L-LOOKS LIKE...
...YOUR LEGS ARE FROZEN!
THAT BALL IS MINE!

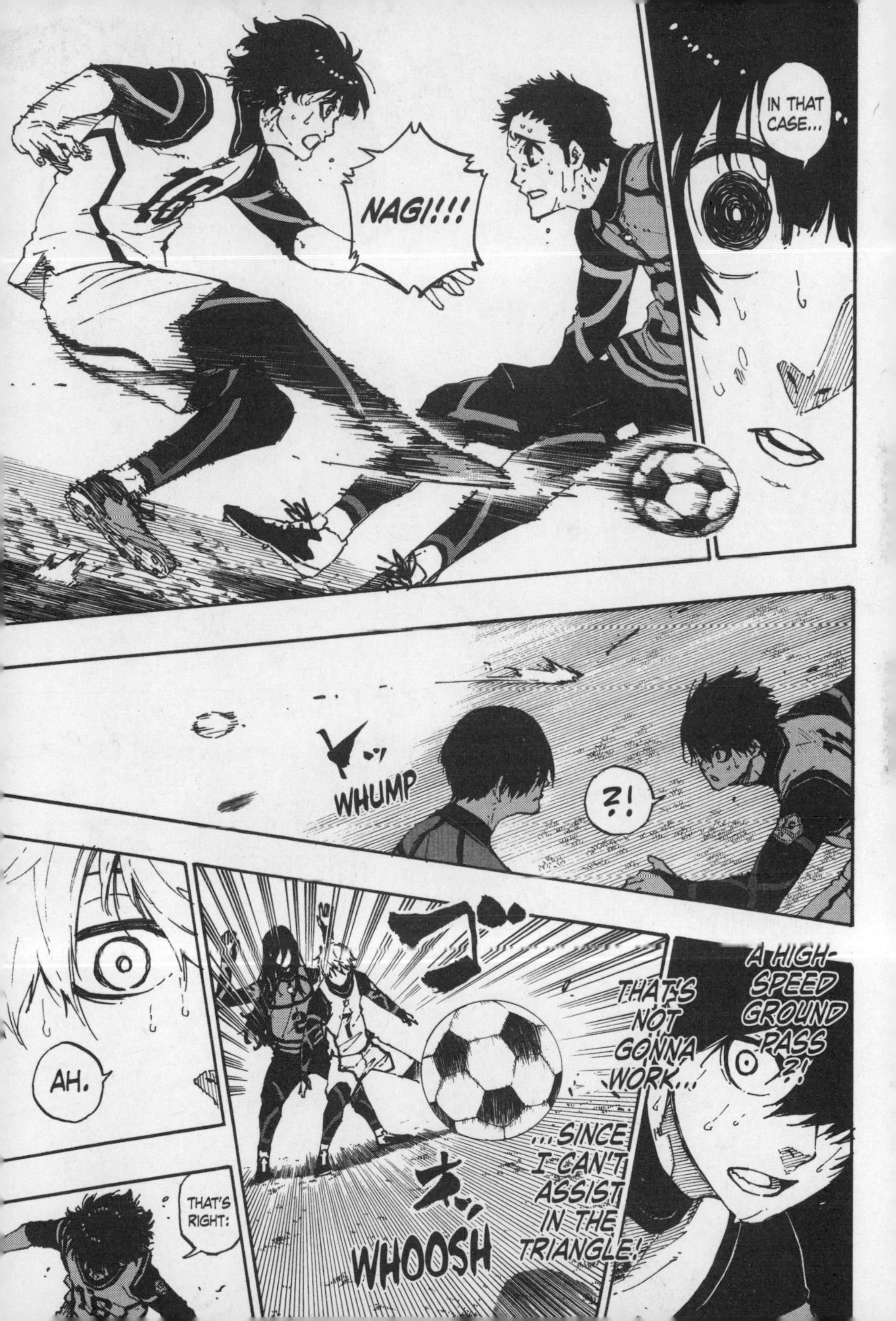
IN THAT CASE...
NAGI!!!
?!
WHUMP
A HIGH-SPEED GROUND PASS?!
THAT'S NOT GONNA WORK...
...SINCE I CAN'T ASSIST IN THE TRIANGLE!
WHOOSH
AH.
THAT'S RIGHT:

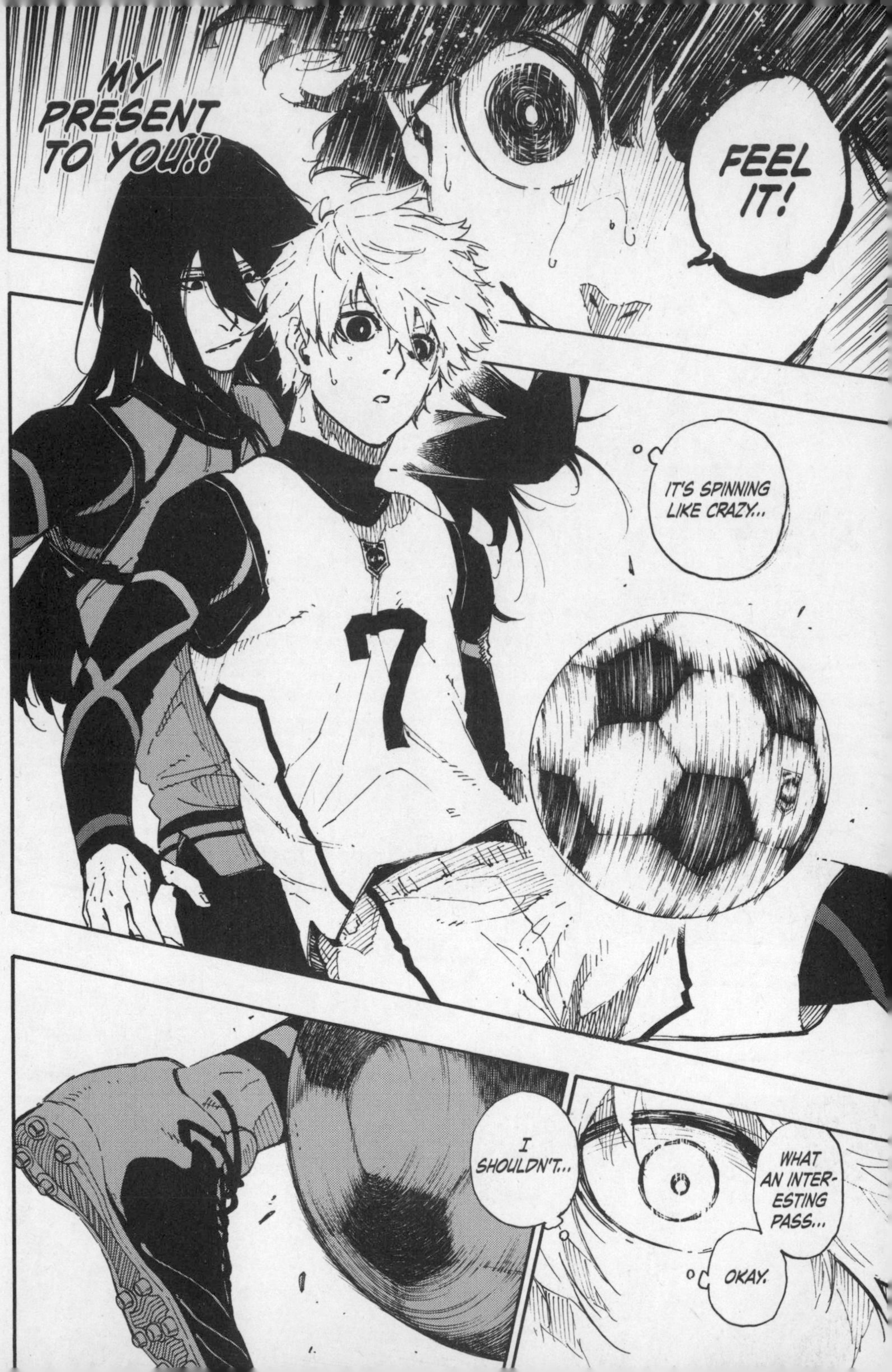

FEEL IT!
MY PRESENT TO YOU!!
IT'S SPINNING LIKE CRAZY...
WHAT AN INTERESTING PASS...
I SHOULDN'T...
OKAY.

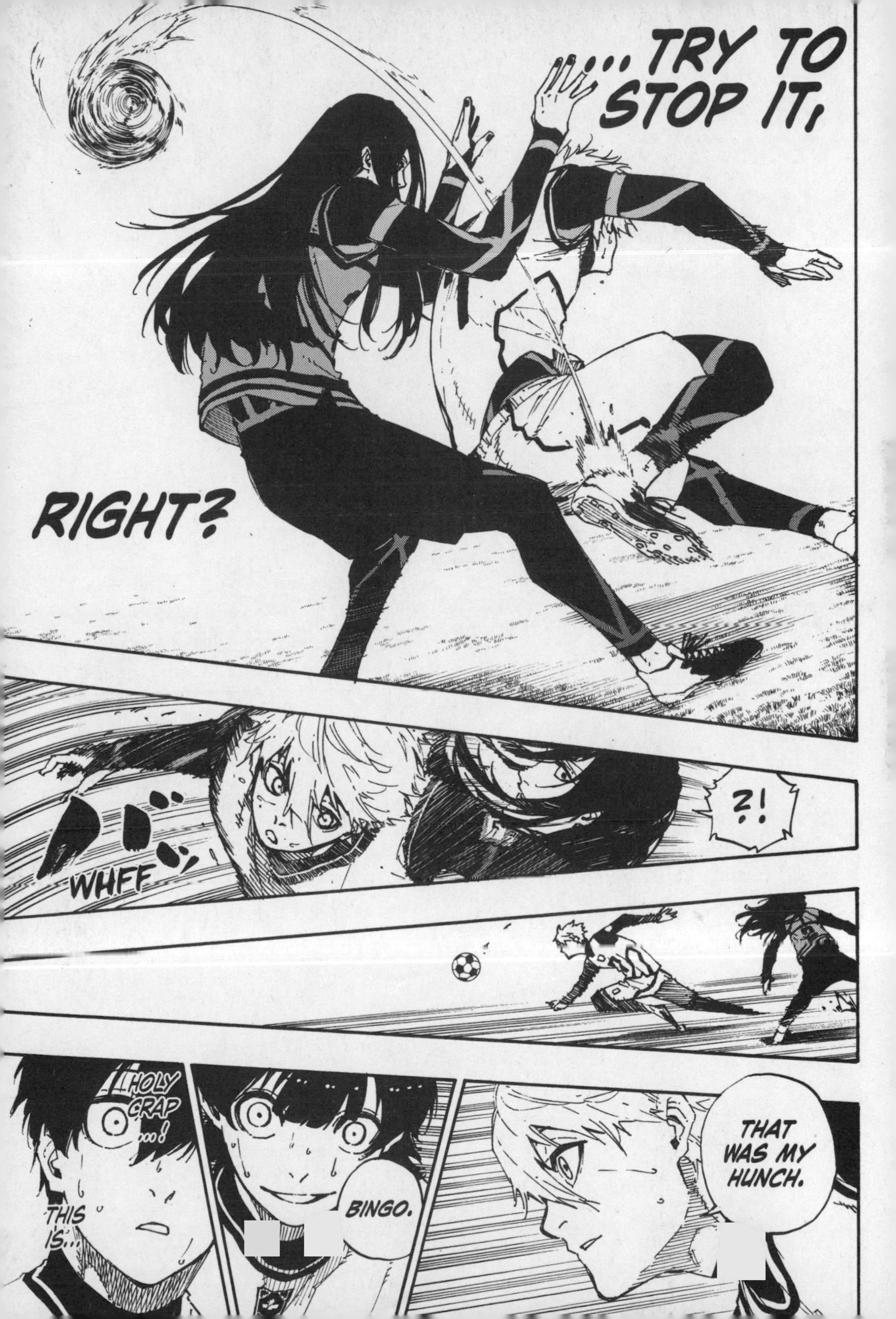
...TRY TO STOP IT,
RIGHT?
?!
WHFF
THAT WAS MY HUNCH.
BINGO.
HOLY CRAP...!
THIS IS...

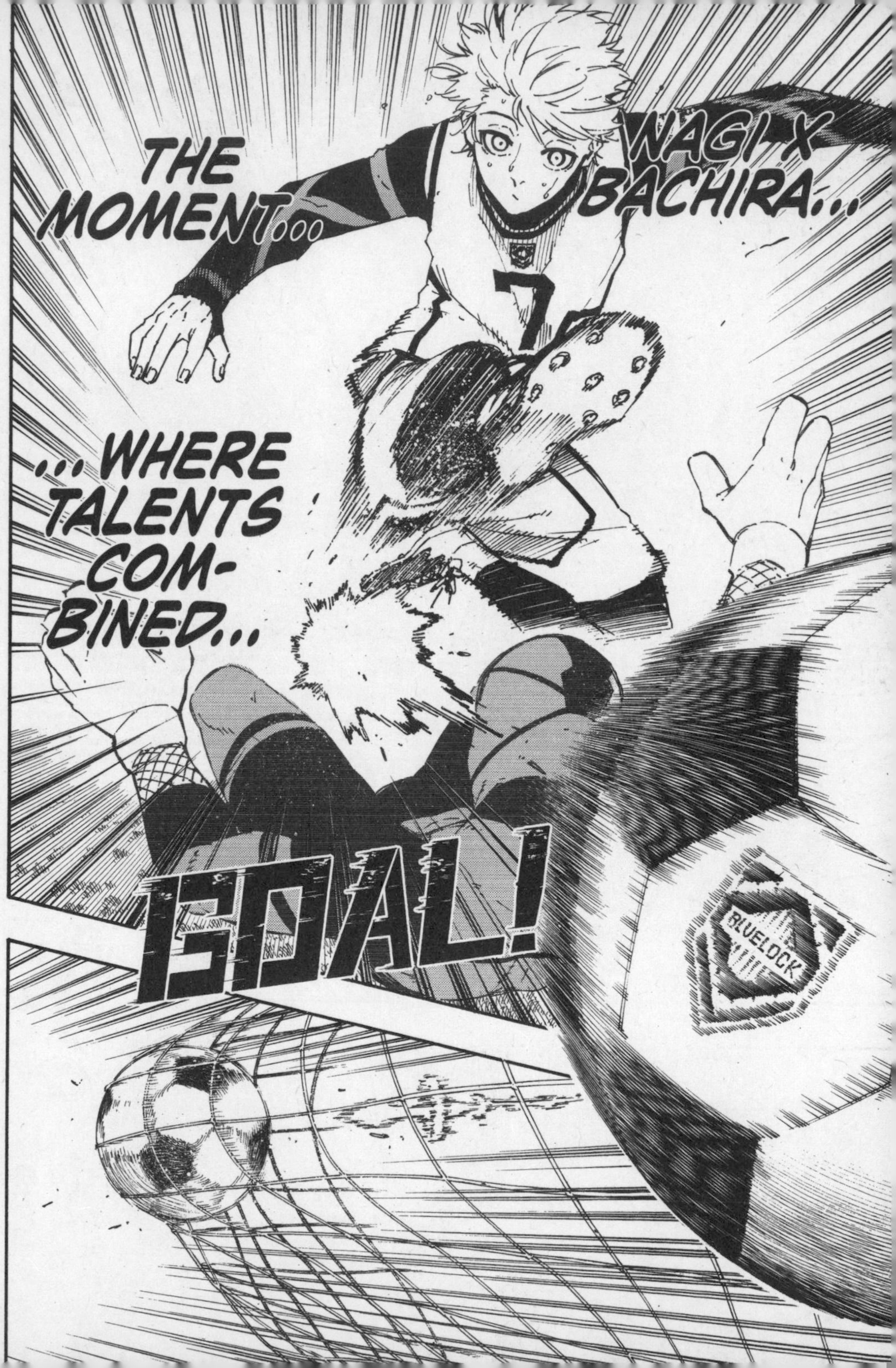
NAGI X BACHIRA...
THE MOMENT...
...WHERE TALENTS COM-BINED...
GOAL!
BLUELOCK

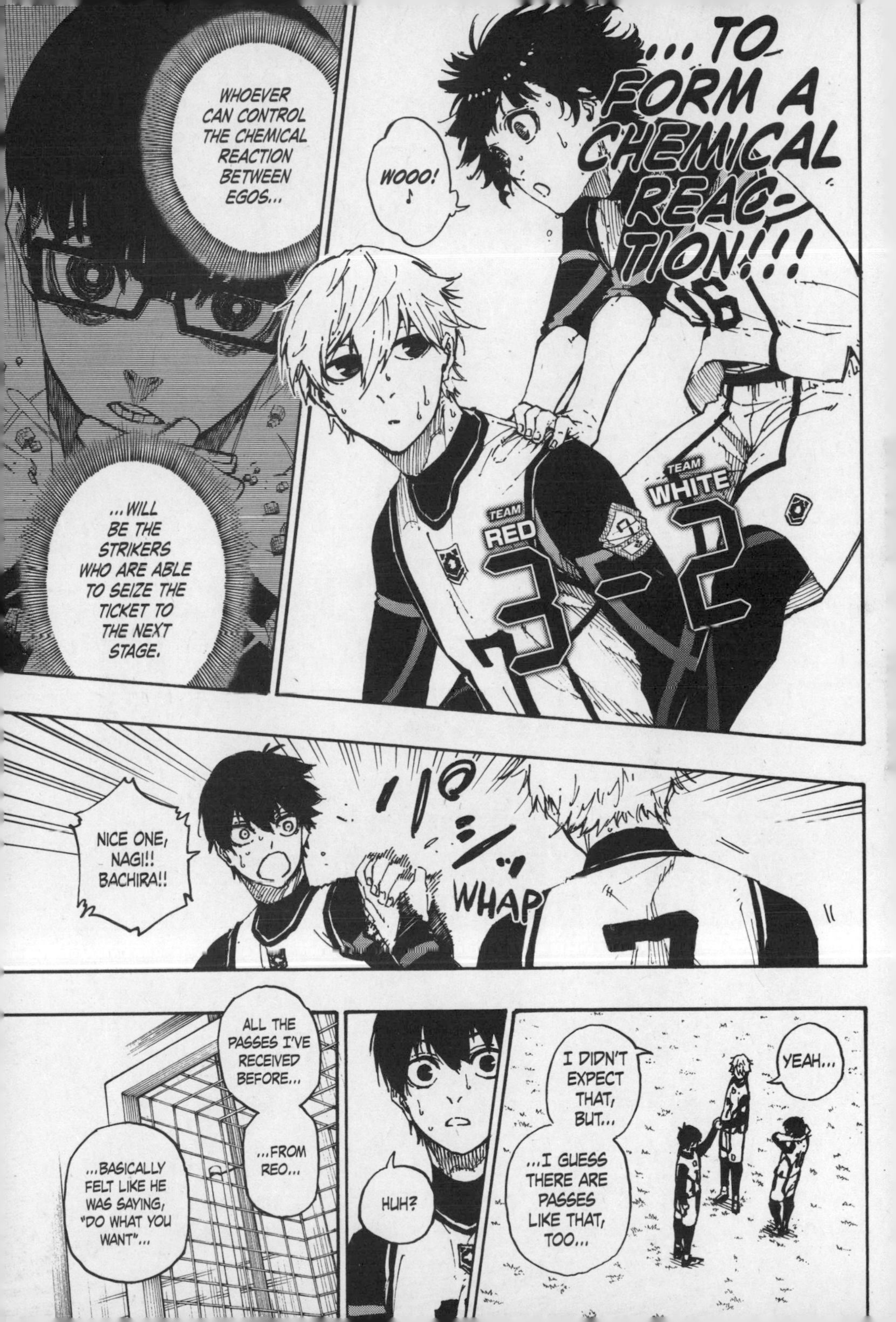
...TO FORM A CHEMICAL REACTION!!!
WOOO! ♪
TEAM WHITE 2
TEAM RED 3
WHOEVER CAN CONTROL THE CHEMICAL REACTION BETWEEN EGOS...
...WILL BE THE STRIKERS WHO ARE ABLE TO SEIZE THE TICKET TO THE NEXT STAGE.
NICE ONE, NAGI!! BACHIRA!!
WHAP
YEAH...
I DIDN'T EXPECT THAT, BUT...
...I GUESS THERE ARE PASSES LIKE THAT, TOO...
HUH?
ALL THE PASSES I'VE RECEIVED BEFORE...
...FROM REO...
...BASICALLY FELT LIKE HE WAS SAYING, "DO WHAT YOU WANT"...

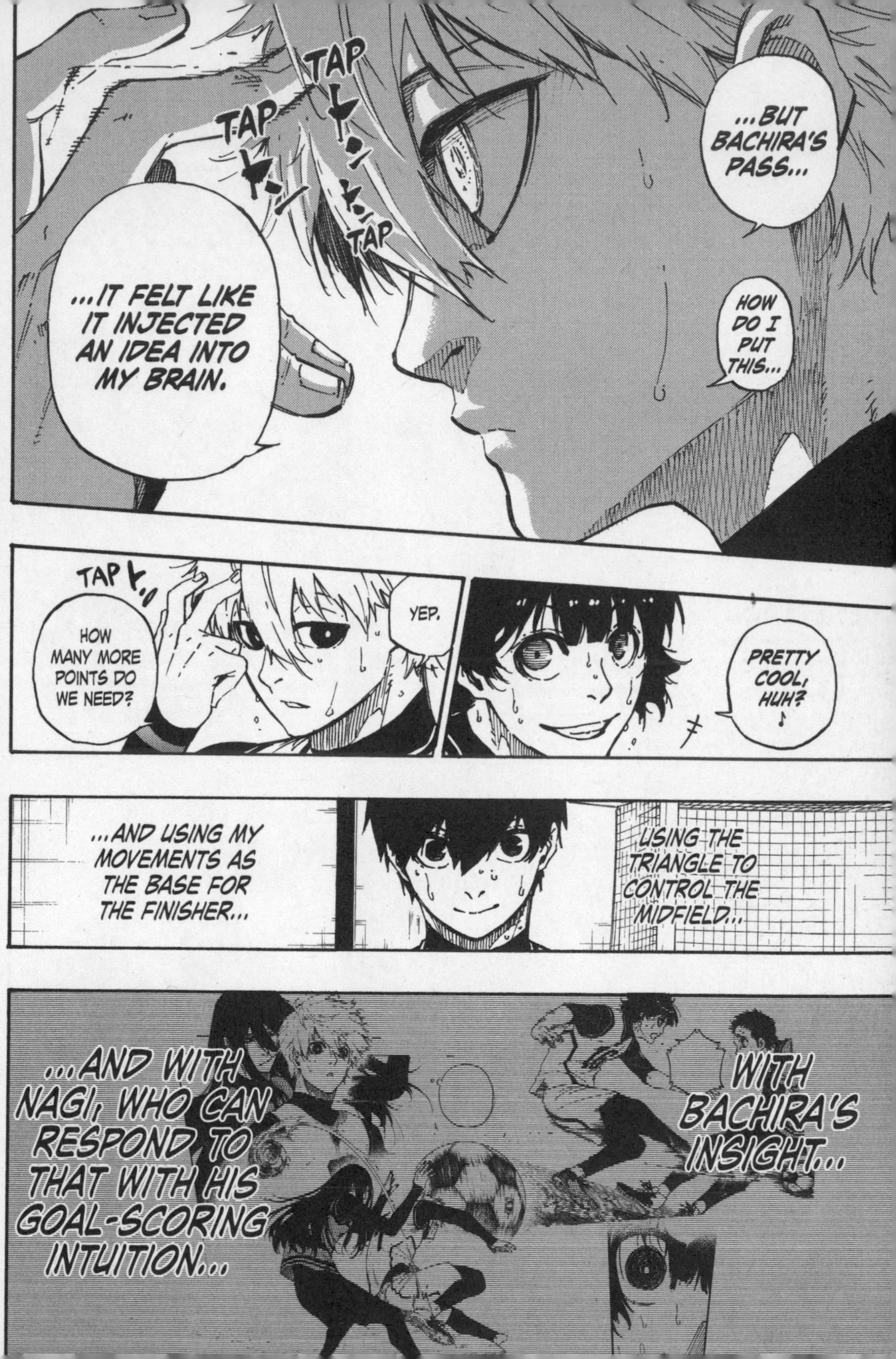
TAP
TAP
TAP
TAP
...BUT BACHIRA'S PASS...
HOW DO I PUT THIS...
...IT FELT LIKE IT INJECTED AN IDEA INTO MY BRAIN.
PRETTY COOL, HUH? ♪
YEP.
TAP
HOW MANY MORE POINTS DO WE NEED?
USING THE TRIANGLE TO CONTROL THE MIDFIELD...
...AND USING MY MOVEMENTS AS THE BASE FOR THE FINISHER...
WITH BACHIRA'S INSIGHT...
...AND WITH NAGI, WHO CAN RESPOND TO THAT WITH HIS GOAL-SCORING INTUITION...

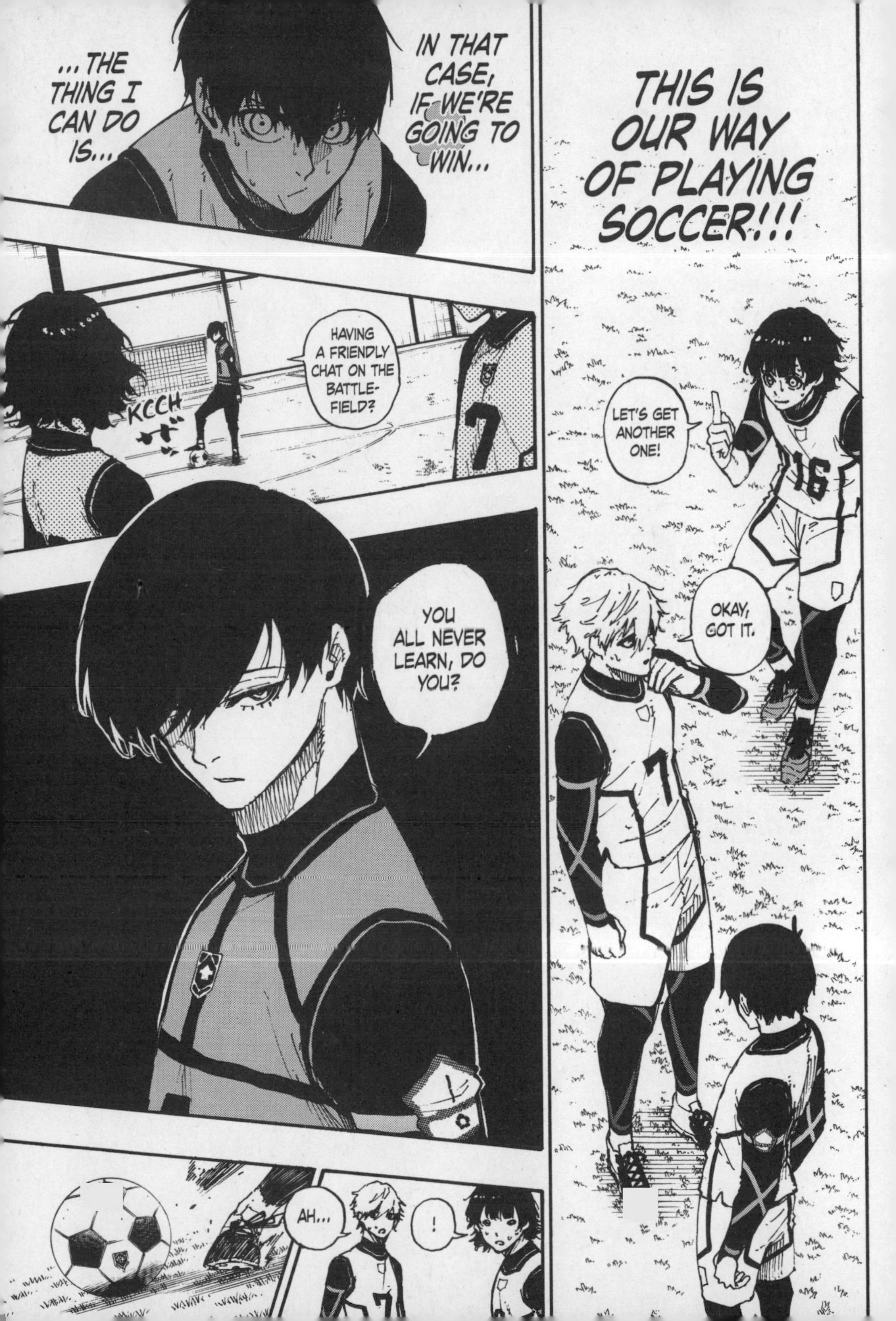
THIS IS OUR WAY OF PLAYING SOCCER!!!
LET'S GET ANOTHER ONE!
OKAY, GOT IT.
IN THAT CASE, IF WE'RE GOING TO WIN...
...THE THING I CAN DO IS...
HAVING A FRIENDLY CHAT ON THE BATTLE-FIELD?
KCCH
YOU ALL NEVER LEARN, DO YOU?
!
AH...

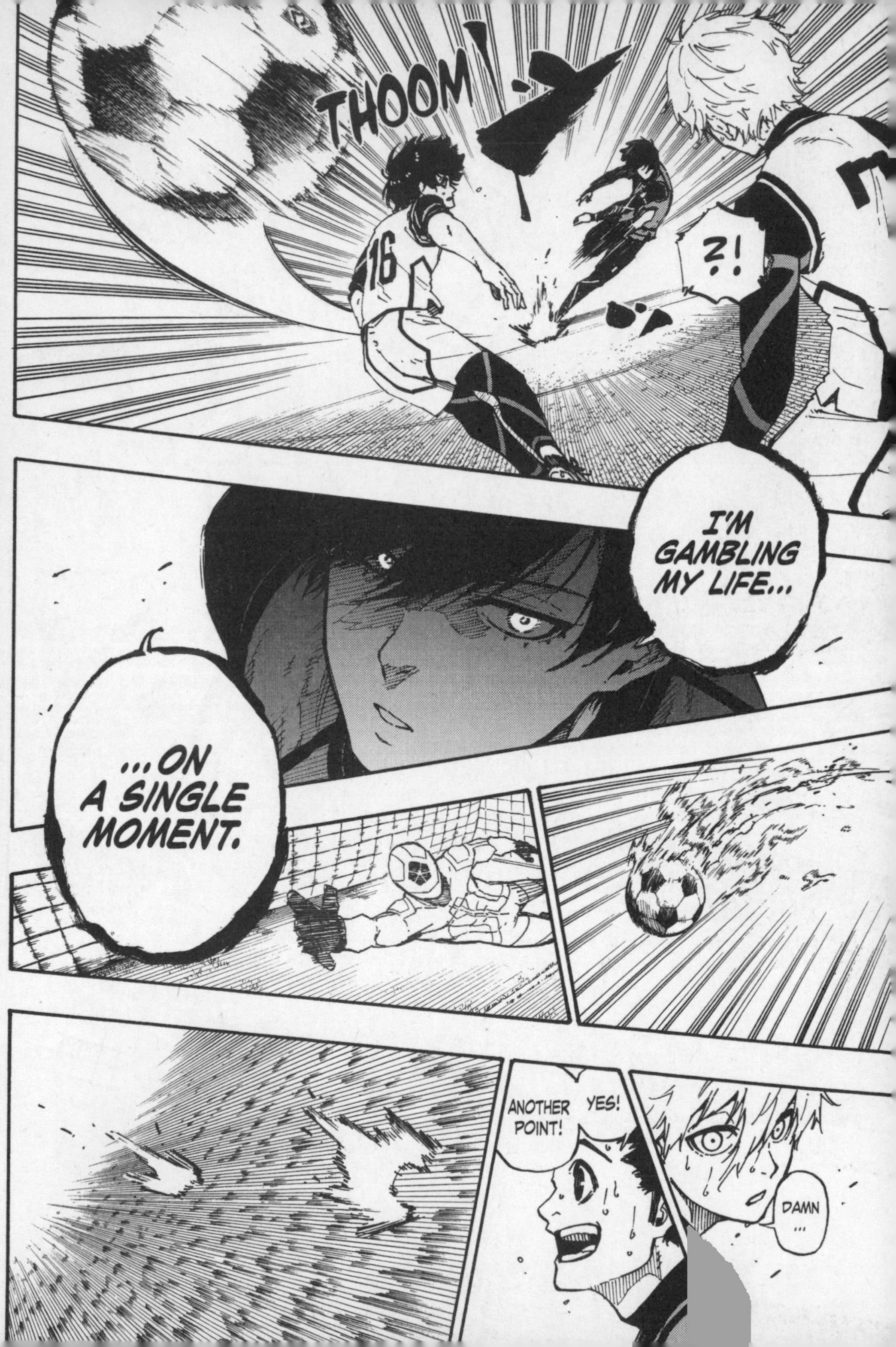
THOOM
?!
I'M GAMBLING MY LIFE...
...ON A SINGLE MOMENT.
YES!
ANOTHER POINT!
DAMN ...

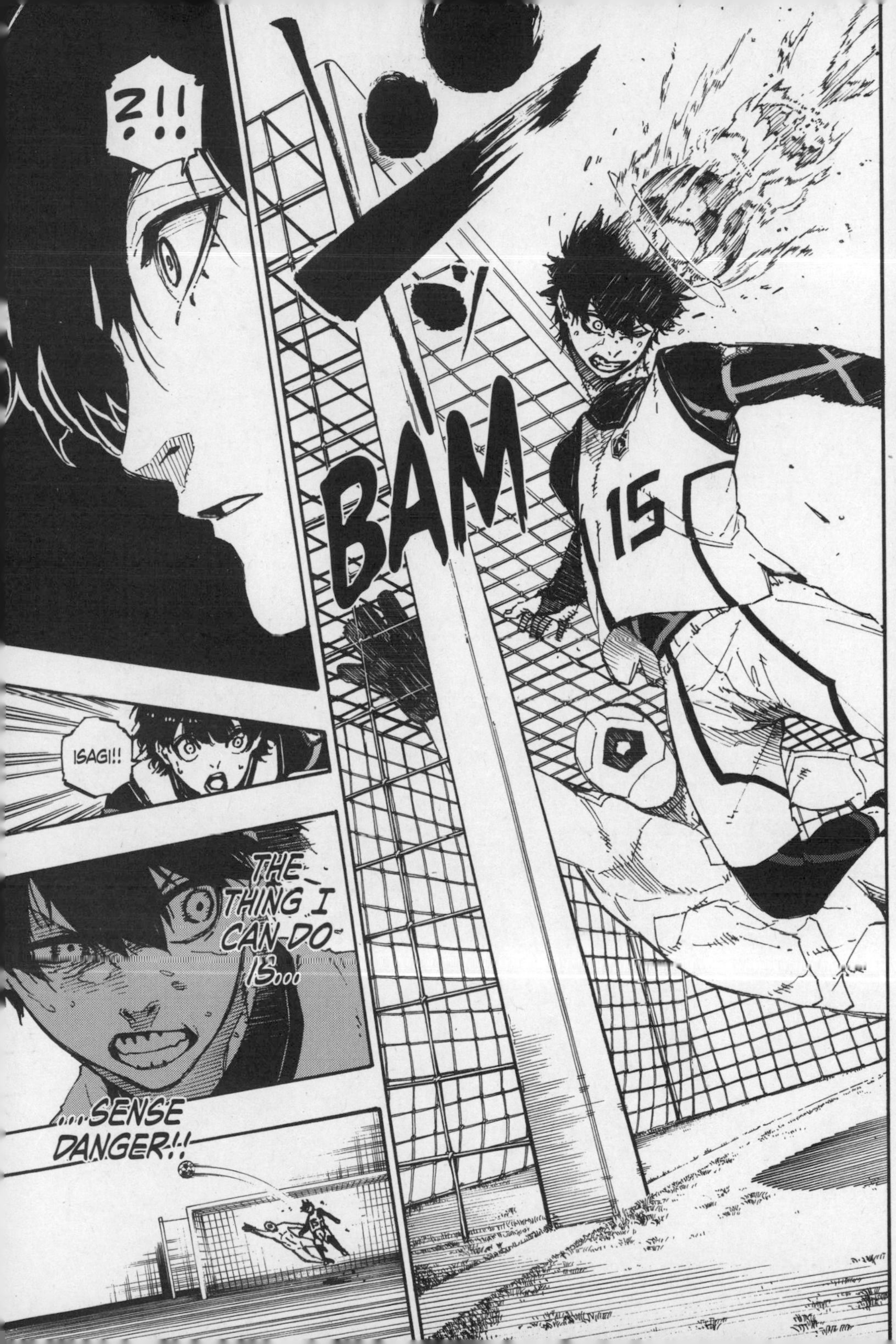
BAM
?!!
ISAGI!!
THE THING I CAN DO IS...
...SENSE DANGER!!

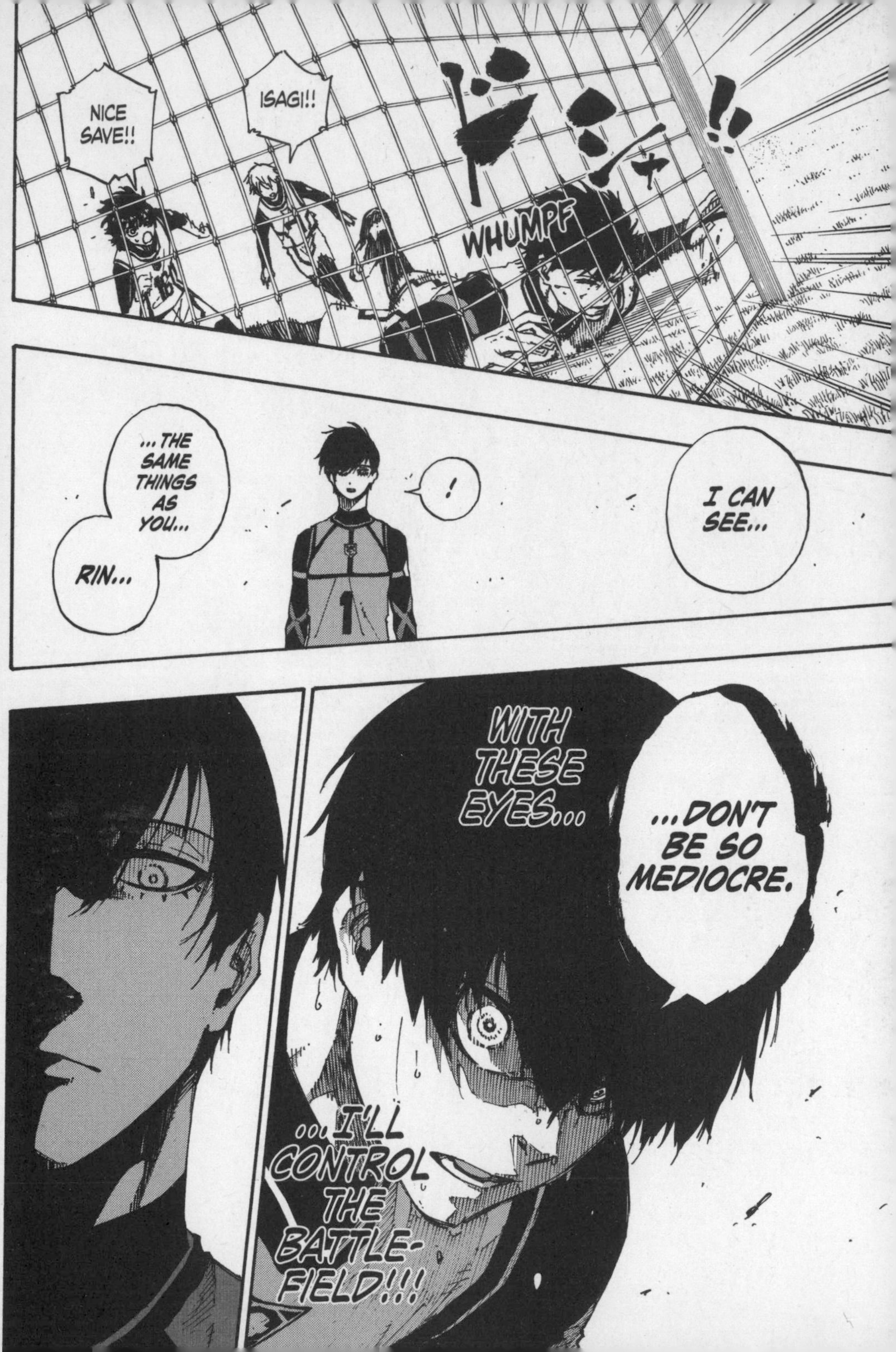
WHUMPF
ISAGI!!
NICE SAVE!!
I CAN SEE...
!
...THE SAME THINGS AS YOU...
RIN...
...DON'T BE SO MEDIOCRE.
WITH THESE EYES...
...I'LL CONTROL THE BATTLE-FIELD!!!

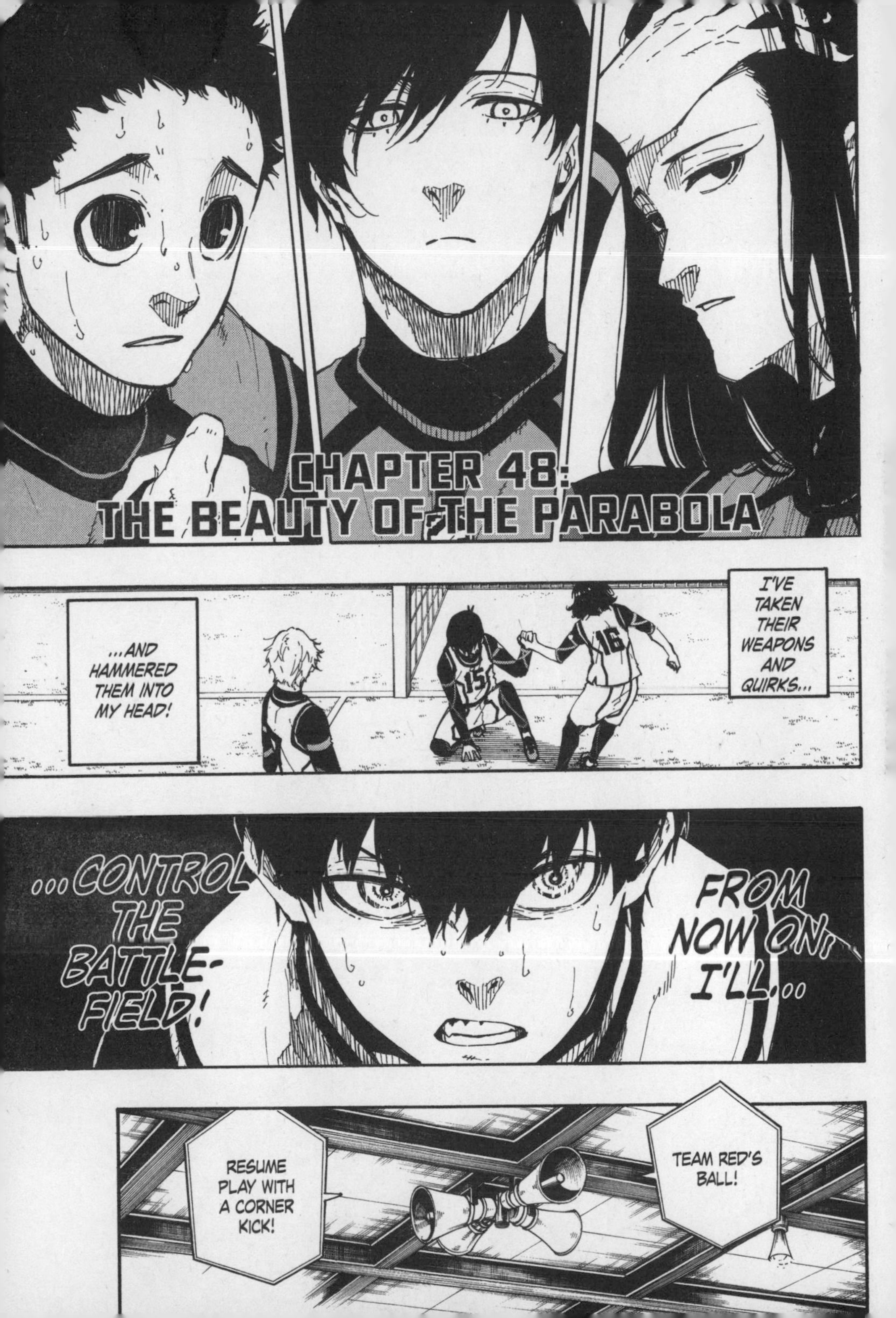
CHAPTER 48:
THE BEAUTY OF THE PARABOLA
I'VE TAKEN THEIR WEAPONS AND QUIRKS...
...AND HAMMERED THEM INTO MY HEAD!
FROM NOW ON, I'LL...
...CONTROL THE BATTLE-FIELD!
TEAM RED'S BALL!
RESUME PLAY WITH A CORNER KICK!

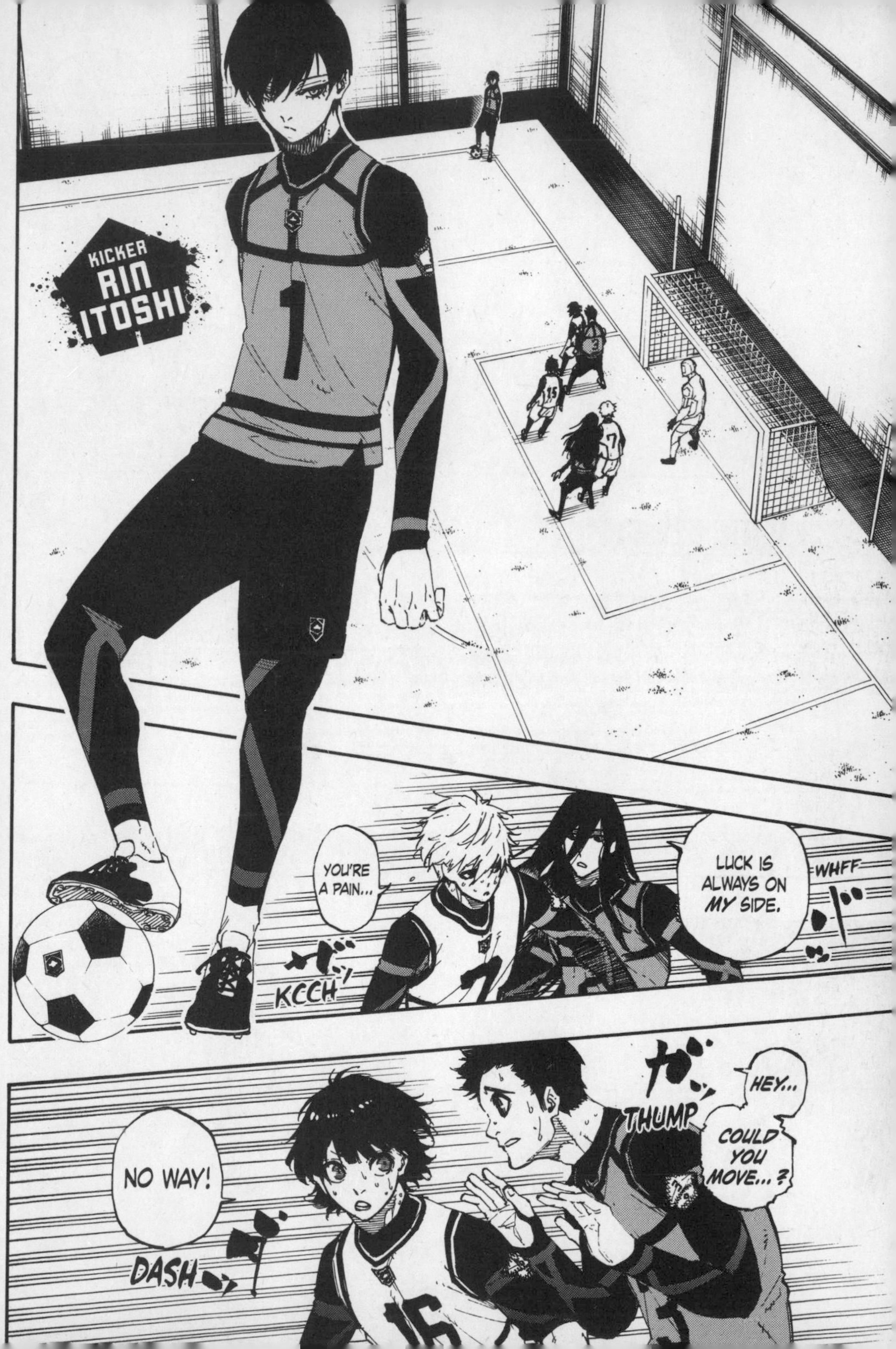
KICKER
RIN ITOSHI
WHFF
LUCK IS ALWAYS ON MY SIDE.
YOU'RE A PAIN...
KCCH
HEY...
COULD YOU MOVE...?
THUMP
NO WAY!
DASH

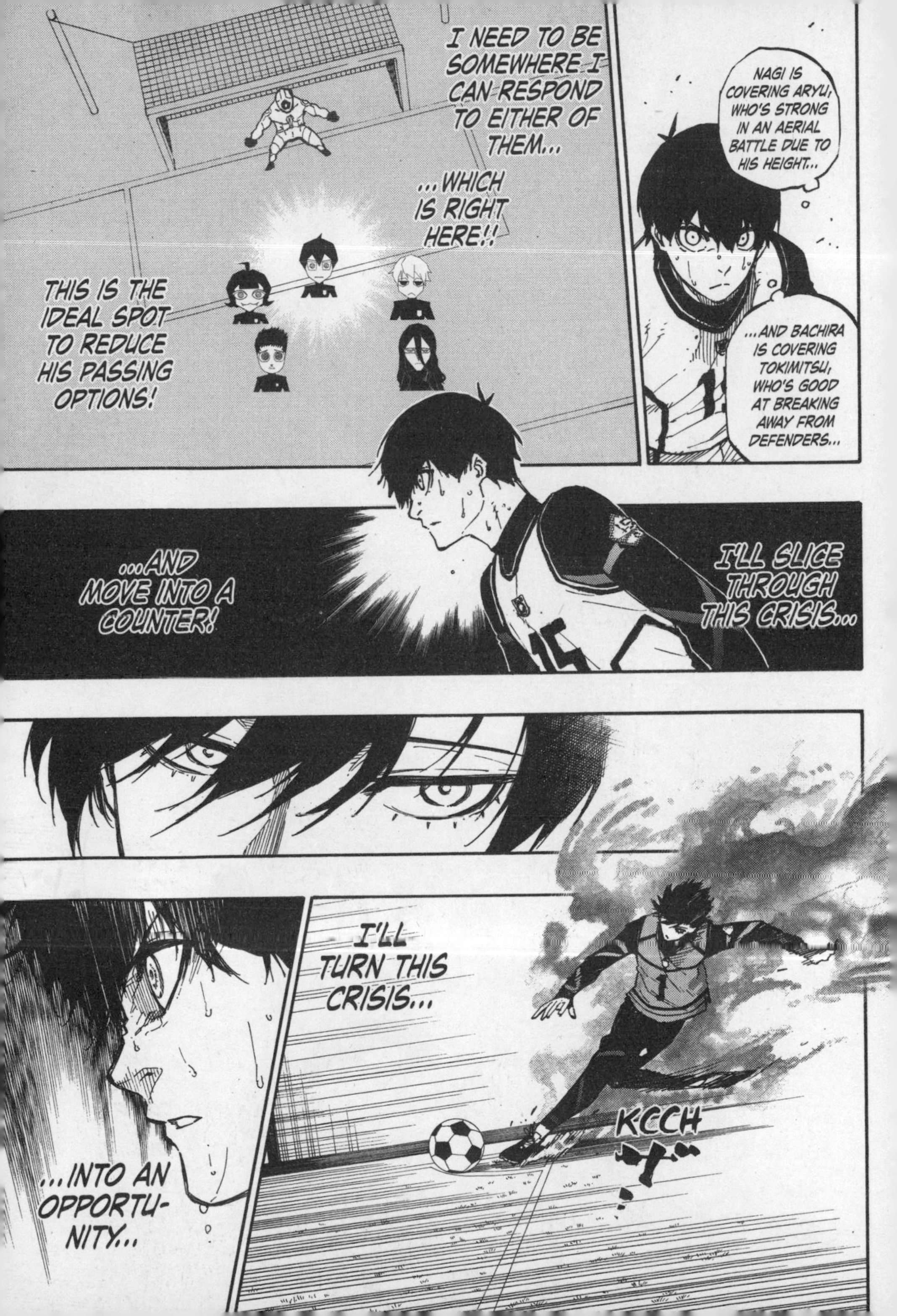
NAGI IS COVERING ARYU, WHO'S STRONG IN AN AERIAL BATTLE DUE TO HIS HEIGHT...
...AND BACHIRA IS COVERING TOKIMITSU, WHO'S GOOD AT BREAKING AWAY FROM DEFENDERS...
I NEED TO BE SOMEWHERE I CAN RESPOND TO EITHER OF THEM...
...WHICH IS RIGHT HERE!!
THIS IS THE IDEAL SPOT TO REDUCE HIS PASSING OPTIONS!
I'LL SLICE THROUGH THIS CRISIS...
...AND MOVE INTO A COUNTER!
I'LL TURN THIS CRISIS...
KCCH
...INTO AN OPPORTU-NITY...

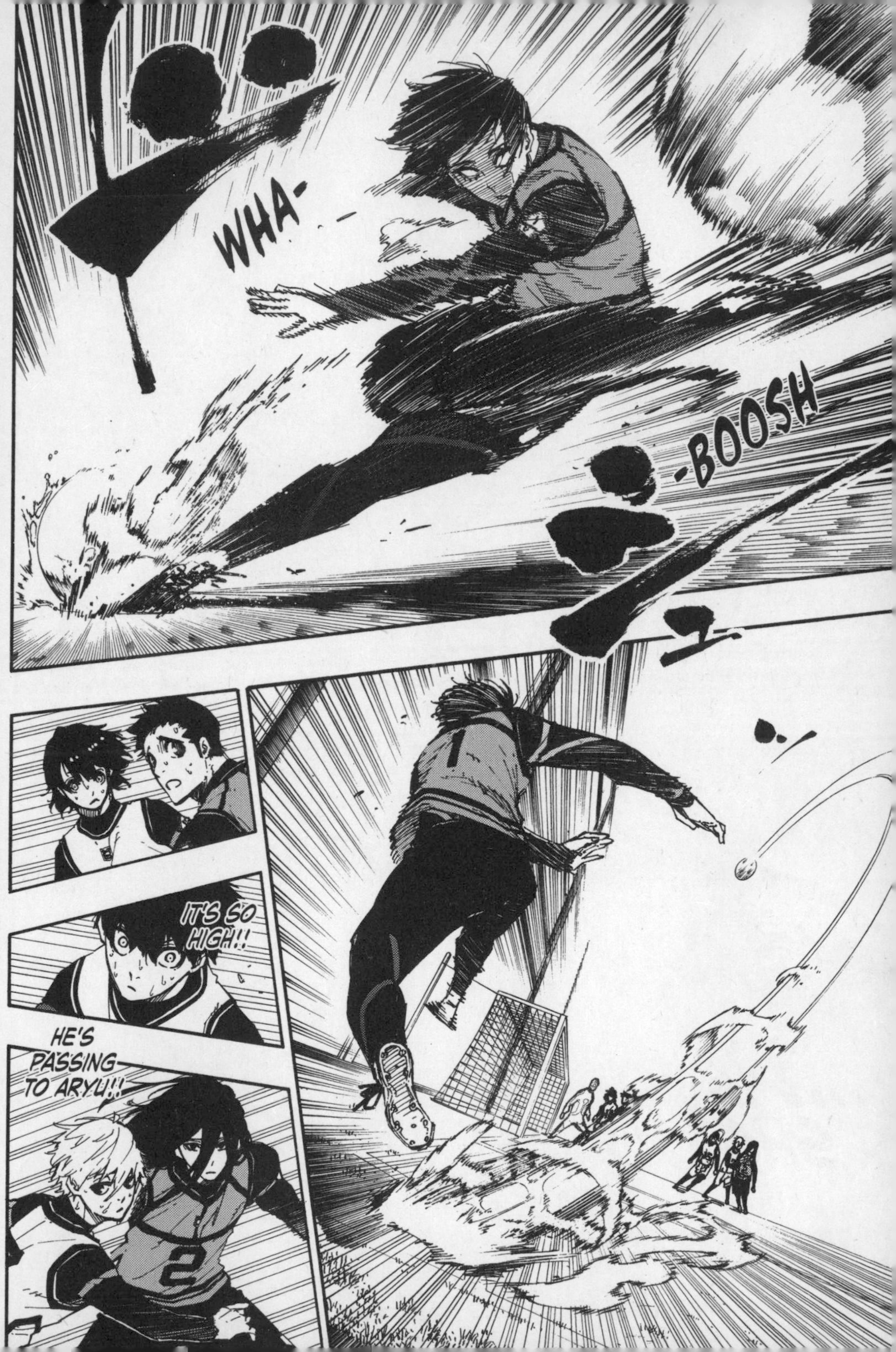
WHA-
-BOOSH
IT'S SO HIGH!!
HE'S PASSING TO ARYU!!

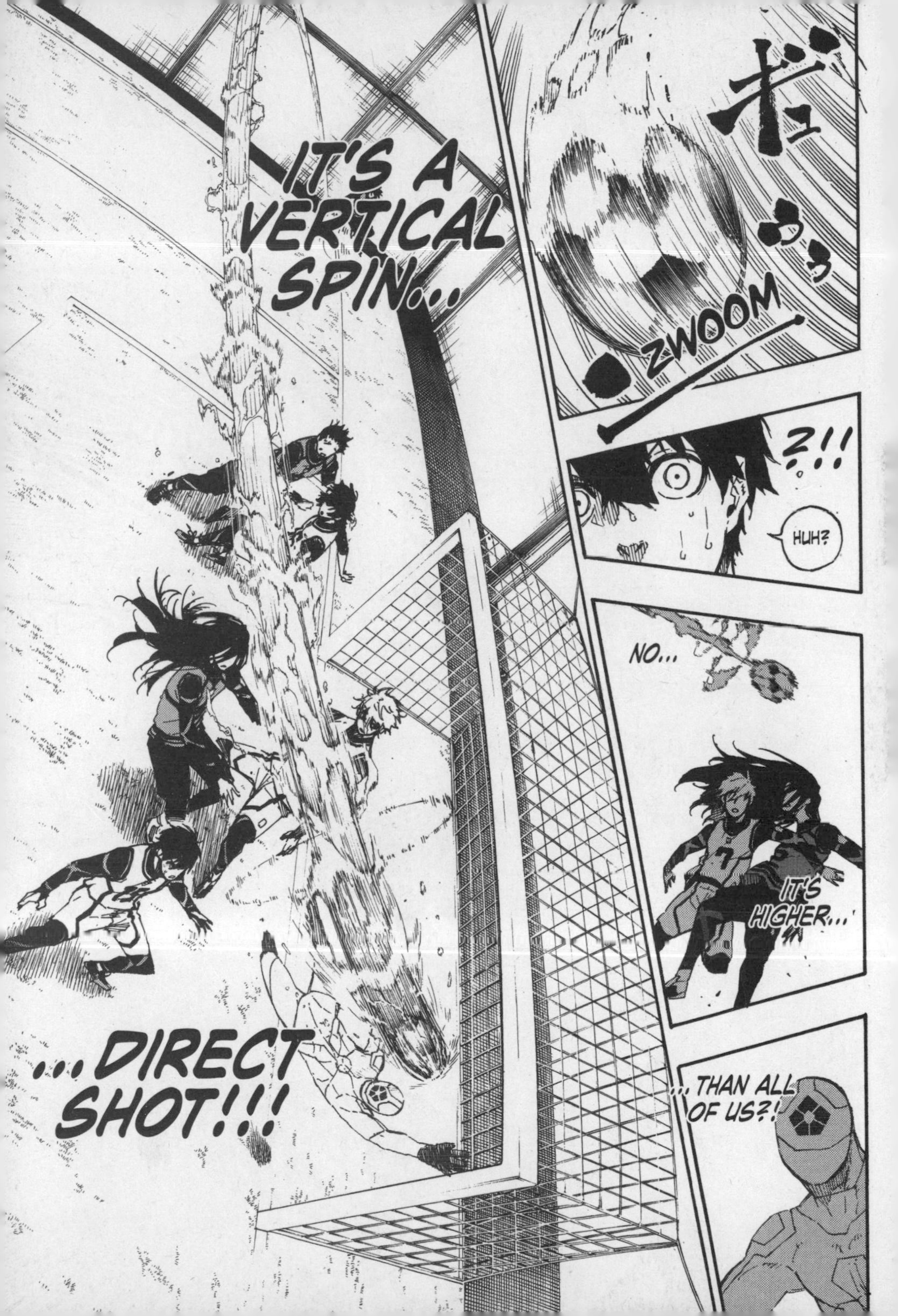
ZWOOM
?!!
HUH?
NO...
IT'S HIGHER...
...THAN ALL OF US?!
IT'S A VERTICAL SPIN...
...DIRECT SHOT!!!

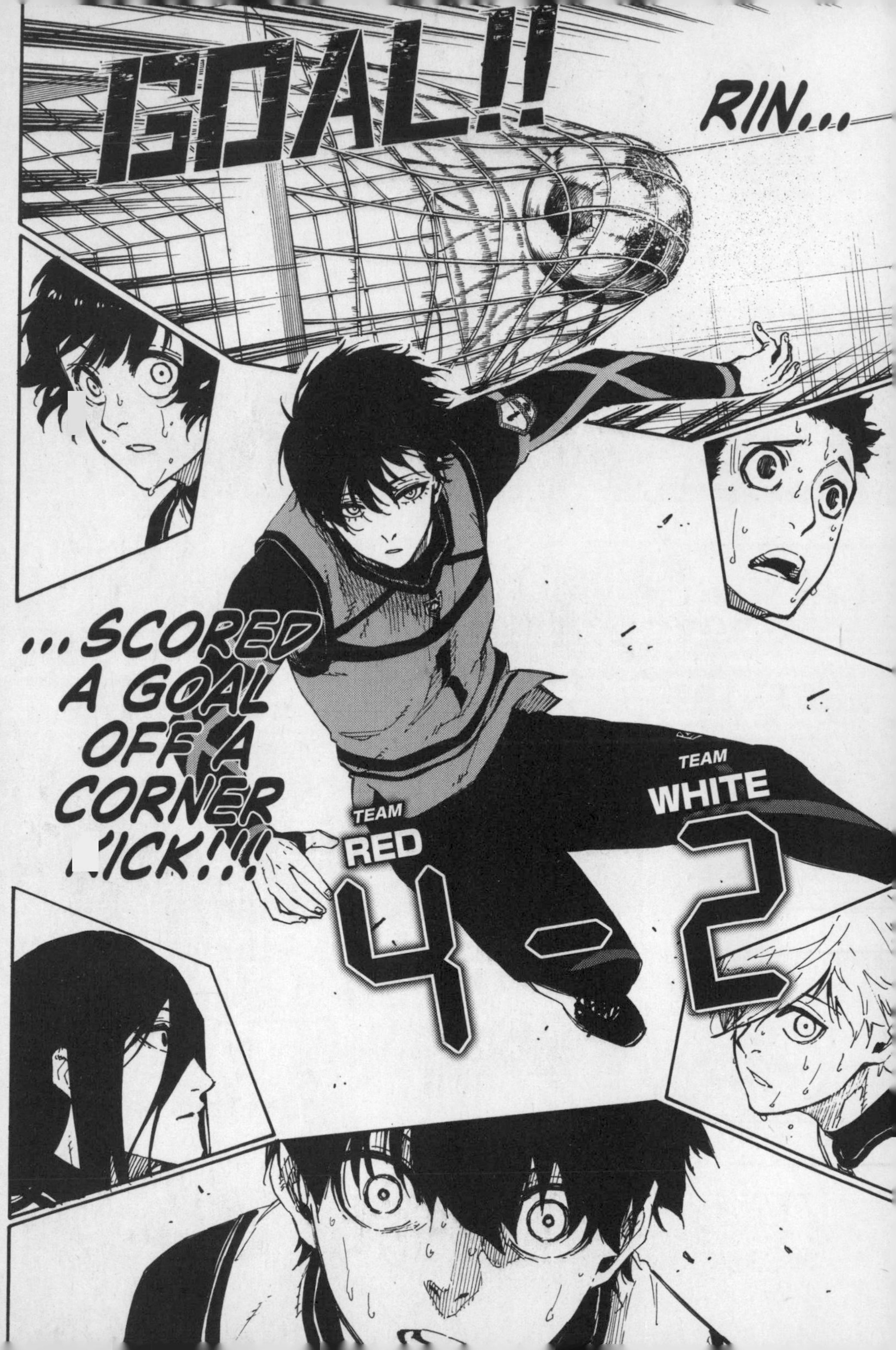
GOAL!!
RIN...
...SCORED A GOAL OFF A CORNER KICK!!!
TEAM RED 4 - 2 TEAM WHITE

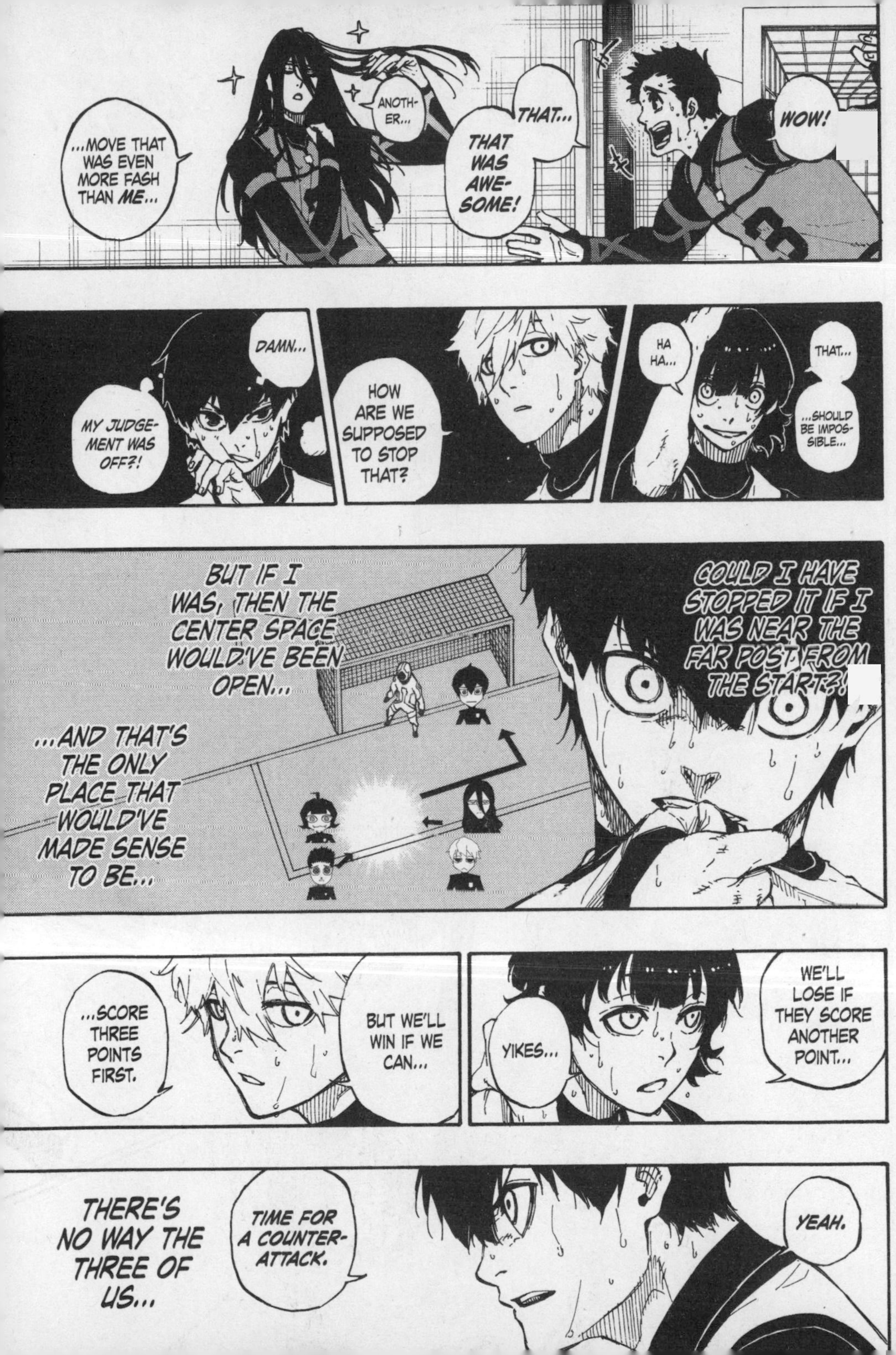
WOW!
THAT...
THAT WAS AWESOME!
ANOTHER...
...MOVE THAT WAS EVEN MORE FASH THAN ME...
THAT...
...SHOULD BE IMPOSSIBLE...
HA HA...
HOW ARE WE SUPPOSED TO STOP THAT?
DAMN...
MY JUDGEMENT WAS OFF?!
COULD I HAVE STOPPED IT IF I WAS NEAR THE FAR POST FROM THE START?!
BUT IF I WAS, THEN THE CENTER SPACE WOULD'VE BEEN OPEN...
...AND THAT'S THE ONLY PLACE THAT WOULD'VE MADE SENSE TO BE...
WE'LL LOSE IF THEY SCORE ANOTHER POINT...
YIKES...
BUT WE'LL WIN IF WE CAN...
...SCORE THREE POINTS FIRST.
YEAH.
TIME FOR A COUNTER-ATTACK.
THERE'S NO WAY THE THREE OF US...

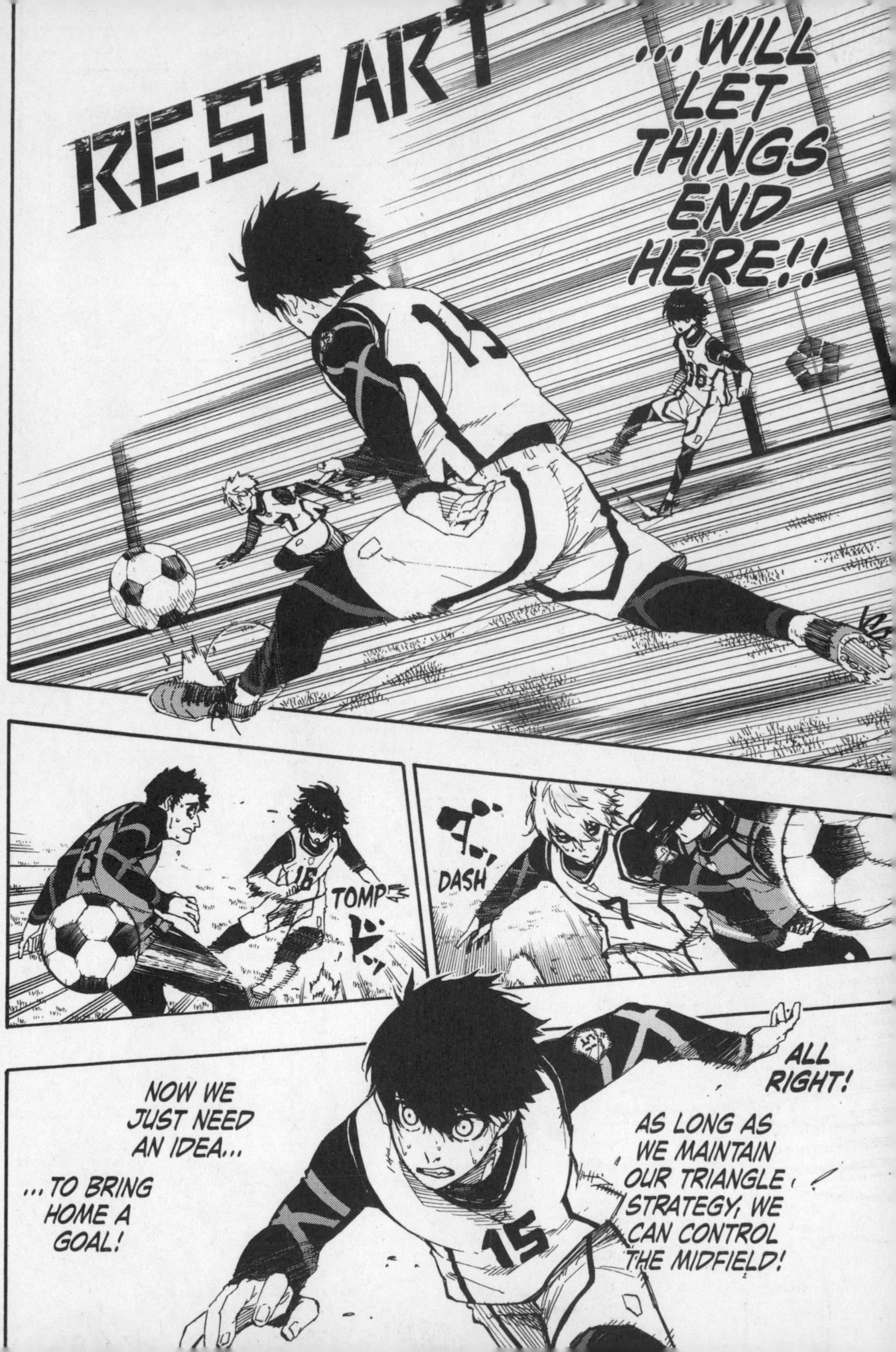
...WILL LET THINGS END HERE!!
RESTART
DASH
TOMP
ALL RIGHT!
AS LONG AS WE MAINTAIN OUR TRIANGLE STRATEGY, WE CAN CONTROL THE MIDFIELD!
NOW WE JUST NEED AN IDEA...
...TO BRING HOME A GOAL!

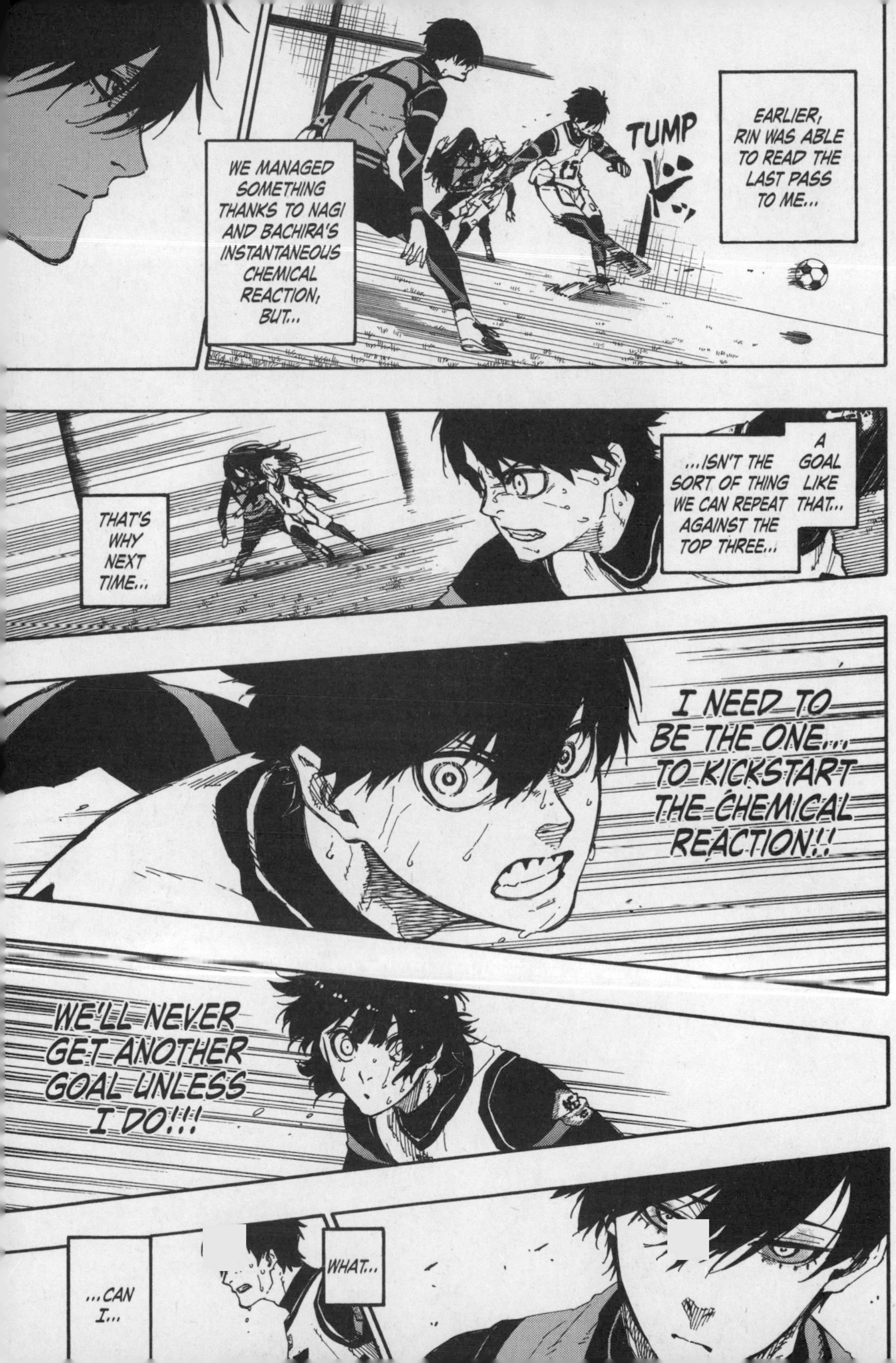
EARLIER, RIN WAS ABLE TO READ THE LAST PASS TO ME...
TUMP
WE MANAGED SOMETHING THANKS TO NAGI AND BACHIRA'S INSTANTANEOUS CHEMICAL REACTION, BUT...
A GOAL LIKE THAT...
...ISN'T THE SORT OF THING WE CAN REPEAT AGAINST THE TOP THREE...
THAT'S WHY NEXT TIME...
I NEED TO BE THE ONE... TO KICKSTART THE CHEMICAL REACTION!!
WE'LL NEVER GET ANOTHER GOAL UNLESS I DO!!!
WHAT...
...CAN I...

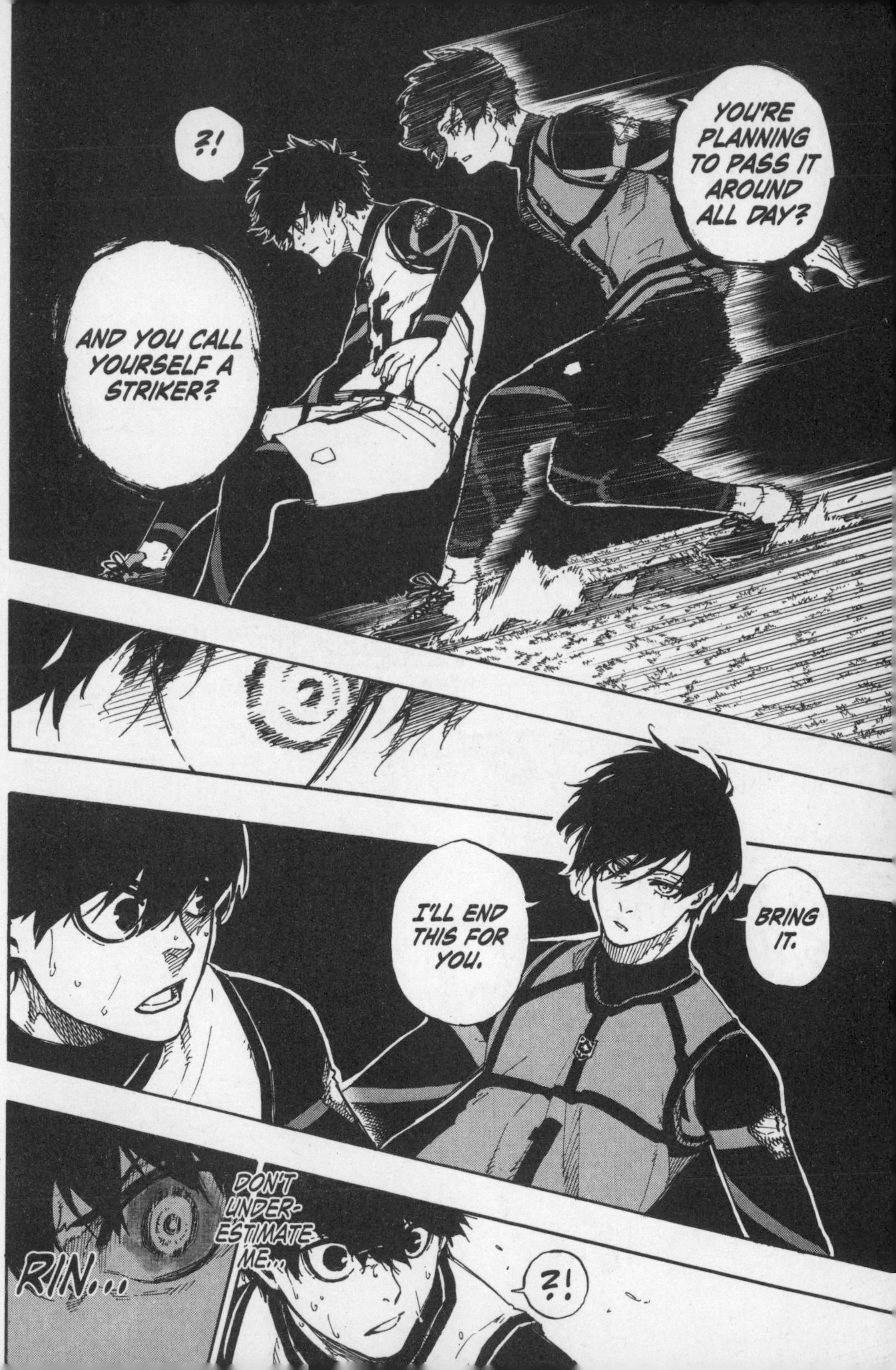
YOU'RE PLANNING TO PASS IT AROUND ALL DAY?
?!
AND YOU CALL YOURSELF A STRIKER?
BRING IT.
I'LL END THIS FOR YOU.
?!
DON'T UNDER-ESTIMATE ME...
RIN...

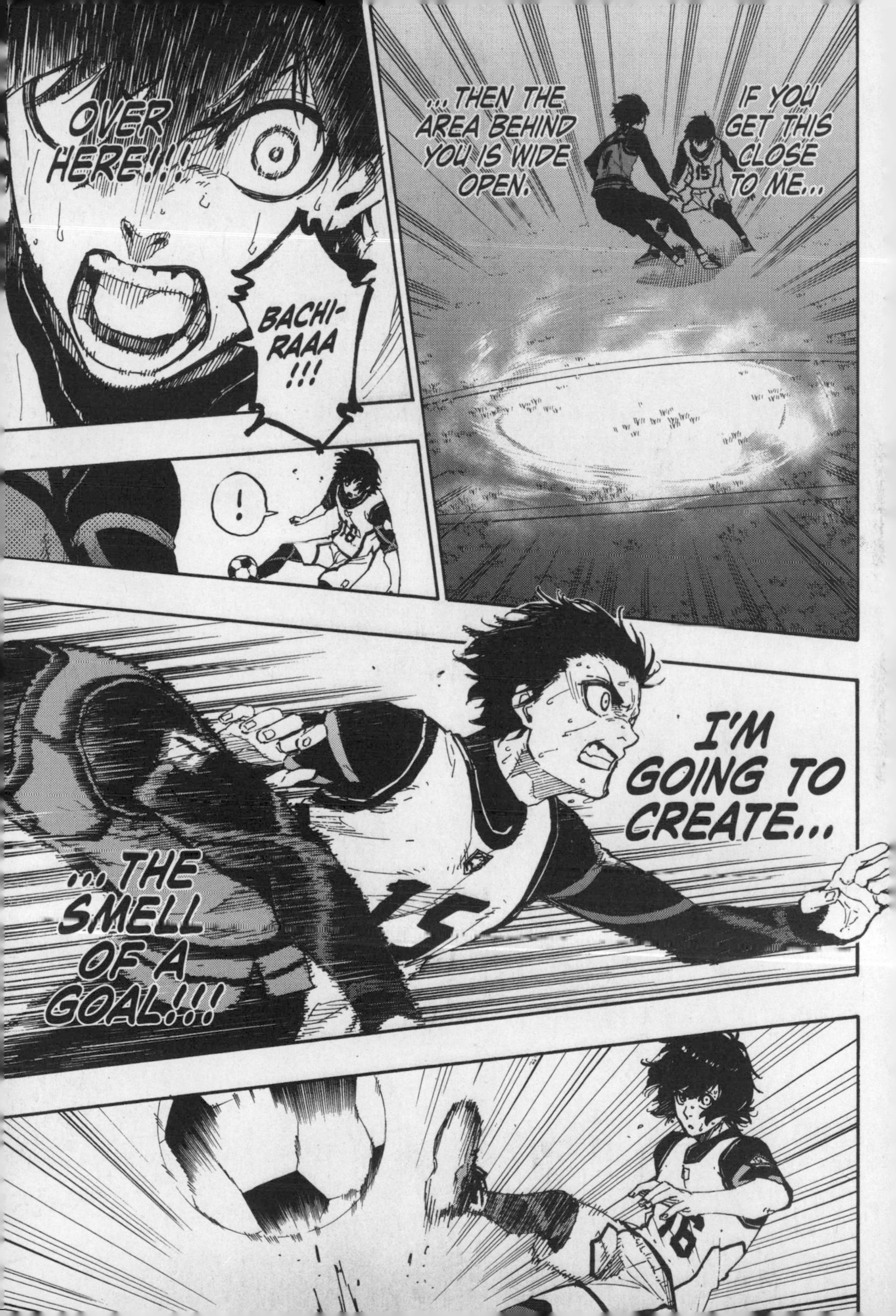
IF YOU GET THIS CLOSE TO ME...
...THEN THE AREA BEHIND YOU IS WIDE OPEN.
OVER HERE!!!
BACHI-RAAA!!!
!
I'M GOING TO CREATE...
...THE SMELL OF A GOAL!!!

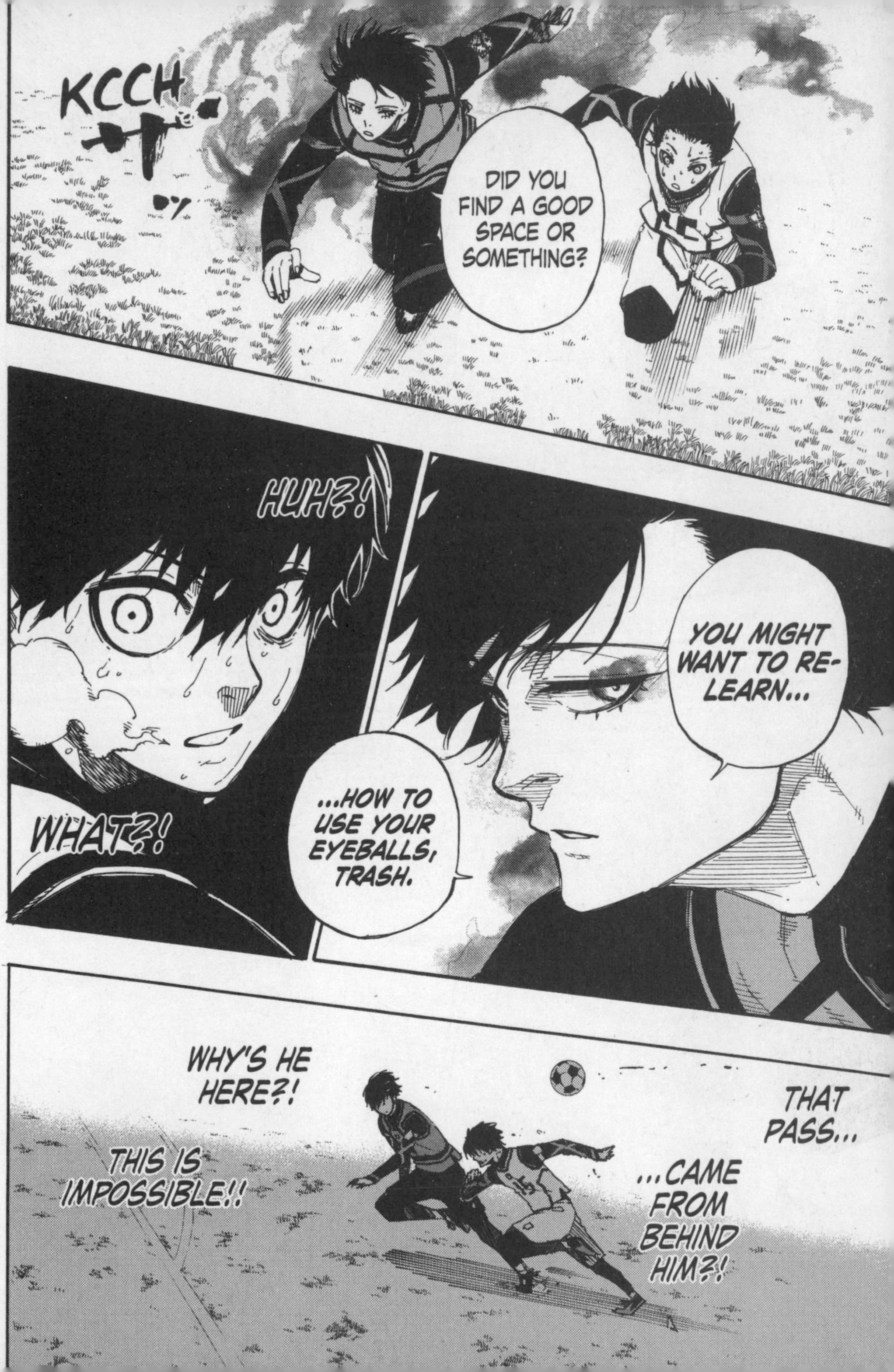
KCCH
DID YOU FIND A GOOD SPACE OR SOMETHING?
YOU MIGHT WANT TO RE-LEARN...
...HOW TO USE YOUR EYEBALLS, TRASH.
HUH?!
WHAT?!
THAT PASS...
...CAME FROM BEHIND HIM?!
WHY'S HE HERE?!
THIS IS IMPOSSIBLE!!

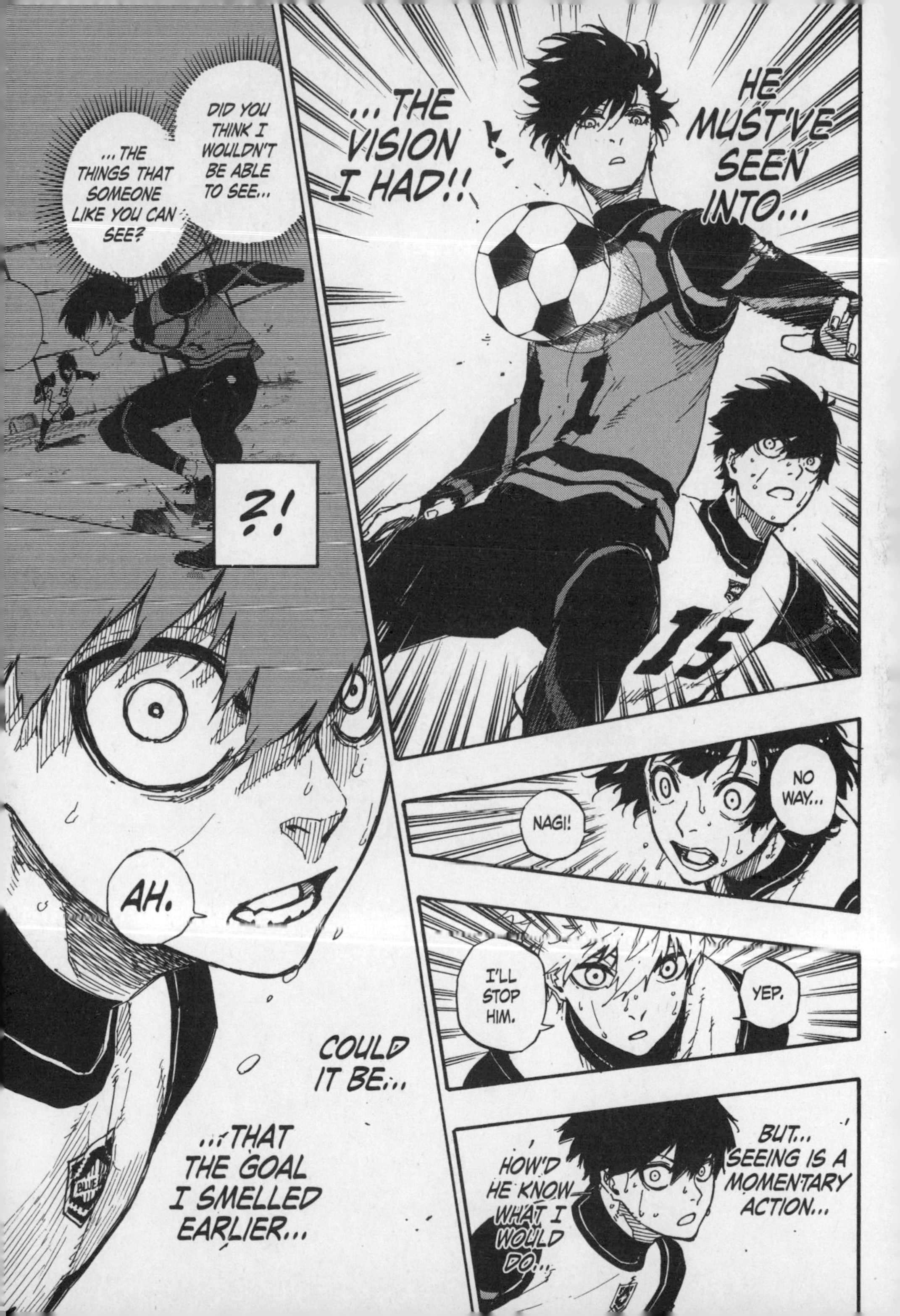
HE MUST'VE SEEN INTO...
...THE VISION I HAD!!
NO WAY...
NAGI!
YEP.
I'LL STOP HIM.
BUT... SEEING IS A MOMENTARY ACTION...
HOW'D HE KNOW WHAT I WOULD DO...
DID YOU THINK I WOULDN'T BE ABLE TO SEE...
...THE THINGS THAT SOMEONE LIKE YOU CAN SEE?
?!
AH.
COULD IT BE...
...THAT THE GOAL I SMELLED EARLIER...

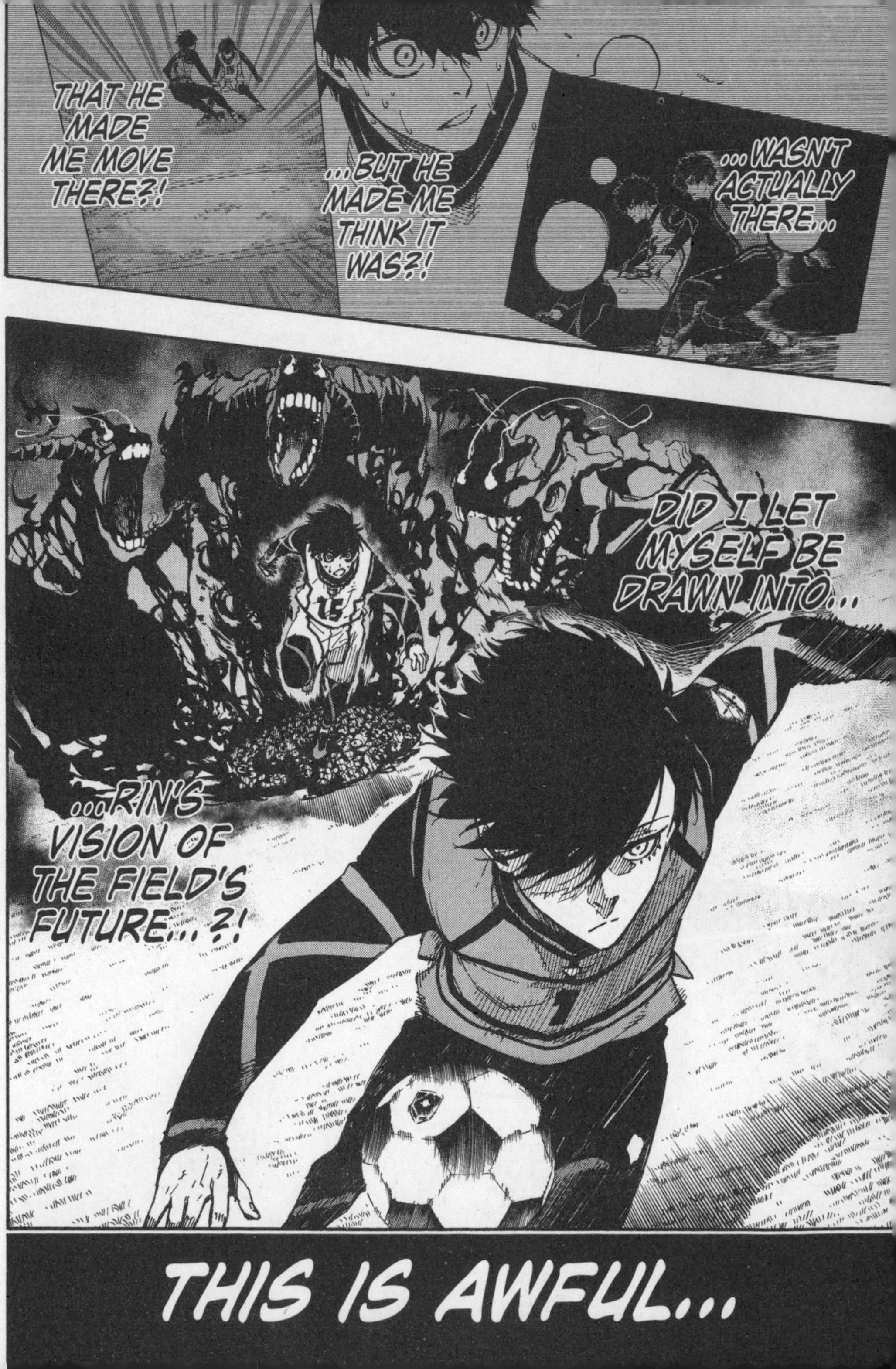
...WASN'T ACTUALLY THERE...
...BUT HE MADE ME THINK IT WAS?!
THAT HE MADE ME MOVE THERE?!
DID I LET MYSELF BE DRAWN INTO...
...RIN'S VISION OF THE FIELD'S FUTURE...?!
THIS IS AWFUL...

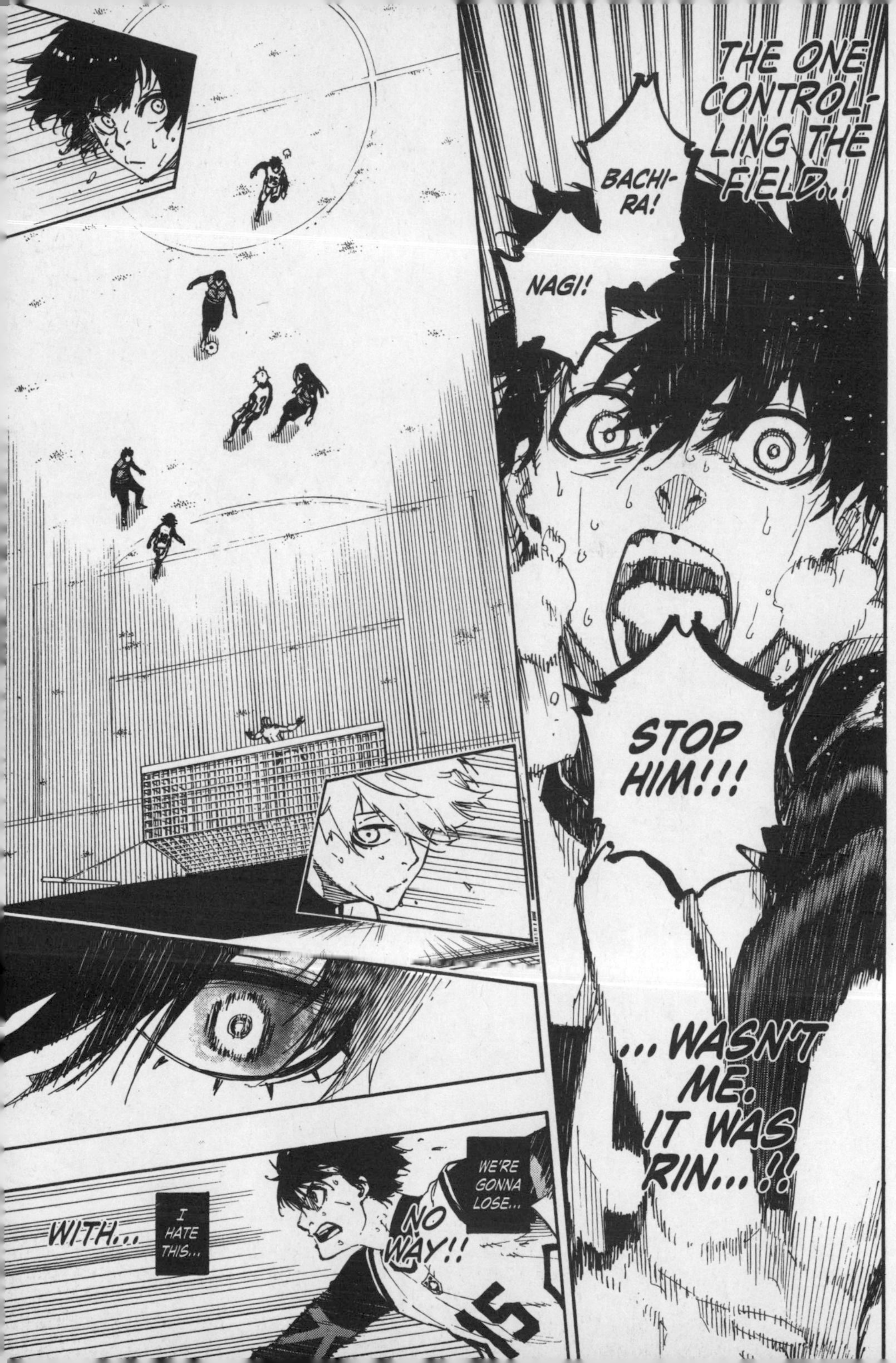
THE ONE CONTROL-LING THE FIELD..
BACHI-RA!
NAGI!
STOP HIM!!!
...WASN'T ME. IT WAS RIN...!!
WE'RE GONNA LOSE...
NO WAY!!
I HATE THIS...
WITH...

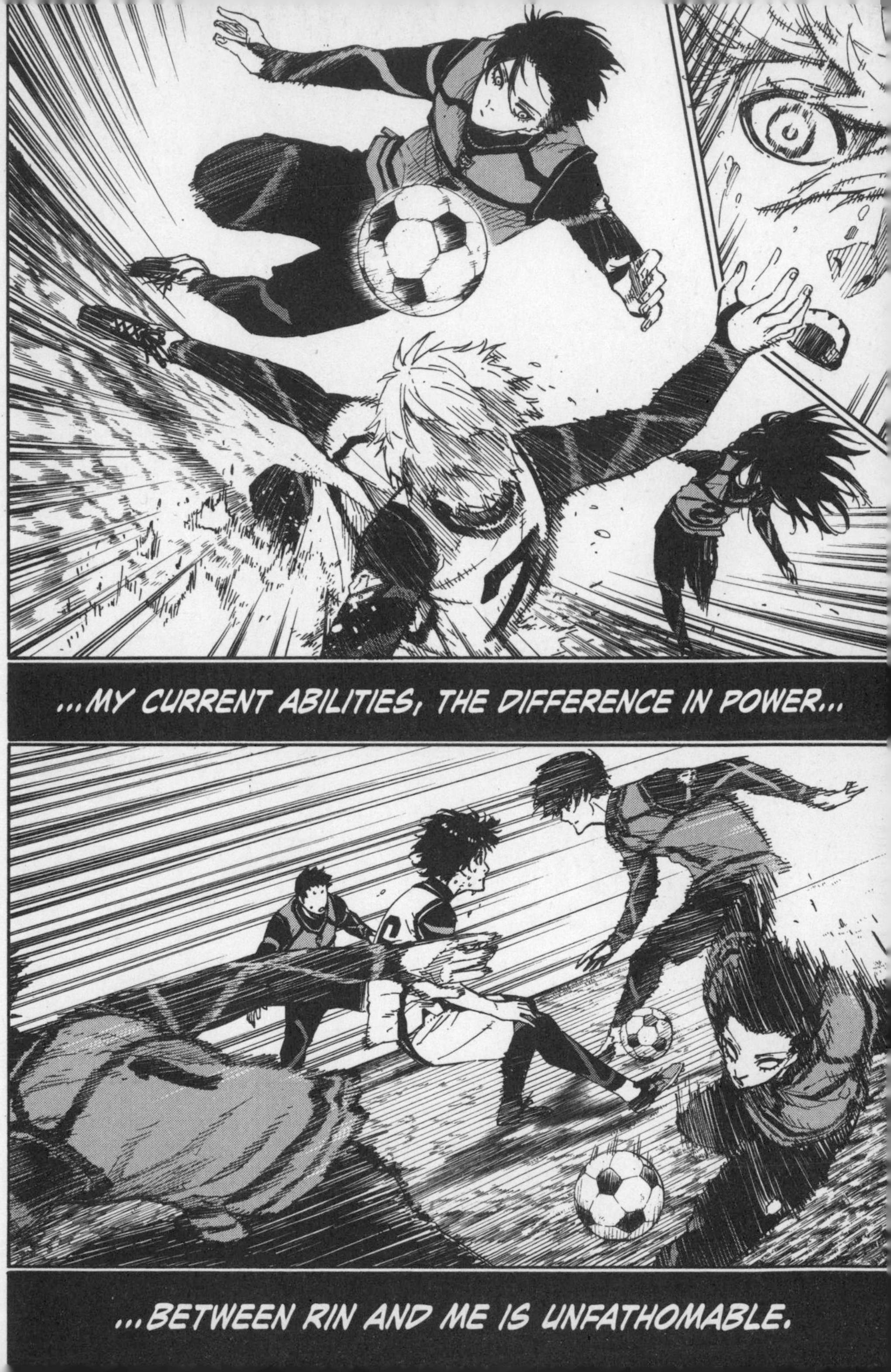
...MY CURRENT ABILITIES, THE DIFFERENCE IN POWER...
...BETWEEN RIN AND ME IS UNFATHOMABLE.

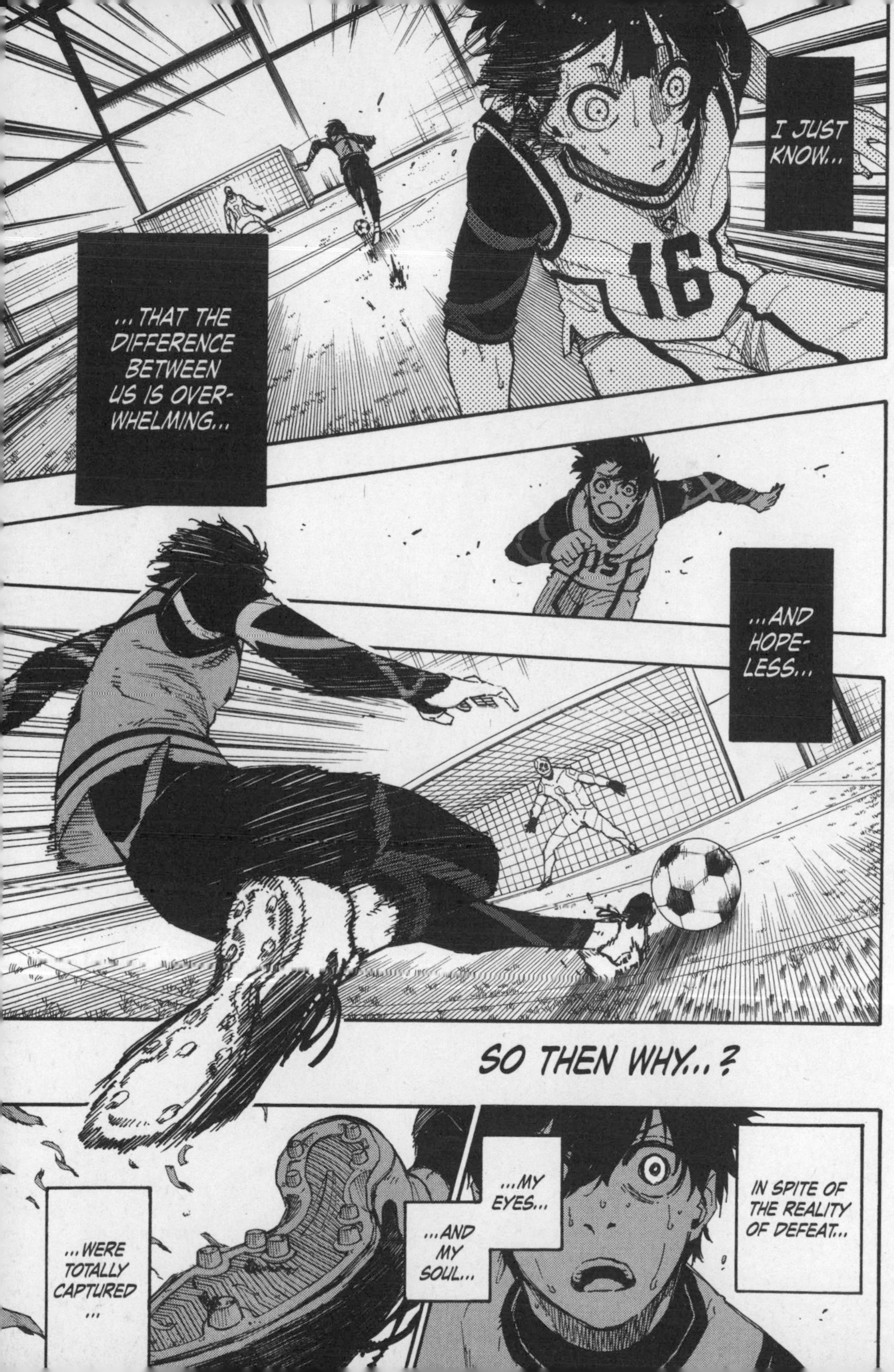
I JUST KNOW...
...THAT THE DIFFERENCE BETWEEN US IS OVER-WHELMING...
...AND HOPE-LESS...
SO THEN WHY...?
IN SPITE OF THE REALITY OF DEFEAT...
...MY EYES...
...AND MY SOUL...
...WERE TOTALLY CAPTURED ...

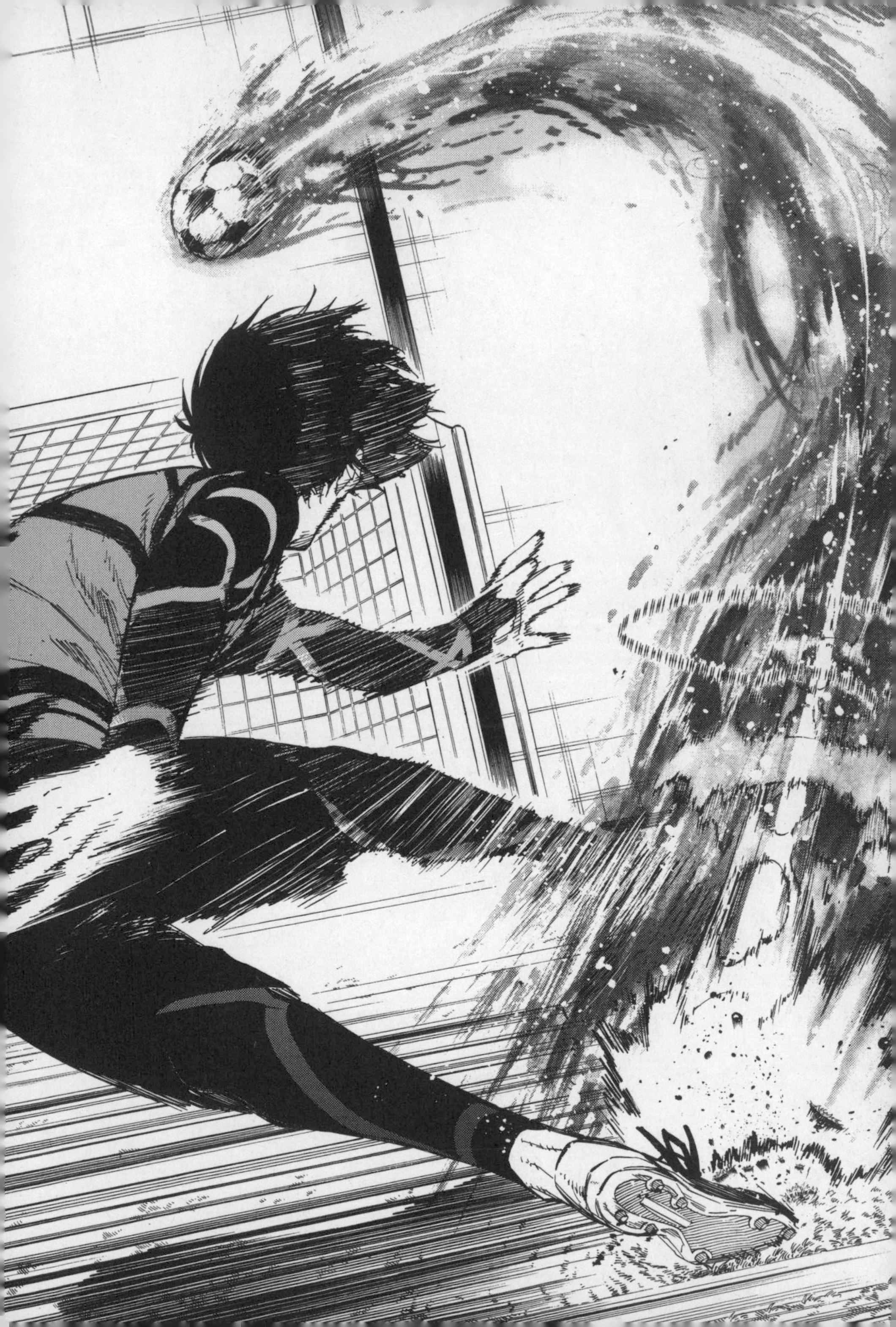

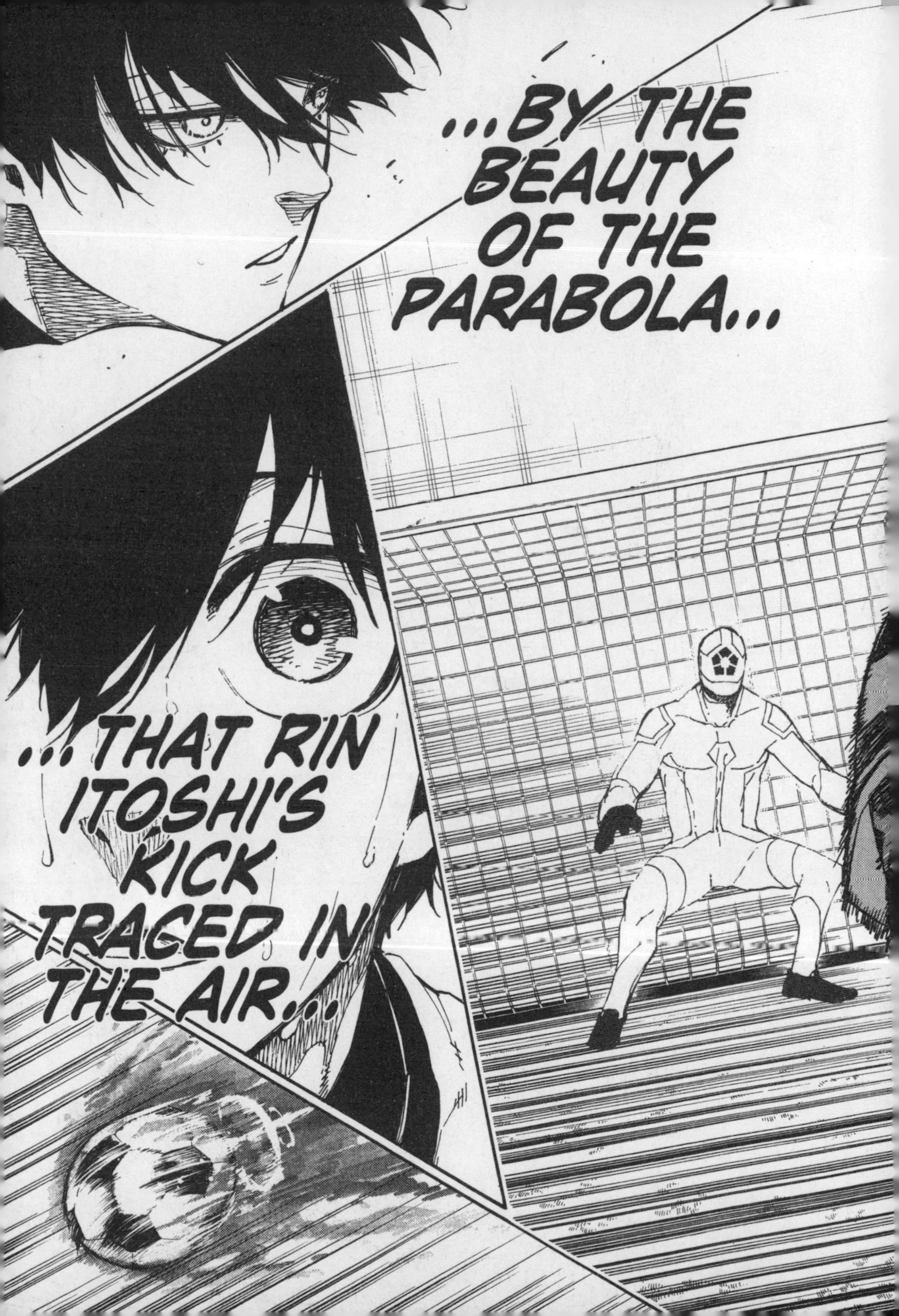
...BY THE BEAUTY OF THE PARABOLA...
...THAT RIN ITOSHI'S KICK TRACED IN THE AIR...

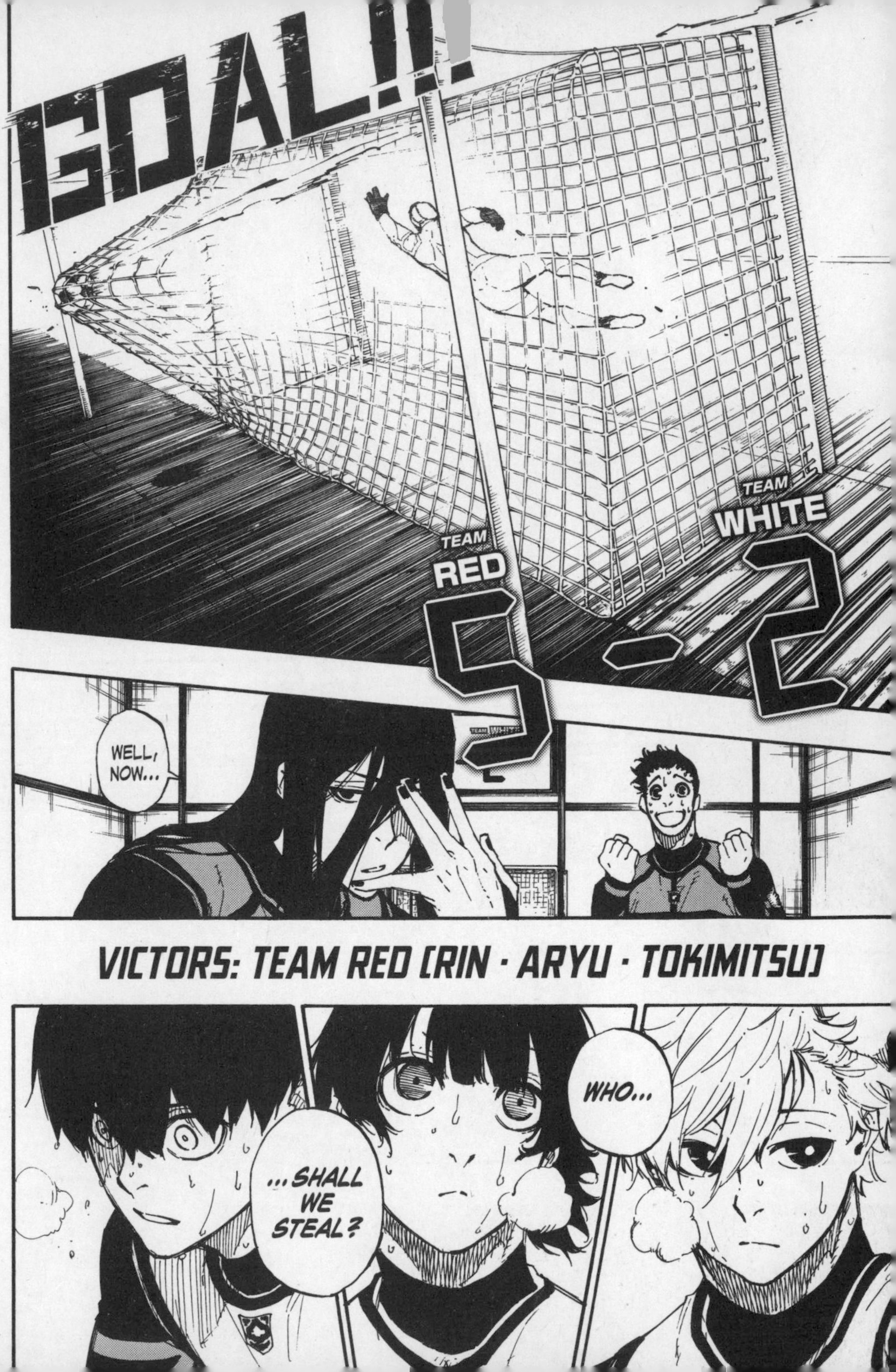
GOAL!!!
TEAM RED
5
-
TEAM WHITE
2
WELL, NOW...
VICTORS: TEAM RED [RIN · ARYU · TOKIMITSU]
WHO...
...SHALL WE STEAL?

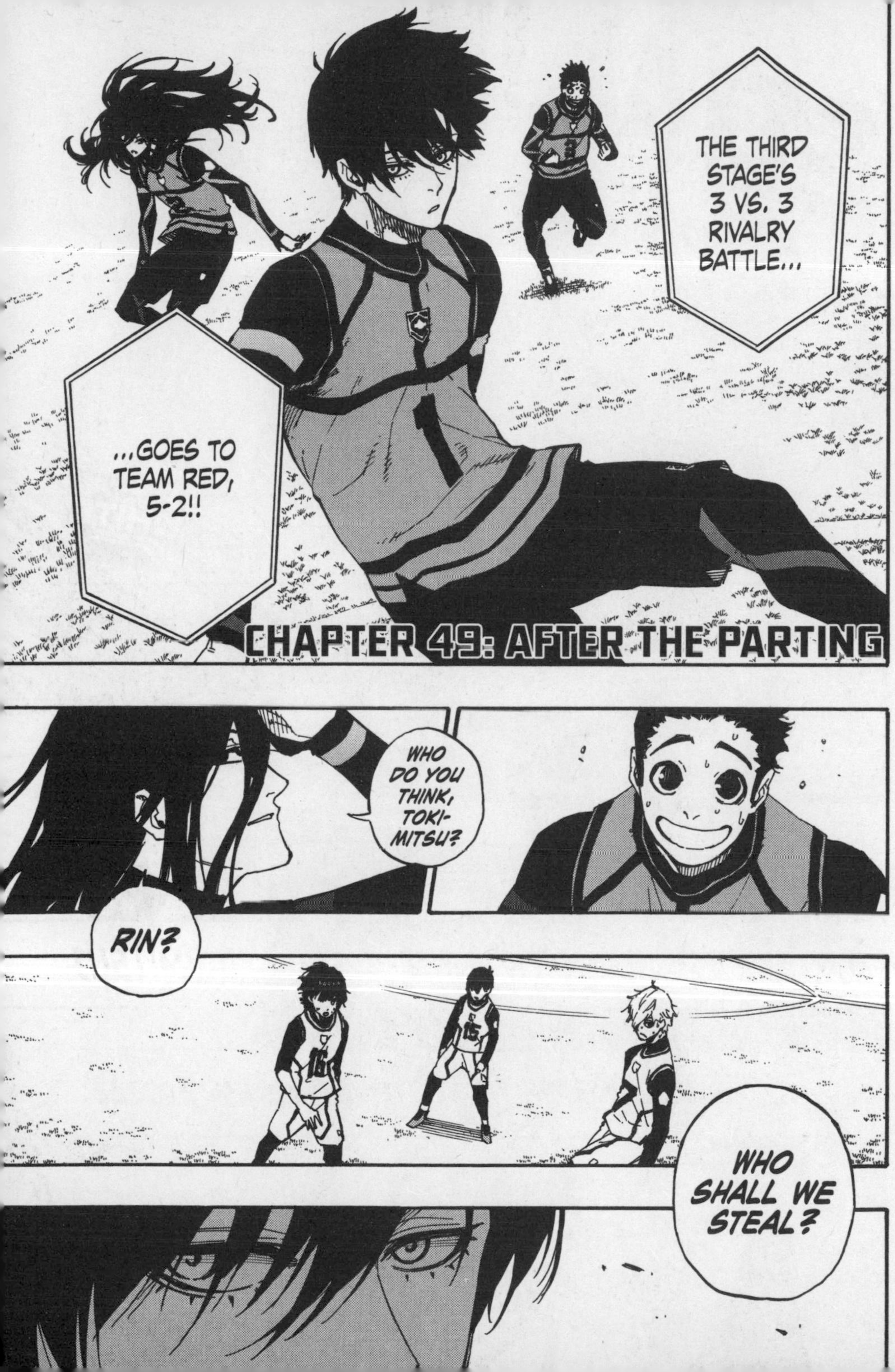
THE THIRD STAGE'S 3 VS. 3 RIVALRY BATTLE...
...GOES TO TEAM RED, 5-2!!
CHAPTER 49: AFTER THE PARTING
WHO DO YOU THINK, TOKI-MITSU?
RIN?
WHO SHALL WE STEAL?

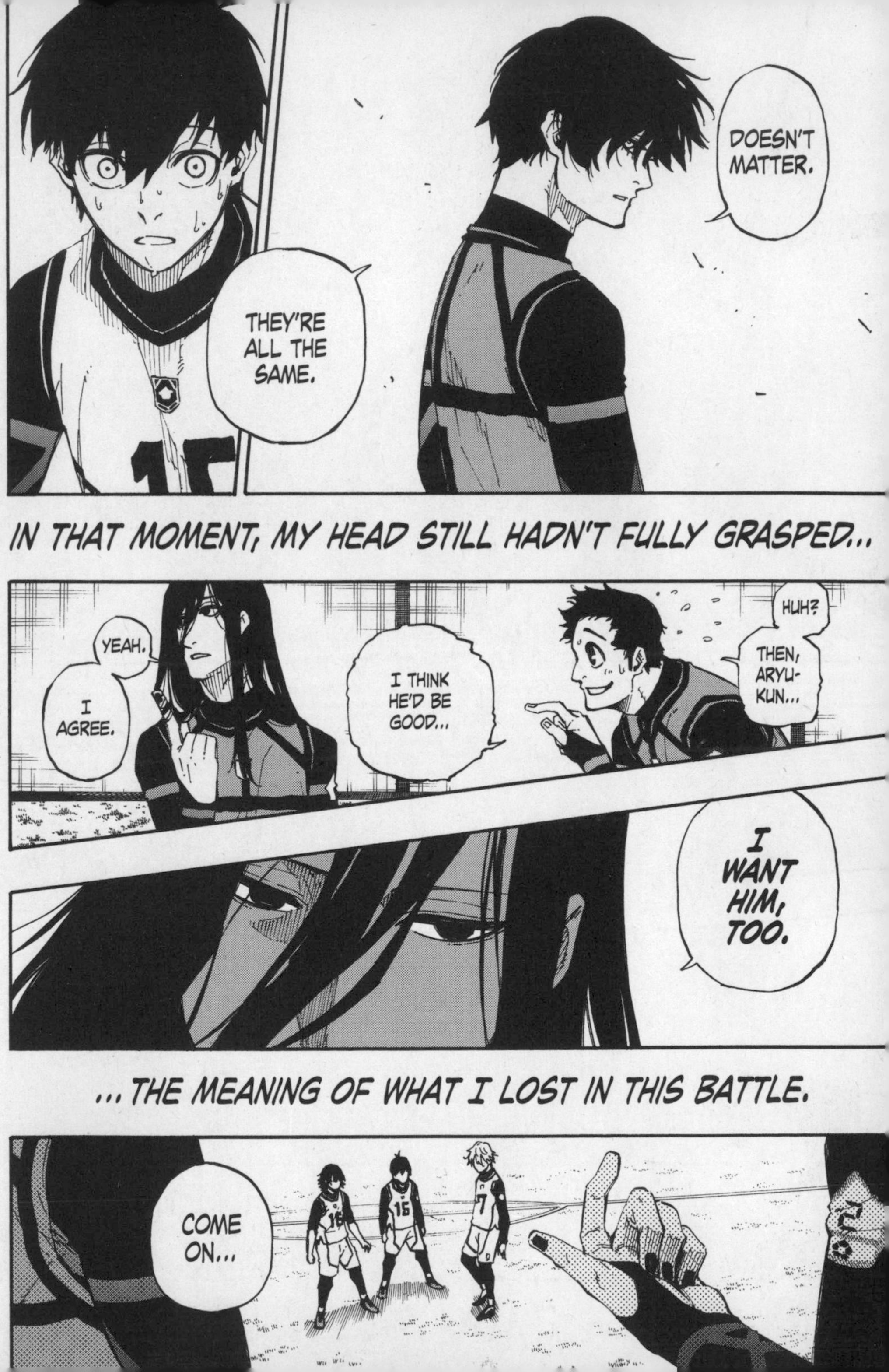
DOESN'T MATTER.
THEY'RE ALL THE SAME.
IN THAT MOMENT, MY HEAD STILL HADN'T FULLY GRASPED...
HUH?
THEN, ARYU-KUN...
I THINK HE'D BE GOOD...
YEAH.
I AGREE.
I WANT HIM, TOO.
...THE MEANING OF WHAT I LOST IN THIS BATTLE.
COME ON...

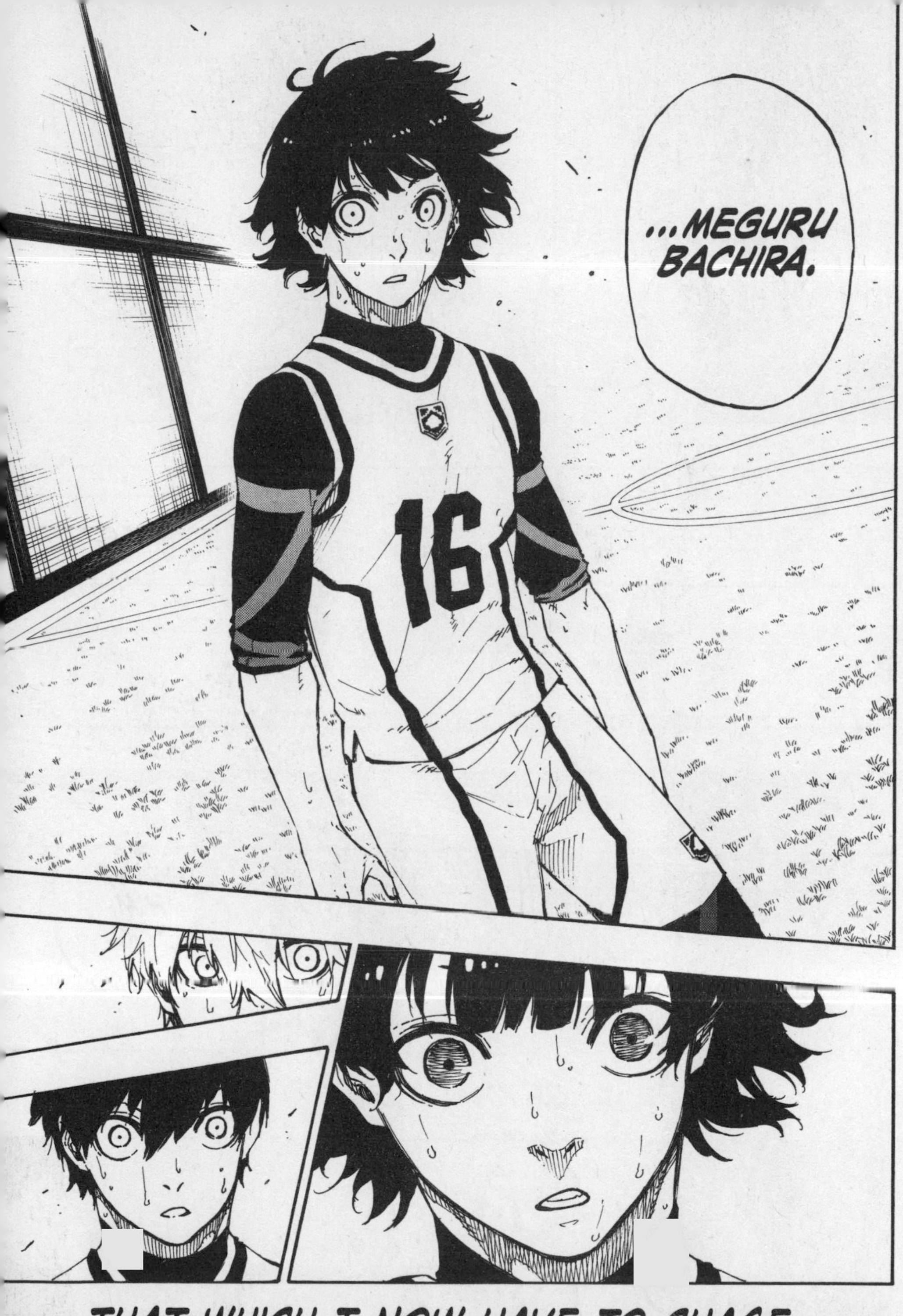
...MEGURU BACHIRA.

THAT WHICH I NOW HAVE TO CHASE.

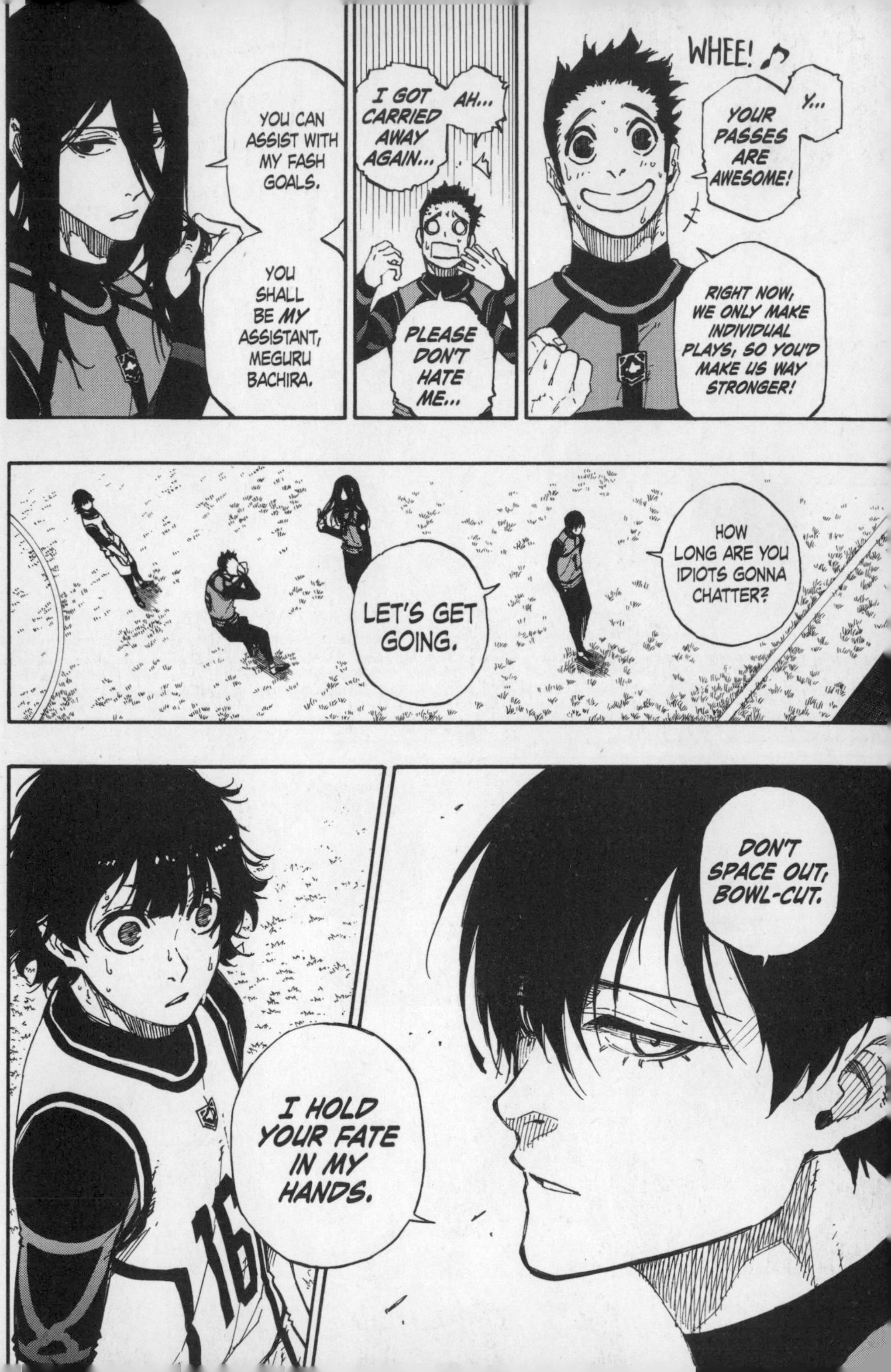
WHEE! ♪
Y... YOUR PASSES ARE AWESOME!
RIGHT NOW, WE ONLY MAKE INDIVIDUAL PLAYS, SO YOU'D MAKE US WAY STRONGER!
AH...
I GOT CARRIED AWAY AGAIN...
PLEASE DON'T HATE ME...
YOU CAN ASSIST WITH MY FASH GOALS.
YOU SHALL BE MY ASSISTANT, MEGURU BACHIRA.
HOW LONG ARE YOU IDIOTS GONNA CHATTER?
LET'S GET GOING.
DON'T SPACE OUT, BOWL-CUT.
I HOLD YOUR FATE IN MY HANDS.

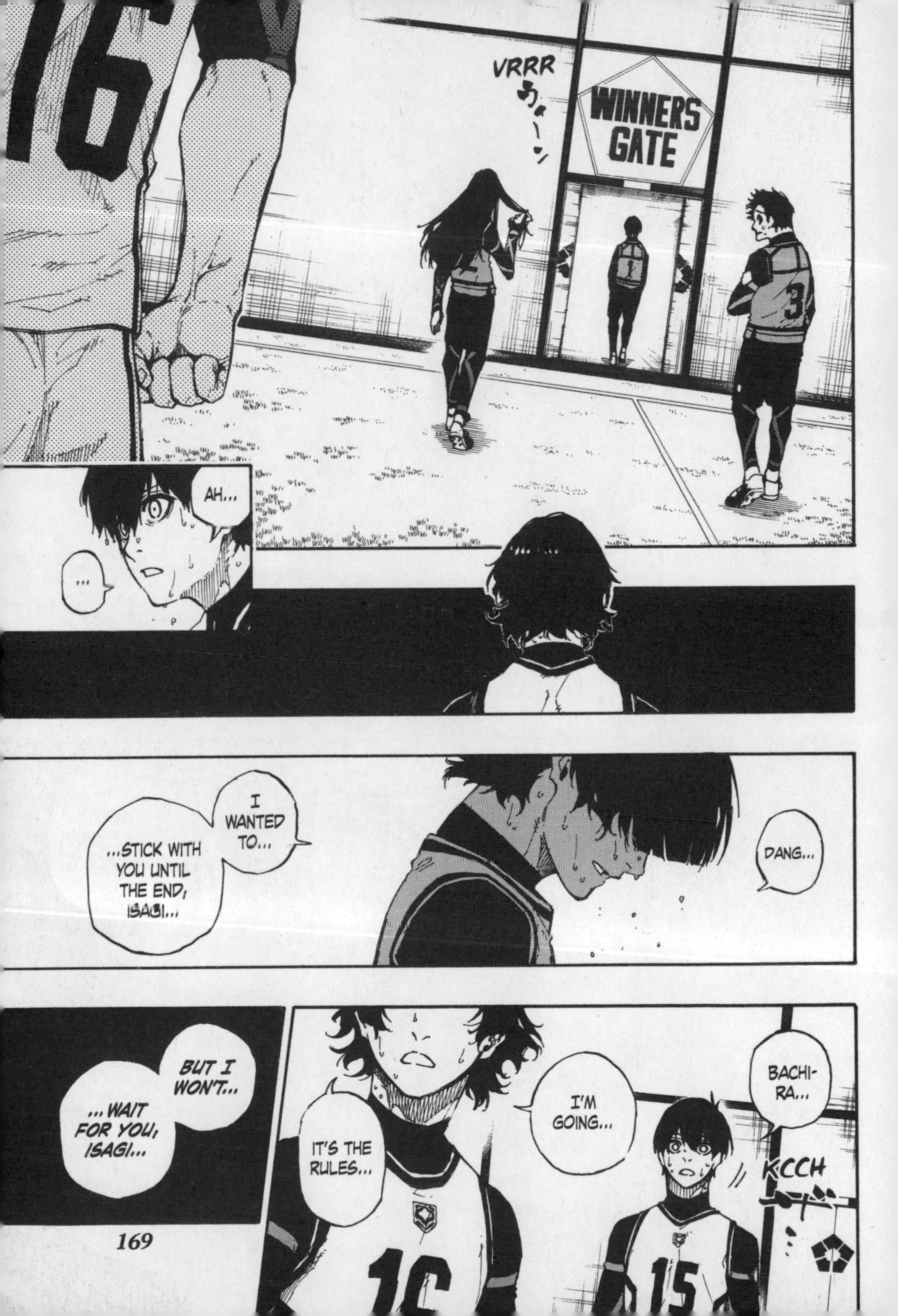
VRRR
WINNERS GATE
AH...
...
DANG...
I WANTED TO...
...STICK WITH YOU UNTIL THE END, ISAGI...
BACHI-RA...
KCCH
I'M GOING...
IT'S THE RULES...
BUT I WON'T...
...WAIT FOR YOU, ISAGI...

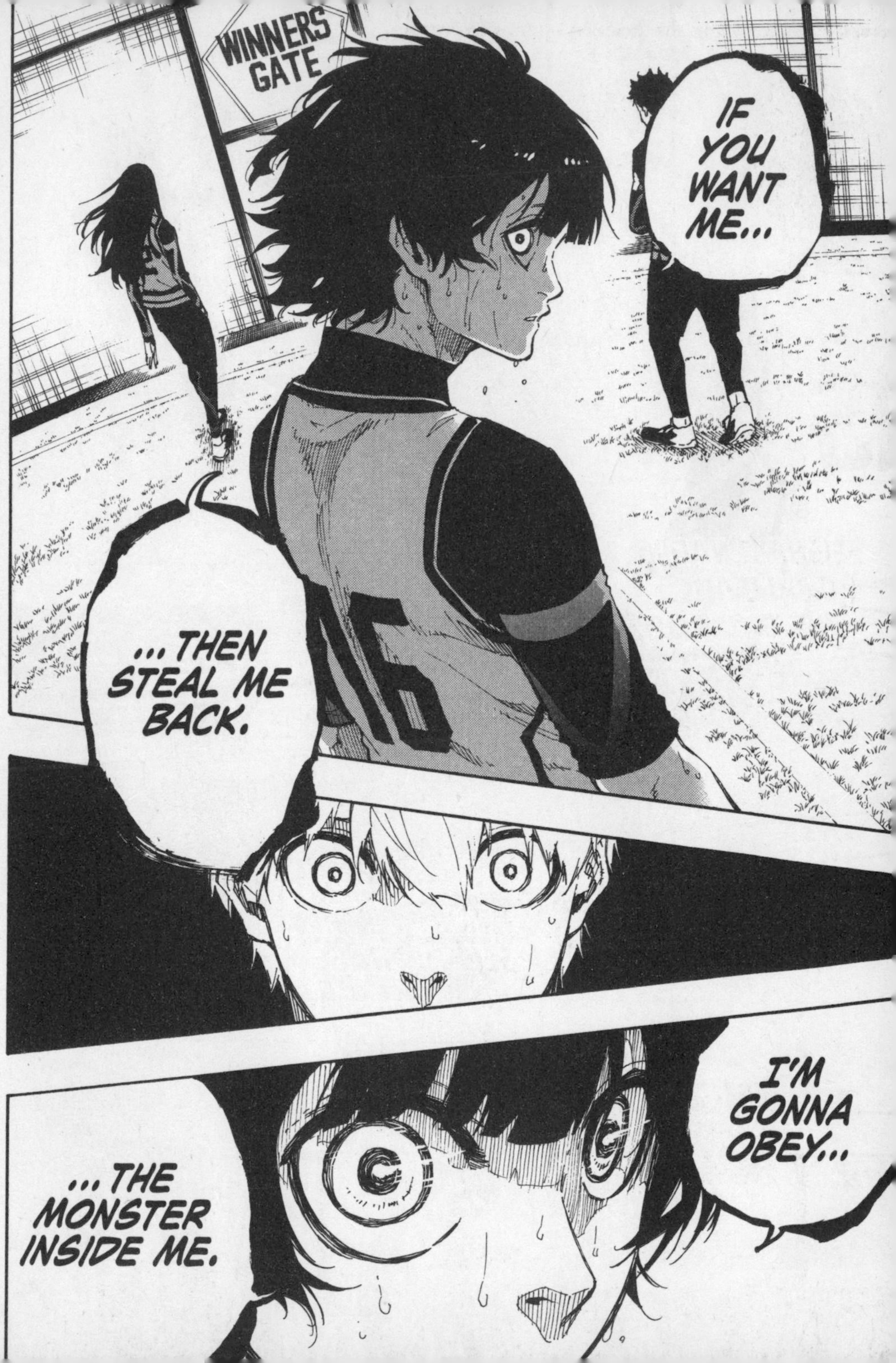
WINNERS GATE
IF YOU WANT ME...
...THEN STEAL ME BACK.
I'M GONNA OBEY...
...THE MONSTER INSIDE ME.

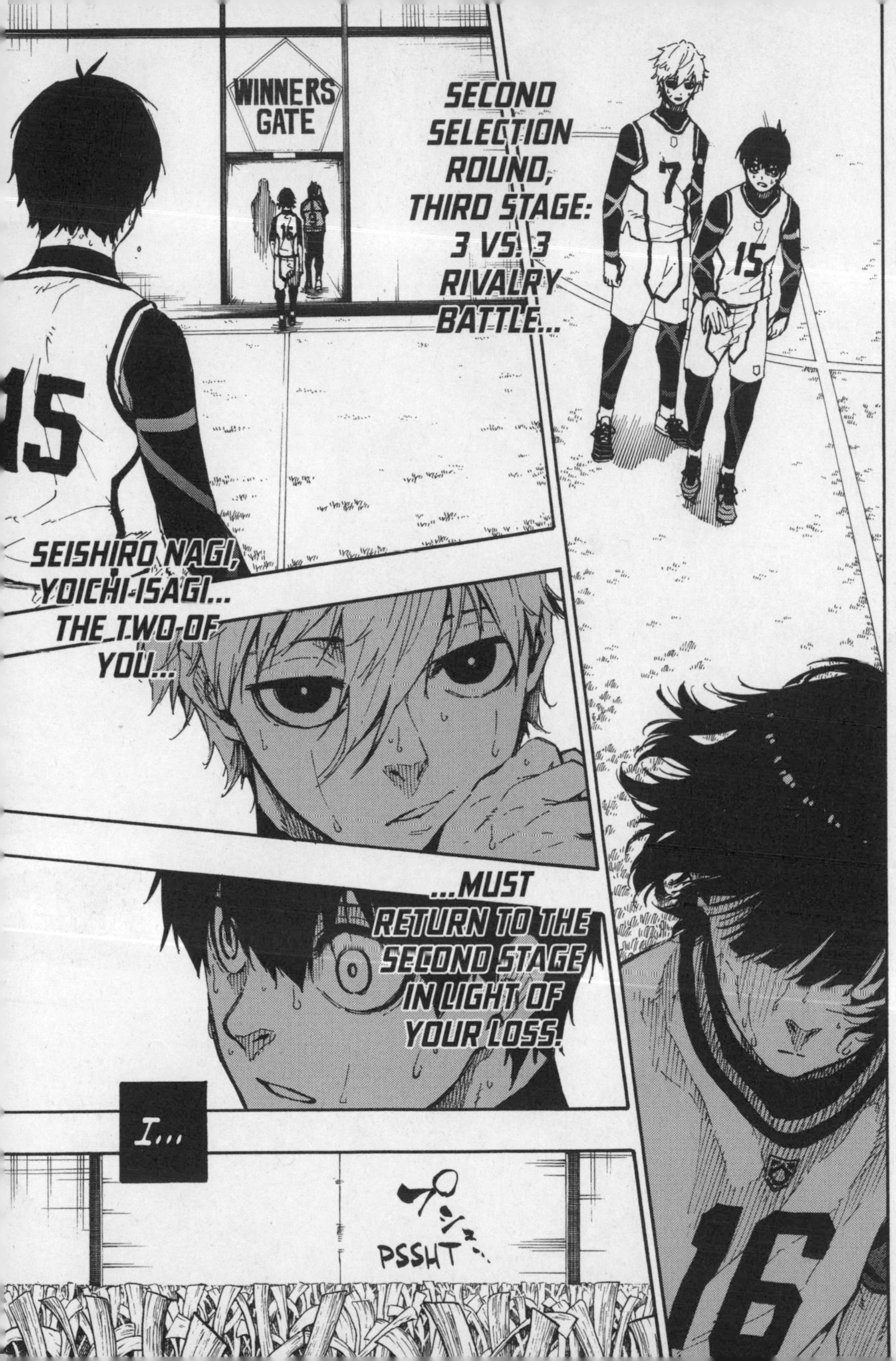
SECOND SELECTION ROUND, THIRD STAGE: 3 VS. 3 RIVALRY BATTLE...
WINNERS GATE
SEISHIRO NAGI, YOICHI ISAGI... THE TWO OF YOU...
...MUST RETURN TO THE SECOND STAGE IN LIGHT OF YOUR LOSS.
I...
PSSHT

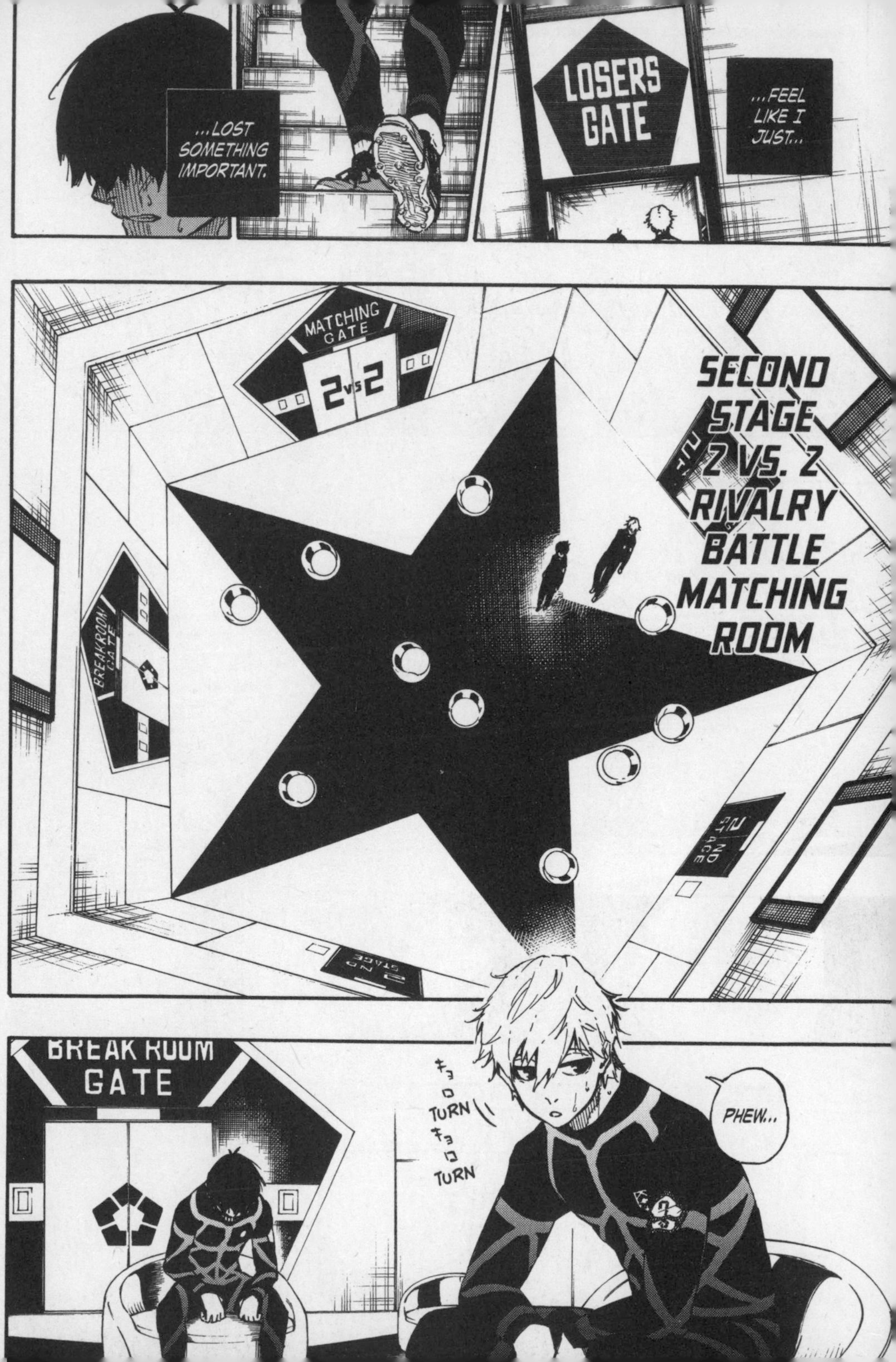
LOSERS GATE
...FEEL LIKE I JUST...
...LOST SOMETHING IMPORTANT.
SECOND STAGE 2 VS. 2 RIVALRY BATTLE MATCHING ROOM
MATCHING GATE
2 VS 2
BREAKROOM GATE
2ND STAGE
PHEW...
TURN
TURN
BREAK ROOM GATE

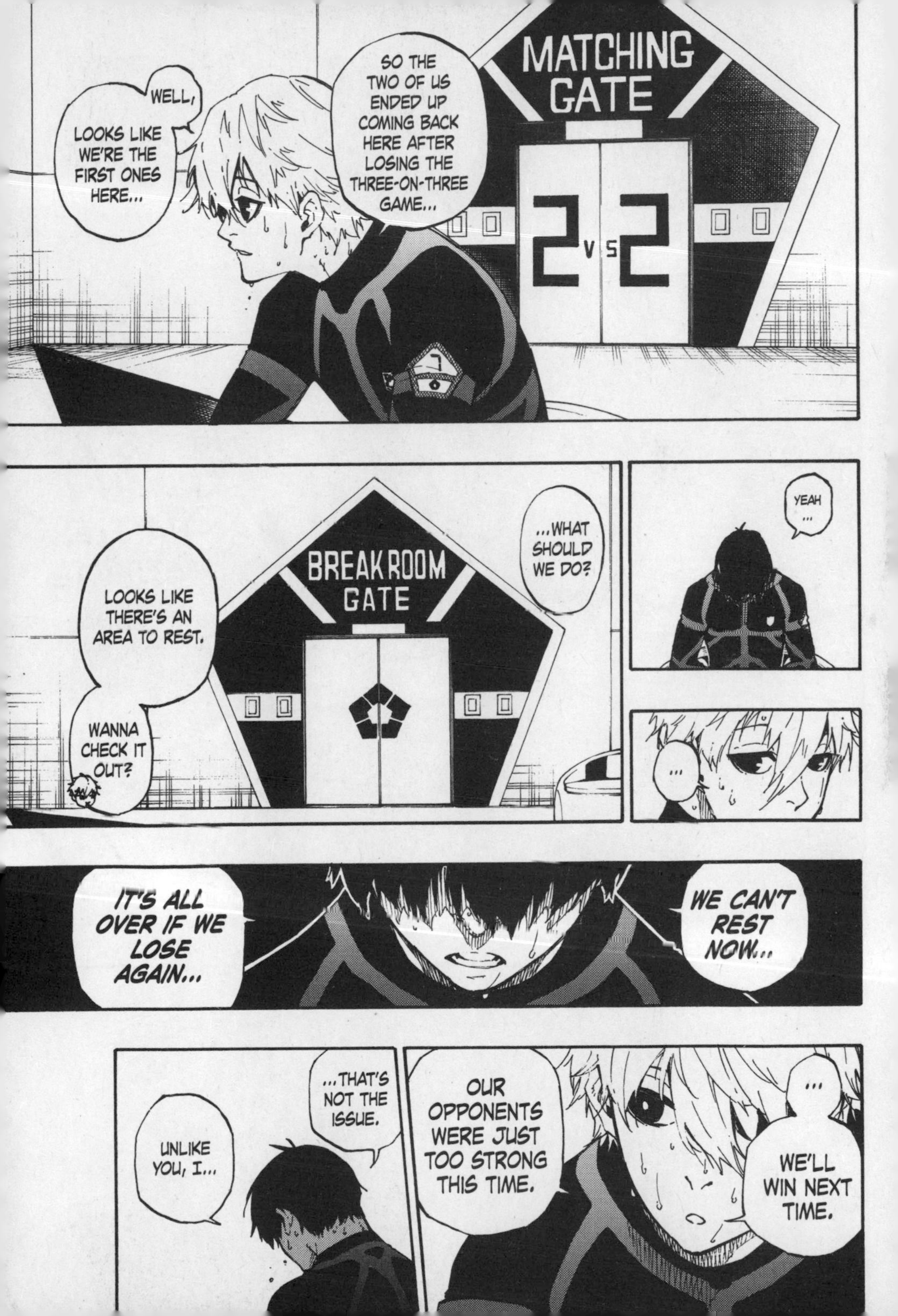
MATCHING GATE
2 VS 2
SO THE TWO OF US ENDED UP COMING BACK HERE AFTER LOSING THE THREE-ON-THREE GAME...
WELL, LOOKS LIKE WE'RE THE FIRST ONES HERE...
YEAH ...
...
...WHAT SHOULD WE DO?
BREAK ROOM GATE
LOOKS LIKE THERE'S AN AREA TO REST.
WANNA CHECK IT OUT?
WE CAN'T REST NOW...
IT'S ALL OVER IF WE LOSE AGAIN...
...
OUR OPPONENTS WERE JUST TOO STRONG THIS TIME.
WE'LL WIN NEXT TIME.
...THAT'S NOT THE ISSUE.
UNLIKE YOU, I...

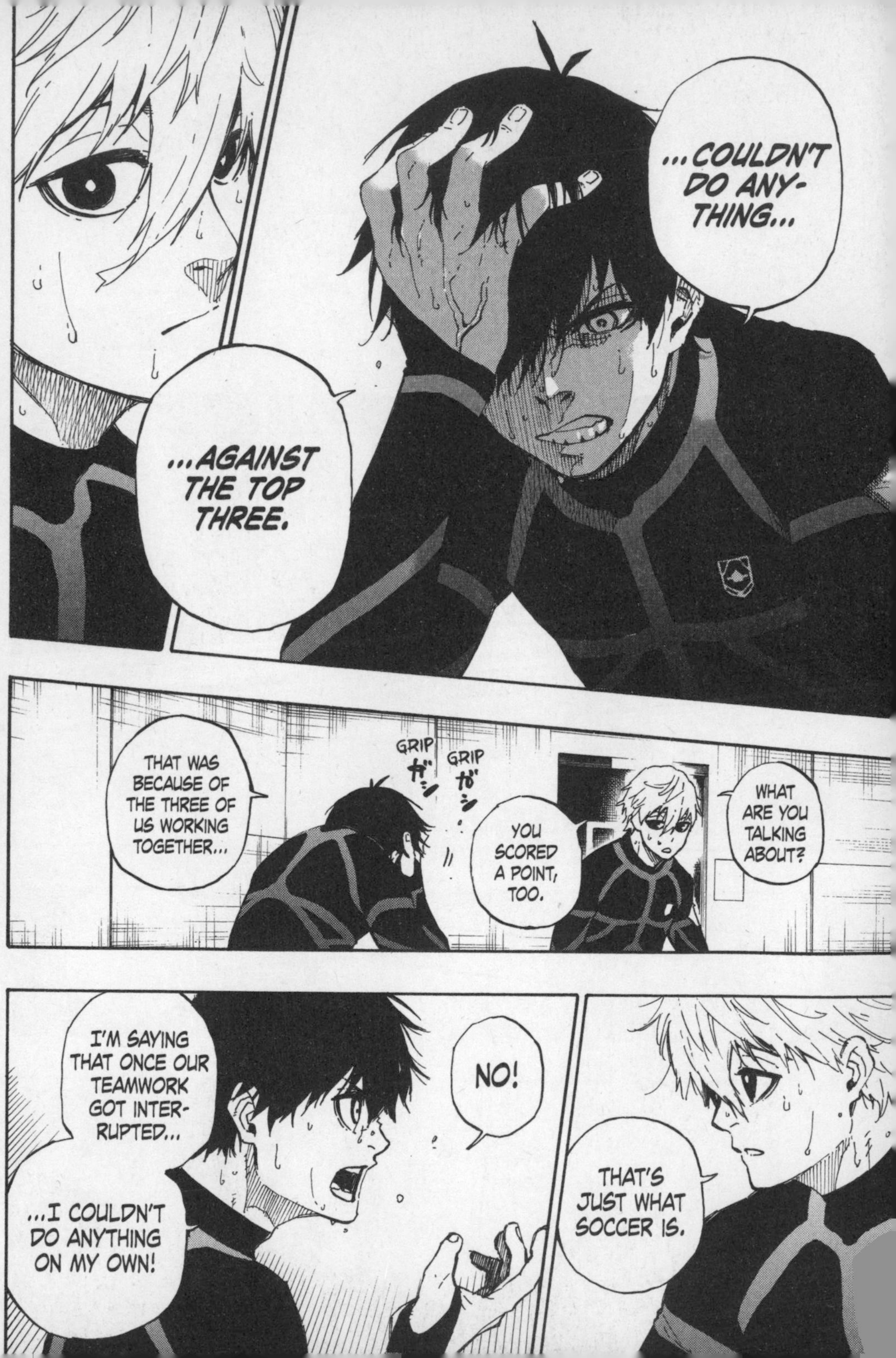
...COULDN'T DO ANY-THING...
...AGAINST THE TOP THREE.
WHAT ARE YOU TALKING ABOUT?
YOU SCORED A POINT, TOO.
GRIP
GRIP
THAT WAS BECAUSE OF THE THREE OF US WORKING TOGETHER...
THAT'S JUST WHAT SOCCER IS.
NO!
I'M SAYING THAT ONCE OUR TEAMWORK GOT INTER-RUPTED...
...I COULDN'T DO ANYTHING ON MY OWN!

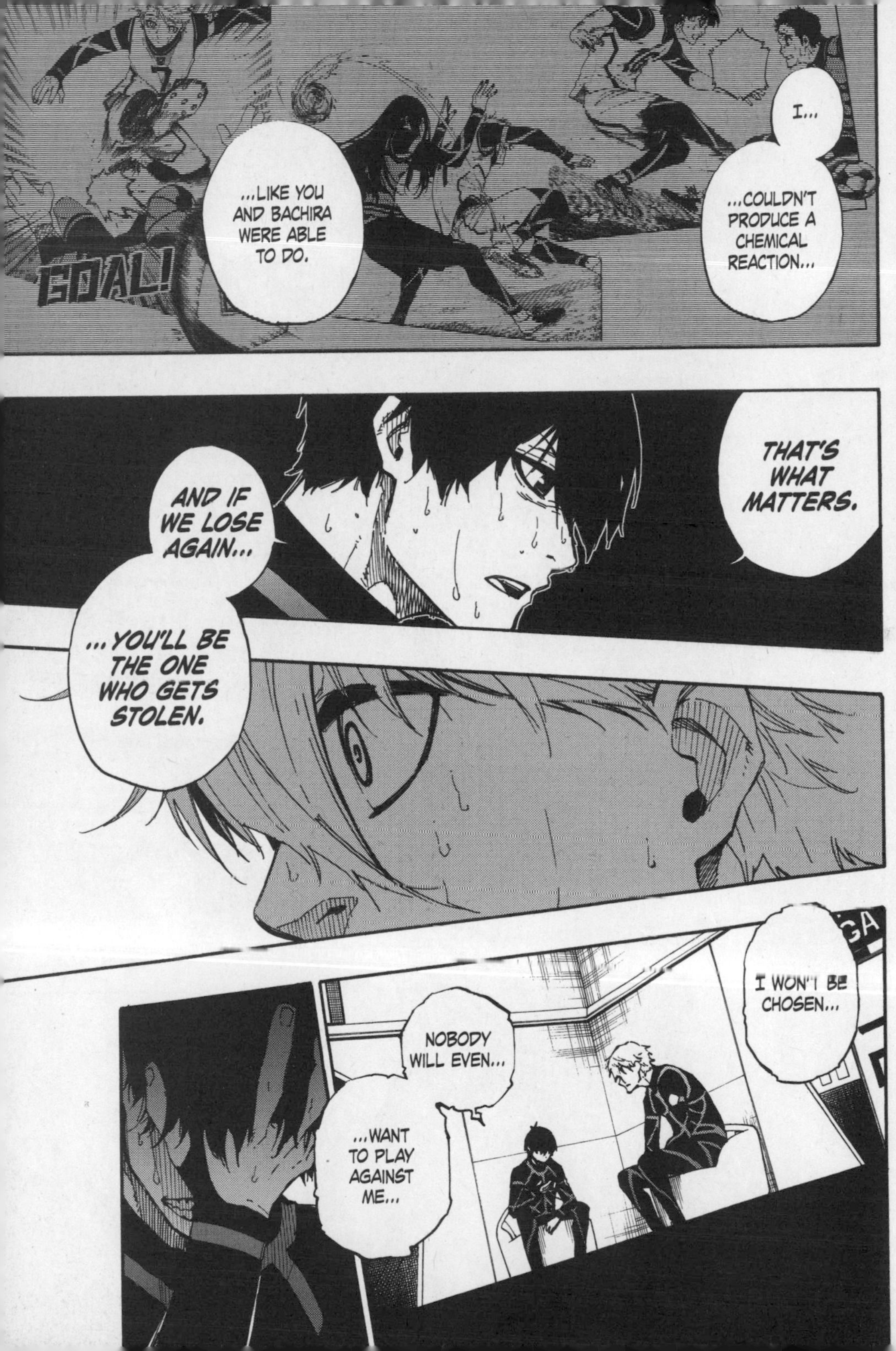
I...
...COULDN'T PRODUCE A CHEMICAL REACTION...
...LIKE YOU AND BACHIRA WERE ABLE TO DO.
GOAL!
THAT'S WHAT MATTERS.
AND IF WE LOSE AGAIN...
...YOU'LL BE THE ONE WHO GETS STOLEN.
I WON'T BE CHOSEN...
NOBODY WILL EVEN...
...WANT TO PLAY AGAINST ME...

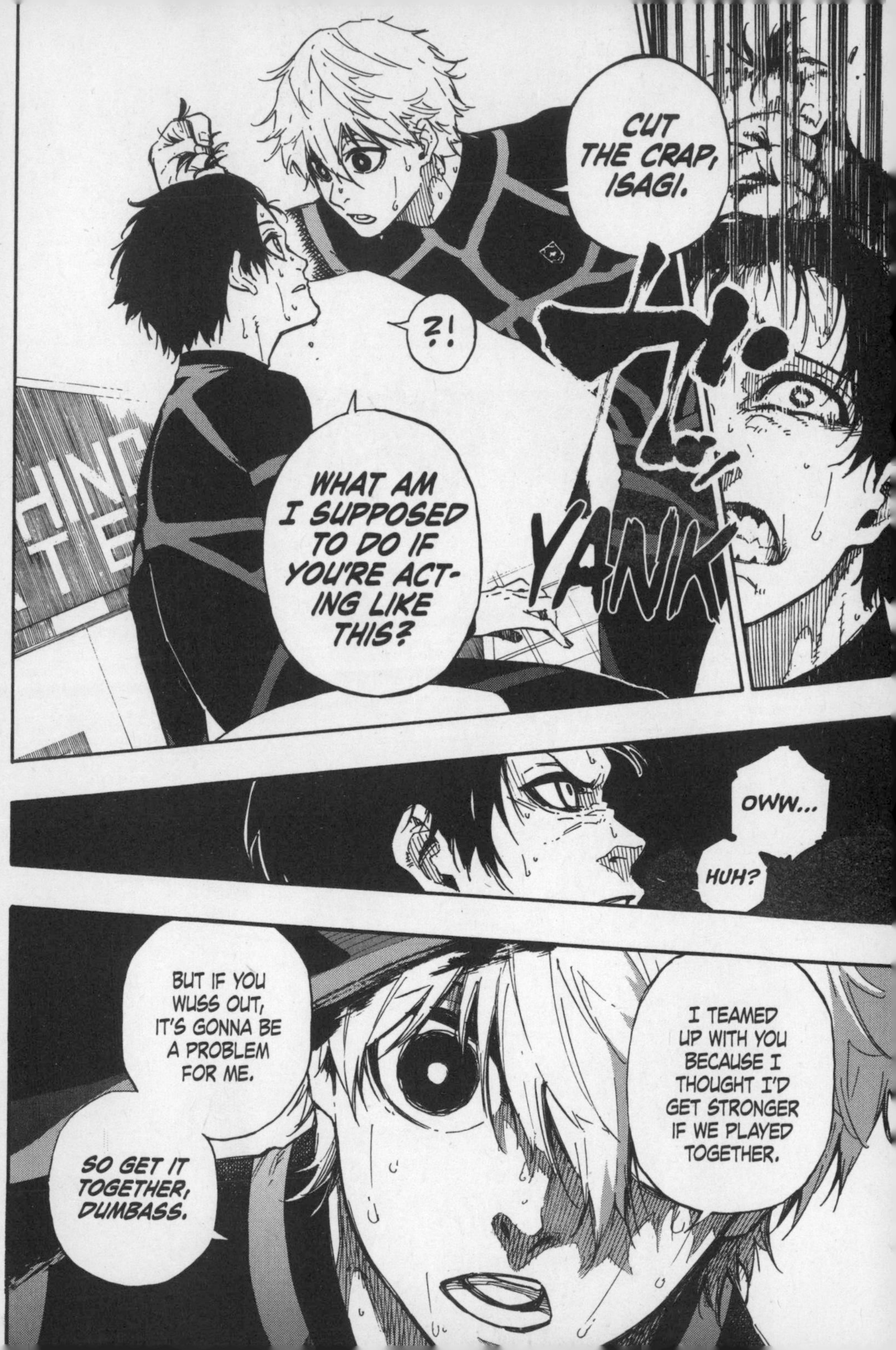
CUT THE CRAP, ISAGI.
YANK
?!
WHAT AM I SUPPOSED TO DO IF YOU'RE ACT-ING LIKE THIS?
OWW...
HUH?
I TEAMED UP WITH YOU BECAUSE I THOUGHT I'D GET STRONGER IF WE PLAYED TOGETHER.
BUT IF YOU WUSS OUT, IT'S GONNA BE A PROBLEM FOR ME.
SO GET IT TOGETHER, DUMBASS.

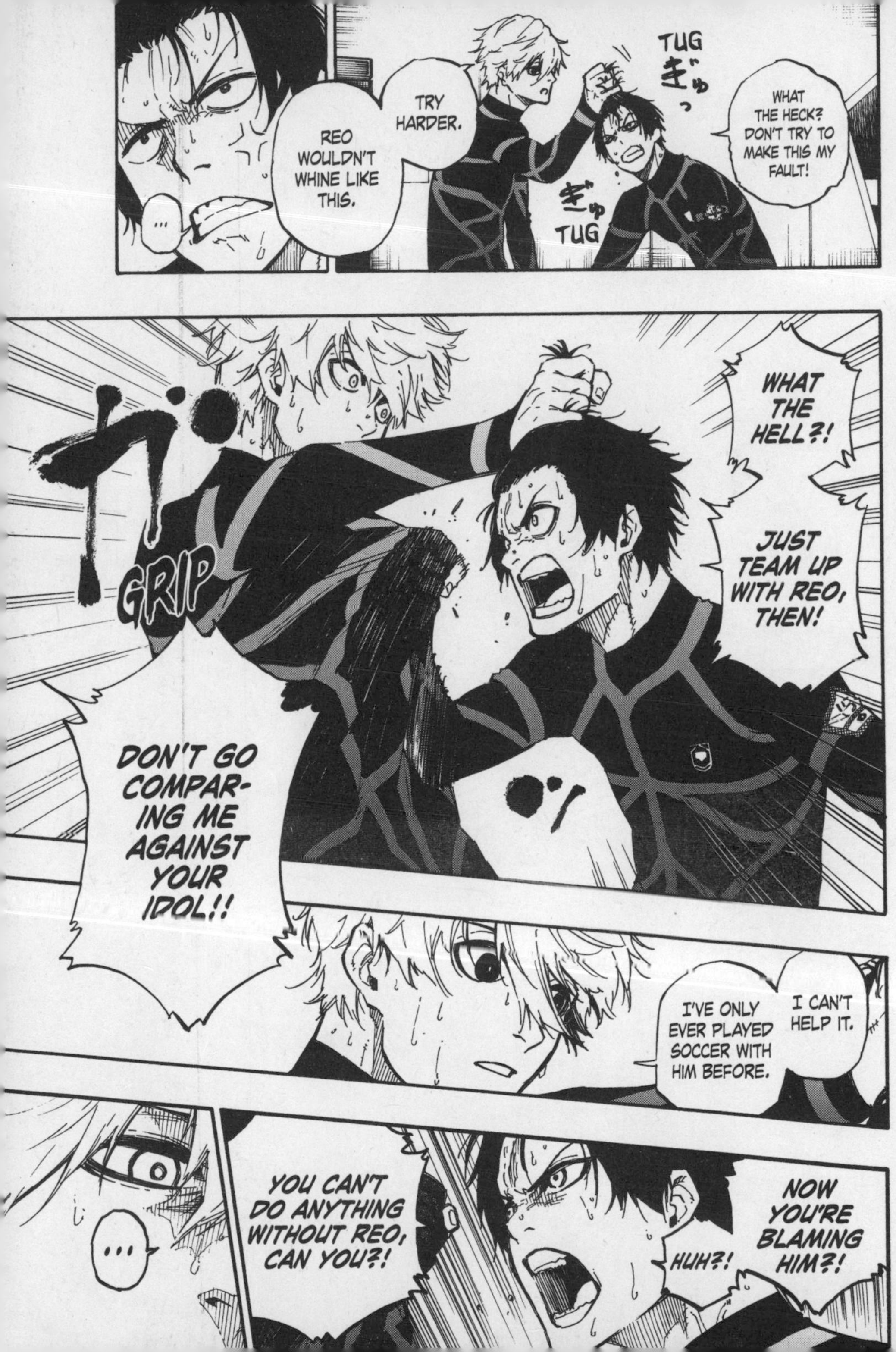
TUG ぎゅっ
WHAT THE HECK? DON'T TRY TO MAKE THIS MY FAULT!
TRY HARDER.
REO WOULDN'T WHINE LIKE THIS.
ぎゅ TUG
...
WHAT THE HELL?!
JUST TEAM UP WITH REO, THEN!
GRIP
DON'T GO COMPARING ME AGAINST YOUR IDOL!!
I CAN'T HELP IT.
I'VE ONLY EVER PLAYED SOCCER WITH HIM BEFORE.
NOW YOU'RE BLAMING HIM?!
HUH?!
YOU CAN'T DO ANYTHING WITHOUT REO, CAN YOU?!
...

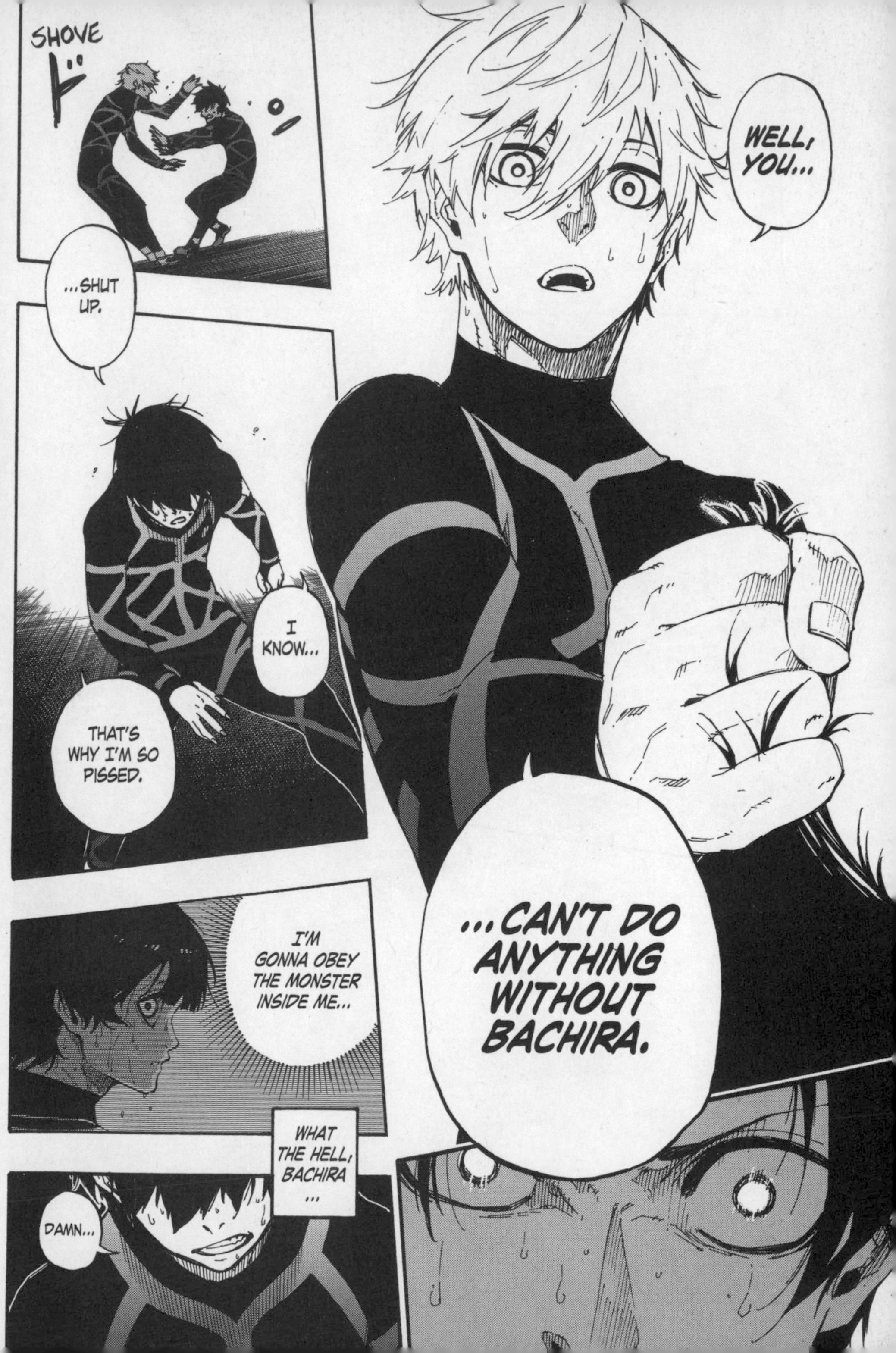
WELL, YOU...
...CAN'T DO ANYTHING WITHOUT BACHIRA.
SHOVE
...SHUT UP.
I KNOW...
THAT'S WHY I'M SO PISSED.
I'M GONNA OBEY THE MONSTER INSIDE ME...
WHAT THE HELL, BACHIRA ...
DAMN...

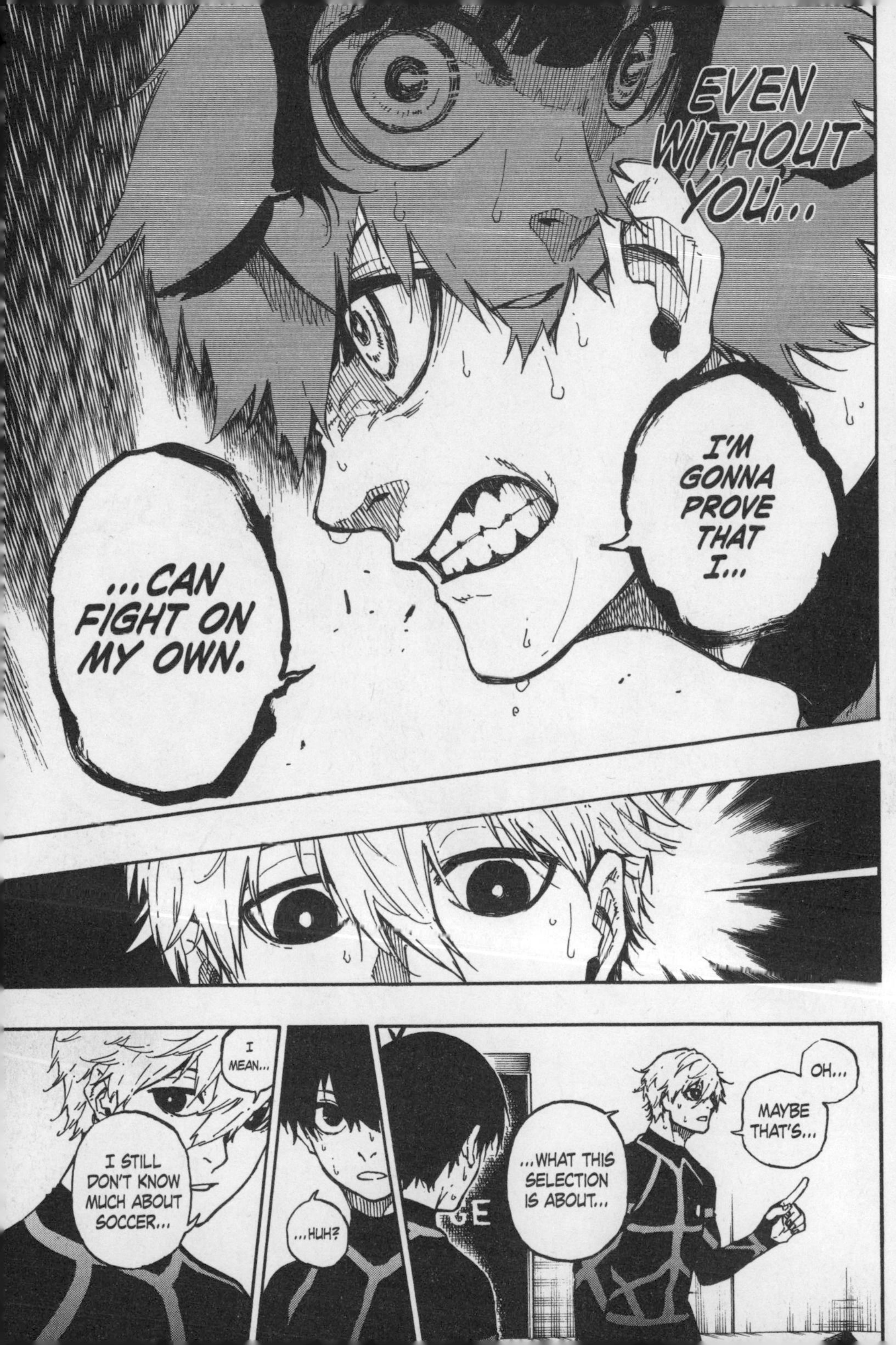
EVEN WITHOUT YOU...
I'M GONNA PROVE THAT I...
...CAN FIGHT ON MY OWN.
OH...
MAYBE THAT'S...
...WHAT THIS SELECTION IS ABOUT...
...HUH?
I MEAN...
I STILL DON'T KNOW MUCH ABOUT SOCCER...

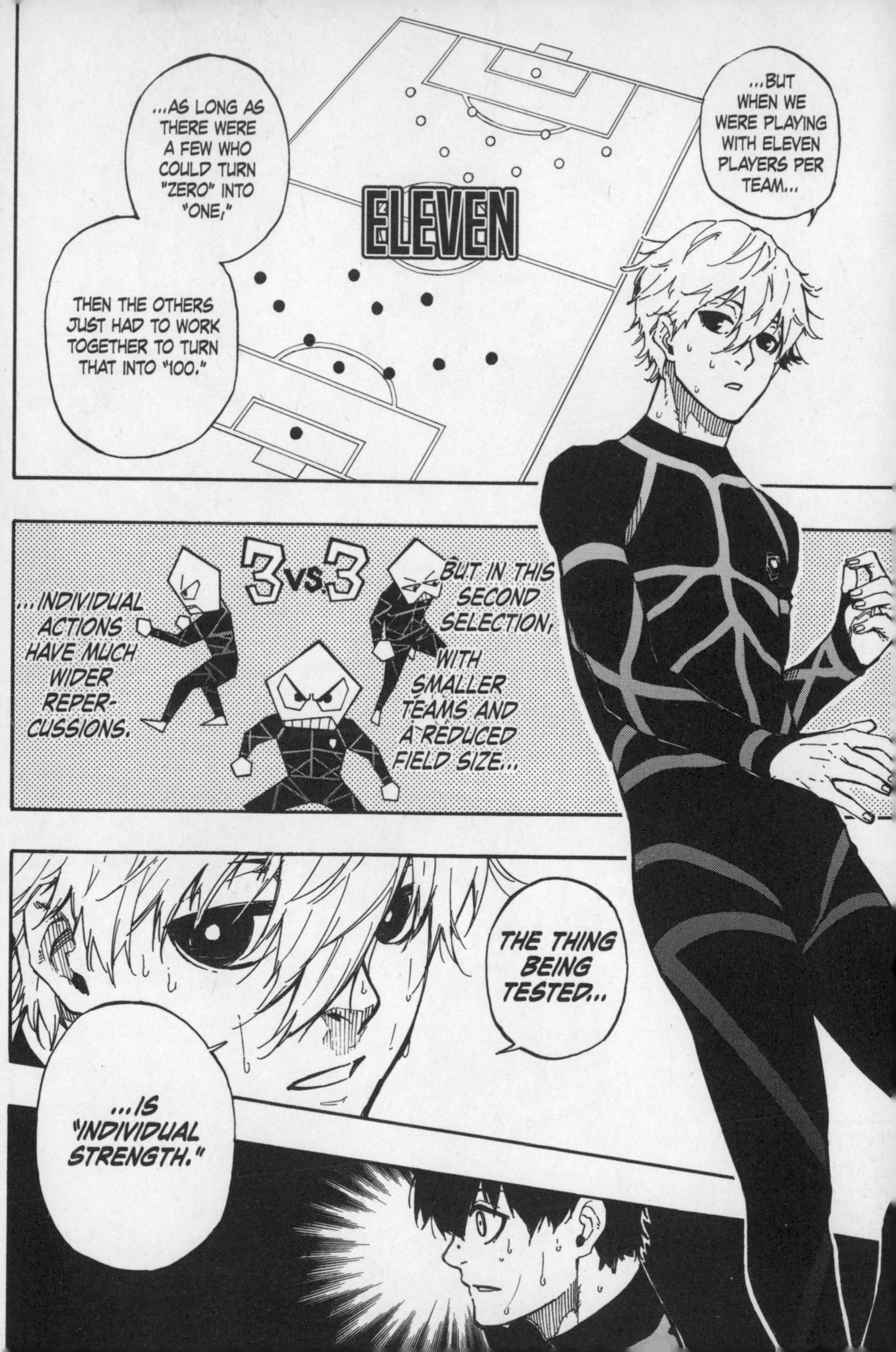
...BUT WHEN WE WERE PLAYING WITH ELEVEN PLAYERS PER TEAM...
ELEVEN
...AS LONG AS THERE WERE A FEW WHO COULD TURN "ZERO" INTO "ONE,"
THEN THE OTHERS JUST HAD TO WORK TOGETHER TO TURN THAT INTO "100."
BUT IN THIS SECOND SELECTION,
WITH SMALLER TEAMS AND A REDUCED FIELD SIZE...
3 VS. 3
...INDIVIDUAL ACTIONS HAVE MUCH WIDER REPER-CUSSIONS.
THE THING BEING TESTED...
...IS "INDIVIDUAL STRENGTH."

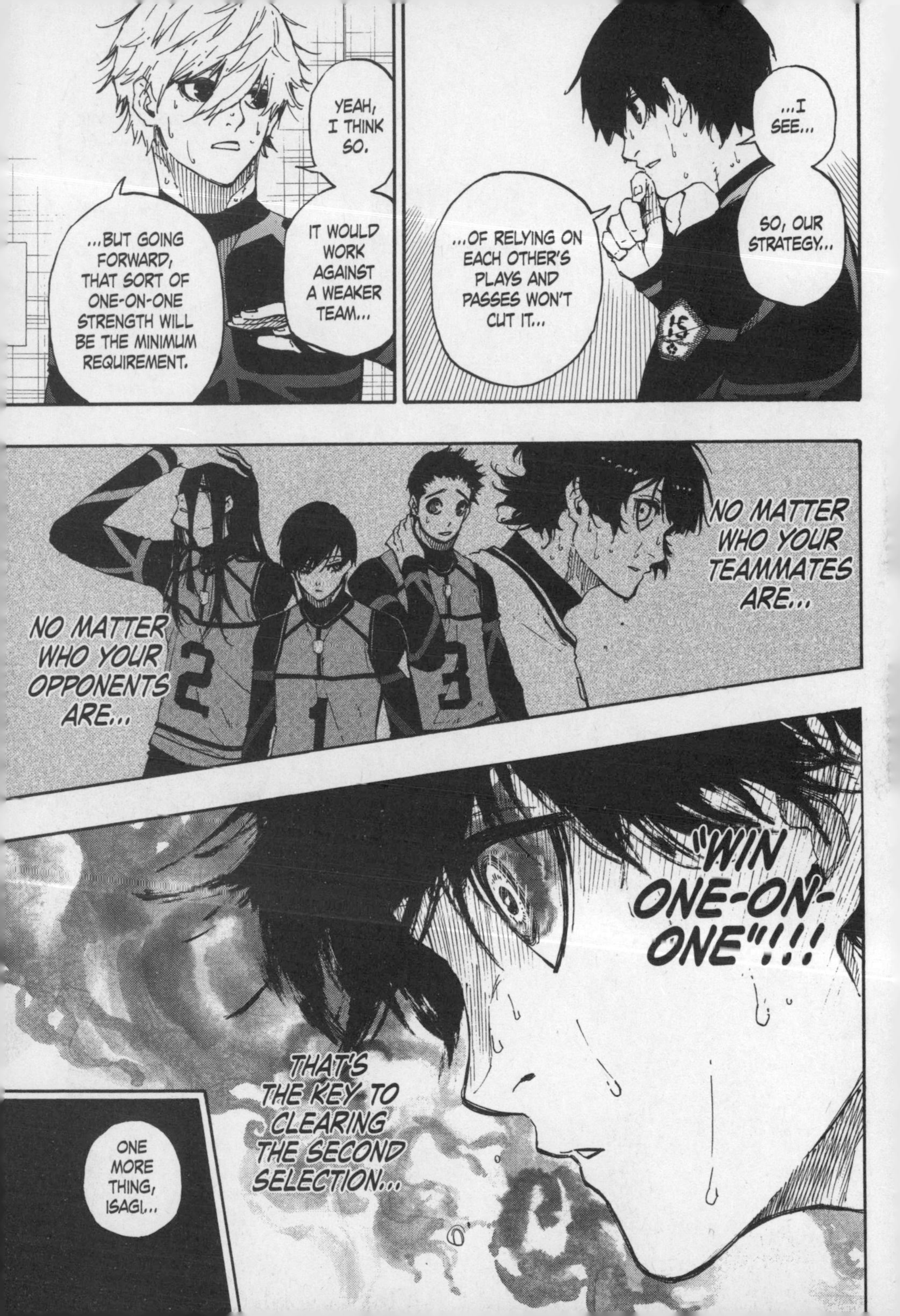
...I SEE...
SO, OUR STRATEGY...
...OF RELYING ON EACH OTHER'S PLAYS AND PASSES WON'T CUT IT...
YEAH, I THINK SO.
IT WOULD WORK AGAINST A WEAKER TEAM...
...BUT GOING FORWARD, THAT SORT OF ONE-ON-ONE STRENGTH WILL BE THE MINIMUM REQUIREMENT.
NO MATTER WHO YOUR TEAMMATES ARE...
NO MATTER WHO YOUR OPPONENTS ARE...
"WIN ONE-ON-ONE"!!!
THAT'S THE KEY TO CLEARING THE SECOND SELECTION...
ONE MORE THING, ISAGI...

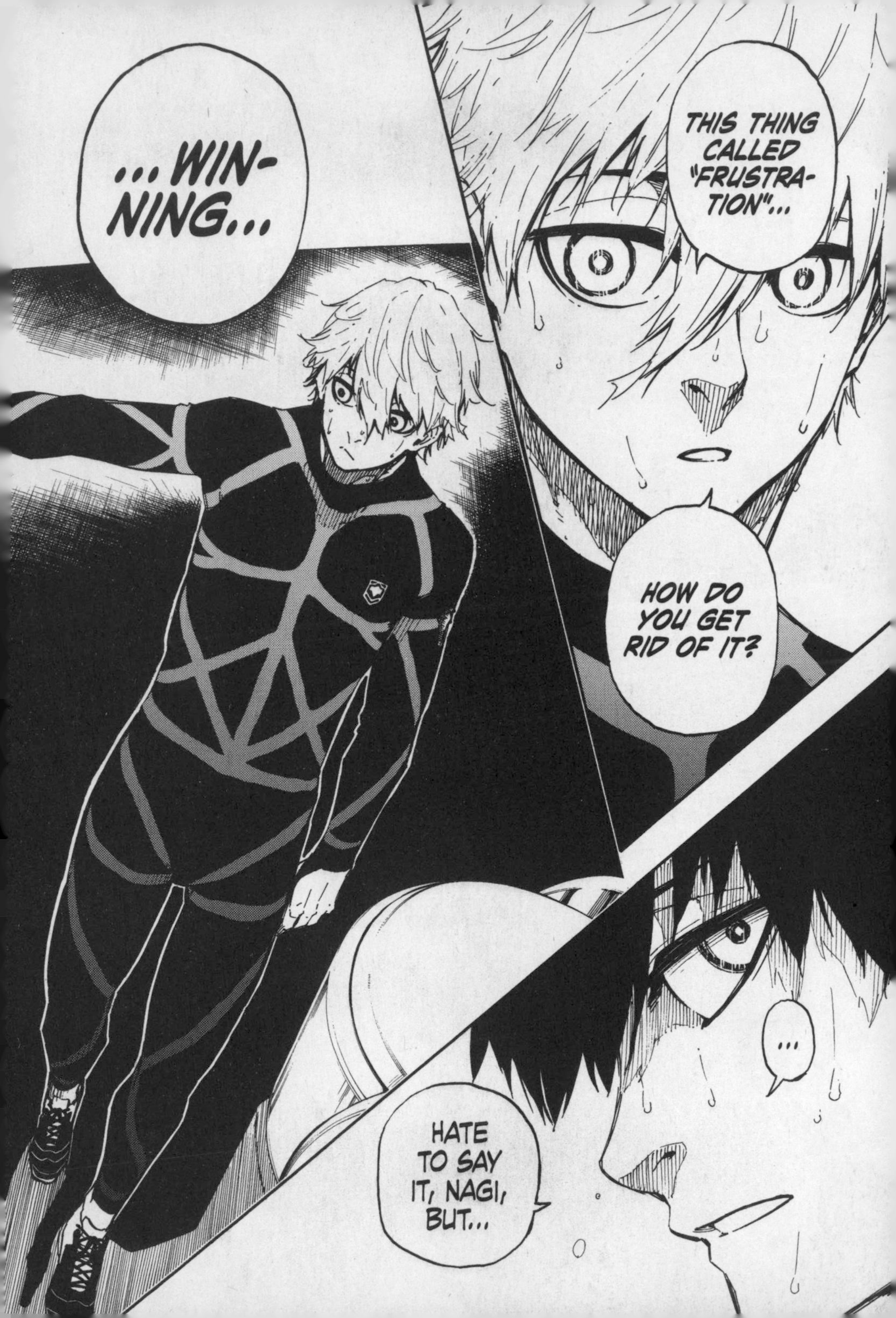
THIS THING CALLED "FRUSTRATION"...
HOW DO YOU GET RID OF IT?
...
HATE TO SAY IT, NAGI, BUT...
...WIN-NING...

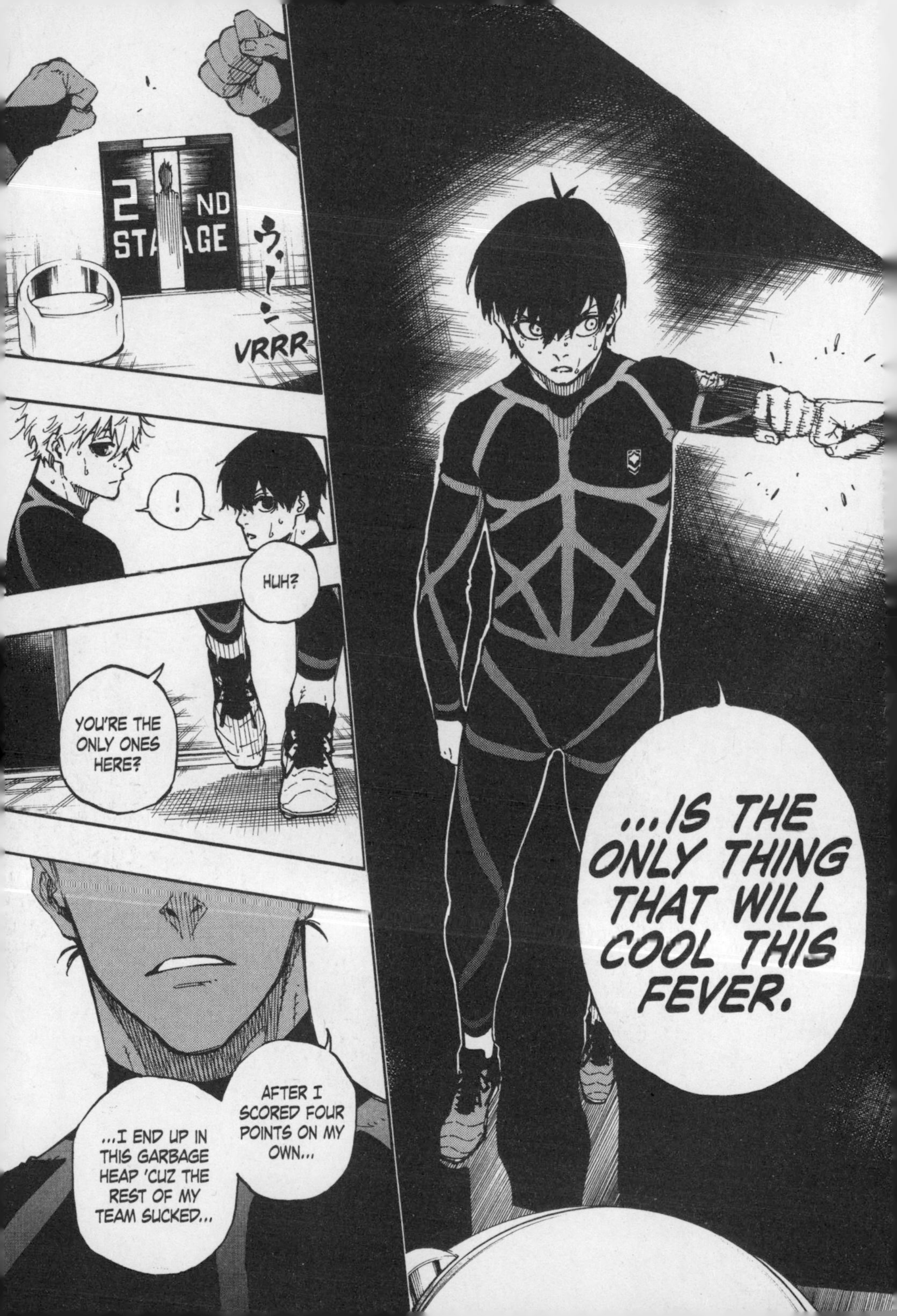
...IS THE ONLY THING THAT WILL COOL THIS FEVER.
2ND STAGE
ウィーン
VRRR
!
HUH?
YOU'RE THE ONLY ONES HERE?
AFTER I SCORED FOUR POINTS ON MY OWN...
...I END UP IN THIS GARBAGE HEAP 'CUZ THE REST OF MY TEAM SUCKED...

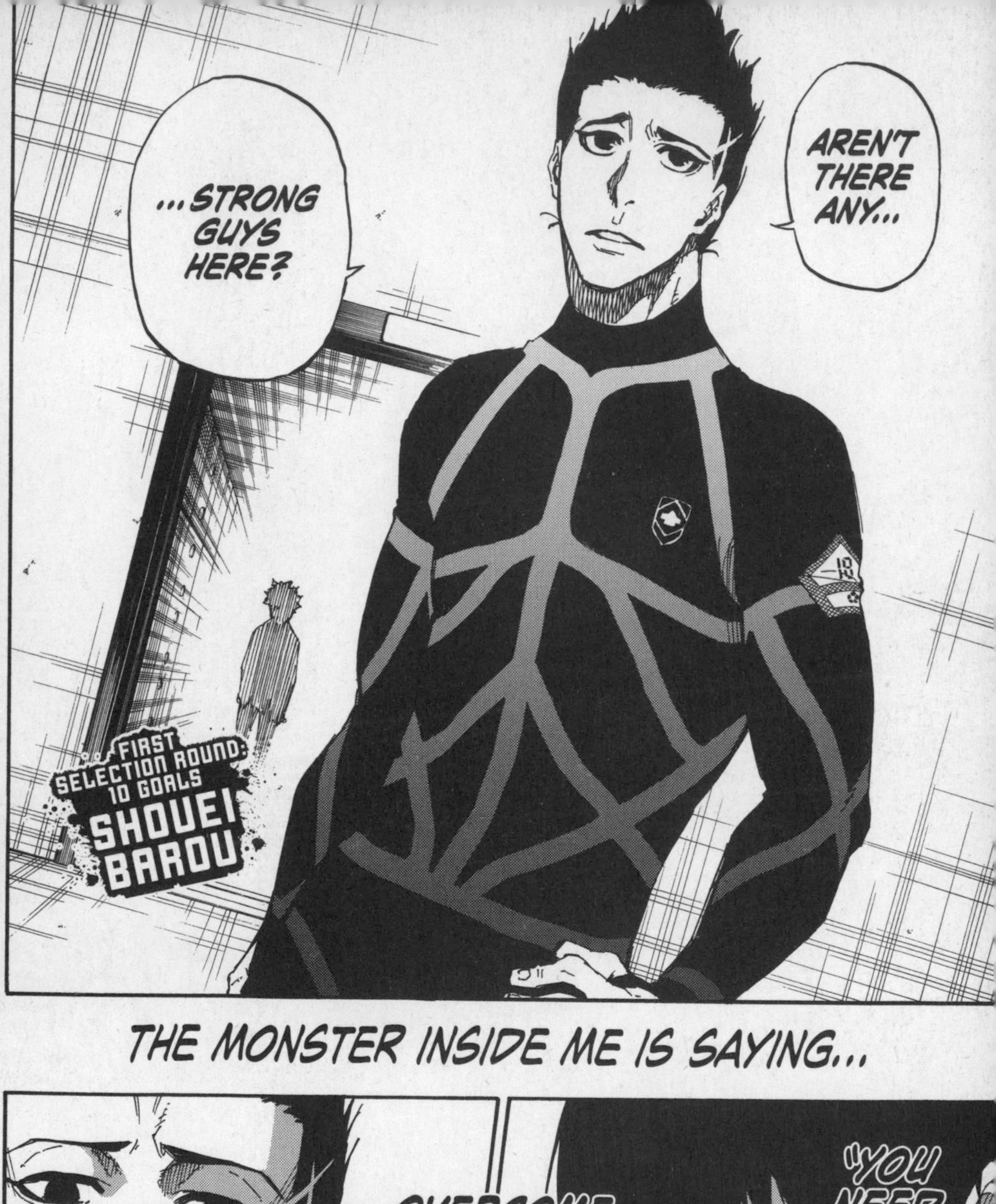
AREN'T THERE ANY...
...STRONG GUYS HERE?
FIRST SELECTION ROUND: 10 GOALS
SHOUEI BAROU

THE MONSTER INSIDE ME IS SAYING...

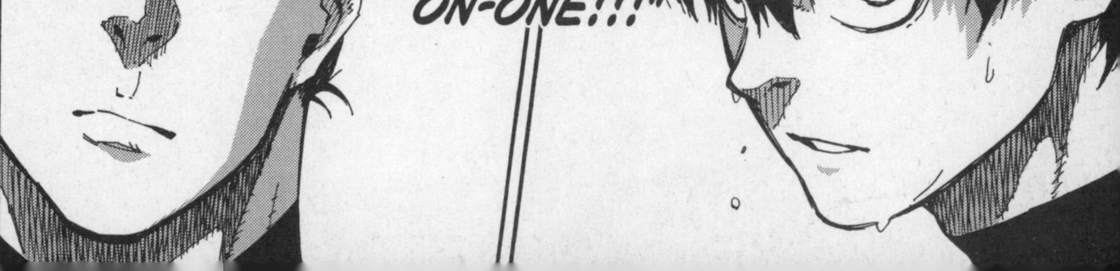
"YOU NEED TO...
...OVERCOME BAROU, ONE-ON-ONE!!!"

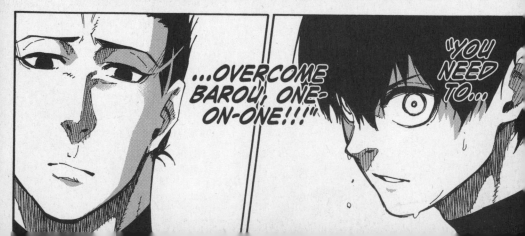

# BLUE LOCK

CONTINUED IN VOL. 7

# THE STORY OF THE TOP 3 TEAM'S FORMATION

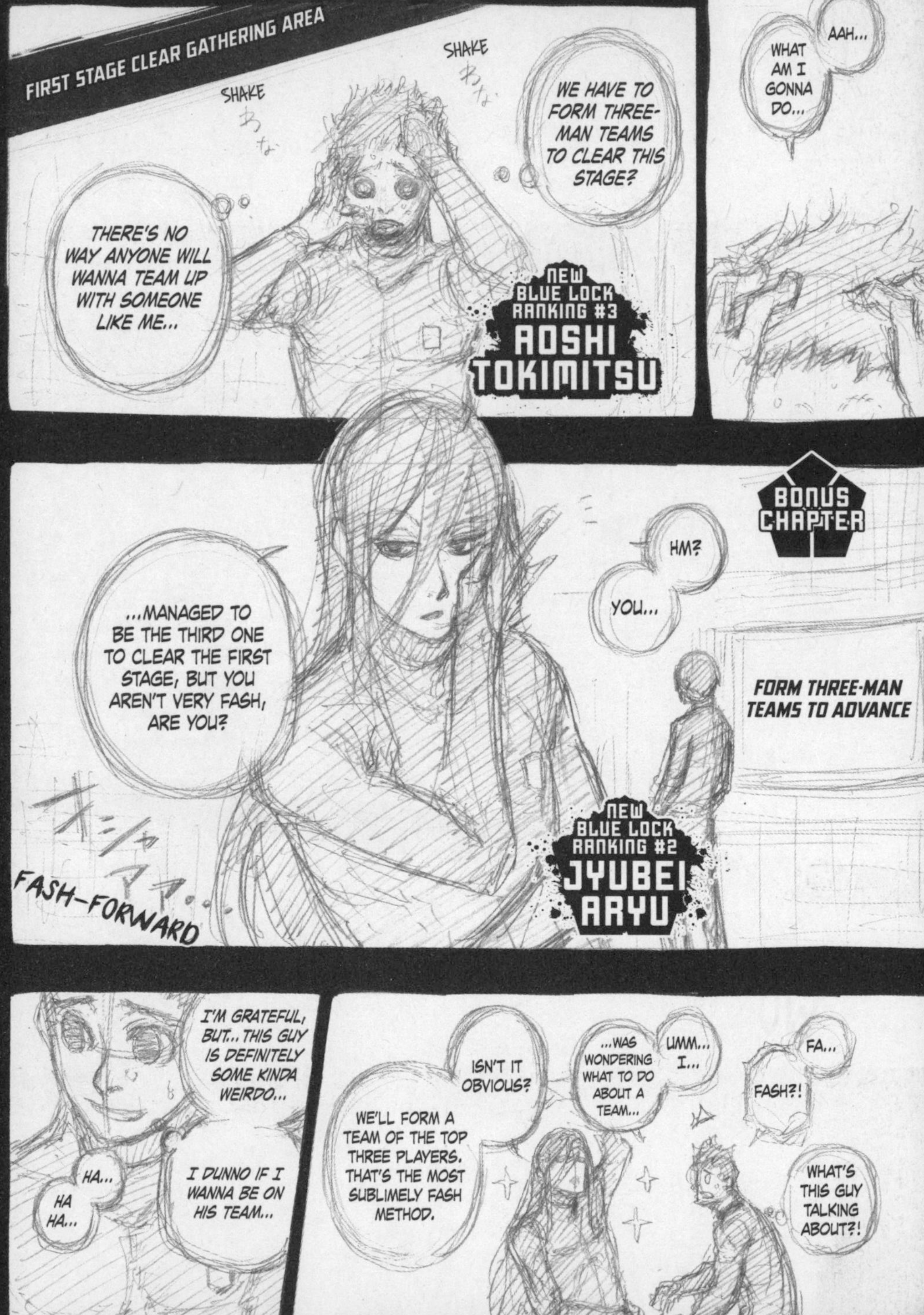
AAH...
WHAT AM I GONNA DO...
FIRST STAGE CLEAR GATHERING AREA
SHAKE
SHAKE
WE HAVE TO FORM THREE-MAN TEAMS TO CLEAR THIS STAGE?
THERE'S NO WAY ANYONE WILL WANNA TEAM UP WITH SOMEONE LIKE ME...
NEW BLUE LOCK RANKING #3 AOSHI TOKIMITSU
BONUS CHAPTER
HM?
YOU...
FORM THREE-MAN TEAMS TO ADVANCE
...MANAGED TO BE THE THIRD ONE TO CLEAR THE FIRST STAGE, BUT YOU AREN'T VERY FASH, ARE YOU?
NEW BLUE LOCK RANKING #2 JYUBEI ARYU
FASH-FORWARD
FA...
FASH?!
UMM... I...
...WAS WONDERING WHAT TO DO ABOUT A TEAM...
ISN'T IT OBVIOUS?
WHAT'S THIS GUY TALKING ABOUT?!
WE'LL FORM A TEAM OF THE TOP THREE PLAYERS. THAT'S THE MOST SUBLIMELY FASH METHOD.
I'M GRATEFUL, BUT... THIS GUY IS DEFINITELY SOME KINDA WEIRDO...
I DUNNO IF I WANNA BE ON HIS TEAM...
HA...
HA HA...

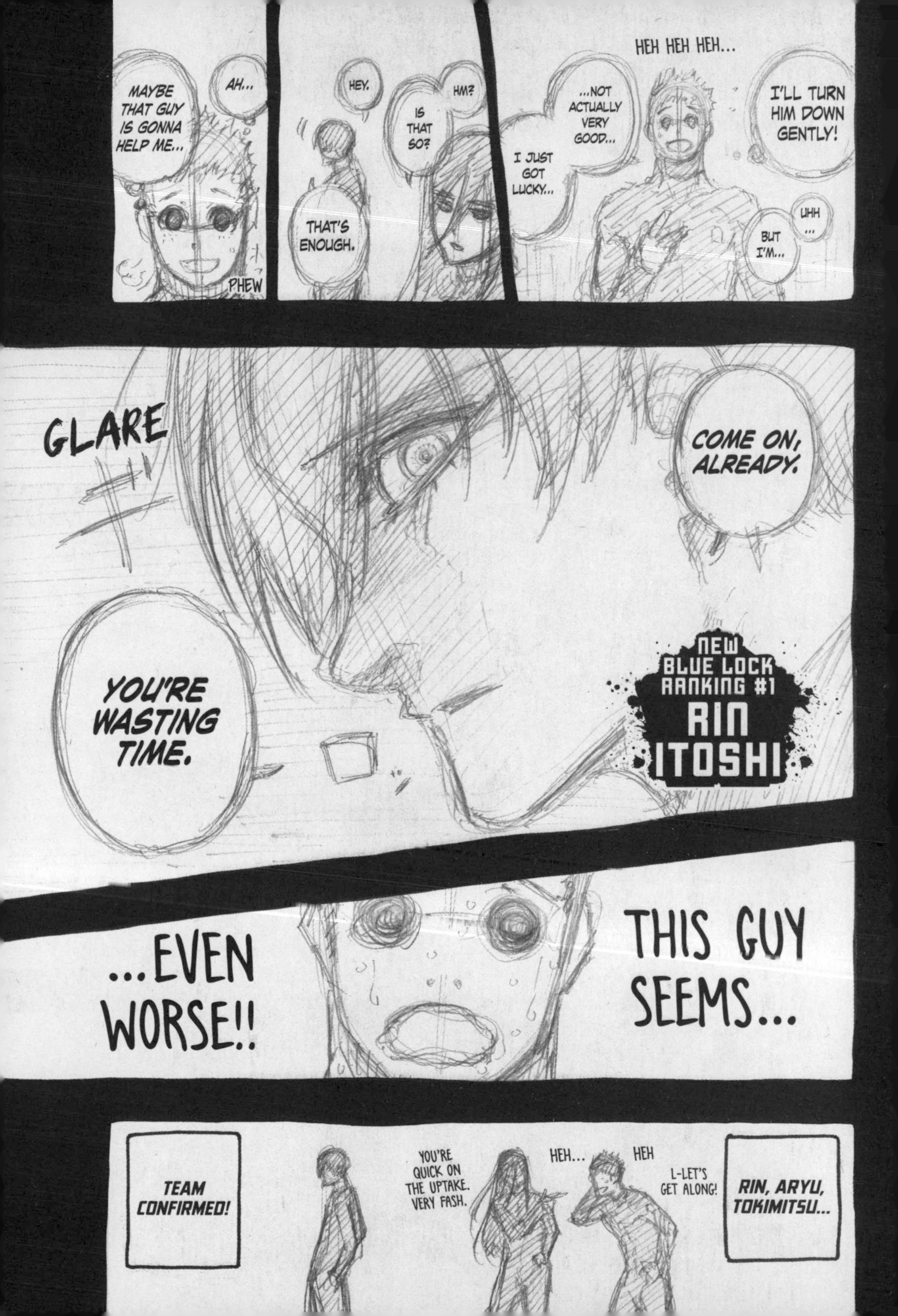
I'LL TURN HIM DOWN GENTLY!
UHH...
BUT I'M...
...NOT ACTUALLY VERY GOOD...
I JUST GOT LUCKY...
HEH HEH HEH...
HM?
IS THAT SO?
HEY.
THAT'S ENOUGH.
AH...
MAYBE THAT GUY IS GONNA HELP ME...
PHEW
COME ON, ALREADY.
GLARE
YOU'RE WASTING TIME.
NEW BLUE LOCK RANKING #1
RIN ITOSHI
THIS GUY SEEMS...
...EVEN WORSE!!
RIN, ARYU, TOKIMITSU...
L-LET'S GET ALONG!
HEH
HEH...
YOU'RE QUICK ON THE UPTAKE. VERY FASH.
TEAM CONFIRMED!

# BLUE LOCK MAN
## COMPLETE EXPLANATION

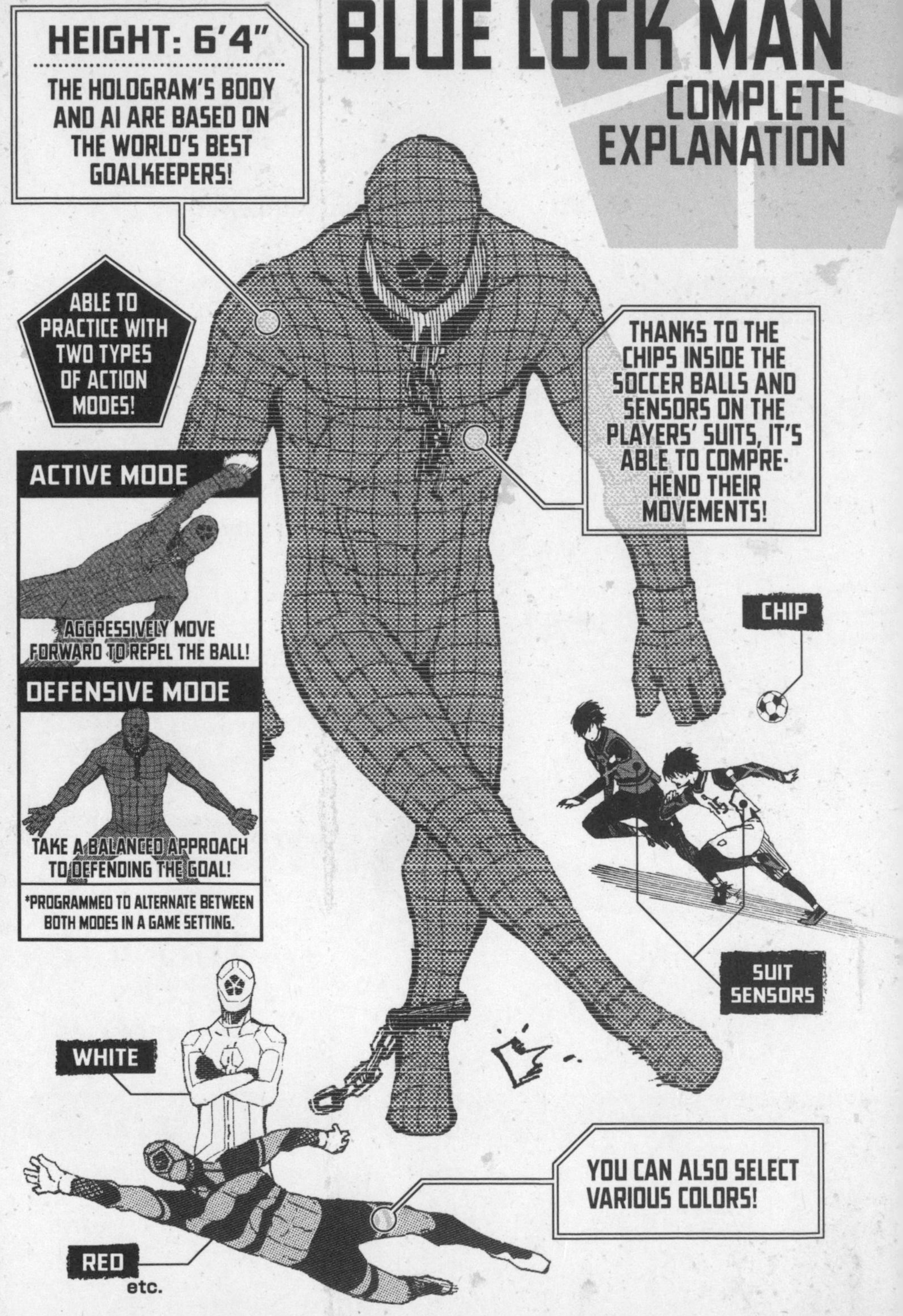
HEIGHT: 6'4"
THE HOLOGRAM'S BODY AND AI ARE BASED ON THE WORLD'S BEST GOALKEEPERS!
ABLE TO PRACTICE WITH TWO TYPES OF ACTION MODES!
THANKS TO THE CHIPS INSIDE THE SOCCER BALLS AND SENSORS ON THE PLAYERS' SUITS, IT'S ABLE TO COMPRE-HEND THEIR MOVEMENTS!
ACTIVE MODE
AGGRESSIVELY MOVE FORWARD TO REPEL THE BALL!
DEFENSIVE MODE
TAKE A BALANCED APPROACH TO DEFENDING THE GOAL!
*PROGRAMMED TO ALTERNATE BETWEEN BOTH MODES IN A GAME SETTING.
CHIP
SUIT SENSORS
WHITE
YOU CAN ALSO SELECT VARIOUS COLORS!
RED
etc.

◉ STORY  **MUNEYUKI KANESHIRO**

◉ ART  **YUSUKE NOMURA**

◉ ART ASSISTANTS

| | |
|---|---|
| ARATAMA-SAN | AOI-SAN |
| TAKANIWA-SAN | AYATSUKA-SAN |
| SATOU-SAN | HARA-SAN |
| OTAKE-SAN | MUTO-SAN |
| HARADA-SAN | SANGU-SAN |
| KAWAI-SAN | (LISTED RANDOMLY) |

◉ DESIGN  KUMOCHI-SAN

OBA-SAN

(HIVE)

THANK YOU FOR BUYING VOLUME 6!
AS YOU CAN SEE BY LOOKING AT THE STAFF CREDITS,
ABOUT HALF OF OUR ORIGINAL ASSISTANTS HAVE GRADUATED FROM
OUR TEAM TO START THEIR OWN COMICS AND SERIALIZATIONS.
I FEEL LIKE A MOTHER WHO'S BEEN LEFT BEHIND AT HOME...

BLUE LOCK

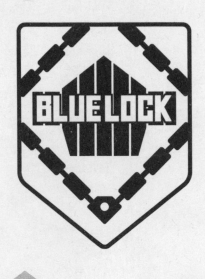

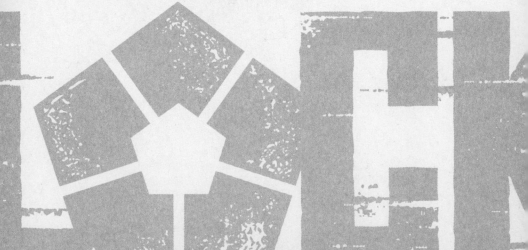

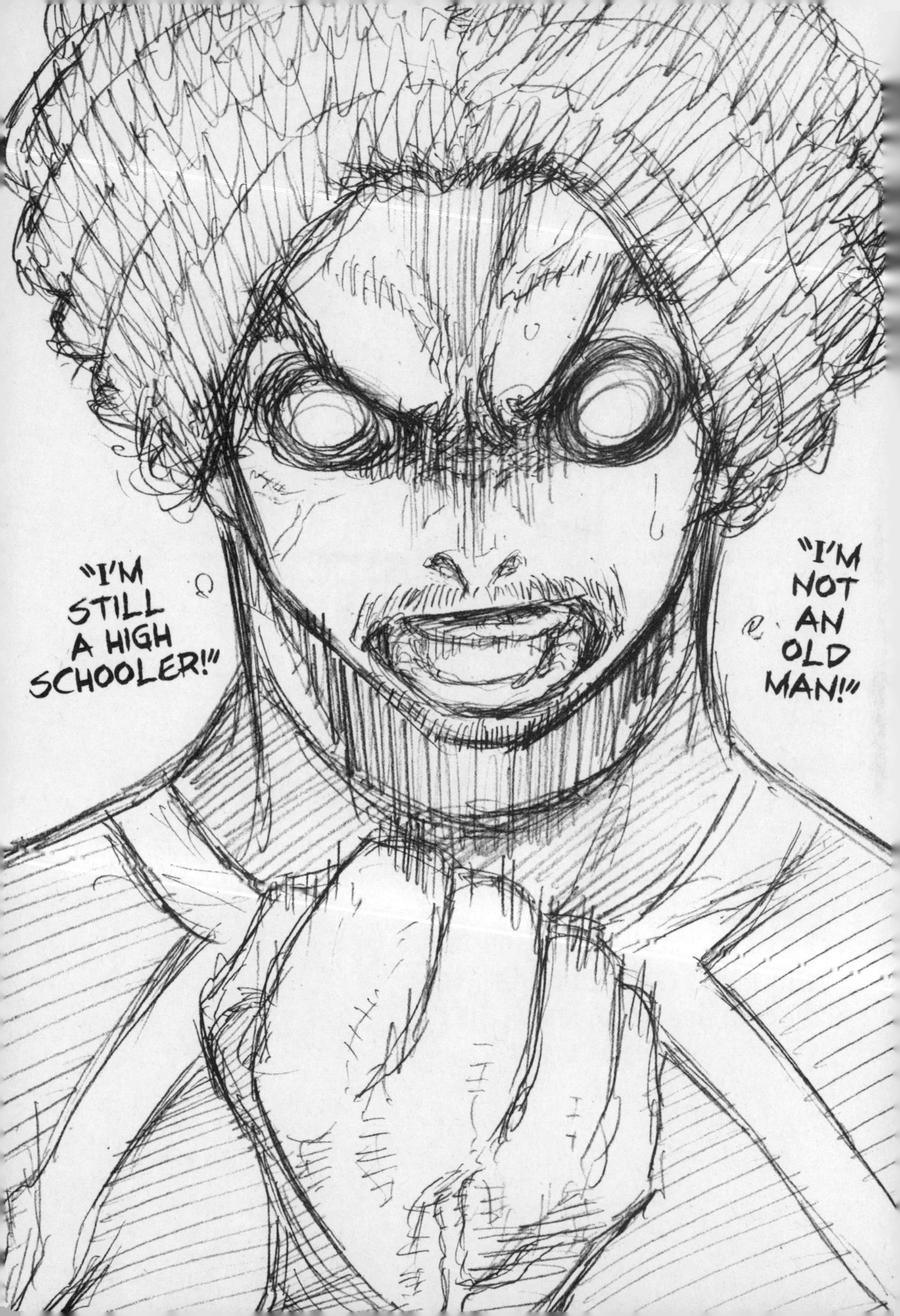
"I'M NOT AN OLD MAN!"
"I'M STILL A HIGH SCHOOLER!"

# Yusuke Nomura

*"I like action movies. I like action anime. To our dear readers, I hope you can see the action come alive in our manga."*

Yusuke Nomura debuted in 2014 with the grotesquely cute cult hit alien invasion story *Dolly Kill Kill*, which was released digitally in English by Kodansha. Nomura is the illustrator behind *Blue Lock*.

# Muneyuki Kaneshiro

*"Unlike life, sports have winners and losers. I like that it's cruel, pure, and intense. This is what I thought while watching TV and drinking a beer."*

Muneyuki Kaneshiro broke out as creator of 2011's *As the Gods Will*, a death game story that spawned two sequels and a film adaptation directed by the legendary Takashi Miike. Kaneshiro writes the story of *Blue Lock*.

# TRANSLATION NOTES

## "Hana Ichi Monme"

### page 69

In the original Japanese, Nagi references a traditional Japanese children's game called "Hana Ichi Monme," which is similar to "Red Rover." Instead of trying to break through a link of hands, the two groups sing the lines of a song and then team leaders step forward and do rock-paper-scissors. The winner goes back to their team, and they discuss who they want to add from the other team.

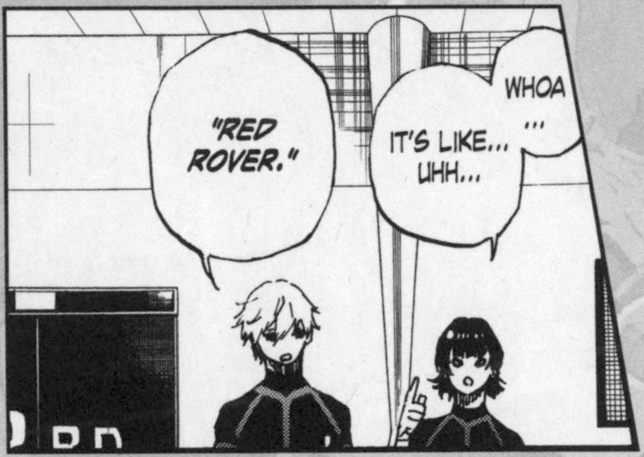
WHOA ...
IT'S LIKE... UHH...
"RED ROVER."

## Brows

### page 114

The characters frequently call out rival players by their appearances. In the original Japanese, Bachira calls Tokimitsu's eyebrows as looking like the kanji character for number eight [八].

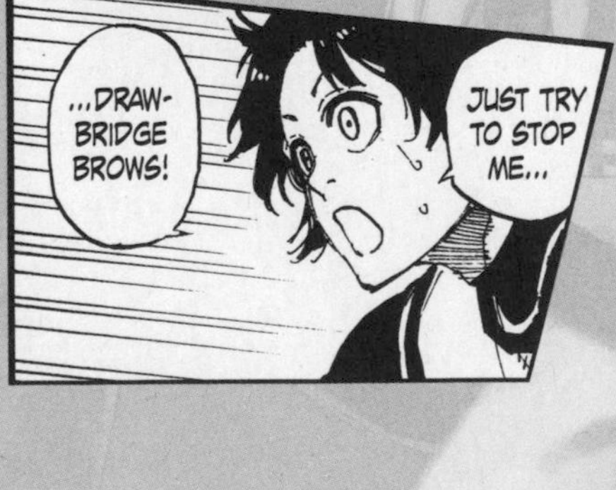
JUST TRY TO STOP ME...
...DRAW-BRIDGE BROWS!

# Young characters and steampunk setting, like *Howl's Moving Castle* and *Battle Angel Alita*

Beyond the Clouds © 2018 Nicke / Ki-oon

A boy with a talent for machines and a mysterious girl whose wings he's fixed will take you beyond the clouds! In the tradition of the high-flying, resonant adventure stories of Studio Ghibli comes a gorgeous tale about the longing of young hearts for adventure and friendship!

Knight of the Ice ©Yayoi Ogawa/Kodansha Ltd.

# SKATING THRILLS AND ICY CHILLS WITH THIS NEW TINGLY ROMANCE SERIES!

A rom-com on ice, perfect for fans of *Princess Jellyfish* and *Wotakoi*. Kokoro is the talk of the figure-skating world, winning trophies and hearts. But little do they know... he's actually a huge nerd! From the beloved creator of *You're My Pet* (*Tramps Like Us*).

Chitose is a serious young woman, working for the health magazine *SASSO*. Or at least, she would be, if she wasn't constantly getting distracted by her childhood friend, international figure skating star Kokoro Kijinami! In the public eye and on the ice, Kokoro is a gallant, flawless knight, but behind his glittery costumes and breathtaking spins lies a secret: He's actually a hopelessly romantic otaku, who can only land his quad jumps when Chitose is on hand to recite a spell from his favorite magical girl anime!

# A SMART, NEW ROMANTIC COMEDY FOR FANS OF *SHORTCAKE CAKE* AND *TERRACE HOUSE!*

A romance manga starring high school girl Meeko, who learns to live on her own in a boarding house whose living room is home to the odd (but handsome) Matsunaga-san. She begins to adjust to her new life away from her parents, but Meeko soon learns that no matter how far away from home she is, she's still a young girl at heart — especially when she finds herself falling for Matsunaga-san.

# PERFECT WORLD

### Rie Aruga

A TOUCHING
NEW SERIES
ABOUT LOVE AND
COPING WITH
DISABILITY

An office party reunites Tsugumi with her high school crush Itsuki. He's realized his dream of becoming an architect, but along the way, he experienced a spinal injury that put him in a wheelchair. Now Tsugumi's rekindled feelings will butt up against prejudices she never considered — and Itsuki will have to decide if he's ready to let someone into his heart...

"Depicts with great delicacy and courage the difficulties some with disabilities experience getting involved in romantic relationships... Rie Aruga refuses to romanticize, pushing her heroine to face the reality of disability. She invites her readers to the same tasks of empathy, knowledge and recognition."
—Slate.fr

"An important entry [in manga romance]... The emotional core of both plot and characters indicates thoughtfulness... [Aruga's] research is readily apparent in the text and artwork, making this feel like a real story."
—Anime News Network

Perfect World © Rie Aruga/Kodansha Ltd.

# The boys are back, in 400-page hardcovers that are as pretty and badass as they are!

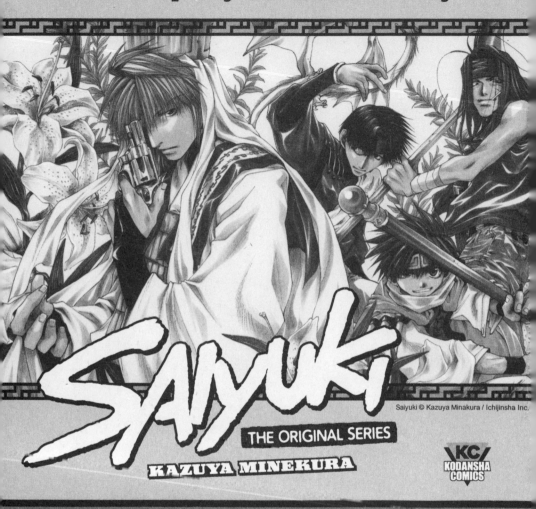

Saiyuki © Kazuya Minakura / Ichijinsha Inc.

**SAIYUKI**

THE ORIGINAL SERIES

KAZUYA MINEKURA

KC KODANSHA COMICS

## "AN EDGY COMIC LOOK AT AN ANCIENT CHINESE TALE." —YALSA

Genjo Sanzo is a Buddhist priest in the city of Togenkyo, which is being ravaged by yokai spirits that have fallen out of balance with the natural order. His superiors send him on a journey far to the west to discover why this is happening and how to stop it. His companions are three yokai with human souls. But this is no day trip — the four will encounter many discoveries and horrors on the way.

## FEATURES NEW TRANSLATION, COLOR PAGES, AND BEAUTIFUL WRAPAROUND COVER ART!

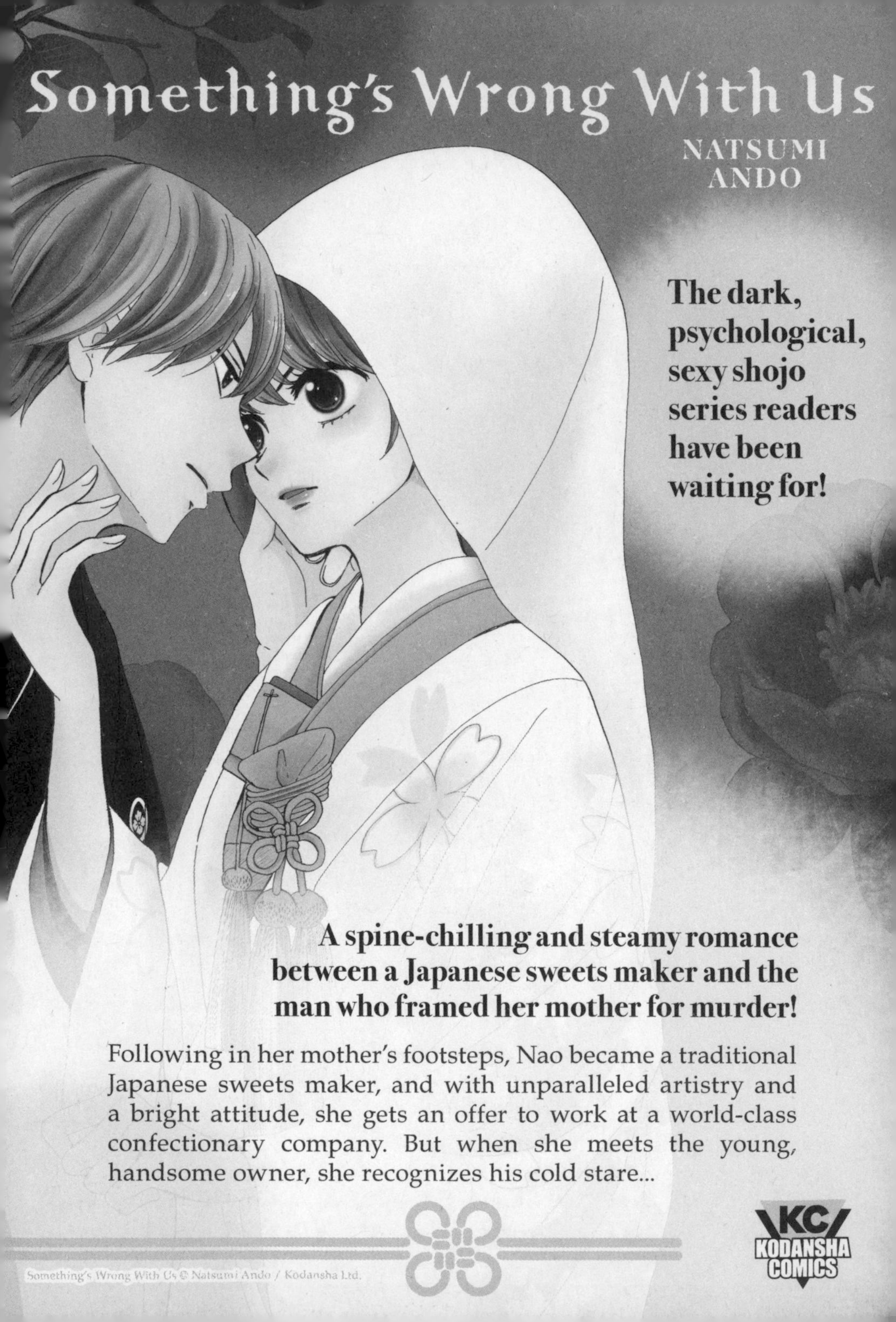
Something's Wrong With Us
NATSUMI ANDO
The dark, psychological, sexy shojo series readers have been waiting for!
A spine-chilling and steamy romance between a Japanese sweets maker and the man who framed her mother for murder!
Following in her mother's footsteps, Nao became a traditional Japanese sweets maker, and with unparalleled artistry and a bright attitude, she gets an offer to work at a world-class confectionary company. But when she meets the young, handsome owner, she recognizes his cold stare...
KC KODANSHA COMICS
Something's Wrong With Us © Natsumi Ando / Kodansha Ltd.

# THE SWEET SCENT OF LOVE IS IN THE AIR! FOR FANS OF OFFBEAT ROMANCES LIKE *WOTAKOI*

Sweat and Soap © Kintetsu Yamada / Kodansha Ltd.

In an office romance, there's a fine line between sexy and awkward... and that line is where Asako — a woman who sweats copiously — meets Koutarou — a perfume developer who can't get enough of Asako's, er, scent. Don't miss a romcom manga like no other!

# SAINT ☆ YOUNG MEN

## A LONG AWAITED ARRIVAL IN PREMIUM 2-IN-1 HARDCOVER

After centuries of hard work, Jesus and Buddha take a break from their heavenly duties to relax among the people of Japan, and their adventures in this lighthearted buddy comedy are sure to bring mirth and merriment to all!

"Brilliant...the physical comedy and facial expressions will make you literally LOL."

—Sam Humphries
(host of *DC Daily*; writer, *Green Lanterns*, *Legendary Star-Lord*)

Saint Young Men © Hikaru Nakamura/Kodansha Ltd.

**The adorable new odd-couple cat comedy manga from the creator of the beloved *Chi's Sweet Home*, in full color!**

Praise for *Chi's Sweet Home*

**"Nearly impossible to turn away... a true all-ages title that anyone, young or old, cat lover or not, will enjoy. The stories will bring a smile to your face and warm your heart."**

—School Library Journal

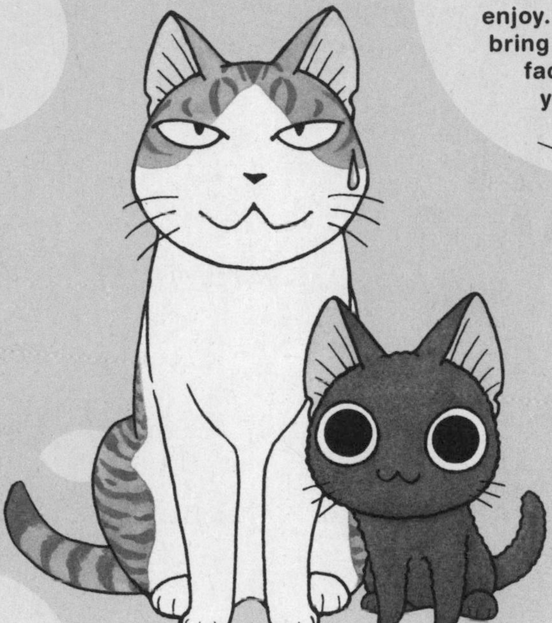

# Sue & Tai-chan

**Konami Kanata**

Sue is an aging housecat who's looking forward to living out her life in peace... but her plans change when the mischievous black tomcat Tai-chan enters the picture! Hey! Sue never signed up to be a catsitter! *Sue & Tai-chan* is the latest from the reigning meow-narch of cute kitty comics, Konami Kanata.

KC KODANSHA COMICS

# The beloved characters from *Cardcaptor Sakura* return in a brand new, reimagined fantasy adventure!

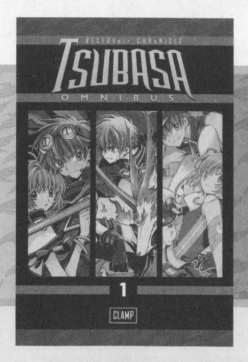

"[*Tsubasa*] takes readers on a fantastic ride that only gets more exhilarating with each successive chapter." —Anime News Network

In the Kingdom of Clow, an archaeological dig unleashes an incredible power, causing Princess Sakura to lose her memories. To save her, her childhood friend Syaoran must follow the orders of the Dimension Witch and travel alongside Kurogane, an unrivaled warrior; Fai, a powerful magician; and Mokona, a curiously strange creature, to retrieve Sakura's dispersed memories!

“Clever, sassy, and original....*xxxHOLiC* has the inherent hallmarks of a runaway hit.”
—NewType magazine

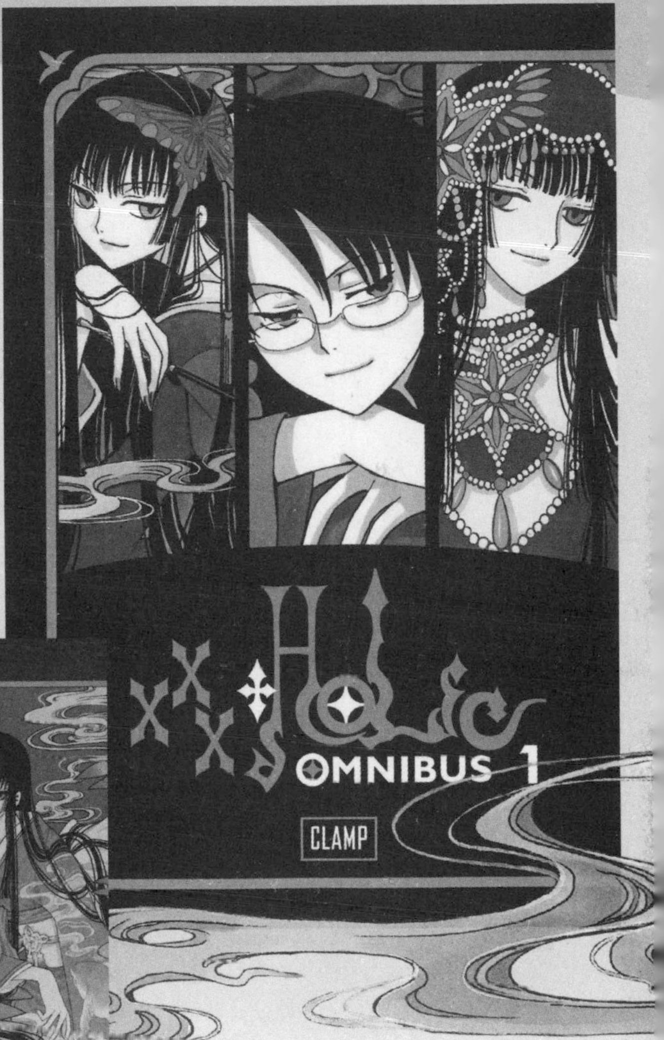
xxxHOLiC
OMNIBUS 1
CLAMP

**Beautifully seductive artwork and uniquely Japanese depictions of the supernatural will hypnotize CLAMP fans!**

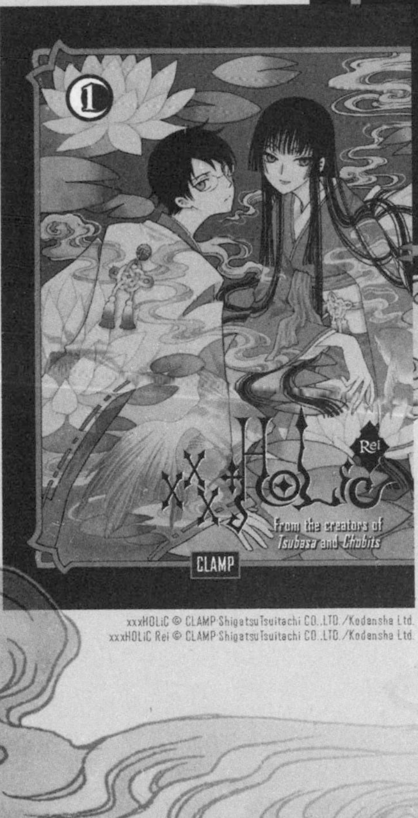
1
xxxHOLiC
Rei
From the creators of Tsubasa and Chobits
CLAMP



Kimihiro Watanuki is haunted by visions of ghosts and spirits. He seeks help from a mysterious woman named Yuko, who claims she can help. However, Watanuki must work for Yuko in order to pay for her aid. Soon Watanuki finds himself employed in Yuko’s shop, where he sees things and meets customers that are stranger than anything he could have ever imagined.

KC
KODANSHA COMICS

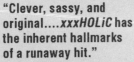

◄ KAMOME ►
SHIRAHAMA

# Witch Hat Atelier

A magical manga
adventure for
fans of Disney
and Studio
Ghibli!

*Witch Hat Atelier © Kamome Shirahama/Kodansha Ltd.*

## The magical adventure that took Japan by storm is finally here, from acclaimed DC and Marvel cover artist Kamome Shirahama!

In a world where everyone takes wonders like magic spells and dragons for granted, Coco is a girl with a simple dream: She wants to be a witch. But everybody knows magicians are born, not made, and Coco was not born with a gift for magic. Resigned to her un-magical life, Coco is about to give up on her dream to become a witch...until the day she meets Qifrey, a mysterious, traveling magician. After secretly seeing Qifrey perform magic in a way she's never seen before, Coco soon learns what everybody "knows" might not be the truth, and discovers that her magical dream may not be as far away as it may seem...

# The art-deco cyberpunk classic from the creators of *xxxHOLiC* and *Cardcaptor Sakura*!

"Starred Review. This experimental sci-fi work from CLAMP reads like a romantic version of *AKIRA*."
—Publishers Weekly

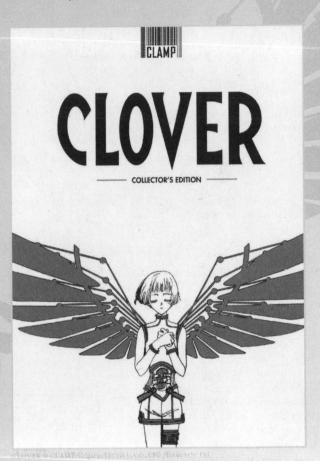

CLOVER © CLAMP·ShigatsuTsuitachi CO.,LTD./Kodansha Ltd.

Su was born into a bleak future, where the government keeps tight control over children with magical powers—codenamed "Clovers." With Su being the only "four-leaf" Clover in the world, she has been kept isolated nearly her whole life. Can ex-military agent Kazuhiko deliver her to the happiness she seeks? Experience the complete series in this hardcover edition, which also includes over twenty pages of ravishing color art!

A Kodansha Trade Paperback Original

*Blue Lock 6* copyright © 2019 Muneyuki Kaneshiro/Yusuke Nomura
English translation copyright © 2023 Muneyuki Kaneshiro/Yusuke Nomura

Published in the United States by
Kodansha USA Publishing, LLC, New York.

Publication rights for this English edition arranged through
Kodansha Ltd., Tokyo.

First published in Japan in 2019 by Kodansha Ltd., Tokyo
as *Buruu rokku*, volume 6.

ISBN 978-1-64651-663-6

Printed in the United States of America.

9 8 7 6 5 4 3 2 1

Original Digital Edition Translation: Nate Derr
Original Digital Edition Lettering: Chris Burgener
Original Digital Edition Editing: Thalia Sutton
Print Edition Lettering: Scott O. Brown
Print Edition Editing: Maggie Le
YKS Services LLC/SKY JAPAN, Inc.
Kodansha USA Publishing edition cover design by Matthew Akuginow

Publisher: Kiichiro Sugawara

Director of Publishing Services: Ben Applegate
Director of Publishing Operations: Dave Barrett
Publishing Services Managing Editors: Alanna Ruse, Madison Salters,
with Grace Chen
Production Manager: Jocelyn O'Dowd

KODANSHA.US

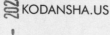

**KODANSHA**